Praise for *Eisenhower*

"*Eisenhower 1956* is a gripping account of Ike's masterful handling of the Suez crisis. Set against the backdrop of the president's two life-threatening illnesses, David A. Nichols's penetrating examination of a potentially disastrous incident in the tinderbox of the Middle East reveals how Eisenhower's decisive actions averted a deadly war and deterred the Soviet Union from intervening during some of the darkest days of the Cold War."

—Carlo D'Este, author of *Eisenhower: A Soldier's Life*
and *Patton: A Genius for War*

"A richly contextual reappraisal of a telling year in the presidency. . . . A suspenseful study that moves chronologically through the days in which the U.S. government was on tenterhooks. . . . A solid revisiting of this compelling leader about whom we are still learning."

—*Kirkus Reviews*

"David Nichols's book on Eisenhower's momentous year is fresh and insightful—and powerful and exciting. The more we know about Ike's subtle but masterful ability to keep the peace, the more we miss his kind in politics and government."

—Evan Thomas, author of *The War Lovers*

"Superb. . . . An intricate and highly readable work on an utterly crucial moment in our history. . . . It's hard to imagine it will ever be surpassed as the authoritative work on the subject."

—Stephen Benedict, former assistant staff secretary
in the Eisenhower White House

"Nichols lays to rest the common misconception that Secretary of State John Foster Dulles ran foreign policy while Eisenhower played golf. It was Eisenhower's leadership that helped bring an end to a conflict that threatened to widen into a larger war. . . . Will appeal to both 20th-century presidential history specialists and general presidential history buffs. Recommended."

—*Library Journal*

"*Eisenhower 1956* is the ultimate inside story of Ike's exemplary leadership during the world's first nuclear crisis. Surprisingly, it is also a riveting tale that reads like a suspense thriller, ending with a narrow escape from disastrous consequences."

—Daun van Ee, editor, *The Papers of Dwight David Eisenhower*

ALSO BY DAVID A. NICHOLS

A Matter of Justice: Eisenhower and the Beginning of the Civil Rights Revolution

Lincoln and the Indians: Civil War Policy and Politics

THE PRESIDENT'S YEAR OF CRISIS

★

SUEZ AND THE BRINK OF WAR

EISENHOWER 1956

DAVID A. NICHOLS

SIMON & SCHUSTER PAPERBACKS

NEW YORK   LONDON   TORONTO   SYDNEY   NEW DELHI

Simon & Schuster Paperbacks
A Division of Simon & Schuster, Inc.
1230 Avenue of the Americas
New York, NY 10020

Photo credits appear on page 333.

First Simon & Schuster trade paperback edition February 2012

SIMON & SCHUSTER PAPERBACKS and colophon are registered trademarks
of Simon & Schuster, Inc.

For information about special discounts for bulk purchases,
please contact Simon & Schuster Special Sales at
1-866-506-1949 or business@simonandschuster.com.

The Simon & Schuster Speakers Bureau can bring authors
to your live event. For more information or to book an event,
contact the Simon & Schuster Speakers Bureau at
1-866-248-3049 or visit our website at www.simonspeakers.com.

Designed by Ruth Lee-Mui

Manufactured in the United States of America

3   5   7   9   10   8   6   4   2

The Library of Congress has cataloged the hardcover edition as follows:
Nichols, David A. (David Allen), 1939–
Eisenhower 1956 : the president's year of crisis : Suez and the brink of war /
David A. Nichols. — 1st Simon & Schuster hardcover ed.
p. cm.
Includes bibliographical references and index.
1. Eisenhower, Dwight D. (Dwight David), 1890–1969. 2. Egypt—
History—Intervention, 1956. 3. United States—Foreign
relations—1953–1961. 4. Political leadership—United States—Case
studies. 5. International relations—Decision making. I. Title.
E836.N529 2011
973.921092—dc22   2011000771

ISBN 978-1-4391-3933-2
ISBN 978-1-4391-3934-9 (pbk)
ISBN 978-1-4391-4699-6 (ebook)

To my grandsons—Joey, Lance, Thomas,
Nate, Luke, William, and Spenser

We cannot and will not condone armed aggression—no matter who the attacker, and no matter who the victim. We cannot—in the world any more than in our own nation—subscribe to one law for the weak, another law for the strong; one law for those opposing us, another for those allied with us. There can be only one law or there will be no peace.

—Dwight D. Eisenhower, November 1, 1956

CONTENTS

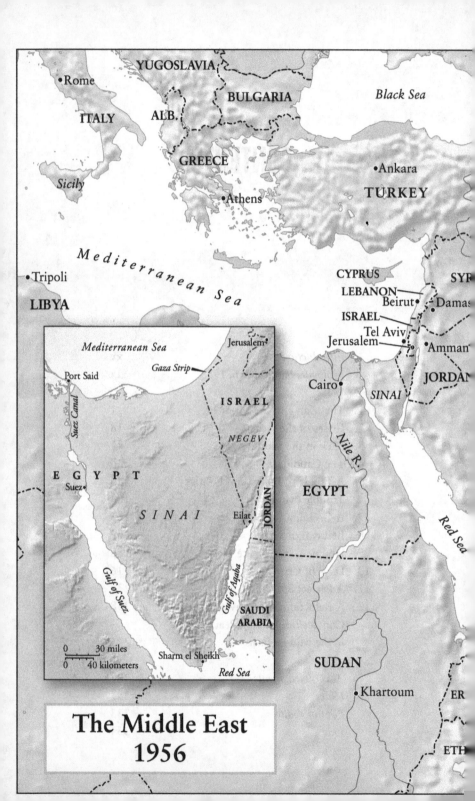

ITALY

•Rome

YUGOSLAVIA

BULGARIA

ALB.

GREECE

Sicily

•Athens

_M e d i t e r r a n e a n   S e a_

•Tripoli

LIBYA

Black Sea

•Ankara

TURKEY

CYPRUS

LEBANON

Beirut• •Damas

ISRAEL

Tel Aviv

Jerusalem

SYR

•Amman

JORDAN

Cairo•

SINAI

EGYPT

Nile R.

Red Sea

SUDAN

•Khartoum

ER

ETH

Mediterranean Sea

Jerusalem•

Port Said•

Gaza Strip

ISRAEL

Suez Canal

EGYPT

NEGEV

Suez•

SINAI

JORDAN

Eilat•

Gulf of Suez

Gulf of Aqaba

SAUDI
ARABIA

0   30 miles
0   40 kilometers

Sharm el Sheikh•

Red Sea

The Middle East
1956

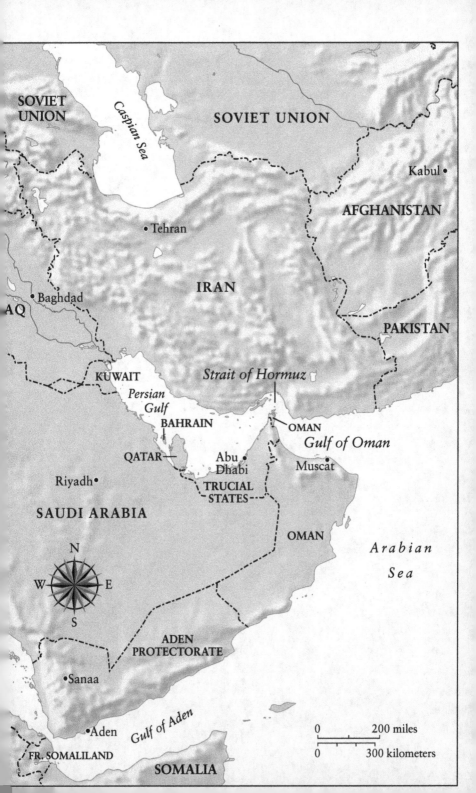

INTRODUCTION

★ ★ ★ ★ ★ ★

EISENHOWER 1956 is the intensely personal story of how the thirty-fourth president of the United States dealt with the most dangerous foreign crisis of his eight years in office. It's a tale of international intrigue and betrayal by wartime allies caught in the cross fire of collapsing colonial empires and intense, rising nationalism in the Middle East—all played out in the context of the Cold War with the Soviet Union.

Historians have long treated the Suez crisis as a minor episode in the dissolution of colonial rule after World War II, but it was much more than that. The crisis climaxed in a tumultuous nine-day period just prior to the 1956 U.S. presidential election, when Great Britain, France, and Israel attacked Egypt, and the Soviet Union sent a huge invasion force into Hungary to put down a popular rebellion there while threatening to intervene in the Middle East. Dwight D. Eisenhower—grappling with the most traumatic health crises of his life and in the midst of a reelection campaign—took a principled stand against aggression and skillfully guided the United States through the Suez crisis and averted global war.

For London and Paris, and for the Western democracies as a whole, Egyptian president Gamal Abdel Nasser's nationalization of the Suez Canal Company in July 1956 was potentially calamitous. Much of the oil to power Western Europe's postwar economic recovery and defense, along with other critical goods, flowed through the canal. Eisenhower made his share of mistakes in the months preceding the crisis: he and his intelligence officials failed to foresee Nasser's action and Eisenhower failed to grasp how his administration's policies had set the stage for conflict. But once it happened, Ike and his secretary of state, John Foster Dulles, held off the march to war for months, refused to condone naked aggression, and forced the allies to back down.

This book draws on a myriad of documents declassified in recent decades, including intelligence reports, minutes of National Security Council meetings, and notes on confidential Oval Office conversations. These documents make it possible to tell the inside story of the crisis from the perspective of Eisenhower's White House, giving us an unprecedented opportunity to look over Ike's shoulder and follow him day by day, sometimes hour by hour, as he dealt with a crisis that at times appeared to be spinning out of control and toward a superpower war.

We have learned a lot about Eisenhower's presidency in the past thirty years. There were multiple reasons for its initial neglect by historians: a paucity of rigorous research, a bias in favor of particular models of presidential leadership, and a scholarly preoccupation with presidential rhetoric that did not quite fit Ike's soldierly restraint. Eisenhower's public persona— calm, smiling, almost grandfatherly—contributed to the myth of a less than dynamic president. Behind the scenes, though, Ike was a tough, disciplined, supremely organized leader, fully in command of the challenges that arose during his presidency.[1] That side of Eisenhower is etched in bold relief in *Eisenhower 1956*.

Much has been written about Eisenhower's foreign policy, especially the Cold War in Europe and the Far East, but remarkably little about his policies toward the Middle East. Ike himself noted in his memoirs that, from 1955 onward, "no region of the world received as much of my close attention and that of my colleagues as did the Middle East."[2] Although *Eisenhower 1956* aims to address that neglect, it is not the story of the broad sweep of Eisenhower's actions in the Cold War nor, for that matter, the full scope of issues in the Middle East, commonly referred to in that era as "the Near East." Britain, France, Israel, and Egypt were primary protagonists in the Suez drama, but *Eisenhower 1956* is focused sharply on Eisenhower's role in the crisis.[3]

While there are substantial British studies of the allied side of the Suez episode, the primary American volumes about the crisis were published prior to the declassification of major documents. More recent diplomatic histories, while helpful in understanding the flow of diplomacy for the period, have not focused as directly on Eisenhower as this book does.[4]

In short, *Eisenhower 1956* is what the title says it is—a book about Ike in the most difficult year of his presidency, as he struggled to keep the peace while faced with serious illness in the midst of a presidential election campaign and some of the darkest days of the Cold War.

The Middle East and its problems, especially the Arab-Israeli conflict, are still with us. As a result of the Suez crisis, Eisenhower committed the United States to replacing the British as the guarantor of Middle East peace and security, including Western access to its oil resources. His historic reshaping of American policy toward the region, enshrined in the Eisenhower Doctrine passed by Congress in 1957, still informs the current policy debate.

PROLOGUE

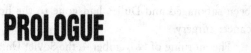

★ ★ ★ ★ ★ ★

November 6, 1956

IT WAS Election Day. Americans were going to the polls either to elect a new president or keep Dwight Eisenhower in that office for another four years.

Just past noon, Ike stepped out of the limousine that had transported him from the airport and strode into the White House. He and Mamie had driven to their home in Gettysburg, Pennsylvania, that morning to vote, only to be urgently called back. The president had just endured the most stressful week of his presidency, coming on the heels of one of the most difficult years, at least physically, of his life. He had suffered and recovered from both a heart attack and major intestinal surgery, the latter in the midst of his campaign for a second term.

When Gamal Abdel Nasser of Egypt nationalized the Suez Canal in July, the British and French had begun preparing for war. For months, Eisenhower and Secretary of State John Foster Dulles had held them off. Ike now knew that his World War II allies had double-crossed him, hatching their own secret plot to take military action against Egypt.

On October 29, as part of an elaborate plan to wrest control of the canal from Nasser, Israel had attacked Egypt, followed by British and French bombing—all without consulting Eisenhower. Ike had protested, had taken the issue to the United Nations, and had announced to the American people that "there will be no United States involvement in these present hostilities."

The situation had worsened day by day. As the Israelis advanced, a huge Anglo-French armada sailed toward the Egyptian coast. The morning of November 3, Ike learned that the main oil pipeline through Syria had been sabotaged and Dulles had gone to the hospital during the night for cancer surgery.

The morning of November 4, the Soviet Union had sent 200,000 troops and four thousand tanks into Budapest, Hungary, to put down a revolt. The next day, British and French paratroopers landed in Egypt; by then, the Israelis held five thousand Egyptians prisoner and were occupying the Sinai Peninsula and the Gaza Strip. The Soviet premier, Nikolai A. Bulganin, had sent messages to Israel, Britain, France, and the United States, threatening to intervene in the war in the Middle East. Ike had responded by putting American military forces on alert.

On Election Day morning, Ike's health was still fragile. The previous night, his blood pressure was elevated and his heart was skipping beats. He had awakened after a fitful sleep and called his doctor immediately to examine the infected scar from his surgery. In his first meeting on that day, Ike had recognized that he confronted a situation that could escalate into the world war he had tried so hard to avoid. "Our people should be alert," he had said to a meeting of key advisors that morning. He knew that the presence of Soviet planes in Syria would inevitably trigger British and French attacks on those airfields, possibly followed by Soviet retaliation against America's closest allies—allies the United States was pledged to defend.

When Ike and Mamie had arrived at Gettysburg, he was immediately called to a phone. A helicopter rushed him back to Washington but he did not know the reason until he arrived at the airport—news from Moscow that the Soviet Union was possibly moving toward intervention.

At 12:38 P.M., Eisenhower walked into the White House and, after being briefed, went to the Cabinet Room, where eighteen men waited—the vice president and the top leadership of both the State and Defense departments, including the Joint Chiefs. The purpose of this council of war was to review the readiness of the United States to fight a major war with the Soviet Union.

1

★ ★ ★ ★ ★ ★

THE MAN AND THE MOMENT

"I believed that it would be undesirable and impracticable for the British to retain sizable forces permanently in the territory of a jealous and resentful government amid an openly hostile population."

Eisenhower in his memoir, *Waging Peace*

DWIGHT D. EISENHOWER was sworn in as president of the United States at 12:32 P.M. on January 20, 1953. He had won the election over the Democratic candidate, Adlai Stevenson, primarily because he was an iconic war hero, associated in the public mind with victory in World War II. Elliot Richardson, a war veteran who later led four different cabinet-level departments, sensed Ike's mettle as a crisis leader the first time he saw him. Richardson said to himself: "This guy is a tough son-of-a-bitch!"[1]

Yet, on Inauguration Day, Eisenhower avoided the grand gestures or dramatic rhetoric one might have expected from a flamboyant military figure like Douglas MacArthur. He flashed the famous smile only once during the ceremony. The *New York Times* described his demeanor as "grave and grim," saying he "looked lonely and a little sad" as he assumed "a responsibility no one can bear without trembling." Begun with a prayer, Eisenhower's inaugural speech was a serious, almost philosophical dissertation about faith and principle. Although he was a military man to the core, he said virtually nothing about weapons and armies.[2]

Columnist James Reston noted that forty-one of the forty-eight paragraphs in the speech were devoted to foreign affairs. Eisenhower assured the nations in major regions of the world—Europe, the Far East, and Latin America—of American support in their quest for freedom. He did not mention the Middle East. Listening to Eisenhower's inaugural address, Reston tried to discern whether the general was a "Europe-firster" or an "Asia-firster." On January 20, 1953, no one thought to ask whether Ike was a "Middle East–firster."[3]

"NEVER AGAIN"

Eisenhower could not have anticipated the events that would culminate in the most dangerous foreign crisis of his administration, a crisis threatening world war. Nor could he have imagined that a dispute over the Suez Canal would create a major rift with America's closest allies and personal friends with whom he had fought World War II. Nor could he foresee that all this would occur in a year in which he would be plagued by illness, even as he was compelled to reshape American policy in the Middle East. But while Ike could not envision the coming Suez storm, he was acutely aware that he was assuming the presidency in a dangerous world still shell-shocked from World War II. Those who had endured its ravages had sworn, in effect, to "never again" tolerate the conditions they believed had spawned the conflagration.

The Soviet Union, after suffering an estimated 35 million casualties in the war, exemplified this syndrome. Soviet leaders had resented being forced to carry the burden of the war against Hitler until June 1944. Having fought Germany in two world wars, the Russians had blocked German reunification and set up puppet communist regimes in Bulgaria, Czechoslovakia, Hungary, Poland, and Romania as a buffer against future invasion.

The British and French harbored their own version of the "never again" mind-set, determined to avoid future appeasement of aggressors. Their leaders, especially Prime Minister Winston Churchill, viewed Soviet domination of Eastern Europe as a reincarnation of Hitler's aggression. The postwar disintegration of Europe's colonial empires only exacerbated the paranoia. Later, Churchill's successor, Anthony Eden, would insist to Eisenhower that Gamal Abdel Nasser, the general who took power in Egypt in 1954, was, in effect, "another Hitler."[4]

Britain's and France's former colonies, especially Egypt, waved the flag of rising nationalism, fiercely determined that the European powers would never again dominate their affairs. Arab nationalism had been further fueled by the creation of the state of Israel in 1948, built on the resolve of European Jews to never again submit to a Nazi-like Holocaust.

While the United States emerged from the war stronger than its European allies, the Soviet Union's postwar actions and development of atomic weapons intensified American perceptions of a worldwide communist threat. President Harry Truman, and later Eisenhower, concluded that America must never again embrace isolationism and fail to address a growing peril to world peace.

This bundle of tensions had spawned a "Cold War" almost immediately after the big war. In 1946, Churchill, while out of power, declared that an "Iron Curtain" had descended on Eastern Europe. In 1947, President Truman enunciated the Truman Doctrine to contain communism and launched the Marshall Plan to rebuild Western European economies. By Inauguration Day, Eisenhower had fully embraced the doctrine that world peace depended on American containment of the Soviet Union; indeed, a major reason Ike had decided to run for president was to defeat the isolationist wing of the Republican Party.[5]

"SLOW TO PICK UP THE SWORD"

The new president, on his first day in office, was more fully a citizen of the world than any of his predecessors. He had lived in Panama, the Philippines, England, and France. He had survived two world wars and, in the second, had commanded history's largest military expeditionary force.

As he took the oath of office, Ike had a strategic map of the globe in his head, with the areas of potential conflict with the Soviet Union clearly delineated. Eisenhower possessed a first-class strategic intellect. Attorney General Herbert Brownell, Jr., recalled the feelings of Ike's subordinates that "in the two-thirds of his job dealing with foreign and military affairs he knew more than all of us put together."

Yet Eisenhower the military man was not militaristic. He did not think that there were military solutions to many problems. While prepared to exploit his military credibility in deterring the Soviets, Eisenhower viewed war with them as a last, not a first, resort. The new president was determined to talk about disarmament early and often.

Ike's reluctance to go to war made him intensely skeptical about the wisdom of getting into "brushfire" wars, those "little wars" that he believed could escalate into global conflict.[6] By January 20, he had already decided to end the one he had inherited in Korea, and set out to avoid any others during his presidency.

Still, given the potential horrors of nuclear war, some of Ike's advisors thought that such limited wars were the only ones that could safely be fought. Ike thought it naive to believe it would always be possible to control a small war or even, as he put it, a "nice sweet World War II type of war." He believed that the Soviet Union and the United States would be tempted to use every weapon at their disposal. That was a good reason, in Eisenhower's thinking, to clearly communicate to the other side that massive retaliation would be his response to major aggression. That strategic gambit, a bluff worthy of a skilled poker player, was designed to prevent war, not cause it—to convince his adversary to join hands with him in keeping the peace. General Andrew Goodpaster, his longtime aide and friend, recalled that Ike was "slow to pick up the sword."[7]

A SIGN OF THINGS TO COME

Still, on Inauguration Day, the Middle East was already on Eisenhower's agenda. He had quickly decided against walking in lockstep with the British on Middle East policy. Prime Minister Churchill, who had returned to power in 1951, had visited Washington two weeks prior to the inauguration, imploring Eisenhower to support Britain in negotiations with the Egyptians regarding the British military presence in the Suez Canal Zone. Afterward, Ike expressed concern in his diary that the aging British warrior was "trying to relive the days of World War II." Churchill, he recalled, had talked "very animatedly" about "Egypt and its future" and had particularly sought Ike's solidarity with the British on issues regarding the status of the canal.[8]

The bone of contention was the presence of eighty thousand British troops in Egypt, stationed on a huge base in the Canal Zone. Those British forces had a long history, closely linked to Britain's quasi-colonial domination of that country. Ever since its completion by the French and Egyptians in 1869, the Suez Canal, connecting the Red Sea with the Mediterranean, had been a boon to European economies and a linchpin of British and

French influence in the Middle East. It facilitated commerce between Asia and Europe, but its construction had required the forced labor of thousands of Egyptians, spawning a legacy of lasting bitterness toward the Europeans.

In 1875, financial problems had compelled Egypt to sell its share in the Canal Company to the British, who along with the French parlayed this stake into effective control of Egypt's finances and government. In 1882, the British landed troops to protect the canal during a civil war in Egypt; on Eisenhower's Inauguration Day, they were still there.

In July 1952, a military junta, led by Gamal Abdel Nasser and Muhammad Naguib, had seized power in Egypt, dethroning King Farouk. The new government's leaders immediately began to agitate for the removal of the British forces. Difficult negotiations were already underway when Eisenhower took office and Churchill wanted the new president to commit the United States to full participation.[9]

Three days after Eisenhower was inaugurated, President Naguib escalated the rhetoric about the British occupation of the Canal Zone, publicly calling for the Egyptian people to "get rid of the last traces of British Imperialism" and swearing that "after this day, no tyrant will ever establish himself upon our soil." Eisenhower had already reached a firm conclusion that "it would be undesirable and impracticable for the British to retain sizable forces permanently in the territory of a jealous and resentful government amid an openly hostile population."[10]

Eisenhower was knowledgeable about the Arab world, partly due to his oversight of World War II operations in North Africa. He understood that the Middle East, as the repository of the world's largest known petroleum reserves, was essential to the survival of Western Europe in the Cold War contest with the Soviet Union. Ike embraced a strategic reality, starkly expressed in his memoirs: the Suez Canal was, he wrote, "the most important waterway in the world."[11]

Keeping the canal open in time of war had been an overriding European priority for decades. Eisenhower anchored the legal foundation for his approach to the strategic status of the Suez Canal in two documents, both formally ratified by nations that utilized the canal. The first was the Convention of 1888 signed by the maritime nations, pledging to "guarantee, at all times, and to all Powers, the free use of the Suez Maritime Canal." That agreement assumed that British troops would continue to protect the Canal Zone.[12]

The second agreement was signed in 1950 in the aftermath of the war to establish the state of Israel, fought against five Arab states—Egypt, Iraq, Jordan, Lebanon, and Syria. The United Nations–sponsored armistice in 1949 authorized temporary borders that were the catalyst for repeated violent incidents and reprisals. A particular problem was the Gaza Strip, a small finger of land bordering Egypt, Israel, and the Mediterranean. The Egyptians were granted temporary oversight of Gaza, setting the stage for almost constant conflict with Israel.[13] Given this volatile situation, the British, French, and Americans signed an agreement in 1950 (known as the Tripartite Declaration), attempting to avoid an arms race in the Middle East by prescribing limits on the provision of arms to the protagonists and pledging assistance to any Middle East nation threatened by aggression.[14]

A third legal reality would inform Eisenhower's view of the Suez Canal in the years ahead. In the words of Attorney General Brownell, "The entire length of the Canal lay within Egyptian territory."[15]

On February 24, 1953, Eisenhower called a special meeting of the National Security Council (NSC) to discuss the British-Egyptian negotiations and Prime Minister Churchill's demands for American involvement. Ike told the group that he was "puzzled" by Churchill's expressions of "extreme urgency" regarding the role of the United States in the negotiations. Noting some "frightening phraseology" in Churchill's correspondence, Ike worried aloud that Churchill was "trying to tie our hands in advance."[16]

A PLANNER-PRESIDENT

Ike's reliance on the NSC points to the best framework for understanding Eisenhower's leadership, especially in foreign affairs. He was a planner. That was how he had risen in the military, not by battlefield exploits; Ike never commanded troops in combat. Goodpaster recalled that Eisenhower divided long-range planning and policy development from day-to-day operations because, he said, paraphrasing Ike, "If you try to combine the two, operations will eat up the long-range planning."[17] The NSC was his vehicle for handling the latter.

The NSC had been established by the National Security Act of 1947, and its statutory members included the president, vice president, secretaries of state and defense, and director of the Office of Defense Mobilization. Depending on the subject under discussion, the president could invite other cabinet members and advisors to attend, usually including the secretary of the treasury, the chairman of the Joint Chiefs of Staff, and the director of Central Intelligence (DCI), who, under Eisenhower, normally started NSC meetings with a briefing. Eisenhower underscored the importance he attached to the NSC in his first State of the Union message on February 2, 1953, saying that, "in these days of tension," it was important that the NSC "perform effectively." "I propose," he stated, "to see that it does so." [18]

Unlike his predecessor, Ike intended to chair most meetings of the NSC. That did not mean that the NSC made decisions; Eisenhower did that. He recalled that "a vote was never taken" among its members. Ike said he did not hesitate "to take a different course than that almost unanimously proposed." [19]

Eisenhower's favorite planning aphorism was, "Plans are worthless but planning is everything." In any emergency, he counseled, "The first thing you do is to take all the plans off the top shelf and throw them out the window and start once more." That did not mean that the planning process was pointless. On the contrary, he believed it was essential to plan so you are prepared "to do the normal thing when everybody else is going nuts." [20]

Ike's system dictated planning for any contingency, no matter how unlikely, even all-out nuclear war. That was the point of the NSC's rigorous, seemingly endless flow of studies, policy papers, discussions, and presidential decisions. Under Eisenhower, NSC members would learn to expect the unexpected and, in the words of the poet Rudyard Kipling, "keep your head when all about you, are losing theirs and blaming it on you." [21]

But Eisenhower could not have anticipated on February 24, 1953, how much, three years hence, so many people would be "going nuts" over the Suez Canal. The signs of trouble were already evident, which is why he was involving the NSC in assessing Churchill's demands. By 1956, as a result of the planning process he began that day, Eisenhower would have at his disposal a set of rigorously defined principles and policies for the Middle East that would guide him through an unprecedented crisis.

IKE'S FOREIGN POLICY PARTNER

Eisenhower understood that, once plans were laid, they could only be carried out through delegation. He was a master delegator, giving some subordinates lots of rope and keeping others on a short leash. Ike believed that "any Chief Executive who tries to do everything himself, as some presidents have, is in trouble." He understood that delegating a task was not just dumping it on someone's desk. Goodpaster recalled that, in the Eisenhower system, "if you were delegated a task, you had to know what the bounds of policy were.... With Eisenhower, there was no deviation from policy without coming back for an additional hearing." [22]

Eisenhower applied that approach with a vengeance to his secretary of state, John Foster Dulles. Ike recalled that it "was more or less understood in 1952" that Dulles was in line for the secretary's job. If New York Republican governor Thomas E. Dewey had won the presidency in 1948, Dulles would have been appointed secretary. While that made the appointment somewhat political, Dulles had superior credentials and a reputation for expertise in foreign affairs. The New York attorney's grandfather and uncle had been secretaries of state. He had served in numerous diplomatic capacities for more than forty years, and had written extensively on the issues of war and peace. Ike was heard to joke, "Foster has been studying to be Secretary of State since he was five years old." [23]

There were those who had doubts about Dulles's appointment. His biographer, Richard Immerman, notes that many Europeans believed that Dulles was "a fire-and-brimstone anti-communist fanatic who would risk the nuclear annihilation of the continent in an effort to blow a hole in the Iron Curtain." In particular, Anthony Eden, the British foreign secretary at the time, pleaded with Eisenhower not to appoint Dulles. [24]

Eisenhower had his own doubts, not about Dulles's expertise but regarding his penchant for provocative language. On one occasion during the 1952 election campaign, Ike reviewed a speech that Dulles had made discussing the liberation of "captive nations" in the Soviet bloc. Ike called Dulles and chewed him out for saying that the United States would employ "all means" to secure liberation, when they had previously agreed that Dulles would say, "all *peaceful* means."

Dulles quickly learned to watch his tongue and to stay in constant consultation with Eisenhower. Ike recalled that "there was no one I kept in as close touch with as I did with Foster," claiming that they talked eight to ten times a day. In 1961, Eisenhower told Walter Cronkite, the CBS News anchor, that he never had "a Cabinet officer who consulted me so frequently, who insisted that every single decision be approved by me in advance, who would never make a single speech until I had edited it down to the last word." [25]

Eisenhower purposely set up an extraordinary situation when he appointed John Foster Dulles as secretary of state and his brother Allen W. Dulles as director of the Central Intelligence Agency, responsible for coordinating the collection of intelligence information on worldwide developments affecting U.S. security. Ike had inherited Walter Bedell "Beetle" Smith, a Truman appointee and Ike's former chief of staff in World War II, in the latter position. Following the inauguration, Eisenhower moved Smith to the State Department as undersecretary of state, second in command to Foster Dulles. He then promoted Foster's brother Allen to head the intelligence agency. However, ill health led to Smith's resignation in 1954, and he was succeeded by Herbert Hoover, Jr., the son of the former president, an oil industry engineer who had assisted the administration in negotiating a new oil production consortium in Iran.[26]

James Hagerty, Ike's press secretary, maintained what other staff members confirmed; any implication that Foster Dulles was running American foreign policy was "a lot of nonsense." That did not mean that Eisenhower did not respect and utilize Dulles's expertise. The false impression arose, Hagerty believed, partly because of Eisenhower's frequent use of the secretary of state as his political lightning rod on controversial issues.[27]

Most of Eisenhower's top appointees, often to their discomfort, shared that experience. Eisenhower was a better politician than most historians have understood. He had risen through the ranks by virtue of his mastery of bureaucratic politics, dealing effectively with Douglas MacArthur, Franklin Roosevelt, Joseph Stalin, Churchill, Truman, Charles de Gaulle, and, in his own command, generals George Patton, Omar Bradley, and Field Marshal Bernard Montgomery. On Inauguration Day, Ike was well aware of the political value of his status as a war hero. In order to govern effectively, he believed he needed to protect his popularity with the American people. His new subordinates would soon discover that he would not hesitate to leave them, as Attorney General Brownell remembered, "out on the proverbial limb." In the years to come—indeed right away in 1953—Foster Dulles would often find himself out on that limb, dealing, among others, with the most sensitive issues in the Middle East.[28]

FACT FINDING IN THE MIDDLE EAST

Given his discomfort with the British approach to negotiations with the Egyptians, Eisenhower set out to collect his own intelligence about the Middle East.

In February 1953, he learned that Eugene R. Black, the president of the World Bank, was about to embark on a trip to the region, with Cairo his first stop. The president called Black into the Oval Office and asked him, Black recalled, to "talk to the heads of different governments and come back and tell me what you think might be done."

When Black returned, he made two recommendations to the president. The first was that Ike "begin to deal even-handedly with Israel and the Arabs" in terms of financial assistance. The second related to Egypt, which the World Bank president called "the most important country," whose new leaders were "anxious to build a dam on the Nile." Black called that project "the most important thing that could be done in Egypt." "I wanted to urge him," Black remembered, "to seriously consider sharing in the financing of the Aswan Dam." [29]

Between 1898 and 1902, the United Kingdom had built the first Aswan Dam on the Nile River. Eisenhower learned from Black that the second dam was being planned as the greatest undertaking in Egyptian history. The new project was increasingly in the news. A February 6, 1953, *New York Times* article by Osgood Caruthers was headed: "Egyptian Dam to Dwarf Pyramids." Donald Neff, a journalist and historian of the Suez crisis, characterized the Egyptian situation as "a race between people and hunger." The objective of the dam would be to control the unpredictable flow of the Nile in order to permit cultivation of enough land to feed the Egyptian people. When completed, the High Dam would create a reservoir 350 miles long, provide flood control, irrigate 1.3 million acres of land, and produce more than half of the country's electricity. For the Egyptian people, the symbolic importance of the dam was almost as important as its economic impact. "The land of the Pharaohs," Caruthers concluded, "is taking a giant step into the twentieth century." [30]

After absorbing Black's perspectives, Eisenhower decided to send Foster Dulles on an even larger fact-finding mission to the Middle East. He blended the announcement of this initiative with a bold, high-profile speech on April 16, 1953—a month after the death of Soviet dictator Joseph Stalin—to the American Society of Newspaper Editors. Eisenhower did not discuss the Middle East that night. Instead, he challenged the new leaders of the Soviet Union to join him in moving toward disarmament and to assess the collateral costs of the arms race. "Every gun that is made, every warship launched, every rocket fired," he said, constituted "a theft from those who hunger and are not fed, those who are cold and are not clothed." A fearful world focused on arms was "spending the sweat of its laborers, the genius of its scientists, the hopes of its children." The costs of the arms race, Eisenhower concluded, had left "humanity hanging from a cross of iron."[31]

Eisenhower's Middle East agenda became clear when, two days later, Secretary Dulles revealed to the same group that he and Harold Stassen, the State Department's mutual security administrator, would visit a dozen nations in the Middle East the following month. Dulles noted that "no United States Secretary of State has ever visited any of these countries." Eisenhower's decision to send Dulles to the Middle East was timely; British-Egyptian negotiations over the Suez Canal that had begun on April 28 broke down on May 5. The following week, Dulles and Stassen headed for Cairo.[32]

After Dulles departed, Eisenhower apparently found himself wondering how the secretary of state would handle himself with men like Egypt's General Naguib. Ike confided to his diary that, while he respected Dulles "as an intensive student of foreign affairs" and "a dedicated and tireless individual," Dulles "seems to have a curious lack of understanding as to how his words and manner may affect another personality."[33]

But it was the British leaders, not Dulles, who frustrated Eisenhower. Ike thought he had chosen the perfect gift for Dulles to deliver to President Naguib—from one military man to another—a Colt revolver from the president's personal collection. But in the wake of the stalled negotiations over Suez, British leaders perceived the gift as symbolizing an American intent to provide arms to the Egyptians. Eisenhower hurriedly reassured Prime Minister Churchill that "presenting one Colt .38 to General Naguib did not presage a flow of planes, tanks, and guns to arm that nation."[34]

Dulles spent five hours with Naguib on May 11, and found the situation in Egypt and in the other Arab states more serious than he and Eisenhower had thought. He reported to the president that the nations of the region, with the exception of Israel, were increasingly hostile to the West and ripe for Soviet subversion. Afterward, when Eisenhower pushed the British to be more flexible, Churchill complained, the president recalled, "that we were leaning far too much toward the Egyptian viewpoint."[35]

NEGOTIATING WITHDRAWAL

Meanwhile, the British and the Americans continued their uncomfortable dialogue on whether or how the United States would join in the negotiations regarding the Suez Canal. Eisenhower finally told Anthony Eden, the

British foreign secretary, that General Naguib would need to explicitly approve, in advance, American involvement in the talks. In mid-March, the *New York Times* reported that "the United States has joined for the first time formally in Anglo-Egyptian negotiations over the withdrawal of British troops from the Canal Zone." That report turned out to be premature. In fact, Naguib had declined to approve American participation and Ike pulled the plug on the venture, writing Eden, "I feel we have been clumsy." Rather than openly endorse the British proposals, Eisenhower told Eden that he and Dulles had concluded that the United States should "preserve an attitude of absolute equality with all other nations."[36]

Responding to Eisenhower, Churchill expressed his fear that it would appear that the United States was helping Egypt. He later wrote that he felt like the man who, about to be attacked by a bear, had prayed, "O Lord, if you cannot help me, please don't help that bear." Churchill believed that unless the United States and Britain went into the negotiations "speaking with one voice," nothing would get done.[37]

Ike's response was unequivocal: without an invitation from the Egyptians, American involvement would make it appear that "our two governments, together, are there to announce an ultimatum. An uninvited guest cannot possibly come into your house, be asked to leave, and then expect cordial and courteous treatment if he insists upon staying." Eisenhower concluded: "Until it is ironed out, I do not see how we can possibly get into it."[38]

In July, Naguib escalated the tensions, insisting on the immediate evacuation of British personnel in the Canal Zone, refusing to consider any agreement lasting more than three years, and agitating for the sale of American armaments to Egypt. Eisenhower and Dulles eventually persuaded the parties to resume negotiations on July 30, based in part on American pledges of assistance with Egypt's economic development and the upgrading of its armed forces. Once again, Eisenhower skillfully juggled multiple priorities; the new British-Egyptian talks began three days after the July 27 signing of the armistice in Korea.[39]

Eisenhower's advocacy for a settlement of the Suez question achieved slow, incremental progress. In January 1954, the parties agreed that, after vacating the Canal Zone, the British would have the right to reenter the canal in case of war. But the following month, Gamal Abdel Nasser, the young Egyptian officer who had been a leader in the rebellion against King Farouk, moved against President Naguib. A struggle ensued, with Nasser deposing Naguib and assuming the presidency in April. Once again the negotiations on the evacuation of British troops from the Suez Canal Zone had been derailed. The charismatic Nasser chose to anchor his presidential prestige on the building of the Aswan High Dam. "Tomorrow," Nasser said, "the gigantic High Dam, more magnificent and seventeen times greater than the Pyramids, will provide a higher standard of living for all Egyptians." [40]

Nasser would prove to be an enigma to the West. The young president delivered fiery speeches, yet two American ambassadors to Egypt who knew him well—Henry A. Byroade and Raymond Arthur Hare—found Nasser gracious and often reasonable in private conversation. He was not, Hare recalled, "the typical hard-boiled dictator." The Egyptian president, Hare had concluded, "didn't like blood" and "didn't like violence." He found Nasser "quite approachable if you were willing to talk to him in a normal way" although, "born of conspiracy," the Egyptian leader was "always suspicious." [41] Both ambassadors never thought that their superiors in Washington quite understood Nasser.

Finally, Eisenhower's relentless pressure on the British paid off. On October 19, 1954, Britain signed an agreement with Egypt to cede control of the Suez Canal Zone to Egypt, with a proviso making the base available again to the British if necessary to defend the canal against foreign aggression. The date of June 18, 1956, was set for the withdrawal of the last British soldier from Suez. The agreement recognized, in the words of a *New York Times* report, "that the Suez Canal is an integral part of Egypt and at the same time of international importance." It would be in force for seven years, and allow the British to maintain a force of twelve hundred civilians, including a minimum of four hundred Egyptians, for operating the canal. One fundamental fact had not changed: the British and French still controlled the lion's share of the stock of the Suez Canal Company and, therefore, its overall operations. [42]

A YEAR OF UNCERTAINTY

As 1955 began, change was in the air. By February, it was evident that Nikita Khrushchev had consolidated his hold on the levers of power in the Soviet Union, ending a struggle that had followed the death of Stalin two years earlier. On February 24, Iraq and Turkey signed a mutual defense treaty in Baghdad, joined in April by the British. The Baghdad Pact had arisen out of an American effort to develop a defensive alliance in the Middle East comparable to the North Atlantic Treaty Organization (NATO), but Egypt and Syria had rejected the proposed Middle East Defense Organization (MEDO). So the United States and Britain had turned to the northern tier of Middle East nations—Turkey, Iran, Iraq, and Pakistan—to form an alliance that would be a bulwark against Soviet expansionism.[43]

Nasser immediately expressed hostility to the Baghdad Pact, interpreting it as anti-Arab and a challenge to his leadership; even Israel was negative toward it. The British pressed the United States to join the pact but Eisenhower was reluctant because, as undersecretary of state Herbert Hoover, Jr., stated, "It would adversely affect our influence in bringing about a reduction in Arab-Israeli tensions."[44]

A Gaza border incident lit the spark that would turn into a Middle East fire. On February 28, 1955, Egyptian infiltrators crossed the border and stole some documents from an Israeli scientific institute. Israel used this minor incursion as a pretext to launch a massive raid on Gaza that killed, according to Cairo, thirty-eight Egyptians, with thirty more wounded. Nasser declared, "That aggression was an alarm bell," forcing him to massively increase Egypt's military expenditures and seek a new source of arms. At the same time, he launched a series of suicide (Fedayeen) raids by Egyptian commandos from Gaza into Israel. The resulting chain reaction of raids and reprisals set the stage for the greater crisis of 1956.[45]

When the newly appointed American ambassador to Egypt, Henry Byroade, met with Nasser on March 11, the Egyptian president protested bitterly about American policy, the Baghdad Pact, and Israeli aggressiveness. Nasser also presented Byroade with a long list of the weapons he needed. The negotiations between the Egyptians and the United States foundered when the Americans insisted on American military advisors and, distrusting the financial viability of the Nasser regime, required cash instead of loans or in-kind payment.

The cast of characters for the evolving Suez crisis was nearing completion. Nasser was entrenched in Egypt and David Ben-Gurion, Israel's founding prime minister, who had retired in 1954, was on a path, as defense minister, to resume that position. And, on April 6, 1955, Anthony Eden succeeded Winston Churchill as prime minister.

The handsome, polished Eden had been Churchill's foreign secretary as far back as 1940 and, at age fifty-eight, had been the Conservative Party's prime-minister-in-waiting for many years. Physically, and perhaps mentally, Eden was past his prime. A botched gall bladder operation in 1953 had left him with an incurably infected bile duct, necessitating his treatment with antibiotics for recurrent bouts of fever. As prime minister, overwork and inadequate sleep made Eden increasingly impatient and temperamental—even, some of his colleagues feared, irrational.[46]

THE ALPHA PLAN

The Eisenhower administration was preoccupied during July 1955 with planning the first postwar summit of the so-called Big Four. The meeting took place July 18–23, in Geneva, Switzerland, and was attended by Eisenhower, Eden, Prime Minister Edgar Faure of France, Premier Nikolai Bulganin of the Soviet Union, and Soviet Communist Party first secretary Nikita Khrushchev. Eisenhower seized the headlines with a dramatic proposal for disarmament, including his "open skies" proposal for aerial reconnaissance over the Soviet Union and the United States to guard against surprise attack.[47]

While it was not on the formal agenda for the Geneva Summit, the Middle East was a backdrop. For a year, the Eisenhower administration had been working on a plan designed to resolve the Arab-Israeli conflict. As a result of Eisenhower's NSC planning process, the president had signed a secret Middle East policy, labeled NSC 5428, on July 23, 1954.[48] That document began: "The Near East is of great strategic, political and economic importance to the free world," and noted: "The area contains the greatest petroleum resources in the world." Therefore, "Efforts to prevent the loss of the Near East will require increasing responsibility, initiative, and leadership by the United States in the area."[49]

A commitment to develop a comprehensive Arab-Israeli peace plan, code-named Alpha, was launched by the supplementary section of NSC 5428, stating that "a definitive peace between the Arab States and Israel should continue to be the ultimate objective of the U.S." As it evolved, the plan was intended to address the major issues in the conflict, most of which survive to this day—the plight of Palestinian refugees, access to the waters of the Jordan River, access to the holy places of Jerusalem, resolution of boundary disputes (especially regarding the Gaza Strip), and military and economic aid to the parties. The latter included the possibility of assistance to Israel in financing compensation for displaced Palestinian refugees and to Egypt for construction of the Aswan Dam.[50]

While attending the Geneva Summit, Eisenhower, Dulles, and Eden held private meetings about the Alpha plan. When Eden wanted to postpone announcement of the plan, Secretary Dulles countered that waiting any longer was dangerous because the Egyptians, in a frantic quest for arms, had insinuated that "they would buy from the Russians if we didn't sell to them." On August 5, Dulles informed Eisenhower that he was ready to notify Nasser "that we would sell certain military equipment to Egypt as desired by him." Dulles was still worried that "if Egypt cannot buy here, they might buy in the Soviet Union." [51]

Originally, the announcement of the peace plan was scheduled for late September 1955, but Eisenhower and Dulles moved it up, responding to growing Arab-Israeli tensions and increased Soviet activity in the area. Dulles told Eisenhower that he feared a Soviet-Arab arms deal might force the United States "to back Israel more strongly and drop our role of impartiality." If Alpha were to have a chance for success, Dulles said, "it should be done while we can speak as the friend of both." [52]

Dulles granted that "the initial reaction of both sides will be negative." He lamented that "the Arabs do not really want to have peace with Israel, and Israel does not want to consider any boundary adjustments." The secretary also said what Eisenhower, the politician, wanted to hear: "We need to make such an effort before the situation gets involved in 1956 politics."

On August 19, Dulles sent the president the statement he intended to make a week later, and Eisenhower approved it. But, three days later, a series of violent incidents detracted from Dulles's presentation before it could be delivered. Egyptian and Israeli border guards exchanged shots at the edge of the Gaza Strip, and an Israeli motorized patrol retaliated and occupied Egyptian positions, killing three Egyptians. On August 25, the Egyptians responded with a weeklong series of raids that killed eleven Israelis and wounded nine. [53]

Dulles plowed ahead anyway. On August 26, 1955, he presented the broad outlines of the Alpha plan to a Council on Foreign Relations meeting in New York City. Dulles's speech was long on generalities and short on specifics. He asserted that "the problem of the Suez Base has been successfully resolved" but did not mention aid for the Aswan Dam. He stated that the president had authorized him to say that the United States would be prepared to join in formal treaty arrangements to guarantee the security of Israel and its neighbors. Harrison Salisbury of the *New York Times* discerned politics in the unveiling of the plan, "a shrewdly conceived political stroke designed to remove from next year's Presidential campaign a possible charge that the Administration was pro-Arab and anti-Israel." [54]

Salisbury was correct—politics was involved. Ike knew that reaction to the Alpha plan would be, as Dulles had remarked to a friend, "hot." The way the announcement was handled ensured that reporters would assume that Alpha was primarily Dulles's proposal, not the president's. Ike kept his distance from the speech, flying to Colorado on August 14 for an extended vacation. Russell Baker's column in the *New York Times* reported that the president intended to get "as far away from his job as it is possible to get." On August 26, reports of the secretary of state's speech were forced to compete with stories of the president taking "a day off," fishing on the South Platte River.[55]

Four days later, Foster Dulles expressed to the press his concern that the Soviet Union might intervene in the Arab-Israeli conflict by providing arms to Arab states. The rumors multiplied throughout September and, on September 20, Dulles met with Soviet foreign minister Vyacheslav Molotov and Soviet ambassador Georgy Zaroubin at the secretary's suite in the Waldorf-Astoria hotel in New York. The secretary warned them that if the Soviet Union made "large armament grants to Arab countries," it would destabilize the Middle East. Molotov disingenuously insisted that any such ventures were "not being approached on political grounds but rather on a commercial basis." He assured Dulles that his government intended "no complication of the situation in the area."[56]

The night before that meeting, President Eisenhower had arrived at the Byers Peak Ranch in Fraser, Colorado. Ike, in the words of the popular song recorded by Bing Crosby and Louis Armstrong, had once again "Gone Fishin'."[57]

2

★ ★ ★ ★ ★ ★

CRISES OF THE HEART

September 23–November 11, 1955

"Well, I walked over to the wall and sat down and came back. I am getting to be a big boy now."

Eisenhower to Sherman Adams, October 26, 1955,

a month after his heart attack

DWIGHT EISENHOWER had not enjoyed a vacation so much in years. He had pleased Mamie by agreeing to spend the six-week vacation at the home of Mamie's mother, Elvira Doud, in Denver, but his part of the bargain was a five-day, men-only fishing trip to Byers Peak Ranch. Once at the ranch, Eisenhower, as his physician Howard Snyder put it, was "as full of contentment as I had ever seen." The group was made up of old friends—the host, Aksel Nielsen, a friend, George E. Allen (not to be confused with assistant secretary of state George V. Allen), assistant press secretary Murray Snyder, and the physician. They were later joined by another longtime Eisenhower friend, Robert L. Biggers of Chrysler Corporation.

As the outing's final day approached, Ike made a decision worthy of a commander-in-chief: on Friday, September 23, the president of the United States would cook breakfast. The night before, he challenged the men to show up the next morning with "a he-man's appetite" because he was planning to cook a "despideda" (farewell) breakfast.[1]

Eisenhower bounded out of bed at 5:00 A.M., ready to commence his culinary duties. Dr. Howard Snyder was the first to arrive at the president's cabin. He had enjoyed the walk, gazing at the blue-gray outline of Byers Peak in the distance, and breathing in the crisp, cool, 35 degree morning air. When Snyder entered the cabin, the president was just emerging from his bedroom, in full stride toward the kitchen. The president boomed a greeting: "What are you doing up so early, Howard?"

As the others arrived, Eisenhower decreed that no one but he would be permitted in the kitchen. About 6:30, they sat down and indulged, according to Snyder, in "special Eisenhower corn cakes, eggs, sausages, ham, blackeyed peas, and red-eye gravy." After breakfast, their vehicles already packed, the party journeyed over the twelve-thousand-foot Berthoud Pass, arriving at the Doud home about 8:30 A.M. The group split up and Eisenhower continued on to his office at Lowry Air Force Base in Denver.

Intent on playing golf, Ike conducted his presidential business expeditiously. Colonel John H. McCann provided the president's morning intelligence briefing, including news that gave Eisenhower pause. Ike betrayed no hint of that concern to Ann Whitman, who had "never seen him look or act better."[2]

About 11:00 A.M., the president departed for the Cherry Hills Country Club, where he teed off at noon for an 18-hole round. Up to the 14th green, Eisenhower was, Howard Snyder recalled, "exuberant" about his game. Then he was interrupted with a message that he had a phone call from Secretary of State Dulles. Returning to the clubhouse, Ike was told that the secretary was en route to an engagement and would call again in an hour. The president returned to his golf game. Snyder overheard Ike grumbling about "an unnecessary call" and his game, in Snyder's terms, "went to pot" between the 14th and 18th greens. Ike returned to the clubhouse "in a bad humor" for lunch.[3]

About 2:30 Ike teed off for a second round but his game was disrupted three more times by calls from Dulles, two of them unsuccessful in connecting Ike with the secretary. Dr. Snyder noted that the president was so irritated at these intrusions that "the veins stood out on his forehead like whipcords." The one call that got through was important. The day before, Dulles had addressed the United Nations General Assembly on the

American proposal for Arab-Israeli peace in the Middle East—code-named Alpha—that Dulles had announced on August 26. Now that plan was in jeopardy. Dulles confirmed to Eisenhower in his phone call that the Soviet Union was preparing to provide "a massive lot of arms" to the Egyptians. He had experienced "a little rough time" in New York, discussing the matter with Molotov, the Soviet foreign minister. The British and French were "alarmed"; Dulles feared the Israelis might launch a preemptive attack on Egypt because "today they can lick them easily."[4]

Eisenhower replied that he had been briefed about "the Egyptian thing" that morning and had been "churning it around." The president expressed concern that the Russians "are considering giving arms to a country in an area where it will cause trouble." Dulles suggested a presidential communication to Soviet premier Bulganin. Eisenhower agreed—he was already obligated to respond to a September 19 message from Bulganin on disarmament—but he wanted to think about it overnight. Ike told Dulles he would call him the following morning.[5]

That phone call was never made.

DUAL CRISES

After the conversation with Dulles, Ike returned to his golf game but quit after nine holes. The president began to experience what he thought were symptoms of indigestion. His discomfort gradually increased during the rest of the day. Eisenhower declined his usual evening drink because, Dr. Snyder recalled, "he did not feel well in the middle." The president had little appetite at dinner and retired early.[6]

On Saturday morning, September 24, just after nine, Secretary Dulles discussed the Egyptian situation with the CIA director, his brother Allen, who reported that "the facts seem pretty firm" about the Egyptian arms deal. Foster did not think they would get far in talking with the Egyptians. Any protests should be directed at the Soviets.[7]

The brothers were unaware that another crisis had been building for hours in Denver. At the Doud home in the middle of the night, Mamie Eisenhower had arisen to go to the bathroom. She passed the door of the president's room, heard him making noises in his sleep, and stopped by his bed to ask whether he was having a nightmare. Ike replied, "No dear, but I thank you." Ten minutes later, he was at her bedside, saying, "I've got a pain across the lower part of my chest." Since he had complained about indigestion, Mamie gave her husband milk of magnesia.[8]

At 2:54 A.M., Mamie called Howard Snyder. Snyder recognized the "distinct note of alarm" in the first lady's voice and sent for a car. Eisenhower had suffered frequent stomach upsets through the years; a late-night visit to the president's bedside was not unprecedented. At 3:11 Snyder arrived at the Doud residence. Upon seeing the president, the doctor listened to his chest and took his blood pressure. Ike's pulse was very rapid and the doctor found it difficult to get a good blood pressure reading.

Ike was "agitated and complaining of severe pain across his chest." Over the next few minutes, Snyder gave the president amyl nitrite to sniff and injections of papaverine hydrochloride, morphine tartrate, heparin, and, later, a second shot of morphine. Suddenly the president went into what Snyder later called "a state of shock." His blood pressure plummeted and his pulse became even more irregular.

Instead of calling for an ambulance, Snyder asked Mamie to climb into bed and embrace the president. Snyder later wrote that "this had the desired effect almost immediately." Eisenhower went back to sleep a little after four—probably due as much to the morphine as Mamie's embrace. By this time, Snyder believed that he was dealing with a heart attack, but he chose to let the president rest from the trauma.

At 5:45 A.M., Snyder called Ann Whitman to say the president might not be into the office until ten o'clock or later. Murray Snyder, the assistant press secretary, should tell the press that the president had experienced a "digestive upset." When the fifty-plus reporters clamored for more information, Whitman called the doctor back and asked him how serious the episode was. Snyder responded that the president was asleep and "his digestive upset was not serious." That was a lie; Ann Whitman took the doctor's reassuring response at "face value" and passed it on to Murray Snyder.[9]

The president slept until 11:30 A.M. Dr. Snyder constantly monitored his blood pressure and pulse as he slept; once the pressure dropped to a dangerously low 86 over 56. Only then did Snyder call Denver's Fitzsimons Army Hospital and request a cardiac specialist to administer an electrocardiogram. The cardiologist, General Byron Pollock, arrived about 1:00 P.M.

Pollock quickly concluded that the president had suffered "a massive infarct," i.e., significant damage to the tissues of the heart. The president was told that he must go to the hospital. Even then, Snyder did not order an ambulance. Instead, he called for a Secret Service car. Whitman later said that Eisenhower walked down the stairs to the car, but Snyder's account says that, due to the difficulty of using a stretcher on the stairs, two big Secret Service agents carried the president down the stairs. He then walked to the car.

Arriving at the rear entrance of Fitzsimons, Eisenhower was placed in a wheelchair and rolled to an elevator, ascending to the eighth floor, where the VIP suite was located. Once in his room, the president was placed in an oxygen tent—an action that surprised him. This may have been the moment when Ike began to realize that he was being treated for a serious heart attack.

About 1:45 P.M., Ann Whitman, Murray Snyder, and other staffers left Lowry Air Force Base for the Famous Chef, a nearby restaurant, for a late lunch. As they began to eat, Murray was called to the phone. He returned to inform the group that the president had suffered "a mild anterior coronary thrombosis." Ann Whitman also received a call; the message was that the president wanted her to call the attorney general to ask him how authority could be delegated during his illness. They paid for their uneaten lunch and rushed back to the base. Ann Whitman believed that "we—and perhaps the world—knew that he had an attack of thrombosis before the President himself knew."[10]

GOVERNING WITHOUT IKE

The administration's first crisis in Middle East policy, mixed with the president's heart attack, only exacerbated the disarray that afflicted the Eisenhower team. In the months to come, the Egyptian arms deal would evolve into a major threat to peace. And the president was out of action at its inception.

Such situations seem destined to arise on a weekend when key people are unavailable. Congress was in recess. The chief of staff, Sherman Adams, was in Europe at the president's request, reviewing NATO operations. Attorney General Herbert Brownell, Jr., was on vacation in Spain. On that rainy Saturday in Washington, Jim Hagerty, the press secretary, was enjoying his first vacation in years, although he had stayed in the capital. Hagerty returned home from golfing about four o'clock and picked up the afternoon edition of the *Washington Star,* noting a two-column box at the bottom of the page, reporting that a digestive upset had kept the president from going to his office that morning. Hagerty, assuming nothing serious, lay down for a nap.[11]

About 4:30 P.M., Hagerty's special White House phone began to ring incessantly—a signal the call was urgent. The press secretary picked up the receiver and Murray Snyder was on the other end: "Jim, Dr. Snyder has just called me and told me that the President has suffered a heart attack." Hagerty felt like he had been "slugged"; he was sure his own heart was skipping beats. Snyder told Hagerty that he intended to tell the press that the president had endured "a mild coronary thrombosis."

Hagerty knew he must leave for Denver immediately. While his wife packed his clothes, the press secretary frantically scribbled a to-do list on a scratch pad. The phone rang; it was Vice President Richard Nixon. "Dick, sit down," Hagerty said. "The President has had a heart attack." "Oh, my God," the vice president responded. "When, how bad is it?" Hagerty did not know. Nixon expressed the feelings of the Eisenhower team: "We all need the President."

The conflicting accounts of those first hours reflect the turmoil that afflicted the Eisenhower staff. In Denver, Ann Whitman was stacking up five or six phone calls at a time. Hagerty and Wilton B. "Jerry" Persons, the assistant chief of staff and congressional liaison, agreed that the press secretary would call the secretaries of state and treasury, and cable Sherman Adams. Whitman's memory later was hazy; she thought she had called Milton first, then the other Eisenhower brothers, but Hagerty recorded in his diary that Ann had tearfully called him, relaying Mrs. Eisenhower's request that he be the one to contact the family.[12]

Hagerty recalled that Foster Dulles "was deeply shocked" when he told the secretary of state of Eisenhower's condition. "Jim, this is terrible news. It is terrible news for the President's family and for the country. But it is equally terrible for the free world." Dulles worried about the possibility that the nations of the world "will adopt an attitude of waiting and seeing who will be the next President" and decline to make commitments.

Dulles had reason for concern. A foreign ministers meeting was scheduled in Geneva starting October 27, designed to follow up on the July meeting of American, British, French, and Soviet heads of state. Eisenhower's first summit with the Soviets had generated hope for progress toward peace, especially disarmament. Dulles feared that the president's illness would make the foreign ministers' negotiations "more difficult than ever" and give the Soviets freedom "to play the usual game of stalling."

Hagerty's voice was "choked up" as he reached Milton Eisenhower on the phone. Milton suggested that, for public confidence, they bring in a civilian heart specialist, one not associated with the Army. Dr. Snyder and the

Fitzsimons physicians had already reached the same conclusion and had settled on one of the leading cardiologists in America—Paul Dudley White, the Boston specialist.[13]

About 5:15 P.M., a frustrated Murray Snyder informed Hagerty that he had been instructed to remove the word "mild" from further announcements to the press. He and Hagerty groused about Dr. Snyder's messages, which had migrated from "a mild digestion upset" to "a mild coronary thrombosis." Would the next message reveal something more serious? At Dr. Snyder's request, Hagerty arranged for Thomas W. Mattingly, the cardiologist at Walter Reed Hospital, to fly with him to Denver. Merriman Smith, the lead reporter with United Press International, had heard the news, called, and persuaded Hagerty to permit him to fly to Denver with them.[14]

At ten minutes until eight o'clock, Hagerty, Mattingly, and Smith boarded their plane. A torrential rainstorm at Lowry Air Force Base forced them to land at Stapleton Airport in Denver. Arriving at Fitzsimons about midnight, Hagerty quickly confirmed his worst fear—the president's heart attack was "more than mild."

Ann Whitman, after a sleepless night, described Sunday, September 25, as "a daze—mostly telephoning." Hagerty, equally weary, arrived at the hospital at 6:30 A.M. He shared a medical bulletin with the press that read: "The President had a very satisfactory night. His blood pressure and pulse continued stable. There were no complications."[15]

As the hours passed, Hagerty's anger smoldered over Howard Snyder's handling of the situation. He grumbled to his diary that "there is no such thing as a mild coronary thrombosis." Hagerty could not comprehend the manner in which Ike had been transported to the hospital. "You just don't let a person with a heart attack walk from his house to the car," he wrote.[16]

In the months to come, Jim Hagerty would perform an extraordinary feat—maintaining Eisenhower's image as an active president when the reality was otherwise. His partner in this pumped-up presidential narrative was Sherman Adams. Years later, Adams claimed in his memoirs that Dr. White had prescribed that the president should "be given as much official work as possible." In fact, for weeks the doctors severely restricted the president's work-related activities.[17]

The alarm in the country was mirrored in the stock market. On Monday the 26th, stocks on the New York Exchange declined $14 billion, half of the market's 1955 gain. Press speculation was rampant that the president's heart attack guaranteed that he would not be a candidate for re-election in 1956. The administration attempted to project normalcy by announcing a cabinet meeting, to be presided over by the vice president. Treasury Secretary George Humphrey, hoping to calm the markets, issued a statement saying "there is no reason to anticipate any change" in administration policies or programs.[18]

Mamie and son John were the president's first nonmedical visitors. "You know," Ike said softly to John, "these are things that always happen to other people; you never think of their happening to you." At such moments, patients often fret over trivial matters. The president pointed John to a table and asked for his billfold. He had won a bet with George E. Allen a couple of days earlier; it was his custom to pass on his winnings to John's wife, Barbara. Mamie later told John that Ike had been obsessed with the billfold throughout his trip to the hospital.[19]

Dr. Paul Dudley White's plane landed at Lowry at 1:30 that Sunday afternoon. After examining the president, Dr. White authorized Hagerty to release a statement that the president had suffered a "moderate" heart attack "without complications." The next day, Monday, September 26, White held a news conference at which he skillfully fended off questions regarding Dr. Snyder's handling of the situation, how long the president's convalescence might take, and whether the president would be able to run for a second term. White had proposed what for that era was standard treatment—a month of complete rest in the hospital, and severely limited activity for a second month.[20]

On the morning of Wednesday, September 28, on Dr. White's orders, Eisenhower was twice lifted out of his bed to sit in a chair for fifteen minutes, and again the following morning. That third time, the president experienced chest pains and was hastily returned to his bed. Snyder recorded that thereafter the president suffered "a return of acute manifestations" caused by "a pericardial adhesion" in the damaged area of the heart. Hagerty glossed over the episode in his briefing for the press, saying that the president was "a little tired this evening and did not feel as well as usual. Otherwise his condition is good." The physicians were not so sanguine. They decided, Snyder recalled, to "start the treatment over again and that the convalescence would be prolonged."[21]

That shook Eisenhower's faith in his doctors. Howard Snyder recalled that for years afterward, the president "waxed vehement in his criticism" of his treatment at Fitzsimons. Eisenhower, he said, held him "guilty of a grave error in judgment in not protecting him from this abuse." The physician knew better than to argue with Ike when he was in that kind of mood. "To arouse the President's anger," Snyder wrote, "would seem like committing murder to me." [22]

ANXIETY OVER IKE AND THE MIDDLE EAST

In Washington, Richard Nixon, John Foster Dulles, and Sherman Adams scrambled to figure out what to do without their leader. For three years, Eisenhower's influence, orders, and preferences had dominated every minute of their service. While Ike appointed strong subordinates and encouraged open debate, his word was always final. Now he was unavailable at the very moment when the Soviet Union had made an audacious move in the Middle East, possibly setting the stage for war.

Foster Dulles had already concluded that this was no time for timidity. He remembered vividly what had happened when Woodrow Wilson suffered a stroke after World War I, and Mrs. Wilson had prevented access to the president. That, he told Nixon, "had been awful." They agreed that Adams should fly to Denver to oversee access to the president. The vice president's planned trip to the Middle East should be canceled. Dulles warned Nixon that, with the president out of the public eye, he "should watch himself more closely as to what he did." [23]

On Tuesday, September 27, Foster Dulles's anxiety was undiminished. Sherman Adams, upon returning from Europe, opined that "Foster seems lost without the Boss." The secretary was suddenly on his own, lacking the presidential restraint that had so often prevented him from making rash decisions. He conducted two phone conversations with undersecretary of state Herbert Hoover, Jr., worrying that the Egyptian arms transaction might give the Russians a financial "stranglehold" on Egypt. Dulles asserted that "we have a lot of cards to play with Nasser although they are mostly negative." [24]

At 9:30 that night, the foreign ministers of the United States, United Kingdom, France, and the Soviet Union met in New York to discuss their scheduled meetings in Geneva for October. [25] Secretary Dulles and British foreign secretary Harold Macmillan agreed to speak "very frankly" to Soviet foreign minister Molotov regarding the Egyptian arms deal. Macmillan asserted that his country was "very much disturbed" over the arms offer and expressed fears that it could derail progress at Geneva.

Molotov coolly responded that, at the time he had left Moscow, "not a single rifle or bullet had been sold to any country in that area." Any such transactions would be on "a commercial basis." Irritated, Dulles responded "in all candor" that the arms deal was "not a theoretical and academic matter." The American public had believed that the Geneva Summit was a step toward peace but if "there were large shipments of arms to Egypt, the result would be to dissipate all these hopes."

Dulles recalled his conversation with Eisenhower about the arms sale to Egypt the previous Friday, when the president had "expressed his deep concern on this matter" and had planned to write Premier Bulganin. "Because of illness," Dulles concluded, "the letter was not written," but he implored Molotov to convey the president's concern to Bulganin. Molotov found "no grounds for any disturbance or concern on this." He retorted that the West had delivered even larger supplies of arms to other nations in the region, an oblique reference to matériel furnished to Turkey, Iran, Iraq, Saudi Arabia, and Israel.

The next morning, Foster told his brother, Allen, that Molotov had been "evasive." The CIA director did not believe that the Israelis would "sit by and watch" Egypt receive Soviet arms. Israel would want arms from the United States or a security agreement and, failing that, "they may start a war." [26]

The arms deal was made public on September 27. Egypt would procure Soviet-produced arms from the Czechs, in exchange for Egyptian cotton. The *New York Times* reported that Egyptian premier Nasser had sought jet bombers, heavy tanks, heavy artillery, naval craft, and other military equipment from Western powers, but the deal had collapsed when the State Department had insisted on cash rather than in-kind payment. In response to the Soviet arms deal, Israeli leaders had launched a campaign to obtain additional arms from the United States, linked to a security agreement. As Israel's ambassador to Washington, Abba Eban, put it, "Can Israel wait like a rabbit for the snake to get large enough to devour her?" [27]

On Wednesday the 28th, Dulles and Hoover agreed that, even without the president, they needed to communicate American concerns to Egypt. They decided to send George V. Allen, who, as assistant secretary of state for Near Eastern affairs, had developed a personal relationship with Nasser. Allen could stop in other capitals in the region, including Israel, to make the trip appear routine. Allen, rather than the American ambassador to Egypt, Henry Byroade—who Dulles believed had become too cozy with Nasser—would deliver the secretary's letter to the Egyptian premier. [28]

The letter that Allen carried to Nasser was threatening in tone and substance, lacking Eisenhower's editing that had often moderated Dulles's language. Dulles wrote that the arms deal could damage "the existing good relations between our two peoples." The United States might be forced to review existing programs of economic assistance and arms sales to Egypt, and revisit the current management of the American cotton surplus, designed to minimize its impact on Egypt. The arms deal with Moscow was not, the secretary asserted, "a simple commercial transaction"; it had "deep political meaning." Dulles urged Nasser "to ponder carefully the consequences of the course you are now embarking upon." That ultimatum was bound to elicit an angry response in Cairo. Allen's plea was rejected by Nasser, and the diplomat, after five days in Cairo, returned to Washington empty-handed.[29]

Back home, the administration was trudging through a legal no-man's-land. There was no constitutional framework for reassigning authority when the president was incapacitated. The 25th Amendment, which addresses presidential disability, would not be ratified for another dozen years. Deputy attorney general William P. Rogers, acting in Brownell's absence, met with the vice president and Sherman Adams at Rogers's home to avoid reporters. When Brownell returned the following day, he researched constitutional precedents and pending presidential actions, concluding that the situation did not require the vice president to act as president. Sherman Adams recalled that, from this moment onward, the government was essentially managed by a committee consisting of himself, Nixon, Dulles, Brownell, Humphrey, and Persons.[30]

The National Security Council met the morning of Thursday, September 29, to confront the dual crises—the president's illness and the new situation in the Middle East.[31] Nixon told the gathering that important decisions should not be delayed and even unimportant ones "should not be allowed to pile up for the President when he returns to Washington." Important matters normally processed "directly with the president" should now be brought to the NSC. The big problem was defining new directions in policy, especially in the wake of the Soviet-Egyptian arms deal. The NSC would need to operate within "existing presidential policy," Nixon asserted, and any new policy direction "would of course require presidential approval."

The council then plunged into the turbulent waters of deliberation without their captain. Allen Dulles called the Egyptian arms deal "a new kind of Soviet Trojan Horse" that could dump "large inventories of obsolete and obsolescent weapons" into a volatile region. The Soviets were poised to become "merchants of death" on a huge scale. Secretary Dulles feared that the USSR would provide arms not only to Egypt, but also to Syria and Saudi Arabia, shifting the balance of power against Israel. After the meeting, Foster Dulles called Jim Hagerty to inform him that Sherman Adams would serve as liaison between the NSC and the cabinet, and the president in Denver. "We don't want it to drift the way it did in Wilson's time," he said.

The same ground was plowed the next day in the cabinet meeting.[32] Attorney General Brownell stated that he had been asked "to determine how the Presidential load might be lightened in regard to routine actions." He asked cabinet members to prepare a list of actions normally requiring presidential approval that could be delegated. Foster Dulles revealed the plan for governing, stating that "Adams would be at Denver as the channel for presentation of matters to the President."

On Monday, October 3, British foreign secretary Macmillan arranged a meeting on the Middle East with Secretary Dulles and their staffs.[33] Eisenhower's disability hung like a pall over the meeting. The participants agreed that blocking the arms sale to Egypt was probably impossible. Dulles, so ready to threaten Nasser earlier, had reconsidered; the allies, he said, should "not take any threatening or drastic step at this time. There should be no public indication of displeasure." Egypt was trying "to play one against the other" but a neutral Egypt was preferable to a communist state. Dulles thought that any response should be directed at the Soviets. The group agreed that a letter from the president to Bulganin might dispel the impression that the United States "had simply swallowed the Russian intervention in the Middle East."

That same day, Eisenhower signed a letter to Nixon that Adams and Dulles had drafted for his signature: "Dear Dick: I hope you will continue to have meetings of the National Security Council and of the Cabinet over which you will preside in accordance with the procedure which you have followed at my request in the past during my absence from Washington."[34]

On October 4, Hagerty began his press conference with the statement he used almost every day: "The president's condition continues to progress satisfactorily without complications."[35]

EISENHOWER IN REBELLION

The Thursday, October 6, meeting of the National Security Council mirrored the convergence of the crises of presidential disability and Middle East instability.[36] Sherman Adams presented a positive report on the president's condition but he foresaw a long-term need to minimize Eisenhower's stress and workload. Adams insisted that Ike was "as bright and cheerful as he had ever been."

That was not quite accurate. Adams glossed over Ike's growing resistance to his exclusion from matters of state. Eisenhower, Adams informed the NSC, had "asked in particular to have the Vice President return" with him to Denver on Saturday. This visit, Adams insisted, was "not to transact any business" but to allow Eisenhower to express his appreciation for all that the NSC members had done. Adams also announced that, the following Tuesday, the secretary of state would visit the president. The president would be up to discussing serious NSC issues "pretty soon," but there would be "no controversial problems placed before the President in the coming week."

The rest of the meeting addressed the second crisis. The first Soviet arms had arrived in Egypt. Deputy CIA director General Charles Cabell reported that the Israelis felt like "sitting ducks" and were demanding action. Secretary Dulles discussed the need to "find more money and resources" to support U.S. objectives in the Middle East. He worried that the Israelis might launch "a preventive war against Egypt."

Back in Denver, a restless Eisenhower strained at the ropes of his restrictions. At his Friday, October 7, news conference, Hagerty revealed that for the first time the physicians had allowed the president to read. Hagerty described how nurses had rolled a table over to Ike's bed and placed a book rack on it, so all he had to do was turn pages. Even now the reading included no official documents, only "reading for pleasure." A reporter asked: "The President has—has not yet left the bed or taken a step has he?" Hagerty replied, "Taken a step? No."[37]

Dwight Eisenhower had always been an active, athletic man. Now he felt like an invalid. The doctors' attempts to insulate him from stress only fueled his anxieties. Ike finally persuaded them to permit him to dictate short notes to friends. He complained about these restrictions to Edward E. "Swede" Hazlett, his high school friend from Abilene who had been forced into early retirement from the Navy due to a heart condition. Ike wrote that "the doctors have almost completely succeeded in 'divorcing' me from my secretary (and thus effectively prevented the kind of reply I should like to make to your note)." On October 10, Eisenhower complained to Red Blaik, the football coach at West Point, that "I am not allowed to listen to Army football games." [38]

Still, Eisenhower had forced Adams to modify his regimen; the chief of staff gave up on his effort to keep the president isolated from stressful issues. Ann Whitman recorded that, upon Adams's return from Washington, "a new program was inaugurated regarding official business." Adams would continue to bring matters to the president for action, and Whitman could sit in the room and take notes. Nixon's arrival began the new regimen although the visit was limited to fifteen minutes. [39]

The president's new activities began more fully on Monday, October 10, when he signed documents and proclamations. Adams earnestly tried to keep the conversation light but Ike grabbed the chance to address the issue that haunted him and everyone else—whether he should run again. Ike ticked off the names of potential successors—Nixon, George Humphrey, former navy secretary Robert Anderson, U.N. ambassador Henry Cabot Lodge, Jr.—and found them all wanting. Over the next few months, Eisenhower would periodically revisit this litany of potential successors, invariably naming men who lacked the stature and political clout to succeed him. Adams tried to end the conversation, but Ike wanted to share that he had been "pretty depressed" when the doctors had informed him that they wanted him to remain in the hospital six more weeks. He was angry because they had first told him that the heart damage was the "dimension of a dime," but now he had learned that it was "considerably larger." [40]

IKE AND DULLES TOGETHER AGAIN

On Tuesday morning, October 11, the president saw the man who, in many regards, had been running the government's foreign affairs for two and a half weeks. Foster Dulles had been allotted twenty-five minutes by the doctors. [41] His agenda included preparations for the Geneva foreign ministers meeting, disarmament proposals, and plans for encouraging East-West contacts. Dulles presented a draft of an interim reply to Bulganin's September 19 letter on disarmament, to which Eisenhower, due to his heart attack, had not responded. Finally, Dulles raised the subject that was bound to raise the president's stress level—Egypt's acquisition of arms from the Soviet Union. Dulles described its "widespread repercussions" and presented a draft of a short letter to Bulganin.

Dulles rose and prepared to leave, but Eisenhower pulled him back. Ike wanted to discuss "the future" and the possibility that "the country might fall into the hands of persons who had no real principles." He wanted to find a successor "within the inner circle" of his administration, someone "reasonably young, preferably in his forties." Ike regretted that he had failed to identify anyone with "the desired youth and vigor" who was "respected by the country as having maturity of judgment." Dulles urged the president to let the matter rest until next year, following a "full recovery." Dulles, worried that he had exceeded his time limit, told the president that he had to leave. Eisenhower laughed and characterized such restrictions as the "dictatorship" that ruled his life.

Eisenhower's two communications to Premier Bulganin went out later that day. The second expressed the president's concern "about the new prospective arms shipments to Egypt" and his hope for "a peacefully constructive solution of the Arab-Israel problem." Brief though they were, these letters put Ike back in the diplomatic game. Jim Hagerty reinforced the image of an active president, describing Ike's involvement with seven topics of international importance and giving the impression that this had been a "surprisingly long" work session with the secretary of state. Buried in the *New York Times* report was the fact that Dr. Paul Dudley White had insisted that future work sessions still be limited to fifteen minutes.[42]

Two days later, at the meeting of the National Security Council, Foster Dulles broached the delicate subject that he had not raised with the president—what the United States would do if the arms deal with Egypt resulted in war between the Israelis and Egyptians. In such circumstances, Dulles feared it might be difficult "to convince the world that one or another of the two antagonists was guilty of clear-cut aggression." Would the United States dare to contemplate a blockade of the aggressor or the use of NATO forces? Admiral Arthur W. Radford, chairman of the Joint Chiefs of Staff, responded that it would be "relatively easy" to establish a naval blockade, but the unspoken dilemma was that the most likely target of a blockade—the probable aggressor—would be Israel.[43]

In Denver, Eisenhower plotted his escape from the "dictatorship" and the doctors' six-week timetable for his leaving the hospital. Some friends, including the NATO commander, General Alfred Gruenther, urged that

Eisenhower, once he left the hospital, go someplace warm and relaxing like Key West, Florida. Ike was having none of that. He told Sherman Adams on Wednesday that he "had pretty well settled on Gettysburg because Mrs. Eisenhower was set on it." That stretched the truth; the president wanted to be closer to Washington. He justified the decision on the grounds that it "would save Governor Adams' commutation time." Treasury Secretary Humphrey, after a visit to the president, contradicted Ike's explanation. Mrs. Eisenhower, Humphrey told Secretary Dulles, preferred that he stay at Fitzsimons but Ike was determined to leave. She was worried that at Gettysburg he would be too close to Washington and "feel freer to get back into things."⁴⁴

Despite his breakthrough meetings with Nixon and Dulles, Eisenhower's activities were still restricted. On October 14, Ike's sixty-fifth birthday, Mamie gave him a small plastic easel that would fit on his hospital table so he could resume another treasured pastime—painting. He wrote Senate majority leader Lyndon Johnson, a heart attack victim the previous July, that if the Texan were to visit him, "the doctors will probably put a time limit on us to keep us from getting garrulous about our common ailments." The following day, Ike complained to son John that "the doctors are still rather severely restricting my activities." He thanked the painter Thomas Edgar Stephens for the gift of a portrait of his mother. Ike reflected, "I feel rather like a child here, and I can imagine Mother's strong personality telling me to be good, to do what the doctors say, and gently prodding me into the business of a complete recovery."⁴⁵

On his birthday, Ike was still not reading the newspapers. If he had, he would have learned that the *New York Times* had "confirmed" that the Soviet Union had offered to finance the Aswan Dam for Egypt—an overstatement, it turned out, propagated by Egyptian sources. A few days later, the *Times* reported that the United States, according to "diplomatic officials," was considering contributing "substantially" to the financing of the project. The newspaper did not say that President Eisenhower would have to sign off on any such decision. At this time, he was in no position to make it. Even more difficult, Congress would have to approve the appropriation.⁴⁶

On Wednesday, October 19, at 9:00 A.M., John Foster Dulles walked into the president's hospital room and, in preparation for the Geneva foreign ministers meeting, handed the president a statement that would communicate to the world that he and Eisenhower were agreed on policies. Ike dictated a letter for the vice president to read to the cabinet, noting that the secretary of state would be bearing "a heavy load of responsibility" on matters "which Foster and I planned together." The president reinforced that Dulles spoke for him and "with authority for our country." [47]

THE NSC WITHOUT IKE

Thursday was a stressful day for the administration team in Washington. Foster Dulles had flown back from Denver to meet for two hours with the legislative leaders of both parties, briefing them on the upcoming Geneva meetings. Then Dulles attended the most important National Security Council meeting since Eisenhower had been stricken. [48]

At the previous meeting, the NSC had agreed that its planning board staff would review American policy in the Middle East. The board's lengthy report concluded that, because of the introduction of Soviet arms, "the risk of major armed conflict in the Near East is now more acute and more immediate." If the United States took a "hands off" approach to an Israeli attack, Egypt and Syria would surely appeal to the USSR for assistance. [49]

The planning board had reviewed possible economic sanctions to deter a resort to war by Israel or Egypt—a discontinuance of American aid, an embargo on trade, and blocking the transfer of funds from the United States to nations in the region. Military options were more troublesome. The report concluded that "a military blockade of Israel" would be "relatively simple and almost completely effective." The remaining military possibilities were more sobering, involving direct military intervention by the United States and its allies, hopefully with United Nations approval. The sticking point was that, in the event of armed conflict, circumstances might "make it difficult to establish, particularly in the minds of the general public, the identity of the aggressor."

That was bureaucratic talk for the elephant in the room—the probability that Israel would strike first, while it still had military superiority. Pro-Israeli groups had significant political clout in the United States. The suggestion of military action, even a blockade, against Israel threw the NSC into turmoil. Secretary Dulles, sensing the fear in the room, pleaded that they not repeat the mistakes of the Truman administration by dealing with the Arab-Israeli problem "on a purely political basis." He recalled that, in 1948, Secretary of State George Marshall had been humiliated over his opposition to President Truman's recognition of the state of Israel.

None of the alternatives was palatable. A blockade of Israel would generate a political firestorm in the United States. A blockade of Egypt would ignite anger throughout the Arab world, threatening a cutoff of oil to Western Europe. Foster Dulles fiercely argued that for "the United States to sponsor an arms race between Israel and the Arab States would be a very futile action." He preferred to treat the Egyptian arms deal as a "one-shot affair" and decline Israel's requests for weapons. CIA director Allen Dulles opined that neither the Israelis nor the Arabs "really desired a permanent solution." Vice President Nixon, who had been silent to this point, heatedly argued that the United States would have "a hell of a time" getting Congress to support sending American forces to fight the Israelis.

This contentious debate deteriorated without Eisenhower there to mold consensus. The discussion bogged down over whether the established policy toward the Middle East, NSC 5428—adopted initially in 1954—could be changed without the president's approval.[50] Finally, Nixon concluded that the NSC "had reached an impasse in its consideration of this policy." They had given Secretary Dulles very little to say to other world leaders as he traveled to Geneva. The group finally settled on the weakest possible option—Hoover's proposal that "in view of the President's absence," Dulles be authorized to inform the Israeli prime minister of the nonmilitary sanctions that would be possibilities in the event of war, fulfilling the spirit of existing policy. Military options, including a blockade, were sent back to the planning board for further study.

That same day, Soviet premier Bulganin's response to the president's message on the arms deal arrived. Bulganin transmitted a copy of what he had written to Anthony Eden, in response to the British prime minister's protest, contending that there was no need for serious concern. Eisenhower countered that "this large transaction has greatly increased danger of a major outbreak of violence in the area." The president held Bulganin's government directly responsible, ignoring the Soviet tactic of channeling the arms for Egypt through Czechoslovakia. In a meeting with the American ambassador, Charles E. "Chip" Bohlen, Bulganin repeated Molotov's claim of Soviet innocence, expressing surprise at the importance the United States placed on the deal between Egypt and Czechoslovakia. The Soviet premier pointed out that the Western allies had sold arms to Turkey, Iran, Iraq, and Saudi Arabia and the Soviet Union had not complained.[51]

PLOTTING THE RETURN

Wednesday, October 26, was a busy day for the impatient president. He had taken his first steps the day before. When Adams entered the president's suite, Ike proudly announced, "Well, I walked over to the wall and sat down and came back. I am getting to be a big boy now."[52]

Eisenhower, encouraged by this watershed event in his recovery, began to plan, in some detail, his escape from Fitzsimons Hospital. Later on the 26th, Eisenhower fussed over a matter that was still a long way off—the State of the Union message, tentatively scheduled for delivery on January 5. Ike had been informed by his doctors that, four months from the date of his attack—approximately the end of January—they would administer a battery of tests designed to ascertain how much of his previous activities he could resume. "For myself, I don't care," he said to Adams. "I have had a pretty good life, I am not too concerned with me." But Ike feared that the strain of delivering the speech in person might jeopardize the tests. He concluded: "If I could give the speech on the first of February, regardless of the verdict of the doctors, I would."[53]

Later that day, Eisenhower dictated several letters. One was to Swede Hazlett, who had written Ike regarding the 1956 election.[54] "Of course, you won't run," Hazlett had asserted, "and I am glad of it!" The "stresses and strains" of the job were "much too great for anyone in your condition." Eisenhower should leave the choice of a successor "to the primaries and the convention, without any high-pressuring for any individual." Hazlett also opined that Milton Eisenhower would be a "natural" for president.

Eisenhower had no intention of abdicating. He rejected the hands-off approach Hazlett had suggested because he would want a successor who would carry on his program if he decided not to run. Ike also questioned Hazlett's assumptions about his physical condition. "Today I am walking a few steps," he wrote, and his recovery was following "the normal pattern." In four months, the doctors could reach "an accurate prognosis of the level of activity a heart victim can sustain without incurring any damage." Eisenhower had clearly settled on a timeline for his decision about running. He would make a final determination after that four-month checkup, in late January or early February. If the results were positive, Ike had effectively decided to run.

TROUBLE IN GENEVA

The leadership team in Washington could not get their commander-in-chief back soon enough. The Middle East situation continued to deteriorate. The NSC learned on October 27 that, without informing the Americans, the British had landed troops in the Al Buraimi area of Saudi Arabia in a dispute over oil interests. In Geneva, Foster Dulles and Harold Macmillan confronted demands by the Israeli government that Egypt withdraw from its arms deal with Czechoslovakia and that the Americans sign a security treaty with Israel.[55]

Eisenhower was receiving disturbing cables from the secretary of state in Geneva. With the foreign ministers conference barely underway, July's "Spirit of Geneva" had evaporated. The Soviet Union's leaders had apparently been emboldened by their Middle East initiative and by the disability of the man they most feared—Eisenhower. Ike commented to his diary that it was evident that the Soviets were "going to make no concessions." They were "playing a game" while "they double cross us in the Middle East." The president ordered Adams to tell Dulles that "the United States must not be a party to a false peace or to prolongation of any kind of conference when obviously the other side is acting in bad faith."[56]

On Sunday, October 30, Secretary Dulles met with Soviet foreign minister Molotov alone regarding the arms agreement with Egypt. Molotov repeated the Soviet contention that the Western powers were already providing arms to nations in the region. The threat of aggression, Molotov argued, "was not from Egypt but from Israel." Dulles responded that the "danger of war should concern us all." When Dulles reported to the British and French foreign ministers the next morning, Macmillan summarized the allies' dilemma; in protesting the arms sale, the danger was that the allies might unwittingly bestow on the Soviets the status of "partners in Middle Eastern affairs."[57]

Israel continued to lobby aggressively for arms to counter the Soviet-Egyptian deal. On October 31, Israeli prime minister Moshe Sharett called on Dulles in Geneva with a list of "defensive" arms his government wished to purchase and renewed the request for a security agreement. Otherwise, Israel "would have to place greater reliance than ever on its arms." Dulles replied that such a request would have to be considered by the Defense Department and the cabinet. He said he doubted that Congress would approve a security treaty. The secretary warned the prime minister that Israel would lose much of its goodwill in the United States if it launched a preventive war. Dulles worried particularly about "one border incident leading to another with a crescendo culminating in war."[58]

The next morning, Eisenhower read the reports of Dulles's meetings. He lamented in his diary that Arab and Israeli leaders had long ignored his warning of what would happen if they did not make peace. He had "begged to be allowed to be friends of both sides" but had continually run into "that flaming antagonism." [59]

That antagonism exploded into violence again. The Israelis decided to call Foster Dulles's bluff. Allen Dulles informed the November 3 NSC meeting that the Arab-Israeli conflict had taken "a serious turn for the worse during the night." [60] The Israelis had attacked Egyptians in the El Auja area, a one-hundred-square-mile demilitarized zone bordering Egypt, established as part of the armistice negotiated by the United Nations in 1949. This episode was just one more of a series of violent flare-ups along the Jordanian, Syrian, and Egyptian borders with Israel that had frequently occurred since the armistice. At El Auja, the Israelis, allegedly because the Egyptians had established illegal checkpoints inside the demilitarized zone, launched an attack that killed fifty Egyptian soldiers in the bloodiest incident since 1949. The Egyptians had fought back and claimed a great victory but news correspondents doubted the accuracy of their reports.

Only that morning, David Ben-Gurion, assuming the prime minister's office for the second time, had provided cover for the assault by telling the Israeli Knesset that he was willing to "meet with the Prime Minister of Egypt and every other Arab leader" to settle the Arab-Israeli conflict. Admiral Radford told the NSC that the Israelis were mobilizing; Allen Dulles added that Israel had 86,000 men under arms and could rapidly expand to 200,000. Vice President Nixon demanded to know "what excuses" the Israelis had to offer for perpetrating this attack after a discussion with the secretary of state. [61]

A TRIUMPHAL RETURN

Dwight Eisenhower, still in Denver, was only marginally engaged with this increasingly dangerous situation. He was focused on ridding himself of the restrictions that were keeping him at the hospital. [62]

Eisenhower succeeded in cutting in half the doctors' recommended six additional weeks at Fitzsimons. The president targeted the first week in November for a brief return to Washington before proceeding to Gettysburg. The physicians insisted that, if Eisenhower tried to travel that soon, he would have to be pushed to the airplane in a wheelchair. Ike had no intention of returning to the White House looking like an invalid. He reluctantly agreed to additional days and, accompanied by Ann Whitman, increased his walking and practiced climbing fourteen steps in a nearby stairwell to convince himself that he could make it up the ramp to his plane. [63]

Eisenhower was also determined to minimize the restraints once he settled in at Gettysburg. On November 6, he sent a detailed letter to Dr. White, with specific questions regarding what he could and could not do regarding golf, bridge, shooting, walking, group meetings, paperwork, and rest periods after he left the hospital. Ike asked, "If I don't go to sleep could I lie down and still talk, if I wanted to?" The president still felt like a caged animal. He was privately determined to put one toe over any line that White drew.[64]

Adams continued to protect Eisenhower from the most disturbing reports from the Middle East, informing the president on Monday, November 7, that there were no new intelligence reports on the Middle East, indicating that "both sides are giving fairly serious attention to the warnings they have been getting." Ike cabled Foster Dulles, thanking him for his reports on the Geneva meetings and breaking the news of his departure from Fitzsimons, planned for the following Friday.[65]

Tuesday, November 8, Dulles informed Eisenhower that Molotov, after returning to Geneva from consultations in Moscow, had "delivered one of the most cynical and uncompromising speeches" he had ever heard, rejecting all the Western proposals for guaranteeing European security and reunifying Germany. The president expressed to Dulles his astonishment at the Soviet leaders' "deliberate repudiation of prior intentions and, in fact, a breach of good faith." Ike reluctantly concluded: "There seems to be little value in dragging out the conference." Eisenhower admitted to Herbert Hoover that he had "much depression" about what had happened at Geneva. "You can't trust them, the Soviets, when they are talking nice and you can't trust them when they are talking [tough]," he said. Dulles, in response, proposed to "recess" the Geneva conference. Eisenhower agreed that it was important to give an opponent an escape hatch. "We should be careful," he cautioned Dulles, "not to say we are through."[66]

While concerns over Europe and Germany had been flashpoints for the collapse of the Geneva meetings, the new situation in the Middle East was the backdrop. Two events since July had shaken the foundations of the "Spirit of Geneva"—the arms deal with Egypt and Eisenhower's heart attack.

On the morning of Wednesday, November 9, in Geneva, Secretary Dulles and Harold Macmillan sought agreement on joint policy directions regarding the Middle East. They discussed a proposed statement by Eisenhower that would resist the Israeli appeal for additional arms. In spite of the Soviet arms deal with Egypt, Macmillan and Dulles still hoped to pursue a general settlement of issues between the Israelis and the Arabs. Macmillan suggested offering Nasser a "package deal." Egypt would be asked to work with them on an Arab-Israeli settlement and, in return, the Western powers would assist with construction of the Aswan Dam.[67]

The president's statement, as finally released, viewed "with deep concern the latest developments" in the Middle East. "The recent outbreak of hostilities," he stated, "has led to a sharp increase in tensions." The United States, the statement read, did not intend "to contribute to an arms competition in the Near East." Eisenhower invoked the Tripartite Declaration of 1950, which had committed Britain, France, and the United States to repelling aggression across armistice lines and to maintaining a balance of arms between Israel and the Arabs. America's goal in the Middle East, he said, was "a just peace," as presented by the secretary of state in his August 26 speech proposing an Israeli-Arab settlement. If those conditions were met, the United States would be willing to "join in formal treaty engagements to prevent or thwart any effort by either side to alter by force the boundaries between Israel and its Arab neighbors." "Recent developments," Eisenhower concluded, "have made it all the more imperative that a settlement be found."[68]

Meanwhile, Eisenhower planned his return to Washington like it was a campaign event, micromanaging the plans for his landing at Washington National Airport. He wanted Nixon to come two thirds of the way up the ramp to meet him, then say a few words, with the president responding. He approved the plan for members of the cabinet, diplomatic corps, and leaders of Congress to be in attendance. Ike asked for a bubble car so he could stand and wave at the crowds. He reviewed all arrangements, including radio and television coverage.[69]

Friday, November 11, was Veterans Day—an appropriate day for an old soldier to return in triumph to the nation's capital. Ike had a flair for the dramatic at such moments. He intended his return to be reassuring to the American people at the very moment when the Geneva conference was collapsing and tensions in the Middle East were the worst of his presidency.

A crowd of five thousand was waiting when the president's plane, the *Columbine*, landed at Washington National. Mrs. Eisenhower appeared first at the door, followed immediately by the president, dressed in a camel hair topcoat over tan slacks and a sport coat, and wearing a soft brown hat, which he removed to wave at the crowd. Vice President Nixon and

John and Barbara Eisenhower greeted the president and Mrs. Eisenhower. Ike later thanked Nixon for organizing "one of the truly red-letter days of our lives." He greeted the gathering, joking that his vacation stay in Colorado had "been a little longer than we had planned." Eisenhower said he was pleased "that the doctors have given me at least a parole if not a pardon, and I expect to be back at my accustomed duties, although they say I must ease my way into them and not bulldoze my way into them." [70]

But Ike was confronted with the doctors' restrictions even as he and Mrs. Eisenhower entered the bubble top limousine. The top was closed, contrary to the president's wishes. When Ike asked about it, he was informed that, for medical reasons, he should not stand up. Eisenhower later complained that he was "forced many times to kneel on the floor of the car in order to make myself seen." When the nine-car motorcade arrived at the Lincoln Memorial, an Air Force band struck up a march, and two thousand servicemen, five paces apart, stood at attention between there and the White House. A large banner was strung across Pennsylvania Avenue, announcing, "Welcome Home, Ike!" The president's car arrived at the South Portico of the White House at 4:23. [71]

The Eisenhowers were welcomed by Chief Robert Murray of the Washington Police Department and the White House domestic staff. The president greeted them, walked to the elevator, and went to his room on the second floor, where he was immediately surrounded by four doctors. Their examination revealed no serious fatigue. His blood pressure was 126 over 84 and his pulse was 72. But by now, Ike was thoroughly irritated. He turned to Howard Snyder and snarled, "Damn it Howard, why did you not let me stand in the car? It would have been far less exhausting for me had I been able to do so." [72]

With the world in turmoil and his doctors still hovering, Dwight Eisenhower's seven-week nightmare was drawing to a close. That evening, he ate dinner with the family and Dr. White. While the rest of the group watched a movie—an activity still denied the president—Ike retired to sleep in his own bed. [73] He would go to the Oval Office for a while the next day. It was good to be back, even for a brief stay.

3

BACK IN THE SADDLE AGAIN

November 12, 1955–January 23, 1956

"It would appear that the world is on the verge of an abyss."

Eisenhower Diary, January 10, 1956, the second
day after returning to the White House

ON MONDAY morning, November 14, Eisenhower was determined to do something presidential before departing for Gettysburg. He called a meeting in the Oval Office with Herbert Hoover, Sherman Adams, and James Hagerty to review what Secretary Dulles should say upon his departure from Geneva.[1] Dulles, Eisenhower asserted, should say that the American policy of "peace through strength" would continue, and that the Russians must understand that following a path toward greater conflict was "pure suicide." The secretary should conclude with something like: "We came here seeking nothing for ourselves, only seeking decency and justice for Europe and the world." Ike lamented that "the results of this Conference mean that you can't let down an inch."

The president instructed Hoover to have Dulles report to him in Gettysburg as soon as the secretary returned from Geneva. Ike wanted the media to capture "the drama of having the Secretary change planes in Washington, hop into [the] little plane and come directly to Gettysburg." Their consultation should be billed as "a calculation of what the Secretary is going to do now, what the President is going to do now, and what our country should do now."

At eleven, the president's motorcade departed for Gettysburg, where he and Mrs. Eisenhower were greeted in the town square by the mayor and an enthusiastic crowd. Ike withstood the trip well and participated in an informal birthday dinner for the first lady that evening. While the large house's amenities made life relaxing for the Eisenhowers, the weather limited Ike's activities. He recalled the urging from doctors and friends that he recuperate in a warmer climate, writing a friend that the weather in Gettysburg had turned "murky, damp and cold." [2]

On Tuesday evening, November 15, Ike returned to his pre–heart attack practice of enjoying one or two highballs in the evening, although Dr. Snyder's insistence on taking the presidential blood pressure three times a day reminded him of his condition. Perhaps Ike wanted those drinks that night for a reason. A potential successor had decided not to wait to see how the president's recuperation progressed. That day, Adlai Stevenson, the former governor of Illinois and 1952 Democratic standard bearer, announced in Chicago that he would be a candidate for the presidency in 1956. [3]

A GROWING MIDDLE EAST PROBLEM

Eisenhower tried to follow the light schedule his doctors had prescribed, but the turmoil in the Middle East would not leave him alone. A large rally in support of arms for Israel was scheduled for Madison Square Garden in New York City that evening. In the morning, the president had approved a message to be read at the rally by Rabbi Abba Hillel Silver, who had offered a prayer at Eisenhower's inauguration in 1953. The statement affirmed that "a threat to peace in the Near East is a threat to world peace," but emphasized the United States' unwillingness to "contribute to an arms competition" in the Middle East. Israel's only hope for "lasting security," the president concluded, was "a just and reasonable settlement" of the Arab-Israeli conflict. [4]

A new National Intelligence Estimate—reflecting the consensus of the intelligence community (including the CIA and other agencies) regarding specific threats to national security—was delivered to the State Department the day of the pro-Israel rally. [5] The report confirmed that the Egyptian arms deal with the Soviet Union had "substantially increased the risk of

Egyptian-Israeli hostilities." Its authors concluded that the primary impact of the arms deal on Egypt's military capabilities "has been to raise morale"; the Egyptians were still no match for Israeli capabilities. The NIE suggested that a "relatively mild" reaction by the United States would be in order. Any attempt to punish Cairo by withdrawing aid or increasing the flow of arms to Israel would probably produce "an angry and emotional reaction," resulting in "violent anti-US disorders" that could push Egypt into greater reliance on the Soviet Union.

The Aswan Dam project was a major topic in the NIE. The intelligence community accepted as fact an unconfirmed rumor that the Soviet Union had already offered Egypt the equivalent of $600 million in aid for the dam over thirty years at 2 percent interest; if completed, the Aswan Dam would "constitute an enormous monument to Soviet industry." Still, the NIE reported no evidence that Egypt had accepted the offer. Nasser appeared to be committed to avoiding foreign domination, including "political alignment with the Soviet Bloc." The Egyptians would probably welcome an American and World Bank decision to assist with the project.

THE RESTLESS PATIENT

Eisenhower had not seen that NIE when he approved the plan for Foster Dulles, upon his return from Geneva, to visit Gettysburg on November 17. The president also approved the first meetings at which he would preside since his heart attack—the National Security Council on Monday, November 21, and the cabinet the following morning. These would be held at Camp David to insulate the president from Washington pressures.[6]

Dr. White worried about Ike's increase in activity. The heart specialist wrote the president that it would be "wiser to go a bit slowly than to rush the completion of your convalescence." It was normal to be "a little depressed or a little impatient." That letter was placed in Ike's hands the very day Secretary Dulles was scheduled to arrive. Ike acted quickly to keep his overprotective medical team at bay, dispatching reassuring messages to several of them, including Dr. White. The gap between what Eisenhower claimed he was doing and the reality was a small chasm. He wrote the heart specialist: "So far as a feeling of impatience on my part is concerned, I believe that I conquered that weeks ago." On the contrary, Ike said, "I am afraid I am beginning to like the 'lazy life' " and "beginning to practice procrastination."[7]

In fact, he hated it. The president could hardly wait for the secretary of state's visit. Foster Dulles's return to the United States followed the president's script to the letter, even though one engine of his plane had "conked out" over the Atlantic. At the airport, Dulles declined to comment on the collapse of the Geneva meetings except to say that his first duty was "to report to the President." The secretary flew immediately to Gettysburg, arriving at four in the afternoon for a ninety-minute conference with Eisenhower. The president had arranged for Dulles to deliver a nationwide television and radio report the following night, and Dulles stayed overnight in Gettysburg in order to further review his presentation with the president. Dulles's report to the American people on November 18 was moderately optimistic—he did not believe that the recess of the Geneva meetings meant the Soviets and Americans were closer to war. The secretary ended his presentation with a statement from the president pledging that "no setback, no obstacle to progress will ever deter this Government from the great effort to establish a just and durable peace."[8]

Foster Dulles did not mention the Middle East in his television report, but it was on Dwight Eisenhower's mind. The president understood that the new situation in that region, signaled by the arms agreement with Egypt, had been integral to the collapse of the Geneva talks. On November 19, Eisenhower wrote Prime Minister Eden contending that "the only real solution to the dangerous situation in the Middle East is an Israeli-Arab settlement."[9]

The following Monday, Eisenhower, for the first time since he was stricken, went to Camp David to chair his favorite policymaking body, the National Security Council.[10] Secretary Dulles reported on the "new cold war front in the Near East." The Egyptian arms deal, Dulles asserted, "confronted the West with a very grave situation." The stakes were high: "The loss of the oil of the Middle East would be almost catastrophic for the West." Dulles restated his and Eisenhower's hope for "a general solution of the quarrel between the Israelis and the Arabs."

After the meeting, instead of resting, Ike returned to his lodge to confer with Dulles, and they were later joined by Nixon, Secretary of Defense Charles E. Wilson, and Treasury Secretary Humphrey. The president had eleven guests for dinner and played bridge until eight. Eisenhower said very little at the cabinet meeting the following morning, while Foster Dulles repeated his assertion that the Soviet Union "has opened a new front in the cold war."[11]

These had been two demanding days for the recovering heart patient.

In his memoirs, Eisenhower claimed that, after these meetings, "I felt no fatigue or weariness." In fact, when he arrived back in Gettysburg, he was exceedingly weary. He was so fatigued that Dr. Snyder suggested that he attend only one of the meetings next time or separate them by a day, advice that Eisenhower reluctantly accepted, canceling his participation in the December 2 cabinet meeting.[12]

Still, a popular country song of the day—sung by movie cowboy Gene Autry—expressed how the president must have felt; Ike was "back in the saddle again." The day after the November 22 cabinet meeting, Eisenhower approved a flurry of meetings for December, including NSC and cabinet meetings at Camp David on Thursday and Friday, December 8 and 9, before traveling to Walter Reed Hospital for a checkup that weekend. He planned to remain in Washington to attend legislative planning meetings scheduled for Monday and Tuesday, December 12 and 13.[13]

THE ASWAN DILEMMA

On Sunday, November 27, Anthony Eden cabled Eisenhower about "the likelihood of an Egyptian-Russian deal over the Aswan Dam." The Egyptians were in Washington negotiating with the World Bank's subsidiary, the International Bank for Reconstruction and Development (IBRD). American officials had dominated World Bank policies since its creation in 1944, and they now wanted to make competitive contract bids a condition for providing aid to Egypt to build the dam. But the Egyptians were already negotiating construction of the dam with a European consortium that included British firms. Eden feared that if the Egyptians left Washington without an agreement, "the Russians are certain to get the contract." "I hate to trouble you with this," Eden concluded, "but I am convinced that on our joint success in excluding the Russians from this contract may depend the future of Africa."[14]

Until Eden's cable, Eisenhower had not focused on the Aswan Dam. He later called Hoover about it. Hoover said that State Department leaders were "fairly well agreed" that the United States should provide aid to the project. Hoover called the venture "the largest single project yet undertaken anywhere in the world." Ike said that until now he "had no appreciation of the magnitude of the proposal" to build the dam. Eisenhower asked Hoover to urge Foster Dulles to call him at his office the next morning.[15]

On Tuesday, November 29, the secretary called Eisenhower, who inquired whether "there was any reason not to go all out for the Dam in

Egypt?" The secretary did not dissent. Both men worried that Nasser was playing the United States against Russia to get a higher bid. If the United States was going to put up "the bulk of the money," Ike wanted American engineers to inspect the plans for the dam to be sure they were feasible. "We are not going to pay double for something we can get much cheaper," he said.[16]

Eisenhower presided at the Thursday, December 1, NSC meeting, leaving the cabinet meeting the next day for the vice president to chair.[17] He derailed the scheduled agenda and asked Dulles and Hoover to report on "assistance to Egypt in financing the High Aswan Dam." While the Soviets might duplicate the American offer, Hoover said without contradiction by Dulles, it was "essential to make this serious and liberal offer to the Egyptian Government." Treasury Secretary George Humphrey—fiscally conservative and isolationist in his outlook—objected, contending that increased Egyptian competition in the cotton market would be potentially damaging to American producers. Humphrey asserted that the project was bound to cost more than estimated. Supporting the Aswan Dam, he said, was "a terrific example of the United States devoting itself to building up a socialized economy in Egypt for all the world to look at."

Eisenhower had made up his mind. He responded to Humphrey that the years required to build the dam would minimize any impact on American cotton producers, assuming American population growth. As for supporting socialism, Ike cited the Hoover Dam and asserted that the only way the United States had ever been able to develop such projects had been "through the instrumentality of the Government and Government financing." Secretary Dulles added that "implicit" in the program of assistance would be that the Egyptians would agree "to reach some genuine understanding with Israel." He believed that the Egyptians would be incapable of financing the project while simultaneously preparing for war with Israel.

Humphrey was still skeptical. He prophesied that, however meritorious the Aswan project might be, a half dozen other countries would knock on the president's door, claiming their projects were just as worthy. Eisenhower turned to Humphrey, flashed that famous smile, and asked if the secretary remembered a World War I cartoon, the caption of which read: "If you knows a better 'ole, go to it." Humphrey muttered that, on such issues, he "died hard."

Eisenhower's putdown of his old friend ended the discussion. The NSC summary assumed that, in addition to an IBRD loan of about $200 million, the United States and Britain would provide $200 million over a ten-year period for the project. The minutes noted specifically "the president's approval" of American participation.

The following day, December 2, Hoover drafted policies for financing Aswan. Britain would be expected to fund not less than 20 percent of the allied contribution. The World Bank, at American insistence, would require competitive bidding, Egyptian agreement with Sudan on the disposition of the waters of the Nile, and "sound fiscal and monetary polices." The covert agenda was to induce the Egyptians to spend their resources on the dam instead of weapons to oppose Israel, and to finance the remaining costs themselves rather than seek funds from the Soviet Union.[18]

A NEW FRONT IN THE COLD WAR?

To Eisenhower, the Egyptian arms deal had been a fire bell in the night. On Monday, December 5, he wrote Foster Dulles that "nothing has so engaged my attention the past few weeks as the change in the international situation." As Ike saw it, the struggle between communism and the free world had changed. Under Stalin, the Soviets had relied on the threat of force to achieve their goals. The new Russian leaders "seem to have determined to challenge with economic weapons," he told Dulles. Democracies like the United States changed policies publicly and slowly, whereas a dictatorship could "move secretively and selectively."[19]

These worries took a toll on the recovering president. Later in the day, Dr. Snyder "remonstrated" with Eisenhower about "excessive office commitments." Ike went to bed that night at 6:45 and had his supper there. He suffered physical discomfort in his chest until 3:00 A.M., although he and Snyder eventually agreed that the cause truly was indigestion. The next morning, the doctor again warned the president that he was overdoing it. Snyder recorded in his log that his examination indicated "cardiac fatigue."[20]

At Camp David on December 8, Eisenhower and Foster Dulles walked together toward the lodge where the 10:00 A.M. NSC meeting would be held. Dulles informed the president that the Defense Department had nearly completed its review of Israel's request for arms, and the need for a decision was imminent. The proposed aid would be limited to defensive weapons. Eisenhower commented that the United States "could not very well refuse to let the Israelis buy some defensive weapons." But Dulles was concerned; he warned the president that "any sale of arms to Israel would be misinterpreted in the Arab world as support for Israel against her Arab neighbors." The political fallout could "drive the Arabs more and more into the arms of the Soviet Union." [21]

Eisenhower and Dulles chose not to raise this explosive issue with the NSC. The Thursday meeting was focused on a report from a committee chaired by Dr. James Killian of the Massachusetts Institute of Technology established by Eisenhower in 1954 to review defense capabilities. [22] The Killian report underscored the "unacceptable" vulnerability of the Strategic Air Command to Soviet attack. The authors recommended a massive spending program. Eisenhower said he was skeptical that increased military spending would make the country safer. He could conceive of no sure way to protect the nation from unthinkable horrors if the enemy launched an all-out attack. Secretary Wilson observed that "the stark facts" were that the pace of American and Soviet weapons development meant that "in time both will be able to destroy the world, including the birds."

Eisenhower issued a somber warning. The United States, he said, was "engaged in defending a way of life over a prolonged period." The government could force higher spending and "our abundant economy could stand it—for a while; but you cannot do it for the long pull without destroying incentives, inflating the currency, and increasing government controls. This would require an authoritarian system of government, and destroy the health of our free society."

Eisenhower convened a meeting with Dulles, Humphrey, and Wilson over lunch to discuss how they could use foreign aid to respond to the new Soviet economic tactics. To Dulles, the government's present aid program lacked both flexibility and continuity. [23] Humphrey argued that Congress would defeat any specific request for the Aswan Dam because it would affect American agriculture; any congressman who wanted a dam for his district "would press against giving a big dam to the Egyptians." Dulles hoped to seek "general authority" without asking Congress to approve specific projects—similar to the Marshall Plan for Europe. Eisenhower endorsed that approach, aware that it would be difficult to obtain such authority from a Democratic Congress in an election year.

THINKING ABOUT RUNNING

Ike's checkup at Walter Reed Hospital on Saturday, December 10, went well enough to stimulate his thoughts about running again. Eisenhower discussed the coming election with Jim Hagerty as they drove back to the White House. The president said he was "appalled by the lack of qualified candidates on the Democratic side." He did not believe that Adlai Stevenson, Averell Harriman, or Estes Kefauver had the "competency to run the office of President." Ike wanted more discussion with Hagerty when they found time, on a strictly "confidential" basis.

Hagerty later called Sherman Adams to report that the doctors had found Eisenhower in "good shape," but wanted the president to cut back on his schedule. Ike had already scheduled luncheon meetings for Monday and Tuesday, the days set aside for legislative meetings to review budget proposals. Adams and Hagerty were able to persuade Ike to cancel the luncheon engagements, one of which had been scheduled with Thomas Dewey, the former New York governor and GOP presidential standard-bearer in 1944 and 1948. Eisenhower quipped to Hagerty, "He might not be a bad Presidential candidate." [24]

Although Ike canceled the luncheons, December 12 and 13 were his most arduous days of work since the heart attack. The president met with Republican congressional leaders both morning and afternoon on Monday, and for four hours with bipartisan congressional leaders the next morning. Eisenhower pushed for an expanded program of foreign aid, which the administration preferred to call "mutual security." [25]

These meetings were the prelude to Secretary Dulles's announcement a few days later that the administration would, in the new fiscal year, seek $4.9 billion for foreign aid—an unprecedented 81 percent increase over the previous year's budget. Dulles warned that the new Soviet offers of economic assistance to the countries in the Middle East and South Asia could become a "Trojan horse to penetrate and then take over independent countries." The administration tried to bury the funding for the first increment of U.S. assistance for construction of the Aswan Dam in a general $100 million fund for the Middle East, although no official offer had yet been made to Egypt. [26]

Eisenhower was still spending most of his week at Gettysburg. During the return trip from Washington, he resumed his discussion with Hagerty about the 1956 election. [27] When Hagerty asked, "Mr. President, do you know what you're going to do in 1956?" Ike responded with a favorite, less-than-candid mantra: "Jim, you've always known that I didn't particularly want to be President." Eisenhower again deplored the lack, in his perception, of qualified successors. "I don't want to run again," he insisted, "but I am not so sure I will not do it." Ike repeated, as if to himself: "I don't want to, but I may have to."

In Gettysburg the next day, Eisenhower and Hagerty continued their conversation. Eisenhower ticked off every candidate he could approve—Dewey, Democratic governor Frank Lausche of Ohio, and, from his inner circle, Treasury Secretary Humphrey, Attorney General Brownell, chief of staff Adams, and former deputy defense secretary Robert Anderson. Ike and Hagerty generally agreed that none of them could hope to obtain the nomination or be elected. The final two possibilities were Chief Justice Earl Warren and Ike's brother Milton. Regarding Warren, Ike snapped, "Not a chance"; he would not approve of a chief justice leaving the bench to run for president. That left the president's brother, but Ike and the press secretary agreed that the American people did not like dynasties. As if on cue, Hagerty declared that his favorite ticket was still "Eisenhower-Nixon."

Afterward, in his diary, Hagerty was deferential to Ike's self-promoting analysis. He believed the president was "moving now in the direction of feeling that it will be his duty regardless of his health to try to keep this nation free of war and on the right path." In other words, if his health issues could be resolved, Ike had decided to run.

This plan was not new, except to Hagerty; Eisenhower had outlined the same scenario in his October 26 letter to Swede Hazlett. Perhaps Ike was testing his arguments on Hagerty, preparing the press secretary to handle the issues later with reporters. Still, Eisenhower had his worries. The president had confided to Hagerty that what concerned him most was that if he won a second term, "people will think they will have to take care of me—I would hate that. I could not live with myself as an invalid or a semi-invalid."

MORE MIDDLE EAST TROUBLE

Election year and Middle East politics were becoming more entangled. On December 13, the Syrian ambassador to the United Nations called for a special Security Council meeting because, on December 11 and 12, Israel had attacked Syrian forces at Lake Tiberias (also known as the Sea of Galilee) near the Golan Heights. The Israelis claimed that they had acted in response to the shelling of Israeli fishing boats and their police escorts. This incident resulted in a series of contentious Security Council meetings until, on January 19, the council passed a resolution condemning the Israeli action.[28]

Such incidents underlined the importance of launching a diplomatic offensive to implement the Middle East strategy that Eisenhower had rammed through the NSC on December 1—trading support for the Aswan Dam for Egypt's willingness to join in efforts to make peace with Israel. On Wednesday, December 14, undersecretary Hoover explained the implications of the new policy in a meeting with an Egyptian delegation, the British ambassador, Roger Makins, and Eugene Black, the World Bank president. The Egyptians, Hoover later wrote Dulles, responded "warmly" to the proposal, but reacted "violently" to Hoover's insistence that American funds could be used only to support contracts that were the result of competitive bids. Egyptian negotiations with a consortium of British, French, and German companies were well advanced, and a bidding process would force them to start over and delay the project. Hoover informed Secretary Dulles that the Egyptians were being "strongly pressured" by the British to make a deal with the consortium. He feared "a violent reaction in Congress" toward granting American aid should the deal with the consortium be concluded.[29]

Eisenhower's legalistic attitude was partly responsible for this impasse. He had firmly instructed Hoover that the United States could not "violate our basic procedures and customs of handling US Government funds by eliminating competition for the Aswan Dam contract, such as awarding it to the consortium on a 'negotiated' basis." Ike expressed his frustrations with Anthony Eden's government to Ann Whitman: "The British have never had any sense in the Middle East."[30]

The American offer was formalized in a December 16 meeting with Hoover, Makins, Black, and Abel Moneim el Kaissouni, the Egyptian finance minister. Hoover handed Kaissouni an aide-mémoire—a document detailing the Anglo-American commitment. The United States proposed to provide a $54.6 million grant to assist with the first stage of construction, matched by $5 million from the British, in addition to working with the World Bank to facilitate further lending. The document reaffirmed that this aid would be available only if construction contracts were issued on a competitive basis. Kaissouni expressed his "deep gratitude" and indicated Egypt's willingness to try to "work out their problems" with this approach. One phrase in the American aide-mémoire would be important months later: "These proposals are, of course, subject to review by [the] USG [U.S. government] in [the] event extraordinary circumstances intervene." Those circumstances would revolve around the critical question of whether the

American Congress would be willing to finance the proposal. The news of the American and British commitment to the Aswan Dam could not be kept secret. A December 18 *New York Times* page-one story was headed, "West Will Help Egypt Build Dam."[31]

Meanwhile, Eisenhower's subordinates were frantically planning for January and the president's permanent return to the White House. The issue was how to minimize presidential burdens. At the Friday, December 16, cabinet meeting, in the president's absence Vice President Nixon called for limiting cabinet and NSC meetings to two hours with carefully prepared presentations, reviewed ahead of time with the president's staff secretary. Sherman Adams presented a draft of a schedule for the president that reflected, in mid-December, the doctors' judgment that the president's condition showed "some feeling of overwork." Serious matters and significant meetings would be addressed in the mornings, with the president reserving 12:30 to 2:00 for lunch and rest. He would then use the remainder of the afternoon for less stressful, routine business, such as dictation.[32]

Ike's priority was maintaining his involvement with the NSC. He presided at the Thursday, December 22, meeting, where Allen Dulles reported that the British were "flexing their muscles" in the Middle East and "creating problems for the United States."[33] The context for this situation was an overall decline in British influence in the region since the end of World War II, reflecting the dissolution of old colonial ties and increasingly fragile relations with states where the British retained residual influence, such as Jordan. That decline had been visibly symbolized in 1954 by the agreement for the withdrawal of British troops from the Suez Canal Zone, a step the Eisenhower administration had negotiated. In October 1955, the British had landed troops in the Al Buraimi area of Saudi Arabia in a dispute over oil rights, and had pressured Iran into joining the Baghdad Pact. Their insistence that the Jordanians join the pact had stirred protests among that country's huge population of pro-Nasser Palestinians, resulting in riots on December 15. All of this, the CIA director reported, had been "a severe blow to the British and, to some extent, to Western prestige." Foster Dulles said he believed that the British were trying "to restore something of their lost prestige in the Middle East."

The next day, Secretary Dulles instructed George V. Allen, the assistant secretary for the Near East, to inform the Israelis that, because of their attack on the Syrians on December 11–12, the United States was "suspending action" on their request for arms. Dulles urged Allen to make the argument that, no matter how many weapons they procured, the Israelis were still a population of 1.5 million surrounded by forty million Arabs with access to surplus Soviet weapons. "Under these circumstances," Dulles continued, "there is no choice to Israel but to rely upon international influences to protect it." [34]

This was the Eisenhower-Dulles strategy—to restrain the Israelis while pressuring the Egyptians, using the Aswan Dam as an enticement to work toward a comprehensive peace settlement. The pieces were in place to launch an American diplomatic offensive in the new year, when Robert Anderson would visit the parties as a personal emissary from the president. [35]

STILL A PART-TIME PRESIDENT?

Meanwhile, Eisenhower was haunted by the question of running again. The day that Dulles suspended consideration of the Israeli arms request, Ike wrote Swede Hazlett that the "principal topic" of their last exchange—whether he should run in 1956—was "still unresolved, swirls daily around my mind and keeps me awake at night.... I am afraid," he wrote, "that I have had far too great a preoccupation with my own health these past months.... The one thing I need is exercise," he said—undoubtedly thinking of golf—which was impossible because of the Gettysburg weather. [36]

Ike wrote Dr. White on December 27 that he had decided to take the physician's advice. He planned to leave the next day for Key West in search of some sun and distance from the escalating responsibilities that migrated daily from Washington to Gettysburg. The bargain was that, when Ike returned, it would be to the White House, not to Gettysburg. The Key West trip might be one of his last chances to think, without distractions, about running for a second term. Before departing, he instructed Ann Whitman to organize a "top secret" dinner of key advisors to address the election issue on Tuesday, January 10, the day following his scheduled return to the White House. [37]

At 7:15 A.M. on the 28th, as the Eisenhowers prepared to depart, the doctors checked the president and twice found his heart skipping beats. Once in Florida, Ike seemed to relax; that evening, after two highballs, dinner, and a movie, Howard Snyder found no more evidence of irregularities. On New Year's Eve, the president relaxed in the evening with a western movie, and welcomed the New Year by playing poker until one in the morning. When Snyder took the president's blood pressure at bedtime, he found it stable but his pulse was skipping beats. [38]

In deciding to go to Florida, Eisenhower had acquiesced in the decision not to present the State of the Union message in person. On January 5, 1956, it was read by a clerk of the House of Representatives.[39] That decision reflected that, three and a half months after Eisenhower's heart attack, the nation still did not have a full-time president.

The State of the Union document itself was uninspiring, reflecting its preparation, more than usual, by others. The message noted that "Communist tactics against the free nations have shifted in emphasis from reliance on violence and the threat of violence to reliance on division, enticement and duplicity." The Middle East would be the test case for the implementation of these tactics. The president pledged to "spare no effort in seeking to promote a fair solution of the tragic dispute between the Arab States and Israel, all of whom we want as our friends." He made no mention of the Aswan Dam, trying to keep that specific project off the congressional radar in an election year. Eisenhower concluded with a favorite theme: "The sum of our international effort should be this: the waging of peace, with as much resourcefulness, with as great a sense of dedication and urgency, as we have ever mustered in defense of our country in time of war."

On Sunday, January 8, Eisenhower returned to the White House, this time to stay. That day, Foster Dulles was informed that more riots had broken out in Jordan, raising the possibility that the Jordanian government might collapse. While the riots were partially a response to British pressure to join the Baghdad Pact, exacerbated by Egyptian agitation, George Allen informed Dulles that "there was evidence that the Communists were mixed up in it." More than ever, it was imperative to get Robert Anderson launched on his secret peacemaking mission in the Middle East.[40]

FULL-TIME IN THE WHITE HOUSE

The private dinner that Ike had planned for the evening of January 10 to discuss his candidacy encountered difficulty. The president had invited his most trusted political advisors—secretaries Dulles and Humphrey, Attorney General Brownell, Postmaster General (and former party chairman) Arthur Summerfield, current GOP party chairman Leonard Hall, Jim Hagerty, Sherman Adams, Howard Pyle (the president's liaison with governors), United Nations ambassador Henry Cabot Lodge, appointments secretary Tom Stephens, and the president's brother Milton. When Brownell scheduled a luncheon meeting with the invitees to review what they would say to the president, word leaked to the press about both meetings. As a consequence, Brownell called off the luncheon and Eisenhower canceled the dinner, instructing Whitman to tell each individual to say, for the record, that "no dinner had ever been contemplated."[41]

Despite the cancellation, Ike was pumped up for discussion of his candidacy. That day, for an hour and a half, he tried out campaign themes with Foster Dulles that he amplified afterward in his diary.[42] Eisenhower had apparently used the secretary's input to refine a litany of achievements since 1953, ranging from ending the Korean War to steps toward disarmament and, in the Middle East, removal of British troops from the Suez Canal base in Egypt. He identified "the Israeli-Arab situation" as the administration's critical unsolved problem, complicated "by the fact that Britain and ourselves have not seen eye to eye in a number of instances." Overall, Dulles had reinforced Ike's rationale for running, citing international realities that were "not too pleasant to contemplate."

Ike concluded in his diary that he and Dulles had not identified "a single conclusive sign that the world is actually moving toward universal peace and disarmament" and that "it would appear that the world is on the verge of an abyss." The conversation had assisted Ike in crystallizing a duty-based rationale for running again. In that scenario, "an individual who so earnestly wants to lay aside the cares of public office" must "carry on regardless of any other factor." This was a man who, despite his protestations, fervently wanted to stay in office. Years later, Adams put it succinctly: "The real reason a President wants to run again is because he doesn't think anybody else can do as good a job as he's doing."[43]

But the doctors—those damned doctors—continued to urge Eisenhower to ease up, raising fresh doubts in his mind. On Wednesday morning, January 11, the day after his long talk with Dulles, Doctors Snyder, Mattingly, and Pollock surrounded the president and pressed him to stick to a nearly fat-free diet, take a nap every day at noon, and engage in only "non-aggravating" discussion for an hour after lunch. He was instructed to spend a maximum of an hour in a meeting without a ten-minute break, and his schedule should be adjusted for any evening social engagement.

Eisenhower resented these restrictions. He complained to Ann Whitman that doctors could tell him "this is best for you" but, he continued, "it looks to me more and more that if a fellow has a job he has to do it in his own way." Ike was determined not to permit health issues to force him to retire from public life. He shared an extraordinary rationale for running with Whitman, saying that "before his attack in September, he was more determined to quit than he was now."[44]

The doctors had opined that morning that "the little silly annoyances" stressed the president more than "the big problems." To Ike, that sounded ludicrous. The physicians misinterpreted the practiced calm that Eisenhower exhibited when faced with a calamitous situation. As general or president, he could not afford to lose his temper over the big issues; the small ones were safe for blowing off steam. Ike later wrote Swede Hazlett that he had been ordered "to avoid all situations that tend to bring about such reactions as irritation, frustration, anxiety, fear and, above all, anger," and had snapped at the doctors, "Just what do you think the presidency is?"[45]

THE ANDERSON MISSION

During that turbulent first week back in the White House, Eisenhower became increasingly aware of the deteriorating situation in the Middle East. On January 9, he signed letters introducing Robert Anderson as "a trusted friend in whom I have complete confidence" to Egypt's president Nasser and Israel's prime minister Ben-Gurion. Anderson was an Eisenhower favorite. "He is one of the most capable men I know," Ike recorded in his diary. "My confidence in him is such that at the moment I feel that nothing could give me greater satisfaction than to believe that next January 20, I could turn over this office to his hands."[46]

The afternoon of January 11, Eisenhower and Secretary Dulles briefed Anderson in preparation for his top secret mission.[47] Dulles urged Anderson to exploit Egypt's fears about the Baghdad Pact because Nasser "would be willing to pay a considerable price" to limit that alliance and maintain his leadership of the Arab world. Other bargaining chips could include American competition against Egypt in the world cotton market and funding for the Aswan Dam. The Israelis, on the other hand, were badly outnumbered and, given Soviet arms peddling, their situation could deteriorate. Dulles urged Anderson to press upon the Israelis that they needed to "play the part of a good neighbor to the Arabs" and give up on prevailing through force. Otherwise, they were "doomed."

Meanwhile, Foster Dulles was quietly trying to convince Congress to provide funds for the Aswan Dam. The Senate Republican minority leader, William Knowland of California, confessed to Dulles that he was "having a tough time with that one himself" and he had encountered "a great deal of feeling on the Hill on the matter." Dulles told Knowland that he, the president, and Treasury Secretary Humphrey had agreed that it would be best to seek a "capital fund" inside the foreign aid bill that could be drawn upon without specifying that the money would go to financing the Aswan Dam. Knowland warned the secretary that, in Congress, that "will be a rough one." [48]

Impatience had moved back to the White House with Dwight Eisenhower. That first week, Ike found it increasingly difficult to tolerate the simplistic assumptions of his colleagues. At the January 12 NSC meeting, Eisenhower went on the warpath about the naïveté of NSC members who believed that a nuclear war would be over in thirty to sixty days. [49] Based on that assumption, some of them wanted to cut back on the current program of maintaining a five-year stockpile of raw materials to sustain the country in a global war. Ike cited wars, including World War II, when populations had supported continuing warfare despite enormous devastation. He reminded the council members that, in the wake of nuclear destruction, with American ports "in ruins," it might be "three or four years" before the United States could again import needed raw materials. To Eisenhower, basing stockpile objectives on the projected length of a future war was "nuts." [50]

Ike complained that "none of the members of the Council had withdrawn into a quiet room and contemplated for a period of time the real nature of a future thermonuclear war." They could not conceive of "the chaos and destruction which such a war would entail." That did not mean the war or its effects would be over quickly. "The notion that such a war would last for only thirty to sixty days," Eisenhower said, "was just about as specious as the idea of a race between himself and Secretary Humphrey to the moon."

As the meeting drew to a close, Eisenhower recalled his discussion with Secretary Dulles two days earlier about the world being "on the verge of an abyss." He informed the council that he had ordered a confidential study on "the human effects of thermonuclear weapons." The president had been wondering "just how much of such a war the run of people would be willing and able to take." Eisenhower was "dead sure" about one thing: no one would "be the winner" in a nuclear war. "The destruction," he said, "might be such that we might have ultimately to go back to bows and arrows."

RUNNING REVISITED

With that nightmare scenario as a backdrop, Eisenhower returned to politics. The challenges of nuclear war, the Middle East, his fragile health, and the question of running for a second term converged in a rush that week in the president's mind. On Friday evening, January 13, Ike convened the confidential dinner he had canceled on January 10; its details were captured in Jim Hagerty's meticulous notes.[51]

By design or not, Ike had stacked the meeting with people, excepting his brother Milton, whom he surely knew would urge him to run. John Foster Dulles asserted that the president was "God-destined" to protect the peace of the world by continuing in office. Others were more political. Tom Stephens insisted, "We can't elect anyone but you, Mr. President—no one else has a chance." Ike turned to Herbert Brownell, whom he characterized as "an expert at this kind of thing." The New York attorney, who had managed Thomas Dewey's two presidential campaigns and Eisenhower's 1952 run, echoed Stephens's conclusion that only Ike could win—"no one else." The president's absence from the ticket would devastate Republican electoral hopes at all levels and open the door "for a Right Wing capture of the Party—a thing that no member of the Eisenhower Wing would want."

Eisenhower listened quietly to numerous similar comments. He responded that he was aware that "the campaign would be a rough one." The opposition would make his health an issue. "Hell, I know that," he said, "but remember one thing boys—I'm a soldier—and if I had my way I'd rather die with my boots on." When it was suggested that he could delegate campaigning and ceremonial responsibilities to subordinates, Ike responded that "in practice" that would not work; he would inevitably be "pressured to get right back in the old routine."

There was one dissenter in the room. Sherman Adams recalled that, near the end of the meeting, the president joked that "nobody but Milton seemed to be on his side." Ike had assigned Milton to take notes and his brother summarized them afterward in a private meeting and a letter.[52] Milton confirmed the twin arguments, international and political, for running—that Ike's candidacy was essential to keeping peace in the world and to prevent turning over the government to the Democrats. Milton summarized the negative argument—the one he favored—with devastating logic: "You will be 66 when the next Presidential term starts. You've had a heart attack. You could not make a vigorous campaign. It would be calamitous if you had a set-back during the campaign, and difficult for the nation if such occurred any time during your second term."

Milton Eisenhower knew how fiercely his brother coveted his place in history. If he quit now, Milton wrote, Ike would "go down in history as one of our greatest military and political leaders." The alternative: "If you go on, you might enhance your standing, contribute mightily to peace and to sound principles at home; or you might face serious economic setbacks at home and upheavals abroad. You might jeopardize your health and your ability to carry the burdens of office." Milton empathized with his brother's "loneliness" in making such a decision, saying, "I wish I could help."

January 16 was the day that Eisenhower transmitted his annual budget message to Congress for fiscal year 1957. Playing out the strategy he and Secretary Dulles had agreed upon, the document did not mention the Aswan Dam. The president requested "effective flexibility in the use of funds under the Mutual Security Program to enable us to respond to new situations which may arise." He sought "greater continuity in providing economic assistance for development projects and programs which we approve and which require a period of years for planning and completion." Those were code words for Aswan.[53]

THE BRINK AGAIN?

Robert Anderson met with Nasser on January 17.[54] He immediately encountered Nasser's resistance to the World Bank's requirements for financing the Aswan Dam, requirements that might "interfere with the Egyptian power of decision." Nasser provided a stark account of the Egyptian perspective on the Middle East in general. The problem with the Israelis, he said, was "much more difficult than it was a year ago." Israeli violence during 1955 had resulted in "a very strong resentment and anger" among the Arab nations in the region. The Baghdad Pact, announced in January 1955, had come "as a severe disillusioning surprise" and he perceived it as a strategy "designed to isolate Egypt." Given this atmosphere, "any announcement of a settlement between Egypt and Israel would produce a very unpopular reaction both with Egypt and the other Arab countries." Nasser reflected bitterly that, when he had tried to take friendly steps toward the West, he had been attacked by both the British and American press.

After a couple of days, Nasser told Anderson he would consider promoting a "reasonable" settlement with Israel to other Arab nations, provided that he could be "absolutely sure" that the United States, Britain,

Turkey, or Iraq were not allied against him. His second condition addressed the necessity for a period of time, perhaps six months, without additional border incidents or "provocation."

Anderson reported to Secretary Dulles that, based on his talks with Nasser, the best they could hope for would be to persuade Nasser and Ben-Gurion to issue separate letters stating their willingness to keep the peace over a period of months. Dulles responded that while Nasser's position "was not encouraging, it was not completely discouraging."[55]

In Israel, Anderson listened patiently to a two-and-a-half-hour discourse by David Ben-Gurion on the history of the conflict with the Arabs, with war breaking out "the day Israel was declared a state."[56] Ben-Gurion, one of Israel's great patriots and the nation's first prime minister, had retired in 1953 and then returned, recently replacing Moshe Sharett. Anderson asked the prime minister if he would consider writing a letter to the president pledging to avoid border violence provided there was "a similar assurance from Egypt." Such letters could be followed by lower level negotiations, waiting until later to involve the heads of state. Ben-Gurion called that a "first serious step" but worried that the passage of months would allow the Egyptians to increase their arsenal, making it more urgent that the United States provide arms to Israel that "would match Soviet bombers and fighter planes." If the United States continued to decline Israel's requests, it would be "guilty of the greatest crime in our history."

Robert Anderson's job was not made easier by Foster Dulles's penchant for provocative language. Just after Anderson departed for the Middle East, word leaked that the January 16, 1956, issue of *Life* magazine would feature an interview with the secretary of state. Dulles had apparently asserted that three times—in Korea, Indochina, and the Formosa Strait—he and Eisenhower had taken the nation to "the brink of a new war." The article gave Dulles major credit for a bold policy of deterrence based on the threat of nuclear retaliation.[57]

Adlai Stevenson, announced Democratic presidential candidate, accused Dulles of playing "Russian roulette with the life of our nation." The *Life* article was released on the very day that Eisenhower submitted his budget message calling for increased long-term, flexible foreign aid. The newspapers speculated that the controversy could endanger the administration's plan to support the Aswan Dam. A man who could make or break that legislation—House speaker Sam Rayburn of Texas—called Dulles's interview "a pitiful performance."[58]

Dulles initially poured gasoline on the fire by issuing a statement that declined to reject or clarify his statements. On the 17th, the first twenty-three minutes of the secretary of state's news conference were dominated by questions about the article. Dulles tried, without much success, to refute the tone of the magazine article. That day, Stevenson suggested that the president's silence about the article confirmed that Eisenhower approved of the secretary's "saber-rattling, threats of atomic war, and disregard of our Allies." The president, the governor asserted, should repudiate the statements and "fire Mr. Dulles." [59]

Eisenhower had been back in the White House only a few days. Ordinarily, Dulles would have consulted Eisenhower prior to any important public statement, but the interview had taken place in December when the secretary's access to the recovering president was still limited. Even in mid-January, Ike and Dulles had not fully reinstated the day-by-day, sometimes hour-by-hour consultation pattern they had enjoyed prior to the president's heart attack.

Why did Eisenhower not issue a statement immediately? This soon after his return to the White House, Ike was still struggling to juggle as many issues as he once had. He clearly had not read the article, nor had he and Dulles discussed it, even after the controversy arose. Eisenhower seemed preoccupied with preparation for his first news conference since August 4, scheduled for January 19.

As was his custom, Eisenhower held a pre–press conference briefing that morning with advisors. [60] The growing controversy over the secretary of state's statements dominated the session. Eisenhower seemed not to take the matter seriously, saying he planned to say to reporters that he "had not read the article, therefore he did not know the exact words of it," but that he had "the greatest faith in the professional skill of Foster Dulles" and "confidence in his great wisdom." Ike admitted that the "brink of war" phrase "was unfortunate."

Jim Hagerty insisted that the president understand what a brouhaha this had become. He read aloud excerpts from the article that used the "brink" phrase in reference to the three different crises. Hagerty now had the president's attention. Eisenhower expressed "astonishment that the Secretary of State had talked so freely." He had frequently told the NSC that if war became necessary he would go to Congress for approval. Concerned, Ike called Dulles in the middle of the meeting to talk about the problem.

After so many months, Eisenhower knew that this news conference could be a rough one. The president cheerily greeted the reporters, saying that "it's good to see so many faces here again after such a long absence from you." [61] He began by reading the telegram he had sent to the New Hampshire secretary of state, saying that he would "interpose no objection" to placing his name on that state's primary ballot. When asked if he had reached a "tentative conclusion" on running again, the president responded, "No."

Then came the inevitable question about the Dulles interview: "Was any decision reached to use the atomic bomb in those three instances?" Ike followed his original strategy, saying he had not read the article (and neglecting to mention what Hagerty had read to him). Then the president stonewalled, saying he would not publicly discuss secret matters that came before the NSC, but affirming his "complete faith" in Secretary Dulles. Ike insisted that he was in the business of "waging peace, based upon moral principles of decency and justice and right." Taking a strong stand did not automatically mean "being at the brink of something."

William S. White of the *New York Times* asked if the president would comment "on the state of the world, on the state of prospects for peace." Eisenhower reviewed the hopes arising from the Geneva Summit in July and the "great letdown" when the subsequent foreign ministers meeting collapsed. He cited "this growing tension and uneasiness in the Mid-East where American policy is to be friends to all." Then, sounding like a candidate, Ike ticked off his administration's foreign policy successes since 1953 that he had rehearsed with Foster Dulles on January 10, including the agreement for the removal of British bases from Egypt in 1954. The president concluded that, compared to three years earlier, "the situation is better and brighter."

Another reporter asked, "Mr. President, has any date been set for this medical examination that you will have next month?" Eisenhower, who had been building his future around that examination, feigned surprise and turned to Jim Hagerty: "I came over from my office this morning and knew there was something I had forgotten to do. You remember that?" The president turned back to the reporters and said, "No, there hasn't." The room erupted in laughter as the press conference ended.

APOCALYPSE NOW

On Monday, January 23, Eisenhower wrote confidential letters to friends, telling one that he was "not giving any concern as to what, under the changed conditions, this job might do to me" but rather "over a five year stretch what might I do to the job?" Ike repeated that theme with Swede Hazlett and confronted the haunting thought that a man in his situation might become a semi-invalid and "slow up operations, impede the work of all his subordinates, and, by so doing, actually damage the cause for which he may even think he is giving some years of his life." Then, worst of all, loyal subordinates "will not break his heart by telling him of his growing unfitness—they just *try* to make up for it."[62]

That day, Ike blended this consciousness of his own mortality with the "abyss" which he feared the world could sink into without his leadership. He met with retired Lieutenant General Harold Lee George, the staff director of the Net Evaluation Subcommittee of the National Security Council.[63] Eisenhower had charged that group with assessing the devastation that could be expected in the opening stages of nuclear war between the United States and the Soviet Union; this was the confidential report he had warned the NSC about on January 12. Also present were Secretary of State Dulles, Secretary of Defense Wilson, Atomic Energy Commission chairman Lewis Strauss, the chairman of the Joint Chiefs, Admiral Arthur Radford, and National Security Advisor Dillon Anderson.

The hypothetical date for the projected attack was July 1, 1958. General George presented two scenarios. The first assumed no warning of attack until Soviet bombers breached the DEW (Distant Early Warning) line in northern Alaska and Canada. The second assumed the United States had a month of strategic warning, without specific information as to when the attack would come.

The minutes of the meeting record that Eisenhower expressed his "astonishment" at what he heard. He had assumed that, in the second scenario, the delay associated with a strategic warning would provide some opportunity to minimize damage, but General George said that was improbable. Eisenhower agreed with Secretary Wilson that, in such circumstances, the Army would probably be assigned to preserve law and order in the United States. "It would be a long time," Eisenhower said, "before a country so struck would be shipping out any troops to fight any other kind of war."

The president was skeptical about "brushfire" wars. Contemplating this report, he opined anew that the government should avoid "little wars at great distances from the United States" that could slide into a nuclear confrontation. General George commented that, given the president's statement of policy, there would never be another Korea. The president concurred: "I will never commit our forces to battle where I cannot get to the heart of the enemy's power and support."

Afterward, Eisenhower recorded somber, even gloomy thoughts in his diary.[64] George's findings had been horrific. In the first scenario—an all-out attack with little warning—the United States would experience "practically total economic collapse," lasting six months to a year. The leaders of the government would be killed and a new government would have to be improvised by the states. No shipping could come in or go out of the country for months. Particularly shocking, 65 percent of the population would be killed or need emergency medical attention, most of which would not be available. The American damage inflicted on the Soviet Union would be roughly three times greater, but Ike took no satisfaction in that projection. Even in the United States, "it would literally be a business of digging ourselves out of ashes, starting again."

The second scenario would result in a longer war. It was assumed that the Soviets would first attack American airbases but, Eisenhower noted, "there was no significant difference in the losses we would take." Little could be done during the month leading to total war to warn or evacuate populations, protect industries, or improve defenses. The only choice during that month of momentum toward war would be to launch a preventive attack. Ike lamented that this "would be not only against our traditions" but would require a secret session of Congress to vote a declaration of war—something virtually impossible.

The doctors who, on January 11, had observed that the president seemed less stressed by "the big problems" could not have imagined this one. As each day passed, Ike solidified the argument, both to himself and to others, that it was his duty—his destiny—whatever his health, to do what he could to prevent the nuclear nightmare described in General George's report. In the coming months, Eisenhower would become increasingly convinced that the Middle East was a potential flashpoint for Armageddon.

4

★ ★ ★ ★ ★ ★

THE CANDIDATE

January 23–February 29, 1956

"As of this moment, there is not the slightest doubt that I can perform as well as I have, all the important duties of the Presidency."

President Eisenhower, Report to the Nation, February 29, 1956

ON THE evening of Monday, January 23, the same day he reviewed the Net Evaluation Subcommittee's haunting report, the president sat with another George—Walter F. George (D-Georgia), the chairman of the Senate Foreign Relations Committee.[1] Ike had a good relationship with the senator, who had served in the Senate since 1922. Ostensibly, Ike's agenda was to explain about Secretary Dulles's "brink of war" interview in *Life* magazine. But the president's primary agenda was to lobby Senator George to support his extraordinary request to Congress to nearly double the foreign aid appropriation for the next fiscal year.

Eisenhower, clearly thinking about the Aswan Dam, pressed Senator George about the need to support "a limited number of long-range projects" in countries tempted by Soviet promises to build their economies. According to Foster Dulles's notes, the president spoke "with great emphasis and almost emotionally" about the need to "give some hope" to those nations. George responded positively, saying he thought "a formula" could be found to do what the president desired. As it turned out, the senator was too optimistic about Congress's willingness to fund a program that, among other things, would assist Egypt.

TOWARD A DECISION

Subject to health considerations, Eisenhower had essentially decided to run for a second term, but he still had to convince concerned family members and colleagues. His son, John, attempted in a letter, much like brother Milton, to present both sides of the argument. But John's conclusion was terse: "Don't run." "The edge," he wrote, "goes to finding some other line of work." Ike showed the letter to George E. Allen, who responded, "I agree with every word he says—including his recommendation." Mamie Eisenhower appears to have accepted John's analysis initially but, as Ike later recalled, she came to accept her husband's argument that "idleness would be fatal for one of my temperament." [2]

On Wednesday, January 25, in his pre–press conference briefing, Eisenhower rejected, as an abrogation of responsibility, a suggestion that he make no announcement and wait to see if the Republican convention drafted him.[3] Still, he knew that saying yes would set off "the one thing" he must avoid, "running around the country helping every Republican who thinks he needs help." When reminded that the staff could assume more burdens, Eisenhower laughed, citing a meeting scheduled with the Soviet ambassador. "You can't take over what I have to do with Zaroubin today," he said.

For Eisenhower, politics and Middle East tensions were increasingly entangled. He reflected in the pre–press conference session on the fervent plea he had made to Walter George for expansion of foreign aid appropriations. There was already significant resistance in Congress. If reporters asked if he planned to withdraw the request for more funding, Eisenhower intended to say, "by no means." "Projects such as the Dam contemplated in Egypt," he said, "take more than one year."

At his news conference Eisenhower repeated that theme but carefully avoided mentioning Egypt or Aswan.[4] "There are certain projects in certain countries of the world that cannot be executed quickly," he stated. When asked specifically about the Israeli-Arab conflict, the president advocated keeping policy "a bipartisan affair" that would be "above politics." Eisenhower said his "one policy" had been that "America must be friends with both sides" and to encourage "some kind of friendship, at least cooperation between the two sides of the quarrel." Some kind of settlement was the only hope. "There is just no other answer," he said.

When quizzed about running again, Ike repeated his well-rehearsed concern for "the effect on the Presidency, not on me." A reporter asked if he would announce a decision after his scheduled mid-February physical examination. Ike dodged the question and drew laughter when he said, "I don't think there is anything safe to assume about any of my impulses."

The lighthearted banter ended abruptly when a reporter invoked the name of Chief Justice Earl Warren as a possible candidate if Eisenhower chose not to run. Following the president's heart attack, the speculation in the press about a Warren candidacy had gotten under Ike's skin. Rightly or wrongly, he suspected that Warren was complicit in the conjecture. The president reminded the gathering that, when he was nominated by the Republican Party, "I resigned from the Army." "We shouldn't get too great a confusion between politics and the Supreme Court," he said. The message was clear: if Warren wanted to run, the president was saying he should resign from the court.

THE EDEN VISIT

For Eisenhower, making the case for his candidacy required that he visibly resume his role as a world leader. Anthony Eden's state visit, starting January 30, would provide the forum. Just prior to that date, two disparate groups—the leadership of the Soviet Union and the Democratic Party—attempted to embarrass Eisenhower and influence the agenda for his meetings with Eden.

After his news conference on January 25, Eisenhower and Secretary Dulles had met with the Soviet ambassador. Zaroubin delivered a letter from Bulganin proposing a treaty of friendship between the United States and the Soviet Union. After the meeting, an irritated Eisenhower cabled Eden, suggesting that the Soviet proposal "was timed with an eye to our meeting and for that reason the manner of delivery was done to promote wide speculation as to its contents."[5]

On January 28, Eisenhower took the issue off the table prior to the Anglo-American meetings. He wrote Bulganin, rejecting the proposal for a friendship treaty on the grounds that the charter of the United Nations already covered such matters. Eisenhower deplored "a further deterioration" in American-Soviet relations since the Geneva Summit in July, caused by the Soviet government's decision to embark on "a course which increases tensions by intensifying hatreds and animosities implicit in historic international disputes." In other words, the arms deal with the Egyptians was anything but friendly. A treaty was not the answer, Eisenhower wrote, because "it is deeds and not words alone which count."[6]

Eleanor Roosevelt spearheaded an effort to disparage the president's Middle East policies just prior to the meeting with Anthony Eden. The former first lady issued a statement on behalf of herself, former President Truman, and Walter P. Reuther, the vice president of the AFL-CIO labor union coalition. "We must counteract every attempt by the Soviet Union," she said, "to upset the present precarious balance of power" in the Middle East. Roosevelt wanted the United States to supply the arms "needed by Israel to protect itself against any aggression made possible or incited by the introduction of Communist arms."[7]

Israeli ambassador Abba Eban joined in this orchestrated appeal, calling on President Eisenhower and Prime Minister Eden to "rise to the level of their inescapable moral duty" and provide arms to Israel. Adlai Stevenson called for the immediate provision of arms to Israel to restore "an equitable balance of armed strength which will restrain military action from either side. . . . We cannot meet Russian action in the Middle East with inaction," Stevenson stated. "They deliver the arms of war with extraordinary speed. We must counter just as quickly with a long-term and more constructive program."[8]

At one o'clock on Monday, January 30, Anthony Eden and Selwyn Lloyd, the British foreign secretary, arrived at the North Portico of the White House, where they were greeted by the president and Secretary Dulles. After discussion of issues in Europe, the parties shifted their attention to the Middle East. The two leaders achieved a high degree of unity regarding their policies for testing Soviet intentions around the world, but, according to the *New York Times,* spokesmen acknowledged that "there was no comparable unanimity of view on the troubled sweep of the Middle East."[9]

Ever since Eisenhower had assumed the presidency, the British had been uncomfortable with his evenhanded approach to Arab nations, especially Egypt. He had concluded early on that it was "undesirable and impractical for the British to retain sizable forces permanently" in Egypt and had pressed for their withdrawal of troops from the Suez Canal Zone in 1954. That discomfort continued in these meetings as Eisenhower and Eden wrestled with how to keep the peace in the wake of the Soviet arms deal with Egypt. Eisenhower urged the resolution of Britain's unresolved conflicts with Saudi Arabia, including one over oil rights in the Al Buraimi Oasis. Eisenhower and Eden discussed the possibility of stationing United Nations peacekeeping forces on the Israeli-Arab frontiers as a way to prevent war, but reached no consensus. They discussed whether "a show of force" in the Eastern Mediterranean might be helpful. When Admiral Radford suggested that the Sixth Fleet could conduct maneuvers, the president said he preferred something less provocative than aircraft carriers; perhaps "a vessel or two" could make their presence felt without triggering alarm. Eisenhower believed that "the less you can do it with" and still be noticed, "the better."[10]

On February 1, Eisenhower and Eden issued a joint statement affirming their governments' friendship and asserting that "a settlement between Israel and her Arab neighbors is the most urgent need." The leaders expressed concern "at the state of tension in the area" and warned the parties that the Tripartite Declaration of 1950 provided for "action both inside and outside the United Nations" if any nation used or threatened force in violation of the 1948 armistice lines.[11]

The next day, Eisenhower fulfilled his pledge to stage a show of force in the Mediterranean. Rear Admiral T. J. Hedding issued a top secret order, "as directed by the president," to the Sixth Fleet to conduct a "naval demonstration" with destroyers patrolling off the coasts of Israel and Egypt, exchanging calls with passing ships and visiting ports in the area. The recovering heart patient was back on his game, playing diplomatic poker with a military bluff designed to avoid actually going to war.[12]

Eisenhower learned important things about his old ally as a result of the talks. British anxieties about the Middle East were rooted, in no small part, in the dire financial straits that Anthony Eden's government confronted. The British economy had been devastated by World War II and, eleven years later, had not fully recovered, in spite of massive American aid. The United States, on the other hand, had emerged from the war as the world's strongest economic power and its leaders, including Eisenhower, had been slow to comprehend the fragility of the British situation—so desperate that coming up with their 20 percent portion of the funding for the Aswan Dam would be difficult, if not impossible.[13]

Anthony Eden had arrived in the United States at the very moment when British reserves for the pound sterling had reached a dangerously low level. The morning the meetings ended, Eisenhower called Secretary Dulles to discuss a paper the British had presented on their economic situation. Eisenhower told Dulles that the British reserves were "down to 2 billion—which is pretty bad."[14]

Meanwhile, Eisenhower's Middle East policies came under friendly fire. Republicans joined with Democratic congressmen to draft a resolution pressuring the administration to provide arms to Israel. When Republican congressmen, led by Jacob Javits, the Jewish candidate for the Senate from New York, attempted to draw the president into the conflict, Sherman Adams insisted they communicate with the secretary of state. Dulles responded to their letter that the government was committed to "the principle of maintaining our friendship" with both Israel and the Arab states. He insisted that contributing to an arms race would not protect Israel; the Jewish state was badly outnumbered and the United Nations was its primary protection. Dulles cited President Eisenhower and Prime Minister Eden's February 1 statement and his August 26, 1955, speech, "made with President Eisenhower's concurrence." But Dulles equivocated, saying, "We do not exclude the possibility of arms sales to Israel." He rejected the need for a congressional resolution. If congressional action was subsequently warranted, "the President would, of course promptly communicate with the Congress."[15]

Foster Dulles knew that this was no time to rock the status quo regarding arms for Israel. The results of Robert Anderson's secret mission had begun to trickle in. Anderson was informed on February 4 that Nasser had approved a draft of a letter to Eisenhower indicating his country's peaceful intentions. On February 7, the Cairo embassy informed the State Department that Nasser's letter was on its way. Nasser warned American officials that the Egyptian leader would deny the secret discussions with Anderson if there was any leak to the press.[16]

AN UNANNOUNCED DECISION

This had all transpired while Eisenhower was relaxing in Gettysburg after his intense discussions with Anthony Eden. According to Ann Whitman, the president returned on Monday, February 6, "in radiant spirits." She suspected that her boss had made up his mind about running for a second term when he instructed her to call the National Republican Committee chairman, Leonard Hall, "and ask him to come down." Ike met with the

GOP chairman at 5:30 and informed him that, if his health continued to be stable, he would run again.[17]

The day after Ike shared his intent with Hall, he talked with Nixon. "I think Hall is wearing rose colored glasses," the president told the vice president. The chairman had been adamant that Eisenhower's campaign could be limited to three to five talks on television. Ike recalled that in July 1952 the Republican leadership had been confident of winning but "by the time September came around the Republican organization was terrifically frightened." Nixon cited Franklin Roosevelt's minimal campaigns in 1940 and 1944 and opined that a half dozen televised speeches would suffice. But Ike imagined the party leaders pressuring him to campaign "because of your health, to show you are capable." If he campaigned very little, Eisenhower knew that his opponents would say: "See he is an invalid." Ike sighed. "It is going to be really a tough campaign this fall."[18]

Eisenhower focused his pre–press conference briefing for Wednesday on election campaign issues. He was informed that his comments on Earl Warren had caused some stir. Ike resorted to the politician's time-honored tactic of blaming the press, saying he would simply say that "the misinterpretation was the newsmen's own error."[19]

At the news conference, the reporters pressed the president about his political plans. When asked about Milton running, Eisenhower said, "Well," and hesitated, eliciting laugher. Ike said that if his brother had political ambition, "it is unknown to me." Surprisingly, the president unveiled his now favorite rationale to justify running—that he would be better off working than retiring. While gracefully deferring to his doctors' concerns, Ike implied what he was vehement about in private—that the doctors did not know what the job was. He was the one, he said, who knew "what the job demands, and its strains, its emotional strains, its periods of intense concentration." Eisenhower concluded: "I think I will probably trust my own feelings more than I will the doctors' reports." In effect, Ike said to a roomful of reporters that he might run even if the doctors recommended otherwise. Some of the country's most sophisticated journalists naively accepted the president's pretense that the decision had not been made. Ike promised an announcement at a news conference by the 1st of March.[20]

A few days later, Eisenhower candidly discussed the same rationale for running with Sherman Adams and a White House consultant, Kevin McCann. "The biggest reason is that I have always worked one way all my life," he said. He would find life without work "very difficult." Ike fervently wanted to run and he persistently tried to convince both family and colleagues that he would be healthier working than not. The White House was now abuzz with rumors that the president had decided to enter the race. On Friday morning, Jim Hagerty told Ann Whitman that he had discussed it again with the president, and he expected the answer to be yes.[21]

There was still one hurdle to cross—the medical checkup scheduled for four months after the heart attack. Ike, as he had written Swede Hazlett in October, hoped that this particular checkup would clear out any remaining roadblocks to running for a second term. By this time, Eisenhower knew fairly well what the outcome would be, but he needed to play out the drama in public. On Saturday, February 11, Ike and Mamie traveled to Walter Reed Hospital. Unlike earlier checkups, this one only lasted a little over an hour—not the entire weekend. While that was long enough for some basic tests, the probability is that the examination was mostly for show—a ritualistic public exercise about a decision that had already been made.

At the Monday cabinet meeting, the president fueled speculation among the members. Eisenhower had long ago perfected the art of embracing a messianic mission and making it sound like a simple soldier's call to duty. He said to the cabinet that he had tried to avoid the situation "where people say that there is only one man who can do the job." But a man committed to duty, he continued, had to reconsider when, for so many people, "one man comes to personify all their hopes." Ike took note of the rumor that some cabinet members had been talking "about their desire to get back home." He vowed that, if he found himself back in the White House next January, they "would have to be here, too!" Afterward, Whitman overheard appointment secretary Bernard Shanley, Kevin McCann, and Howard Snyder in animated discussion about the president's closing statement, which the doctor opined had been delivered "deliberately." Snyder knew better than most that, deep down, Dwight Eisenhower still relished, as he always had, being that "one man" who personified everyone's hopes.[22]

The dramatic rollout of the examination's results bore the stamp of Eisenhower's penchant for political theater. Ike was scheduled to meet with the doctors on Tuesday to hear the results, then depart for Thomasville, Georgia, to stay at Treasury Secretary George Humphrey's plantation for ten days—a time of rest, recreation, and, it appeared to the public, a last, quiet time to contemplate his decision.

On Valentine's Day, the president followed his usual schedule, arriving at the office just after eight, and overseeing a series of meetings, including one with Republican legislative leaders. But this was no ordinary day. At 11:45, Paul Dudley White stopped at the Oval Office to greet the president. Ike's private meeting with the six physicians who had worked on his case, including White, was scheduled for 2:00 P.M.

At 3:28, the doctors met with the press. Howard Snyder read the physicians' report concluding that the president had made "a good recovery" from his heart attack. Then came Dr. White's time to answer questions. As James Reston put it, "Paul Dudley White did not exactly push President Eisenhower into another campaign for the Presidency today, but he certainly opened the door and invited him in." Indeed, White verbally nailed the proposition to the White House door. He opined that the president should be able to lead a normal life "for another five to ten years." When pressed by the reporters, White repeated his carefully chosen words—that the president should be able to "carry on his present active life satisfactorily for this period, as I have said, for five to ten years." [23]

Now, more than ever, both politicians and newspeople ached for Eisenhower to end the suspense. But Ike had learned long ago how to milk the drama in a situation. His longtime practice, as he confided to Milton the previous year, had been "to wait until the last possible moment before announcing any positive decision." [24]

On the morning of the 15th, Eisenhower held "off the record" meetings with political advisors. Then he and Mrs. Eisenhower motored from the White House to the airport and by 10:35, they were airborne for Georgia where Ike planned to spend the next ten days. Through all this, the president made no public statement about the doctors' findings. Shortly after arriving at the Humphrey estate in mid-afternoon, the president, Humphrey, and Howard Snyder went hunting. *New York Times* columnist James Reston fell for Ike's candidacy charade, writing that the nation now confronted "one of the most important personal spectacles in its political history: a President isolating himself to reach a decision that well may determine the leadership of the Republic and the free world for the next five years." [25]

The news from Eisenhower's doctors was a blow to Adlai Stevenson's strategy for defeating Eisenhower. After a couple of days, Stevenson decided that his best strategy was to continue to imply that the president was not physically up to the job. "I do know his is a hard decision," Stevenson said about the president's deliberations in Georgia. "I don't believe any conscientious man would think of the Presidency of the United States, with its burdens and problems, as a part-time job." [26]

Columnist Arthur Krock speculated on the impact on the Republican Party if Eisenhower decided to be a one-term president. He predicted "a furious battle" between the two Californians, Vice President Richard Nixon and Senator William Knowland, that would divide the party and enhance Democratic chances for recapturing the presidency. Eisenhower's program on Capitol Hill would suffer due to his lame-duck status. And, Krock concluded, the pressure on Chief Justice Earl Warren to reconsider running "will be nation-wide and extraordinarily powerful." This situation, Krock concluded, would be "unique in the political history of first Presidential terms." [27]

THE POLITICS OF TANKS

While everyone, including Eisenhower, was preoccupied with the question of running again, Robert Anderson's mission to the Middle East had begun to bear modest fruit. Nasser's letter to the president arrived the second week in February. The Egyptian leader mentioned the president's "personal representative" and maintained that "Egypt harbors no hostile intentions toward any other state and will never be party to an aggressive war." Nasser recognized "the desirability of seeking to eliminate the tensions between the Arab States and Israel." But, he added, "Egypt must affirm its continuing desire to see the fundamental rights and aspirations of the Arab people respected." [28]

A week later, David Ben-Gurion, still insistently raising questions about Egypt's intent, wrote Eisenhower, stating his government's "full and unqualified readiness" to meet with Nasser or his representatives "to explore possibilities of a settlement or of progress by stages towards an ultimate peace." The Israeli prime minister argued again for the sale of weapons to his country. [29]

Robert Anderson had elicited a small, grudging step toward peace from both nations. More pieces of this delicate mosaic had fallen into place in early February. World Bank president Eugene Black and Egyptian officials announced that they had reached "substantial agreement" on a $200 million loan to assist in building the Aswan Dam. This implied Egyptian rejection of the Soviet Union's offer to finance the project. A week later, Egypt announced that it had dropped its previous opposition to advertising for competitive bids for construction of the dam, as required by the World Bank.[30]

Then, on Eisenhower's second day in Georgia, a controversy erupted. On Wednesday night, February 15, a phone rang at the United Press International copy desk in New York. An anonymous caller reported that on Pier 29 in Brooklyn eighteen light American tanks were about to be loaded on a freighter, destined for Saudi Arabia. The State Department seemed at first to know nothing about the matter. Secretary Dulles was on holiday on a ship in the Bahamas. Pro-Israel factions generated a storm of protest. Israeli ambassador Abba Eban and two Democratic congressmen filed a formal protest with the State Department, alleging that "an Arab country in no danger of attack receives arms. Israel in serious danger of attack has received nothing." Democratic senator Herbert Lehman of New York declared: "This is really adding fuel to the flames."

That evening, Jim Hagerty's phone was ringing off the hook in Georgia. Hagerty hurriedly called acting secretary of state Hoover, who was in charge in Foster Dulles's absence. After they talked, Hagerty drove the seven miles to the Humphrey plantation and interrupted the president's bridge game. Ike made a quick decision. Just past midnight, Hagerty announced that "the Department of State is suspending export licenses to that area." The *New York Times* reported, "The president's action stopped the tank shipment. It did not stop the controversy." Saudi officials protested and Walter George announced that the Senate Foreign Relations Committee would inquire into the matter. Since his arrival at Milestone Plantation in Georgia, the president "has managed to bag twelve quail, play nine holes of golf and stop the shipment of eighteen tanks to Saudi Arabia. What is par for a course of forty-eight hours?"[31]

In the next couple of days, Foster Dulles—blindsided by the president's sudden decision—weighed in. On February 18, the State Department lifted the ban on the shipment of the tanks, on the grounds that the Saudis had purchased them the previous year, had already paid for them, and that the tanks were destined for use in training, not warfare. The *Times* reported that President Eisenhower had personally approved the change of direction. Dulles had also discovered that Eisenhower, in the secretary's absence, had indicated that the United States would not object if the French shipped twelve Mystère fighter planes, ordered in 1955, to Israel—a matter that would come up again.[32]

Back in Washington, after repeated phone conversations with the presi-

dent in Georgia, Foster Dulles prepared to do battle with an aroused Senate Foreign Relations Committee. On Friday, February 24, the Republicans
packed the hearing room with administration supporters. The standing-
room-only crowd burst into applause when the secretary of state entered,
and applauded three more times during his four hours of testimony.[33]

Dulles's testimony was a tour de force.[34] When on his game, no one
could best him in the intricacies of foreign affairs. He refused to apologize
for the mix-up that had caused the tank shipment first to be canceled, then
go forward. Dulles offered what William White called "an aggressive summary" of policies "that had improved the position of the free world." The
secretary insisted that the administration's attempts to mediate Arab-Israeli
conflicts had nothing to do with "domestic politics." While not excluding
the possibility of providing arms to Israel, Dulles worried aloud that Israel
might "precipitate what is called a preventive war." He called the Middle
East situation "a problem of tremendous delicacy and complexity." Asked
why he had not been reached on his boat about the decision to cancel the
tank shipment, Dulles responded that a week's vacation would be worthless if his subordinates were free to phone him all the time.

Dulles received prolonged applause and cries of approval when he
clashed with Senator J. William Fulbright (D-Arkansas) over the question
of whether the overall position of the West had worsened while the Soviet
Union had been advanced. On the contrary, Dulles argued that Soviet leaders were floundering and covering up their own failures by asserting that
the United States was growing weaker, not stronger. "At this moment in
Moscow," he boomed, "they are having to revise their whole program!"
If the United States had to do that, "we would be advertised all over the
world as having failed. They have failed." It was a virtuoso performance.

While Robert Anderson's efforts had generated small rays of hope,
the American ambassador to Egypt, Henry Byroade, feared that peace in
the Middle East would be a casualty of election year politics. Byroade believed that Dulles was overly antagonistic toward President Nasser, while
Dulles distrusted the ambassador's judgment. The ambassador decided to
try to persuade the secretary to take a more balanced approach to Egypt.
On February 23, he wrote Dulles a personal letter, stating that "the last
two days have been one of the most soul-searching periods of my life."[35]
Byroade was "very negative" toward providing arms to Israel. While
the Anderson mission had made some inroads, the administration was
now risking the "impression of floundering hopelessly with a dangerous

situation.... America never has been able to understand the Arab-Israeli issue," Byroade complained. "It was too complicated—too far away, and there has been nothing in America to match the distortion of the Zionists." The ambassador lamented that, for taking this point of view, he had been "labeled anti-Semitic." Byroade called for the president to deliver a "fire-side chat" on the threat from the Soviet Union in the region, and "break the back of Zionism as a political force."

Byroade's plea would fail. Secretary Dulles was dismissive in response, writing the ambassador that he would give his concerns "very careful thought." Byroade correctly sensed that Eisenhower was not going to take on the pro-Israel lobby just when he was ready to announce his candidacy for a second term.

Arriving back in Washington on February 25, Eisenhower was encouraged by the modest achievements of the Anderson mission. Both Ben-Gurion and Nasser had written the letters that Anderson had sought, reciting their fears and grievances but pledging to attempt to avoid friction and incidents that might derail negotiations for a settlement. Eisenhower responded to both on February 27, thanking them for their commitment and informing them that Anderson would soon return to the region to continue discussions. Ike held out an olive branch to Nasser, saying, "I have followed with interest the reports of the negotiations on the construction of a High Dam at Aswan and have been pleased to note the progress which has been made." That project, the president wrote, represented "in finest form the policy of peaceful development for your people of which you wrote." Eisenhower knew the letters from the Israeli and Egyptian leaders were a slender reed. But his overriding mission was to prevent a nuclear war. His instincts told him that the situation in the Middle East, if badly handled, could be the catalyst for that conflagration.[36]

Since January 23, Ike had been considering the gloomy findings of the Net Evaluation subcommittee. A couple of weeks later, on February 10, Eisenhower had called a meeting of the Joint Chiefs, without Secretary of Defense Wilson, to discuss the nuclear threat. Eisenhower referred to the subcommittee's report as he lectured the chiefs on the challenge to work as "a corporate body," serving "the country as a whole," and to avoid getting bogged down in petty service rivalries or administrative detail.[37] Eisenhower asked an ominous question: "How would we fight a war after the amount of devastation shown in that report, or even a small fraction of that amount, had occurred?" They would, he said, need to decentralize emergency services and devise a governance plan that would work if all of them were dead. Eisenhower needed to "shove some of the problems of this kind on to the shoulders of the Joint Chiefs." This would be "a war no one wins," but he didn't "want to lose any worse than we have to." [38]

At the NSC meeting on February 27, Eisenhower was obviously irritated to discover that the Joint Chiefs had not grasped his message. [39] While discussing a document outlining policy in the wake of a nuclear attack, he learned that the chiefs had lobbied the planning board for language that would specify the roles for the Army and Navy in a future war. Ike erupted with frustration—he could not believe what he was hearing. Such language in a policy document would become "almost a military directive," he said. The truth, he asserted, was that "in a future war the chief task of the U.S. ground forces would be to preserve order in the United States." "God only knew," he continued, "what the Navy would be doing in a nuclear attack." They must distinguish, Ike exclaimed, between the precision essential to planning for a nuclear deterrent and the disposition of ground troops and ships after the attack. "If we start now specifying precisely what our Army and Navy are going to do, we'll never stop."

In this meeting, as in numerous others, the enormous costs of the Joint Chief's proposals stirred Eisenhower's passion about what the Cold War could do to American democracy. He wondered aloud whether the United States "must face national bankruptcy and the prospect of a totalitarian control as the only means to deal with an implacable enemy." The president said that this was why he had been telling the Joint Chiefs "that they must behave as statesmen as well as military leaders."

THE CANDIDATE

February 29 comes only once every four years. For effect, Ike liked to make important announcements or take actions on distinctive dates or holidays. Although the decision to run for a second term had essentially been made earlier, the White House staff, led by Jim Hagerty, had successfully kept the lid on that information. The day before Eisenhower had met with congressional leaders without saying a word about his plans. Hagerty tried to squelch rumors that day, saying flatly to the press: "No word one way or another has been relayed to Republican leaders or anyone"—a statement that must have made GOP party chairman Leonard Hall chuckle. Eisenhower and Hagerty had agreed to delay any request for radio and television time until after the news conference—another way of stretching out the drama.[40]

As Wednesday dawned, Middle East policy would, more than ever, be irretrievably entangled with presidential politics. Thinking like a candidate, Eisenhower was tempted to cease treating the Arab-Israeli conflict as "above politics." Just minutes before his news conference, he phoned Hoover, saying he was "a little worried" that the United States was being too rigid in dealing with the Israeli request for arms.[41] He suggested sending "interceptors" and Nike missiles, "if for nothing else to see if they would work." Ike wanted to say to the reporters that the government was making "a really sympathetic study" regarding Israel's needs.

Hoover was stunned. The president's query came only moments before he would be facing the press. There was no time for the undersecretary to talk with his boss, John Foster Dulles. Hoover warned the president that any change of direction might jeopardize the Anderson mission, which was at a delicate juncture. He reminded Eisenhower that Secretary Dulles had repeated the administration's settled policy on February 24 before the Senate Foreign Relations Committee—that the United Nations and the Tripartite Declaration were Israel's primary protection, that the United States did not want to sponsor an arms race, and that the Israelis were so badly outnumbered in the region that providing more arms was no solution. Eisenhower listened, relented, and apparently decided not to make any statement departing from that policy.

Meanwhile the tension deepened outside the ornate gilt and marble Indian Treaty Room in the Executive Office Building, described in the press as a "lofty rectangle of outmoded grandeur in the old gingerbread State Department Building on Pennsylvania Avenue."[42] With the press conference scheduled for 10:30 A.M., reporters started to arrive before eight. Soon there were 311 correspondents, commentators, and radio and television personnel crammed into the room. More than fifty had been turned away. All eyes watched the left of the room, where the president would enter.

Outside, although it was a cold day, Dwight Eisenhower walked without an overcoat across the street from the White House—an obvious attempt to appear physically fit for the cameras. The president strode vigorously into the conference room where reporters later described his appearance as "rested and refreshed." He began the session in a manner similar to other occasions, holding agenda of five items, the last of which was labeled "personal." He dispensed with the first four items in about seven minutes. William White wrote that "the intense impatience of the crowd in the room—though there was not a sound to indicate it—almost screamed to him to get on with it."[43]

Finally, Eisenhower took a deep breath and began to make one of the most important announcements of his life. He did so in language so convoluted that the reporters were initially uncertain about what they were hearing.[44] "I have reached a decision," he said. For what must have seemed like an eternity to the reporters, Ike recited the "many factors and considerations involved." He concluded that he intended to appear on television to explain that "my answer will be positive, that is affirmative." Merriman Smith, trying to be certain about what he had heard, asked the president if they would be allowed to quote: "My answer will be positive, that is, affirmative?" Eisenhower finally said something precise: "Yes."

Ike was prepared with carefully rehearsed witticisms for the rest of the discussion. When asked when he made the decision, Eisenhower sparked laughter when he said that he "was arguing about it yesterday morning." With whom had he discussed the decision? Ike responded, again to laughter, "Everybody that I thought was my friend and some that I wasn't so sure of." What about Mrs. Eisenhower's reaction? He dodged the question, saying only that family members, from the outset, had concluded, "This is your decision. We will conform." More laughter erupted when Hazel Markel of NBC asked if the president had made up his mind to run prior to the heart attack. "You know, Miss Markel," Ike responded, "that is one secret I don't think I will ever tell anybody." Eisenhower concluded by assuring the reporters that "my answer would not be affirmative unless I thought I could last out the 5 years." The news conference had lasted twenty-two minutes. After the traditional, "Thank you, Mr. President," Ike quipped to those near him as he walked out: "Well, at least I had a short conference."[45]

Eisenhower recalled in his memoirs his walk "in the crisp winter air" from the executive mansion to the West Wing that night for the television broadcast. The evidence is compelling; Eisenhower had always intended to run for a second term, both before and after his heart attack. The illness had temporarily derailed his plans, making them contingent upon a reasonable recovery. Ike had spent much time and energy convincing family, colleagues, and, above all, himself, that it was best for him, for the country, and for the world for him to continue in office. He had fended off counterarguments from brother Milton, son John, and friends like Swede Hazlett and George E. Allen. Ike could have chosen in October or November to make a statesmanlike exit that would have allowed other candidates to surface. Instead, he waited so long to make his announcement that no other Republican candidate could hope to build a political base to succeed him.

According to Ann Whitman, the president's remarks that night had gone through at least a half dozen drafts. Waiting to start, Ike went over the address "sentence by sentence." At five minutes until air time, he walked to his desk and, he recalled, "sitting alone in front of a bank of busy, shadowy people, humming equipment, and blinding lights, I spoke as simply as I knew how to millions of Americans."[46]

Unlike the news conference that morning, the president spoke in unequivocal language.[47] If the Republican Party chose to renominate him, Eisenhower stated, "I shall accept that nomination." If elected, "I shall continue to serve them in the office I now hold." Ike stated the conclusive argument he had so carefully honed, that "some" of his doctors believed that "the adverse effects on my health will be less in the Presidency than in any other position I might hold." The president declared: "As of this moment, there is not the slightest doubt that I can perform as well as I have, all the important duties of the Presidency."

Dwight Eisenhower would turn sixty-six years of age on October 14. If elected, he would take office as the oldest president, to that time, to assume office for a second term. But he fervently believed his work was not yet done.

The old soldier's ambition for a second term was still cloaked in duty. "The work that I set out four years ago to do," he said, "has not yet reached the state of development and fruition that I then hoped could be accomplished within the period of a single term in office." In other words, the peace of the world was still at stake. Eisenhower felt called once again to be its peacekeeper.

5

* * * * * *

A TANGLE OF POLICY AND POLITICS

March 1–June 7, 1956

"We have reached the point where it looks as if Egypt, under Nasser, is going to make no move whatsoever to meet the Israelites in an effort to settle outstanding differences."

Eisenhower Diary, March 8, 1956

AT LAST, it was done. Eisenhower's months of agonizing about running were over. He wrote Swede Hazlett that he still worried about what might transpire in the coming months.[1] "I am a competitor, a fighter," Ike confessed. "Politicians begin to get scared about the middle of October." Then he might feel pushed to overdo campaigning, not just by others, but by his own "reluctance to ever accept defeat."

Ike still had lofty goals—"promoting mutual confidence, and therefore peace, among the nations." To achieve that vision, he had to win. In the coming months, politics—the business of getting reelected—would sometimes trump substance for this "fighter" who was so loath "to ever accept defeat." Congress would be the other arena for political machinations. For Eisenhower, his goal of "peace among the nations" was dependent on a Democratic Congress approving his foreign aid proposal—a big order in an election year.

AN UNEASY SECRETARY OF STATE

John Foster Dulles had been spooked by Eisenhower's February 29 phone call to Herbert Hoover about arms for Israel. Before his illness, the president might occasionally overrule Dulles but the secretary had usually felt that they understood each other. Now he was not so sure. Ike had become unpredictable since his return to the White House in January. His president, usually so wonderfully apolitical on the great issues, had been increasingly acting like a political animal.

Foster Dulles belonged to that select group of people who could walk into Eisenhower's office without an appointment. The morning of Friday, March 2, the secretary interrupted a meeting in progress.[2] Dulles correctly assumed that Herbert Brownell and Sherman Adams were there to talk politics and, for that reason, Dulles asked them to stay. The secretary, due to leave the country soon for the Southeast Asia Treaty Organization (SEATO) meeting, impatiently told the president that he hoped that "there would not be White House pressure in my absence to give arms to Israel." Robert Anderson was ready to leave for his second round of talks in the Middle East. While the administration might provide arms to Israel eventually, such a commitment would be "disastrous" in the midst of Anderson's negotiations with Egyptian and Israeli leaders. Dulles suggested that the White House staff was subject "to strong political influences" and would be tempted to "alarm" the president on the issue. Dulles pleaded for no "undue pressure on the State Department during my absence."

Taken aback, Eisenhower asked what was behind the secretary's concern. Dulles cited two times that the president, while vacationing in Georgia and with Dulles out of the country, had taken actions and made statements that had startled the State Department and resulted in unfortunate news stories. Eisenhower had held up the shipment of tanks to Saudi Arabia and had openly expressed approval of the French sending Mystère fighter planes to Israel. Ike confessed that he acted hastily regarding the tanks and recalled that "a good rule in war" was "not to disturb carefully thought out plans in a spirit of sudden emergency without calm review of the whole situation."[3]

Throughout the first half of 1956, Eisenhower and Dulles were increasingly concerned that the incessant border violence between Israel and Egypt might escalate into full-fledged warfare. Ever since the 1949 armistice, violent flare-ups had been frequent along the Jordanian and Syrian borders with Israel, and especially along the border of the Egyptian-occupied Gaza Strip. Immediately following Secretary Dulles's announcement of the Alpha peace plan on August 26, 1955, violence had erupted at Gaza, resulting in a war scare that was a catalyst for Egypt's decision to make an arms deal with the Soviet Union. During February 1956, incidents between Israelis and Egyptians on the Gaza Strip border increased, with especially violent episodes on February 7 and 12. On March 1, King Hussein of Jordan dismissed Sir John Bagot Glubb, the British officer who had commanded, since 1939, the Arab Legion, the British-led Arab army first organized in the 1920s. Glubb's dismissal increased British-Jordanian tensions and enlarged the threat of border violence. On February 19, there were reports that Syria had concluded an arms agreement with the Soviet bloc, and on March 4 Syrians killed two Israeli policemen near the Sea of Galilee. By that time, Robert Anderson was back in Egypt, meeting with Colonel Nasser.[4]

On Monday, March 5, Hoover briefed Eisenhower on the escalating border violence. The president was concerned that "we might rapidly be reaching the point where we would have to take military action in the area." Hoover warned that the United States would have to be careful in order "to avoid the enmity of the Arab nations for many years to come." Apparently Secretary Dulles had instructed Hoover to finally resolve the question of France's desire to sell twelve advanced Mystère IV jet fighters, originally designated for NATO, to Israel. After considering the arguments pro and con, the president said he had "no objection," but it needed to be done quietly, avoiding any appearance that the United States was a party to the transaction. Later that day, there were reports that Syrian machine gunners on the Israeli border had shot down an Israeli plane and new violence had erupted along the Gaza and Jordanian borders.[5]

Eisenhower was harassed by the issue of arms for Israel at his March 7 news conference. William Shannon of the *New York Post* used the American shipment of tanks to Saudi Arabia to ask "why this country refuses to sell arms to Israel?" The president explained that the "few light tanks" for the Saudis had "already been bought and paid for" in 1955 and he was trying to avoid "the initiation of an arms race in that region." When James Reston of the *Times* asked for Eisenhower's assessment of "the trend of world events," the president seized the opportunity to promote his plan for long-term, flexible economic aid that implied support for projects like the Aswan Dam. "I believe," Eisenhower said, "the world has wakened to the fact that global war is getting well nigh unthinkable" and "this uneasy peace"—the "cold war"—was moving in a new, economically oriented direction.[6]

At the Thursday, March 8, NSC meeting, Allen Dulles warned the members that "Arab-Israeli hostilities could break out without further prior warning."[7] Border incidents between Egyptian and Israeli forces were on the increase, he said, citing the Israeli claim that one of their planes had been shot down by the Syrians. The disorder in Jordan, due in part to the dismissal of General Glubb, had added to the region's instability. A new shipment of Soviet arms had arrived in Egypt and there were reports of shipments beginning to arrive in Syria. Nasser's willingness to cooperate in a peace process had "stiffened" and he was "playing now for time." Nasser's ambition, the CIA director asserted, was to be "the leader of all the Arab nations" while the Israelis "see time slipping away" and have "widespread feelings of helplessness and despair." Israel, Dulles stated, had begun "a slow mobilization."

DULLES "THINKING ALOUD"

Foster Dulles, en route to Karachi, Pakistan, for the SEATO meeting, was apparently troubled by his confrontation with the president over arms to Israel. He understood that, in an election year, the president would be relentlessly pressured by supporters of Israel, the Democrats, and the Israeli government. As he traveled, Dulles began to contemplate a shift in policy that might get the administration through the November election and pacify the pro-Israel coalition in Congress that was holding foreign aid legislation hostage.

After the March 8 NSC meeting, Eisenhower read and pondered a "thinking aloud" message from the secretary of state. Dulles suggested that, for the time being, the administration give up on persuading Nasser to support a peace settlement with Israel. The United States should consider joining a modified Baghdad Pact, assist the British in settling their disputes with Saudi Arabia (especially the conflict over oil rights in the Al Buraimi Oasis), and provide military support to Saudi Arabia, Iraq, Iran, and Pakistan. The final step would be to sell defensive weapons to Israel. He proposed, in short, a program designed to isolate the Egyptian leader and hold him primarily responsible for tensions in the Middle East.[8]

Eisenhower's initial response was skeptical. He recalled in his diary that his original strategy had been to "be friends with both contestants in that region." Dulles's ideas were "one line of action" but taking sides now might "destroy our influence in leading toward a peaceful settlement of one of the most explosive situations in the world today." But the president was arguing with himself in his diary entry. Politically, Dulles's proposal was tempting. Ike had concluded that "Egypt, under Nasser, is going to make no move whatsoever to meet the Israelites in an effort to settle outstanding differences." He pondered a divide-and-conquer strategy, trying to persuade the Saudis that "their best interests lie with us, not with the Egyptians and with the Russians."

An anxious communication from Anthony Eden earlier that week had pointed in the same direction as Dulles's "thinking aloud" scheme. "There is no doubt that the Russians are resolved to liquidate the Baghdad Pact," the prime minister wrote, and Nasser was the tool of that policy. "I feel myself that we can no longer safely wait on Nasser. Indeed if the United States now joined the Baghdad Pact this would impress him more than all our attempts to cajole him have yet done." Ike resisted Eden's approach to confronting Nasser, responding, "I do not think that we should close the door yet on the possibility of working with him." That would destroy "any prospects of obtaining an Arab-Israeli settlement." The president wrote that he was reluctant to involve the United States in the Baghdad Pact because that would further alienate the Arab nations.[9]

Dulles's proposals, compared to Eden's, seemed moderate to Eisenhower. On Saturday, March 10, he wrote Dulles that he was tempted by the secretary's proposed change in policy. Ike believed that "if we could get Libya and Saudi Arabia firmly in our camp" and provide some assurances to Israel, the trouble in the Middle East might be "very greatly minimized, if not practically eliminated."[10]

Foreign aid was a cornerstone of the Eisenhower policy but his $4.9 billion request was in trouble with Congress. Even more than the election, Foster Dulles's proposal was designed to address that situation. On March 11, the *New York Times* reported that the administration was gearing up "for a Congressional showdown on its foreign aid program." The newspaper cited the Aswan Dam as the symbol of the administration's plan to support long-term projects in the developing world. Initial responses from congressional leaders had left administration sources "gloomy about the chances of getting through Congress the kind of program that the President and Mr. Dulles have been talking about."[11]

ANDERSON'S FAILURE

On Monday, March 12, Robert Anderson returned from his second trip to the Middle East. Eisenhower told Hoover that he wanted "very much" to see Anderson as soon as possible. At 4:30, Hoover accompanied Anderson to the Oval Office, where Anderson told the president that he had failed. He believed that neither side wanted war but circumstances continued to be "inflammable due to great emotional stress and the immediate proximity of hostile armed forces."[12]

After the meeting, Ike contemplated in his diary the failure of the Anderson mission and Anderson's conclusion that "Nasser proved to be a complete stumbling block."[13] The president was finding Dulles's "thinking aloud" proposals increasingly attractive. Still, Ike knew that making Nasser the villain bordered on crass electoral politics because Israeli officials were hardly innocent bystanders. While claiming they were willing to talk with Egypt, he recalled that the Israelis had been "completely adamant in their attitude of making no concessions whatsoever in order to make a peace." They would give up "not one inch of ground" and were incessantly demanding arms.

Eisenhower could see "no easy answer." The European economies would collapse if Arab oil was cut off. Politically, Egypt had no viable political constituency in the American electorate, whereas Israel had "a very strong position in the heart and emotions of the Western world." Any proposal for making peace was viewed by both sides with suspicion. "It is," the president concluded, "a very sorry situation."

In Cairo, Ambassador Henry Byroade had concluded that Robert Anderson had been too impatient and should have waited longer in Egypt in case Nasser had "second thoughts." The evening of March 13, Nasser invited the ambassador to his home to make the case that Anderson had misunderstood him. "I have written a letter to your President." he said to Byroade. "I will not deceive your President. I will not start a war with Israel. I give to you and to him my word on that issue, not as a politician but as a soldier."[14]

Based on this conversation, Byroade urged Dulles not to abandon the Anderson mission. His plea came too late. Dulles had already ordered the initiation of planning that would implement his "thinking aloud" proposals to the president. The Near East Office had been instructed to reassess Middle East policy on the premise that Nasser was the primary obstacle to peace. On the day that Byroade sent his message, the staff produced draft recommendations in which "delay" was the operative strategy. The United States could delay the approval of export licenses, products, and aid desired by the Egyptians. Above all, the analysts concluded that Americans should "continue to delay the conclusion of current negotiations on the High Aswan Dam."[15]

AN ELECTION YEAR STRATEGY?

The administration's review of Middle East policy coincided with a fresh effort to persuade Congress to approve flexible, long-term foreign aid. That campaign began on March 19, with the president's special message to Congress on mutual security.[16] In order to combat Soviet expansionism in "a somewhat different guise," Eisenhower said it was essential to instill "continuity and flexibility" to the foreign aid program so that the United States could assist "non-military projects and enterprises which will take a number of years to complete." Eisenhower sought $100 million for such projects, lasting as long as ten years, in Africa and the Middle East—with no mention of the Aswan Dam.

That same day, Eisenhower cited in his diary some "very exact intelligence on Nasser's intentions." The source was Anthony Eden, who, on March 15, had forwarded a British intelligence report that described the results of a secret conference of Egyptian ambassadors and ministers held on January 30 in Cairo. Nasser and his subordinates had allegedly laid plans to overthrow the rulers of Iraq, damage the Baghdad Pact, overthrow the monarchy in Libya, and establish Arab republics in Tunisia, Algeria, and Morocco. In particular, the report stated that the Egyptian leaders, after involving the Saudis initially, planned to isolate Saudi Arabia as the remaining monarchy and to eventually remove King Saud. The Soviet Union, the British report said, was fully supporting this "anti-monarchical policy."[17]

Ike never knew quite how to respond to Anthony Eden's frequent anxiety attacks. The following week, he and Secretary Dulles discussed what Dulles called "the rather jittery attitude evidenced by the British by the fact that they were doing a number of things rather hurriedly and without any prior consultation with us." At his news conference on Wednesday, March 21, Eisenhower addressed questions about the Middle East, stating that "any outbreak of major hostilities in the region would be a catastrophe to the world." He succinctly underscored the foundation for British or French anxiety about the Middle East. "As you know," he continued, "all of Western Europe has gradually gone to oil instead of coal for its energy, and that oil comes from the Mid-East." [18]

When Secretary Dulles returned to Washington from the SEATO meetings, Ambassador Abba Eban sought permission to personally deliver a letter from Prime Minister Ben-Gurion to the president. Dulles declined access but, on March 26, put the letter in Eisenhower's hands in White Sulphur Springs, West Virginia, where the president was meeting with North American heads of state. The letter was, as usual, a fervent plea for more arms. Eisenhower decided that, rather than respond immediately, they should wait until the administration's policy review was completed. [19]

Two days later, Dulles called in Eban to tell him he had delivered the letter. Then Dulles did something extraordinary; he hinted that a policy change was in the works. He revealed the administration's intent that "Nasser may no longer be entitled to the preferential treatment he has been getting" in hopes that he would cooperate "in achieving an Arab-Israeli settlement." Dulles said that he and the president had not changed their minds about arms for Israel; there would be no answer on that for the moment. Dulles knew that there were two sides to the matter; he grumbled to the ambassador that Israel's leaders "had not given complete cooperation." [20]

CUTTING NASSER DOWN TO SIZE

Wednesday, March 28, was a day of decision for the new policy direction. At 4:40 P.M., just after the president returned from White Sulphur Springs, Secretary Dulles convened a meeting in the White House. [21] In addition to Eisenhower and Dulles, the group included undersecretary Hoover; George V. Allen and his assistant in the Near East Office, William Rountree; Secretary of Defense Charles Wilson, and deputy secretary Reuben B. Robertson, Jr., Admiral Radford, and Colonel Goodpaster.

Dulles handed the president a memorandum that proposed, in effect, a program to diminish Nasser's influence. [22] Nasser would be forced to "realize that he cannot cooperate as he is doing with the Soviet Union" and still enjoy the same positive relationship with the United States. The secretary recommended that there be no open break in relations, leaving Nasser "a bridge back to good relations with the West if he so desires." Above all, Dulles recommended that the United States and the United Kingdom "continue to delay the conclusion of the current negotiations on the Aswan Dam."

The proposals walked a careful line otherwise. The United States would give increased support to the Baghdad Pact without formally joining it. The administration would continue to deny military aid to Israel but would place no roadblocks to provision of arms by allies. Finally, the administration would seek to strengthen the American position in Saudi Arabia. Dulles recommended contingency plans for more drastic action, such as manipulating American cotton imports to damage the Egyptian market and overthrowing the government of Syria to install a regime friendlier to Iraq and the West.[23]

Eisenhower read the memorandum, basically agreed with it, and placed particular priority on building up King Saud "as a figure with sufficient prestige to offset Nasser." Maintaining access to oil was a cornerstone of the new policy. Saudi Arabia had huge reserves and Egypt had none. The group was especially concerned about the impact on petroleum supplies if Egypt attacked Israel. That might force the United States to consider a military occupation of areas critical to the transport of oil, including pipeline installations in Syria, and the Suez Canal. Dulles asked Radford to conduct a study of the impact of a cutoff of oil on Western Europe. The minutes recorded: "It was the consensus of the meeting that the Near Eastern resources are so vital to the security interests of the United States and the West generally that we could not accept a situation in which access to those resources would be subject to hostile control. Measures, even drastic, would have to be seriously contemplated."[24]

Eisenhower said relatively little during that meeting. His diary reveals that he was troubled.[25] Ike accepted the conclusion that Nasser's "growing ambition" to be recognized as the supreme leader of the Arab nations had led the Egyptian leader to reject "every proposition advanced as a measure of conciliation between the Arabs and Israel." But Eisenhower worried about the feasibility of elevating Saud as a counter to Nasser. "I do not know the man," he wrote, "and therefore do not know whether he could be built up into the position I visualize." But Saudi Arabia contained important holy places and "the Saudi Arabians are considered to be the most deeply religious of all the Arab groups. Perhaps the King could be built up as a spiritual leader."

It can be argued that Eisenhower's grasp of the nature of Middle East nationalism was inadequate, assuming that he could elevate a monarch—one so representative of the old order and so intimately tied to Western oil interests—over Nasser, the charismatic Egyptian leader. Is it possible that Eisenhower had not yet fully regained his pre–heart attack sure-footedness in international affairs? Daun van Ee, coeditor of Eisenhower's published papers, argues for a larger perspective—that Ike's preoccupation with Saud reflects his "great emphasis on the Free World's spiritual strength and on the use of that strength to counter the God-less, spiritually bankrupt communists." [26]

The new policy, code-named Omega, made more sense in terms of domestic politics than enlightened foreign policy. With little support for Egypt in the American electorate, the United States government was embarking on a path designed to punish Nasser for his intransigence that would, in the months ahead, produce a perilous situation in the Middle East.

On March 29, exactly one month after he announced his candidacy for a second term, Eisenhower wrote a long letter to Winston Churchill.[27] The president called the Middle East "the most important and bothersome of the problems that currently confront our nations. . . . The prosperity and welfare of the entire Western world," he wrote, "is inescapably dependent upon Mid East oil and free access thereto." He linked that situation to the possibility of nuclear war. "Each of us should pray earnestly," Ike concluded, "for a bit more wisdom, a bit more understanding, a bit more capacity for dealing with these problems of limitless scope."

In response, Churchill praised Eisenhower for recognizing "so plainly the importance of oil from the Middle East" but he was troubled by Eisenhower's stance on arms for Israel.[28] "I am, of course, a Zionist," he wrote, calling it "a wonderful thing that this tiny colony of Jews should have become a refuge to their compatriots" and had "established themselves as the most effective fighting force in the area." Churchill expressed his fervent hope that, if the Israelis were dissuaded from launching a preemptive attack, the United States would not "stand by and see them overwhelmed by Russian weapons."

A SECRET POLICY?

The policy Eisenhower had approved on March 28 was allegedly secret. Yet its political payoff required leaks to particular constituencies. Secretary Dulles had already alerted the Israelis about the coming change. On Sunday afternoon, April 1, Dulles, Hoover, and Douglas MacArthur II, State Department counselor, briefed British ambassador Roger Makins at the secretary's home—the site the secretary often used to avoid the press.[29] Dulles emphasized the "secret basis" of cooperation with the British. He said that the United States would announce public support for the Baghdad Pact without joining it, attempt to entice the Saudis away from Egypt, and delay action on matters important to Nasser, especially the Aswan Dam. This would be done "without an open break," in hopes of modifying Egyptian behavior. Dulles urged the British to settle outstanding disputes with Saudi Arabia, most notably their conflict over oil rights in Al Buraimi. The administration would continue to resist pressure to supply arms to Israel because, Dulles said, "this would cause the Arab states to unite in open hostility to us." While this stance was "a political liability," Dulles expressed his belief that the president could survive the election campaign "without giving in to Zionist pressures for substantial arms to Israel."

President Nasser sensed that something was up; after months of negotiation, Western support for the Aswan Dam suddenly seemed uncertain. On the same day, April 1, that Dulles had briefed the British ambassador, Osgood Caruthers reported in the *New York Times* on a three-hour interview with Nasser the previous evening. Nasser told the reporter that he still held "in his pocket" a Soviet offer to finance the project. "We have not rejected the Soviet offer," he said, adding that this was not a "threat" or a "bluff." His dealings with the Soviet Union had been "strictly commercial." Nasser charged that the United States would "do great harm to the world if you continue to support colonialism against the philosophy of your own revolution." "We have no intention of attacking Israel," the Egyptian leader asserted. "Our whole thought is on preparedness against an attack from the Israelis." [30]

Nasser may have been responding to news stories about the new American policy. On Tuesday, April 3, the *New York Times* reported that the Eisenhower administration had decided to keep "on ice" the Israeli request for arms—$63 million worth of jet aircraft, tanks, and other weapons. But word had leaked that Israel could appeal for such arms to its traditional suppliers—Britain and France—and, according to "diplomatic sources," the United States would put "no obstacles in their way." [31]

On April 4, the United Nations Security Council unanimously approved a resolution requesting Secretary-General Dag Hammarskjöld to travel to the Middle East to renew armistice agreements that had lapsed as a result of border violence. Before Hammarskjöld could arrive, matters took a turn for the worse. On Friday, April 5, ten hours of fighting along the Gaza armistice line resulted, according to Egyptian sources, in thirty-three civilian deaths and ninety-two wounded. United Nations sources reported that four Israeli civilians had been killed and two wounded. The casualty figures seemed to point toward Israeli responsibility but the Egyptian figures may have been inflated. As so often was the case in these border incidents, the identity of the aggressor was ambiguous. The *New York Times* echoed the phrase that had plagued John Foster Dulles in January, saying the incidents had brought "Israel and Egypt to the brink of war." Colonel Abdel Kader Hatem, a spokesman for Nasser, accused the Israelis of making a "premeditated" attack. "That is a habit of the Israelis," he asserted. "When they hear talk of peace, they always resort to acts of war." The American Zionist Committee for Public Affairs argued that the "Israelis have a right to defend themselves" against "Communist weapons." [32]

In Cairo, Ambassador Byroade believed that the fragile cease-fire in the Gaza Strip could unravel at any moment. The evening of April 9, Nasser told Byroade that complying with a cease-fire would be difficult because he had sent Fedayeen commandos into Israel with orders to kill and maim a number of Israelis equivalent to the Egyptian casualties in Gaza. Those commandos were now beyond his reach. Byroade warned the Egyptian leader that if the Israelis wanted to start a war, he was "walking straight into their trap." [33]

The administration dared be silent no longer on the violence in Gaza. In Augusta, Georgia, where Eisenhower was vacationing, Hagerty read a statement saying that the president and the secretary of state viewed the recent violence "with the utmost seriousness," expressing support for Hammarskjöld's mission and affirming the American commitment to assist any nation that was the victim of aggression. Secretary Dulles announced that he would brief congressional leaders the next day—Tuesday, April 10—on the situation in the Middle East. [34]

Just as Foster Dulles was climbing out of bed that Tuesday, he received an agitated call from Eisenhower, who was angry that the British press was accusing the United States of "vacillating around about the Mid East." "I don't know what they are talking about," Ike complained. He believed that the British government was "handing out some things to the papers about us." Dulles urged the president not to "take on the liabilities of the British position." "They are so panicky," he said. Dulles reassured the president his personal talks with the British were going well, except regarding their conflicts with Saudi Arabia. Eisenhower insisted, "We must find some way to be friends with King Saud." [35]

Later that morning, Foster Dulles met with congressional leaders from both parties.[36] This briefing guaranteed that the new policy would no longer be secret. The secretary explained the politically attractive dual purposes of the initiative—the preservation of the state of Israel and friendly relations with the Arab states "to preserve the flow of oil from the area." Dulles warned: "The Suez Canal can be blocked," a devastating possibility for Western Europe. New developments had forced the administration "to abandon, for the moment, hope of achieving a peaceful settlement of the Arab-Israeli dispute and to turn to the immediate problem of preventing an outbreak of hostilities."

Dulles identified three policies that he and the president had rejected—supplying arms to Israel (although the United States would encourage others to do so), joining the Baghdad Pact, and framing a joint policy with the United Kingdom—the latter due to Britain's increasingly hostile relations in the area, including "a state of undeclared war with Saudi-Arabia" over the Al Buraimi Oasis. The United States would oppose aggression by either the Israelis or the Arabs but, he concluded, "the great difficulty is to identify the aggressor."

Later, Dulles called the president to tell him that the meeting "went pretty well." In an election year, the congressmen had been most worried about the political fallout if Israel were identified as an aggressor. Dulles had chosen his words carefully: "We would not support Israel if it was determined that she was the aggressor." If that principle could not be maintained, he had told the congressmen, "the entire system of world law and order would collapse." During the discussion, Secretary Dulles had not mentioned the Aswan Dam. Eisenhower's and Dulles's immediate concern was protecting American citizens if war broke out. The two men discussed moving American destroyers and carriers in the region into position where they could, if necessary, rescue American nationals. Eisenhower wanted this accomplished quietly, avoiding the impression of preparing for war. He concluded that this "is all we can do for the second."[37]

Eisenhower and Dulles were riding an emotional roller coaster between war and peace. On Wednesday, April 11, Dulles called the president in Augusta to report that "it looks a little better today" because Nasser appeared to be trying to restrain Egyptian commando operations. Ambassador Eban had indicated that the Israelis would not use Egyptian commando raids "as the basis for a new set of reprisals." Byroade had talked with Nasser, to good effect, so "we may be over this particular crisis." But the next day,

Dulles called Eisenhower in Augusta to tell him that "things are not so good today." The Egyptian commandos were still operating. Two planes had been shot down, the latest an Egyptian plane over Israeli territory.[38]

BACK INTO THE ABYSS

Dwight Eisenhower sought to place such international tensions in a larger context, encompassing the Cold War and the threat of nuclear conflict. To him, nuclear war was not a fantasy but a distinct possibility. Therefore, the president did not shrink from contemplating its consequences and he refused to let others do so. He saw the world as a place where the convergence of factors in particular hot spots—Germany, the Far East, and the Middle East—could touch off such a conflict.

On Thursday, April 19, 1956, at 2:35 P.M., the president gathered a large group in the Indian Treaty Room of the Executive Office Building.[39] The purpose was to plan for Operation Alert, a seven-day mobilization exercise scheduled for July and based on a scenario in which ninety-seven nuclear bombs would be exploded over fifty-two major American cities with additional attacks on bases, nuclear facilities, and eleven smaller cities. Eisenhower called the meeting "an historic occasion" because "never before has a President of the United States met with the heads and staff agencies of those departments and offices of government that have mobilization duties in the event of war." Ike recalled drawing up a mobilization plan during the presidency of Herbert Hoover, and the president's staff officers had refused to let Hoover see it. "It was sent back saying to us that they simply weren't going to impose on the President's time to look at such tripe." The room erupted with laughter.

Eisenhower asserted that inflicting "the least possible difficulties on our economy is the reason for this kind of planning." Without devoting attention to such planning, "we could well experience catastrophe in war." A "wise old German" had once observed, Ike said, that "plans themselves are unimportant but planning is everything." The point, the president continued, was "to do the normal thing when everybody else is going nuts." Unexpected things would inevitably happen, like the attack at Pearl Harbor. Agencies were to report their plans for coping with the imaginary war by April 30.[40]

The evening of Saturday, April 21, the president and Adlai Stevenson delivered separate speeches at the meeting of the American Society of Newspaper Editors at the Statler Hotel in Washington.[41] Stevenson described the past three years as a period of retrogression in foreign affairs and grabbed headlines the next day by proposing a moratorium on nuclear tests and channeling foreign aid through the United Nations.

Eisenhower reminisced about his speech to the editors in 1953, when "stories of battlefields and fighting fronts crowded the front pages of our press." Then, "Fear of global war, of a nuclear holocaust darkened the future. To many, the chance for a just and enduring peace seemed lost— hopeless." Now, Eisenhower asserted, the American people had embraced a "cautious hope that a new, a fruitful, a peaceful era for mankind can emerge from a haunted decade. The world breathes a little more easily today."

Eisenhower recited for his audience how, in the past decade, eighteen nations with 650 million people had gained their independence—nations that were "the heirs of many ancient cultures and national traditions," including "the great religions of the world," and speaking in "a hundred tongues." While addressing the need "to resolve disputes between friends we value highly," he said he had committed the United States to refusing to take sides and to "assist in tempering the fears and antagonisms which lead to such disputes."

"My words," the president said, "apply with special force to the troubled area of the Middle East. We will do all in our power—through the United Nations whenever possible—to prevent resort to violence there in that region. We are determined to support and assist any nation in that area which might be subjected to aggression. We will strive untiringly to build the foundations for stable peace in the whole region." The new tensions there had arisen from "a sudden change in Soviet policy," he said. The Russians had moved from threatening force to economic and political subversion, while "wearing smiles around the world."

Ike could not know that the Russians were not the only ones wearing smiles. Two days later, in Paris, the Israelis concluded a secret deal with the French to massively increase the shipment of arms to Israel. The clandestine meetings between Israeli and French officials in the months to come would constitute what historian Donald Neff, in *Warriors at Suez*, has called "one of the most extraordinary secret collusions in modern times."[42]

Eisenhower resumed his correspondence with Churchill on April 27.[43] He told his old ally that he felt fully recovered from his heart attack. "For myself," he wrote, "I sense no difference whatsoever in my feeling of health and strength as compared to my condition prior to the attack." But nuclear war, more than his health, was on the president's mind. Eisenhower rejected Churchill's view that neither side would ever use atomic weapons, knowing how awful the results would be. Ike thought that "it would be unsafe to predict that, if the West and the East should ever become locked up in a life and death struggle, both sides would still have sense enough not to use this horrible instrument." Eisenhower recalled that, in 1945, when Hitler was clearly defeated, "his insane determination to rule or ruin brought additional and completely unnecessary destruction to his country."

THE ASWAN DILEMMA

In spite of Eisenhower's and Dulles's efforts, the administration's foreign aid proposal—$4.9 billion for fiscal 1957, compared with the current $2.75 billion—was in trouble. On April 28, the *New York Times* reported that Representative James P. Richards (D–South Carolina), the chairman of the House Foreign Affairs Committee, planned for his committee to "mark time" until the administration clarified some issues. Senate Foreign Relations Committee Chairman Walter George was adamant in his opposition, especially to the one example of long-term financing authority disclosed by the administration—the Aswan Dam. To George, assistance for Aswan would be "repugnant" because it was "wholly inconsistent" with the need to minimize Arab-Israeli tensions. The senator was also concerned that increased Egyptian cotton production would damage producers in his home state. *Times* reporter William White concluded that "there was little doubt, therefore, that Mr. George's views would prevail" and the legislation would fail. This was bad news for the administration. The new policy of holding Egypt especially responsible for Middle East tensions had been in place for a month, without a positive effect in Congress.[44]

On Monday, Foster Dulles and Eisenhower renewed their campaign on behalf of mutual security legislation, with Dulles testifying before the Senate Foreign Relations Committee. The secretary of state explained the Soviet Union's new tactics aimed at developing nations and argued, quoting the president, that any major reduction in the $4.9 billion request would "gravely endanger the security of the United States." Later that day, Eisenhower charmed congressional leaders at the White House. After the meeting, Senator George and Congressman Richards indicated they had agreed to a "substantial" program. Richards said that, although details remained to be settled, they had "entered a wide area of agreement" with the president.[45]

Eisenhower was still more enthusiastic about the Aswan Dam project than Foster Dulles. On May 2, with the secretary of state in Paris for a NATO meeting, the president sent an "eyes only" memorandum to Hoover. In spite of congressional opposition, Ike was thinking once again about finding a way to support the project. He recalled that his first initiative after returning from his convalescence in December had been to make a "firm offer" to Egypt. "I see no reason," he wrote Hoover, "to change the opinion we then held that the intervention of the Soviets in this proposition would be more or less disastrous." Ike had assumed that the United States was making progress in negotiations with the Egyptians, and he asked: "What has happened?"[46]

Hoover's response startled Eisenhower into realizing that, three months after returning to the White House, he had not fully grasped Foster Dulles's new direction in the Middle East. The undersecretary explained that "progress on the Aswan Dam negotiations is intimately tied up with the question of our overall Near East policy which you will recall the Secretary took up with you on the basis of his memorandum of March 28, 1956."[47] The offer had been made, together with the British, on December 16, 1955, to assist in funding the first phase of the project. World Bank president Black had visited Cairo in January to follow up on possible assistance for the second phase. The Egyptians had made counterproposals that would, among other things, require a commitment from the United States to aid the entire project, not just part of it. Discussions were ongoing in Washington concerning these new Egyptian proposals. Until this moment, the president had either failed to fully understand or was ambivalent about the fact that the anti-Nasser policy he had approved on March 28 had, at its core, an American decision to "delay" progress on those talks.

There was some good news that week. The war scare between Egypt and Israel had receded. On May 3, Secretary-General Hammarskjöld reported to the Security Council that he had secured "reciprocal assurances unconditionally to observe a cease-fire, with a reservation as to self-defense."[48]

POLITICS INTRUDES AGAIN

On Monday, May 7, John Foster Dulles reported to the president on the NATO meetings.[49] They also discussed a draft of the statement Dulles intended to use in a speech the next day to B'nai Brith, the prominent Jewish service organization. Since the controversy over the secretary's *Life* magazine interview in January, Dulles and Eisenhower had resumed their careful consultations about the content of his public presentations. Ike read the statement and approved it, but commented that the audience "would have long faces."

The day of the speech, May 8, James Reston published a column in the *Times* that appeared to be based on background information furnished by Dulles's office. Reston treated the American posture on the Middle East as "Mr. Dulles' policy," hardly mentioning Eisenhower. The journalist repeated precisely what Dulles had told congressional leaders a month earlier—that the administration's goals were to keep the oil-rich Middle East "from falling under Soviet domination" and to preserve the state of Israel without "dividing that area into two hostile blocs—a United States–Israeli bloc and a Soviet-Arab bloc." The State Department had convinced Reston that the policy was designed to protect "the free world's best interests," not "political considerations" in an election year. While noting that the United States would still not provide arms to Israel, Reston nailed the cornerstone of the March 28 policy: the State Department "had revised its optimistic estimates" of Gamal Abdel Nasser and was in the process of delaying, among other things, "the negotiations on aid to Egypt for the Aswan High Dam." Its publication in the *Times* guaranteed that the administration's March 28 policy shift wasn't secret anymore.[50]

Foster Dulles continued to worry about what his boss, in the midst of an election campaign, might say or do. Hoover had undoubtedly informed the secretary concerning the president's confusion about administration policy after March 28 on the dam. Nothing annoyed Dulles quite so much as the debate in Congress over the Bricker Amendment, a proposed constitutional amendment designed to limit the president's treaty-making powers, first proposed in 1953 by Ohio's Republican senator John Bricker. In March, the Senate Judiciary Committee had approved a new version of the Bricker Amendment and sent it to the Senate for action. It read: "A provision of a treaty or other international agreement which conflicts with *any provision* of this Constitution shall not be of any force or effect."[51]

In their meeting on May 7, Dulles had reviewed with Eisenhower a politically moderate statement about the Bricker Amendment, drafted by Attorney General Brownell, which the president had issued the following day. In it, Eisenhower had asserted that "it would be a tragic error to adopt any amendment which would change our traditional treaty-making power or which would hamper the President in his constitutional responsibility to conduct foreign affairs." [52]

That mild statement did not satisfy Foster Dulles. He pushed Ike to openly fight against the amendment. In a meeting on May 9, Eisenhower told Dulles that his advisors thought there was little chance of the amendment coming to a vote and, "therefore, it would be premature to make a direct challenge." [53] Dulles was dumbfounded. He smelled presidential politics in Ike's timidity. He heatedly argued that if Lyndon Johnson quietly picked up votes and then brought the amendment to a vote, "it would be too late for the President's opposition to be effective." Ike called in Sherman Adams, who told the secretary that Johnson and Knowland had assured him there would be no "surprise operation." But Dulles complained that he was "in a very embarrassing position"; he had not answered letters from senators because he thought "the president should take the lead."

After the meeting, Dulles angrily followed Adams into the chief of staff's office, exclaiming that he was "not disposed to preside silently over the liquidation of the treaty-making power and the capacity of the President to conduct foreign affairs on behalf of the nation as a whole." When Dulles again raised the issue of the letters from senators, Adams tersely countered, "Well, why don't you answer them?" Dulles said that would put the president "in a position where either he must adopt my views or I would have to resign. It is up to him to lead and not seem to be forced by me." As it turned out, Eisenhower and his political advisors were correct; Congress would adjourn in July without passing the Bricker Amendment.

The Middle East, not the Bricker Amendment, was what worried Eisenhower. At the Thursday, May 10, NSC meeting, Secretary Dulles reported at length on the recent NATO meeting and his continued concern about new Soviet tactics. [54] Eisenhower called those tactics "a recent manifestation of an age-old problem," that a dictatorship "could change its tactics with no more than a moment's notice." Treasury Secretary Humphrey thought they were taking Soviet actions too seriously, and called the American response comparable to American businessmen who "did not get very excited about a competitor until that competitor really began to bite into their market." Eisenhower turned, looked directly at Humphrey, and responded that there was "one hell of a difference between what the Soviets were doing and business practice": the Soviets were engaged in "the great game of international politics," a game wherein "they didn't have to show a cent of financial profit." Ike said that the Soviet offensive "to secure the allegiance of the uncommitted and underdeveloped nations" might cause American leaders to "wake up some morning and find that Egypt, for instance, had slipped behind the Iron Curtain."

A SILENT ALARM

Late that afternoon, following the NSC meeting, President Eisenhower and Dr. Howard Snyder drove to Walter Reed Hospital, where the president was scheduled to begin a two-day "tip-to-toe" physical checkup the next morning. Snyder noted that "the President looked well and felt well." The White House reinforced positive expectations by announcing that Eisenhower had accepted an invitation to attend a meeting of Latin American heads of state in Panama, June 25–26, his first trip out of the country since the heart attack.[55]

Upon entering the hospital, Eisenhower had joked to reporters that, "when they give you a physical at Walter Reed, brother, they give it to you." The *New York Times* described the president as a "peripatetic patient"— chatting with nurses and doctors, visiting the children's ward, and reading Winston Churchill's book *A History of the English-Speaking Peoples*. He was, Edwin Dale, Jr., reported, "tapped, pinched, pricked, listened to, looked at and written about" in a thorough medical process. The reporter described how "the nation's most famous patient" had been witnessed "padding along the corridors in a bathrobe and slippers."[56]

After the examination was completed, the official hospital record, according to Dr. Snyder, found "the President to be in excellent physical condition." That was misleading. X-rays of Ike's small intestinal tract had revealed "several constricted areas in the terminal ileum." Since barium had passed through without difficulty, the doctors had agreed that the press release could state, "barium studies showed a normally functioning digestive tract." The doctors chose to conceal, not only from the public but from Eisenhower, what Snyder later characterized as "a burned-out terminal ileitis." Snyder recalled that they believed that "the knowledge of this fact would cause the President unnecessary anxiety." Eisenhower, Snyder noted, later "took great exception to our decision in this matter." Snyder justified the secrecy because Eisenhower, since 1945, had suffered from "recurrent attacks of lower abdominal pain and distention." Later, he defended his decision because "between the dates of 12 May and 7 June 1956, the President conducted the affairs of his office without any material distress."[57]

Because the doctors agreed to secrecy, the newspapers failed to pick up any clue about the president's potentially troublesome condition. The White House announced that the president had been found to be in "good" general health, with "no symptoms" of heart inadequacy. Afterward, the president joined Mrs. Eisenhower at the Gettysburg farm, where he was described as "chipper and cheerful after a highly encouraging medical check-up." He was carrying two brightly wrapped packages—presumably a Mother's Day gift for Mrs. Eisenhower and a birthday gift for her mother, Mrs. Doud, who would turn seventy-seven on May 14.[58]

MORE POLITICAL UPHEAVAL

Eisenhower thought he had made a breakthrough on April 30 with Senator George on foreign aid, but the senator decided, at age seventy-eight, not to run for reelection in November. Former Georgia governor Herman Talmadge, an opponent of two Eisenhower priorities—desegregation and foreign aid—immediately announced his candidacy for the vacated Senate seat. While George would continue to chair the Foreign Relations Committee during the remainder of the congressional session, he was now a lame duck, his influence declining. Ike nonetheless still considered him important to the fate of the foreign aid bill. When Eisenhower and George met the evening of May 14, the president offered the senator, once he had retired, a post as the president's personal emissary to NATO. The White House announced that the senator had accepted and had pledged himself, in addition to his NATO duties, to continue to advise the president and the secretary of state regarding "the general development and implementation of a bipartisan foreign policy."[59]

Meanwhile, Egypt had become more aware of the administration's changed policy. Word had leaked that, while the United States was not directly providing arms to Israel, the administration would not stand in the way of other Western powers doing so. Still, one step in support of Egyptian sovereignty transpired, almost without notice. Six airfields built by Britain in the Suez Canal Zone were turned over to Egyptian authority on May 16, fulfilling, a month early, the 1954 agreement for British withdrawal of troops from the area.[60]

But the Egyptians were about to take a step that would further alienate the Western powers. On May 16, the Egyptian government formally recognized the government of communist China. Two days later, the State Department was investigating a rumor that China would be furnishing arms to Egypt. There was speculation that Egyptian government sources had floated the rumor as a warning against providing more fighter planes to Israel. Later, Egypt announced that Nasser had accepted an invitation to visit Beijing.[61]

The news that Egypt had recognized communist China did not help the administration's efforts on Capitol Hill. The House Foreign Affairs Committee voted, on May 17, to deny the president authority to make long-term commitments in foreign aid, and to cut the administration's request from $4.9 billion to $3 billion. The following week, the committee restored some of the cuts but still reduced the request by $1.1 billion. Dulles and Eisenhower now pinned their hopes on the Senate.[62]

That day, a new Middle East controversy erupted. Unknown to the White House or the State Department, on May 10, a Customs Bureau official in New York had blocked the shipment of twenty-one Army surplus half-track vehicles (with caterpillar treads in the back and conventional wheels in front) to Israel because they were not covered by a valid export license. The vehicles were removed from an Israel-bound ship in New York Harbor.[63]

The Israeli embassy decided not to make an issue of the half-track snafu, but Senators Hubert H. Humphrey (D-Minnesota) and Paul Douglas (D-Illinois) charged the Eisenhower administration with pro-Arab favoritism, recalling the government's shipment of eighteen Walker Bulldog tanks to Saudi Arabia in February. Representative Emanuel Celler, a New York Democrat, blasted the action as "part of a studied purpose of the State Department to hamstring and hurt Israel." New York's Herbert Lehman called the removal of the half-track vehicles "unabashed appeasement" of the Arabs. Former Air Force secretary Thomas K. Finletter, an advisor to the Stevenson campaign, issued a statement: "The Eisenhower Administration is firm enough in preventing even the smallest amount of arms from going to Israel. Under such circumstances, what possible justification can they have for sending arms to the Arabs?"

The administration's measured anti-Nasser policy, adopted March 28, had achieved, at best, mixed results in the Middle East. The Sunday, May 20, *New York Times* editorialized that, after years of effort to improve relations with the Arab nations, American policy "has met one rebuff after another from the Arabs." The *Times* said the list was discouraging—the arms deal with the Soviets, Cairo's attempt to break up the Baghdad Pact, Nasser's new "counter-bloc" with Syria and Saudi Arabia, and his pressure on Jordan to join. Now Egypt had "delivered another slap at the United States" by granting diplomatic recognition to communist China. Matters had been made worse by the fuss over the American shipment of arms and ammunition to Saudi Arabia and the announcement about the roadblock to delivering half-track vehicles to Israel.[64]

While Jewish voters were overwhelmingly loyal to the Democratic Party, the GOP was not immune to pro-Israel pressures. Secretary Dulles warned the president on May 22 that Republican congressman Jacob Javits would call at the White House, threatening not to run for the Senate from New York unless the administration changed its policy on arms for Israel. But Dulles said he believed that Israeli ambassador Abba Eban was satisfied that American policy was moving in a more positive direction and that the Israelis "were, in fact, getting from one source or another the arms which they felt they needed."[65]

Still, Foster Dulles dared to hope that his shift in policy had defused some of the political pressures at home. At his news conference later that day, the secretary was not asked about arms for Israel—a reaction to Israel's enhanced ability to obtain arms from American allies, especially the French. When asked about the apparently "much more bearish view" of the administration toward Nasser, Dulles said nothing to dispel that impression and used words, according to the New York Times, "sharper in tone than anything Mr. Dulles had said publicly in the past." He deplored Nasser's promotion of the interests of communist nations. Dulles stepped back from the American commitment to provide aid to the construction of the Aswan Dam, saying he doubted that the United States would find it "practical or desirable" to assist with the dam if the Soviet Union was involved in the project.[66]

The war scare in the Middle East seemed to be receding, thanks to the armistice negotiated by Hammarskjöld on April 19. On June 4, the Security Council passed a resolution commending the secretary-general and calling on the parties to expeditiously implement the armistice agreement. In a calmer atmosphere, Eisenhower met on June 5 with congressional leaders and attempted to persuade them to restore the $1.1 billion cut in his foreign aid request.[67]

A CALL IN THE NIGHT

At his news conference the morning of June 6, Dwight Eisenhower was in a nostalgic mood. This was the twelfth anniversary of D-Day, when he had made the historic decision to land forces in Europe.[68] Ike used the occasion to make a full-throated appeal for foreign aid. "America never got discouraged in that war," he said, because "the objective was so clear; defeat and destroy the enemy; make him stop fighting. In waging a peace, the objectives are not so clear." In a veiled reference to the Middle East, the president described a situation "confused by age-old prejudices and difficulties and mutual antagonisms in different areas of the world.... So," he continued, "the case is not so clear, but the importance is even greater."

"Ladies and gentlemen," Eisenhower proclaimed with passion, "there is no amount of money that you can pour into bombs and missiles and planes and tanks and guns that will assure you peace." Those arms provided "diminishing returns." It made sense to put a "reasonable amount" of money into projects that "tend to make people respectful of the great values that we are supporting, the liberty of the individual, his right to equal opportunity in his own country, to [the] pursuit of happiness."

"If you are waging peace," Eisenhower continued, "you can't be too particular sometimes about the special attitudes that different countries take." Ike was surely thinking about Egypt. The United States, he said, should not assume that "neutral" nations do not deserve assistance. While foreign aid was costly, "as long as we are not shooting, we are not spending one-tenth as much as we would if we were shooting." While the destruction during World War II was extraordinary, Eisenhower told the reporters, "there is no destruction that you have seen that would even give a hint of what another war would bring." The president concluded: "We must continue to wage the peace. We must not be parsimonious. We must support such programs as the Mutual Security Act."

The next day Foster Dulles called Jim Hagerty to tell him that "we are in quite a lot of trouble" because critics had interpreted Eisenhower's statement about neutral nations as an attack on military alliances. Hagerty said he would talk to the president about the problem. Eisenhower pulled back from his ebullient D-Day anniversary mood to edit a politically oriented statement designed to clarify his comments. It asserted that Eisenhower, as former NATO commander, was a great advocate of "the principle of collective security whereby the nations associate themselves together for each other's protection." Eisenhower argued that his "mutual security" proposals to Congress were designed to reinforce that principle. While some nations face "special conditions which justify political neutrality," no nation had the right to be "neutral as between right and wrong or decency and indecency." [69]

Presidential election year reporting can be cruel to candidates, even sitting presidents. Ike's statements on neutralism validated what in subsequent decades has become a Washington truism—that a gaffe is one of those special moments when a politician tells the unvarnished truth.[70]

In spite of the uproar over his statements about neutral nations, Eisenhower was feeling energetic. The morning of Thursday, June 7, he presided over a National Security Council meeting, had another fifteen appointments, and took some time to practice golf. That evening, he attended the White House News Photographers Dinner at the Sheraton Park Hotel, where he drank a couple of Scotches, ate a filet mignon, and laughed at comedian Bob Hope's jokes. Eisenhower stayed up until midnight, a schedule his doctors would have vetoed a few weeks earlier. The president's car dropped Howard Snyder off at his home on Connecticut Avenue. Ike retired to bed almost immediately after arriving at the White house.[71]

The doctor was removing his clothes when the phone rang on his White House home extension. Snyder later recalled reaching for the phone "with a shudder." Only the first lady could be calling at such a late hour, and then, only in an emergency.

6

★ ★ ★ ★ ★ ★

TROUBLE OVER ASWAN

June 8–July 26, 1956

"If we hadn't turned the Egyptians down yesterday, Congress
would have turned them down today, which is another reason
why I think it was a good move on our part."

John Foster Dulles to C. D. Jackson, July 20, 1956

WHEN MAMIE Eisenhower had climbed into bed about midnight, Ike complained of pain. She told Dr. Snyder that the president was having another one of his frequent abdominal upsets. Snyder suggested giving him a tablespoon of milk of magnesia. Twenty minutes later, Mrs. Eisenhower called again, saying the president's discomfort was worse; she had ordered a White House car to pick up Snyder. Five minutes later, the car arrived at his home and, in another five, deposited him at the White House. Just before 1:30, Snyder entered the Eisenhower's bedroom on the second floor of the White House to find Mrs. Eisenhower pacing nervously.[1]

The situation was both familiar and frightening for the doctor. In the past, he had managed to alleviate the president's abdominal distress. But now Snyder could not be certain the president was not suffering another heart attack; his pulse was elevated and his blood pressure was higher than normal. Snyder detected "considerable heart arrhythmia" but the discomfort was focused in the lower abdomen. Snyder got the president back to sleep but Ike awoke at 4:45 and complained of pain for the next three hours.

Just as in Denver, eight months earlier, the physician moved slowly. A few minutes before 8:00 A.M., Ann Whitman's phone rang. Dr. Snyder told her that the president had "a headache and digestive upset" and that she should cancel all of his appointments except the 2:00 P.M. cabinet meeting. To Whitman's ears, that message must have sounded hauntingly familiar. She called Sherman Adams and Jim Hagerty, who then called Foster Dulles, repeating that the president had "an upset stomach and headache" but emphasizing that Dr. Snyder had assured her that there was "nothing wrong" with his heart. Hagerty arrived at the White House at about 8:15 and he, Whitman, and Adams then learned, in Whitman's words, that "the President was far sicker than had been thought." Snyder called the illness "chronic ileitis." Whatever that meant, the staff was shaken; the president of the United States was seriously ill for the second time in eight months.[2]

The two men who knew the most about Eisenhower's physical condition were out of the city. Major General Leonard D. Heaton at Walter Reed Hospital, who had supervised Eisenhower's medical checkups, was on vacation in Virginia. After the White House reached Heaton, Snyder arranged for a plane to fly him to Washington. Colonel Thomas Mattingly, the president's cardiologist at Walter Reed, was driving toward Columbia, South Carolina, sticking to the back roads to enjoy the scenery. He heard about the president's illness on the radio and returned to a main road, where he was intercepted by the state police.[3]

SURGERY ON A PRESIDENT?

By this time, it was mid-morning. At 10:20, Snyder called Walter Reed to request that an ambulance be kept ready in case it was needed. Shortly thereafter, the president vomited. Still, Snyder resisted taking the president to the hospital until he knew that both Heaton and Mattingly would be available. At 12:13, Colonel Goodpaster called the secretary of state to tell him that the cabinet meeting had been canceled and that the president would be taken to the hospital. Fully twelve hours after Snyder arrived at the president's bedside, Ike was put on a stretcher, carried to the South Portico of the White House, and placed in an ambulance, arriving at Walter Reed Hospital fifteen minutes later.[4]

Eventually, some thirteen doctors would be involved in assessing the president's condition. They suspected that there was an obstruction in the president's small intestine. The need for surgery appeared evident but, as Snyder recalled, "no one likes to contemplate operating upon a President of the United States, and especially upon one who has had a serious cardiac infarction within the preceding eight months." [5]

Foster Dulles was agitated over the news. He was about to leave for Iowa State College to deliver the commencement address where he would attempt to further defuse the controversy over the president's off-the-cuff remarks on neutralism at his June 6 news conference. Dulles planned to state that the principle of neutrality had become "obsolete" and "except under very exceptional circumstances, it is an immoral and short-sighted conception." [6]

The secretary had endured great stress during the president's previous illness, and his own health was fragile. When he had heard nothing by mid-afternoon on June 8, Dulles called White House assistant press secretary Murray Snyder, only to be told that the doctors had not provided any new information. Dulles speculated that it had been "a big day" yesterday and that the White House News Photographers Dinner "was enough to do it." He wishfully called it "an attack from dinner." Dulles also made anxious calls to Hagerty and Adams, and wrote a personal note to the president, saying he regretted "leaving you in physical distress." [7]

By 7:15 that evening, the doctors were fully agreed that the president had an "obstruction of the intestine in the terminal ileum." But consensus on performing surgery was elusive because, Snyder recorded, "everyone hesitated to put a knife into his abdomen." Snyder later opined that the surgery would have taken place early in the afternoon of June 8 "if the patient had been plain Mrs. Murphy." At 8:30, Hagerty informed reporters that the president's condition was "progressing satisfactorily" and the doctors had authorized him to say that "there is no indication for immediate surgery." [8]

Still, the doctors procrastinated. By midnight, Howard Snyder was beside himself. He pleaded with the doctors to take one more X-ray, insisting that once they reviewed that image, "you will put the President on the litter and wheel him to the operating room." When the X-ray confirmed the diagnosis, another problem arose. Mamie Eisenhower, who had waited patiently throughout this ordeal, hesitated to sign the permission for surgery. Finally, son John signed. [9]

A little after 2:00 A.M., on Saturday, June 9, the president was lifted from his bed, placed on a gurney and taken to the operating room. General Heaton and Dr. Isidor Ravdin, from the University of Pennsylvania Medical School, performed the operation. Heaton later recalled that Ike, while the anesthetic was being administered, said, "You know, Leonard, I have a lot of bills to sign and I am going to have to be able to sign them within three or four days." The president muttered something about the Constitution—then lost consciousness.[10]

At 2:14 A.M., Hagerty assembled the reporters to tell them that an "exploratory operation" was in progress and that this was "not a heart case," even though Dr. Paul Dudley White had been summoned for consultation. Three hours later, the president was returned to his room in Ward 8. By 8:00 A.M., he had recovered from the anesthetic and Milton Eisenhower emerged from his room, saying the president had "good color."[11]

That morning, the New York Times blazed the headline: "President Undergoes Surgery on Intestine Block at 2:59 A.M.: Doctors Pronounce It Success." General Heaton spoke to a crowded news conference at two o'clock and described the president's condition as "excellent" and said the doctors expected a "rapid and complete recovery" that should not affect his running for a second term. The president would remain in the hospital about fifteen days and resume the "full duties" of his office within four to six weeks. Eisenhower's life expectancy might even be enhanced, thanks to the correction of an intestinal condition that had existed for years. At 7:00 P.M., Hagerty issued another bulletin citing the president's condition as "most satisfactory." Milton Eisenhower appeared and reported that he had "carried on a very friendly, normal conversation" with his brother and the president's spirit was excellent.[12]

Republican leaders moved aggressively to squelch any speculation that the new illness would force Eisenhower to withdraw from the presidential campaign. The Times reported that "some of his closest political advisors" believed, because the surgery had gone well, that there was no question about his running. Democrats asserted that the president's new illness sharpened the issue of whether the sixty-five-year-old president could survive another four years. Republican strategists countered that Adlai Stevenson had undergone gall bladder surgery and New York governor Averell Harriman, another potential presidential candidate, had withstood prostate surgery. One partisan declined to take advantage; Harry Truman announced that he was "very happy" that the president's surgery had gone so well.[13]

DULLES WITHOUT IKE AGAIN

Monday, June 11, was a day of frantic White House meetings confronting, once again, the prospect that the president would be unavailable for four to six weeks. The White House staff agreed that, following any meeting with the president, a written "Memorandum of Conference" should be prepared, submitted to the staff secretary, Colonel Goodpaster, to be filed with Ann Whitman and followed up on by Sherman Adams. The memoranda should place "particular emphasis on decisions reached" and plans for implementation.[14]

Adams, following the doctors' instructions, kept the president's meetings few and short. The first week after the surgery, the doctors insisted that Ike's meetings be limited to one per day, not lasting more than twenty to twenty-five minutes. On June 14, Foster Dulles saw the president for the first time, accompanying Konrad Adenauer, the chancellor of Germany, for a meeting lasting eleven minutes. Dulles himself would not be granted the opportunity for a substantive discussion with the president for another month.[15]

With such a limited schedule, Eisenhower had time to think, to be in pain—and to be depressed. Ike later wrote a friend, "For the first two or three days after this unfortunate business, I not only mistrusted the doctors' prognosis, but I doubted seriously that I would ever feel like myself again." That dark side of his illness was never communicated to the public. The president eventually forgot what those weeks were like, insisting in his memoirs that "although I was truly miserable for several days I was never disturbed, in this instance, by the doubts that beset so many others."[16]

That was not the case. The president was angry when he learned that, following his May checkup, the doctors had decided not to tell him about the abnormality in his intestinal tract, lest it cause him "unnecessary anxiety." He surely wondered what else his doctors were hiding from him. Ike was afflicted with frequent blue moods for much of the six weeks following the surgery. Nixon recalled that Ike "suffered more pain over a longer period of time" and "looked far worse than he had in 1955." The vice president described Eisenhower as "hobbling about, bent over," and uncomfortable.[17]

Eisenhower's personal discouragement, as well as his physical condition, limited his availability to subordinates. John Foster Dulles was scheduled to meet with the president for fifteen to twenty minutes on Friday, June 15, but on Thursday afternoon, following the meeting with the German chancellor, Adams called Dulles to say that the president should have no more visitors until Monday. Adams insisted that the meeting with Adenauer on Thursday "did not have bad consequences—he is just tired." Dulles, frustrated, had hoped to secure an agreement with the president about the schedule for the conference of Latin American heads of state in Panama. That meeting, originally scheduled for the last week in June, had been planned as the president's first foreign trip since his heart attack.[18]

On Friday, the National Security Council was called to order without the president.[19] Allen Dulles reported that Dmitri Shepilov, who had recently replaced Molotov as Soviet foreign minister, was scheduled to arrive in Cairo to attend an event celebrating the departure of British troops from the Suez Canal base area. The CIA director assumed that the Aswan Dam would be on the agenda for Soviet-Egyptian discussion. Secretary Humphrey again expressed his fervent wish "that the United States were out of the High Aswan dam project altogether." He accused the Egyptians of using the American offer as a vehicle for "shopping around to see if they can get a better bargain elsewhere." On Monday, June 18, the newspapers reported that Shepilov had indeed made an offer to Nasser to fund the Aswan Dam project, although it was later learned that the deal had not been formalized.[20]

That day, when Foster Dulles arrived to see the president, the vice president was already there. The three men agreed that Nixon should go ahead with his previous planned trip to represent the government at the anniversary of Philippine independence in Manila. The president approved of proceeding with Indian prime minister Jawaharlal Nehru's visit on July 7 (later canceled), provided Nehru was comfortable with short meetings and the president's unavailability for evening dinners and meetings. Dulles was particularly anxious to discuss the foreign aid legislation and its difficulty in Congress. He did not bring up the Aswan Dam. The entire meeting, including Ike's time with the vice president, lasted just under twenty minutes. Afterward, Jim Hagerty regaled the press with an inflated account of a hardworking president who that day had signed ten bills, vetoed one, and performed a number of other executive duties.[21]

ASWAN AND CONGRESS

Without Ike's counsel, Foster Dulles was left to his own devices. The secretary was increasingly negative about the Aswan Dam because the project had become the flashpoint for congressional opposition to the foreign aid proposal. Dulles warned the Senate Foreign Relations committee on June 19 that reductions in the proposed program could damage the nation's alliances. The *New York Times* reported the bill was in "such trouble" in the Senate that "some of its most powerful friends believed the Administration would be wiser to compromise now rather than risk a heavy setback on the floor." [22]

That Friday, Dulles asked Adams how Ike was and Adams said he was "sitting up and doing business." "While you could detect he was weak," the chief of staff said, "his attitude was the best." The president had reviewed plans for the Republican convention, including who might nominate him and second the nomination. But Ann Whitman, who daily observed Ike more closely than anyone besides his immediate family, was less certain about the president's progress. Eisenhower's mood swings continued in the weeks following his surgery. By the end of the second week, Whitman thought that Ike "seemed much like himself." Then, she noted in her diary, "A new difficulty"—unspecified but probably physical—"arose that seemingly depressed him and set him back." [23]

Eisenhower was certainly not focused on the Aswan Dam. Shepilov's visit to Cairo had not resulted in a formal offer from the Soviet Union, but Colonel Nasser had decided the timing was right to push the West for an agreement. On the night of June 20, he asked Eugene Black, the World Bank president to use his influence to move things along. Black declined to discuss that conversation with the press, except to say that his organization was "fully prepared to finance the High Dam." [24]

On June 25, Secretary Dulles, undersecretary Hoover, and other State Department personnel met with Black, just returned from Egypt, and Andrew N. Overby, an assistant secretary of the treasury. [25] Black reported that the Egyptian leader had been "extremely friendly and courteous" and was "disappointed that there had been no reply to their counter proposals on the Aswan Dam." Nasser, he said, had exhibited "no trace of bitterness." Black opined that Nasser was in no hurry to make a deal with the Soviets. The World Bank president described the situation as "not much different" from December 16, 1955, when the Americans, in his presence, had presented a detailed proposal to the Egyptian finance minister, Abdel Moneim el Kaissouni. [26]

Ever since he had instigated an anti-Nasser shift in policy on March 28, Foster Dulles had been moving toward a decision to withdraw support for the Aswan Dam. He asked Black a loaded question—whether the project was so large that it would impose hardship on Egypt's people. Black responded that some austerity would be required but, if the West did not proceed, Egypt would make a deal during Nasser's upcoming trip to Moscow in August. That "would have a tremendous impact." He went on to say that "Nasser had commited himself politically," and the project was popular with the Egyptian people. Nasser, Black concluded, "gave every indication of preferring to make an agreement with the West; perhaps because he feels the hot breath of the Russians uncomfortably close to the back of his neck."

Dulles described "the knotty difficulties with Congress" and his fear that a rider prohibiting funds for the dam would be attached to the Mutual Security bill. Nasser's project had "cost us too much, not only in Congress, but in the form of political support from friendly countries." Dulles claimed to be undecided—hardly a candid assertion—but he said he "saw a good many hazards." Black later recalled that, at this point in the meeting, he had told the secretary, "If you call it off I think all hell will break loose." At that, Dulles had turned and walked out of the room.[27]

Dulles was increasingly focused on the foreign aid bill. The previous week, he had told Adams that William Knowland and Lyndon Johnson, the Senate minority and majority leaders, were "rather gloomy" about the prospects for the legislation. On June 26, he called Adams, asking if there was any possibility that the president could see the two senators and prepare them for a committee vote scheduled for Friday night, June 29. Adams responded for his depressed boss: "Not much." Dulles also wanted to discuss changes in diplomatic assignments with the president but Adams told the secretary to go ahead on his own—the governor would ask Ike if he had any questions. Among the shifts Dulles was contemplating was the removal of Henry Byroade from Cairo, eliminating Nasser's sole American advocate from the diplomatic dialogue.[28]

Still, Dulles worried about the impact of a Soviet deal to build the Aswan Dam. The morning of June 27, he phoned George V. Allen to ask if he had any information on whether Shepilov had made an offer while in Egypt; Allen replied "none." He believed that Shepilov had arrived in Egypt without an offer "in his pocket." "Nasser is disappointed," Allen concluded. Foster Dulles called Hoover, and they agreed that, if the press asked about Aswan, the secretary would say that "there is no change in the situation."[29]

A SHIP WITHOUT A CAPTAIN

As Eisenhower began his last week at Walter Reed, he was still largely insulated from matters of state. The president was now walking regularly but required extensive bed rest. The limited meetings the doctors permitted were restricted to a few minutes. On Tuesday, June 26, the day that legislative leaders were to meet with the vice president presiding, the president had no appointments at all—not even with Sherman Adams.

Nixon convened the National Security Council at 9:00 A.M. on Thursday.[30] CIA director Dulles now had information that updated George Allen's comment to Foster Dulles the previous day. He shared intelligence, not yet fully confirmed, that Dmitri Shepilov, the Soviet foreign minister, had allegedly offered Egypt a no-interest loan of $400 million for sixty years to build the Aswan Dam, and the Soviet Union would cancel the debt resulting from the arms sold to Egypt the previous year. The report also stated that Shepilov had offered to purchase Egypt's cotton crop—Dulles did not say how much or for how long—and build a steel mill.

In Eisenhower's absence, Foster Dulles and George Humphrey joined forces in questioning support for the Aswan project. Humphrey expressed delight that the Soviets were going to take on the project. That would be "the best possible thing that could happen for the United States," he said. Foster Dulles added that the immediate impact of Soviet support for the dam would be damaging for the United States but "the long-term results might be very good." The secretary of state stuck to his new dogma that American support for the project would become unpopular among the Egyptian people, who "would blame the austerities they suffered" on the United States. Harold Stassen, the president's assistant for disarmament, inquired about the reaction if the United States withdrew its offer of assistance. Humphrey replied that he did not care how it was done; "if there was any way for the United States to back out of the offer," he "desperately hoped that we would seize upon it." Allen Dulles countered that Colonel Nasser "had apparently been very cautious in his dealings with Shepilov," and the CIA director said he doubted that the Russian's visit "had significantly changed the situation in Egypt."

A little before nine in the morning on Saturday, June 30, President and Mrs. Eisenhower left their suite at Walter Reed Hospital to drive to Gettysburg. Ann Whitman, after witnessing the president's bouts of depression, recorded in her diary that "it seemed remarkable, to me, that he could walk out of the hospital as steadily as he did, and look as well as he did." [31] Unlike the previous November, this time there was no grand parade or waving to crowds. The Eisenhowers were driven directly to Gettysburg, arriving just after eleven. After a nap, Ike moved his belongings into the guest cottage, where he would remain during his convalescence. The president endured a restless first night, awakening at 1:30, 2:45, and again at 6:00. Sunday, July 1, was the Eisenhowers' fortieth wedding anniversary. [32]

For the first week in Gettysburg, Ike maintained a light schedule, but his mood improved. He celebrated the July 4 holiday by practicing shots on the putting green for the first time. The next day, Thursday, he conducted his first full-fledged meeting, which lasted over an hour. The one significant matter he addressed directly concerned the CIA's U-2 spy plane flights over the Soviet Union. Ike wanted to be notified if the flights were discovered, because he might have to suspend them. On July 9, Ike wrote to Milton that "steadily I am regaining some strength, and I feel there is no doubt that I shall be able to make the trip to Panama," rescheduled to begin July 21. Eisenhower wrote to his friend William Robinson, the chairman of the board at Coca-Cola, that he was "slowly regaining my strength and manage each day to get a little more exercise." He told Robinson that he had walked that morning almost down to the road and back "without getting tired." [33]

Meanwhile, Foster Dulles had begun to prepare the public and State Department officials for the withdrawal of support for the Aswan Dam. The *New York Times* reported on July 9 that the State Department was "fundamentally re-examining the United States' relations with Egypt," including the Aswan project, and "whether the United States should treat Egypt as a friendly neutral or as a country leaning more and more to the side of the Soviet Union." [34]

That same day, Foster Dulles cabled the embassy staff in Cairo with a detailed, negative assessment of Egyptian responses to American initiatives during the past four years. The administration, he wrote, "has based its Near East policy in large part on cooperation with Egypt often at considerable political cost, both domestic and foreign." The United States had offered to provide arms and assist with the Aswan Dam and the Egyptian response had been an arms deal with the Soviet Union, "recognition of Communist China, and anti-West propaganda and activities." In short, Egypt had followed a path "detrimental" to the interests of the United States. [35]

THE CANDIDATE RETURNS

On Tuesday, July 10, Eisenhower ramped up his activities in preparation for a return to normalcy. As he wrote Sid Richardson, a Texas associate of Robert Anderson's, he had been subject to "such a full regime of treatment, exercise and rest that I have had little time for other matters." Ike's sense of humor had returned. The president told Richardson of his appreciation of Lyndon Johnson for his kindness during his illness and his help on other matters. Ike regretted that he was forced to express such sentiments "on a confidential basis, because no individual of one party is ever supposed to say a nice word about a member of another party." [36]

That morning, Ike presided over a meeting with Republican legislative leaders in Gettysburg.[37] Senator Knowland, the minority leader, reported that the Senate hoped to adjourn by July 21. A major agenda for this meeting was what strategy to adopt regarding the mutual security legislation. On July 6, House and Senate conferees had taken the first of two distinct legislative steps toward approval of a foreign aid bill, agreeing that the program should be authorized to go forward with a preliminary ceiling of $4.014 billion in foreign aid. This was well short of the administration's $4.9 billion request, but more than the House had approved. The second step would involve bills to actually appropriate the money, with particularly important deliberations to be carried out in the Senate Appropriations Committee.[38]

The day before the July 10 legislative meeting, Eisenhower had appealed from Gettysburg for restoration of "a substantial part" of the money that had been cut from the administration's request of $4.9 billion, arguing that the reductions "would definitely injure our efforts to help lead the world to peace based on cooperation and justice."[39]

House minority leader Joseph W. Martin, Jr., of Massachusetts said the question "was whether to make a vigorous fight for the amount agreed upon in conference, and run a chance of a greater cut—or accept the figure the House agreed upon." Eisenhower felt that "it would be better to fight for the sum deemed necessary, rather than just taking the best we can get." The president said that he "did not want it to appear that we were not backing it strongly." Eisenhower added that he intended to "talk vigorously" about the importance of foreign aid "all through the campaign." To fail to appropriate the full amount, he said, would be "the gravest error."

Ike had touched on the question that was on everyone's mind—was he still up to running for a second term? Eisenhower quickly added a personal note. "I have had a rough ride," he said. "But if I was right on February 29, I am now in much better condition." The seriousness of his surgery had mandated "a slow recovery." But, "the thing that was wrong with me, that flared up so many times, has been corrected." He added with emphasis: "This operation was the sternest test that my heart could have." Ike repeated his intent to "talk throughout this campaign" about the "absolutely vital" issue of mutual security aid. Afterward, Knowland, briefing the press about the meeting, recalled that the president had begun his remarks by asking, "Why shouldn't I run?" When reporters pressed the minority leader as to whether that meant the president "would keep his hat in the ring," Knowland responded, "I'm telling you precisely that." [40]

PRELUDE TO A DECISION

The Egyptians were fed up with the months of equivocation. The Aswan Dam negotiations with the Americans were going nowhere. No firm deal had been concluded with the Russians during Shepilov's visit and Nasser still preferred to avoid an intimate relationship with the Russians. Ambassador Byroade reported on July 10 that Nasser had ordered Ambassador Ahmed Hussein to return to Washington to try to persuade Secretary Dulles "to go ahead" with the Aswan project. Initially, Nasser had resisted the conditions imposed by the United States for support of the project as invasions of Egyptian sovereignty—reflected in the World Bank's financial reporting procedures, requirements for competitive contract bids, assurances regarding the Egyptian economy, and its insistence on the resolution of a dispute with Sudan over division of the waters of the Nile. Now Nasser had decided that the changes he had wanted were "not really important." The Egyptian president was irritated that the United States was erroneously assuming a deal with the Soviets was inevitable. Hussein had told Byroade that "Nasser says he truly wishes to be a friend to [the] US." [41]

Byroade confirmed Hussein's message when he visited Nasser's home the night of July 11. He commended Nasser for returning the ambassador to Washington. Nasser responded that nothing, not even the Aswan Dam, was as important as the "lack of mutual confidence" that had arisen between Egypt and the United States. He insisted that he and his people "were not working for any outside power but only for Egypt." Nasser pressed his point: "The Arab world will no longer tolerate colonialism. I am not foolish enough to think that it will tolerate a form of Egyptian colonialism or domination either."[42]

Byroade was motivated by his talk with Nasser to make one last effort to convince Secretary Dulles of Nasser's desire to work with the United States. The ambassador, reacting to Dulles's July 9 recitation of Egyptian misdeeds, wrote on July 13 that there was "an honest difference of opinion as to interpretation between Department and field." Dulles's statement had been essentially factual but "in certain vital aspects we believe the facts themselves are expressed in misleading manner." The "why" of Egypt's actions had been "entirely omitted," he continued. The Soviets had initiated the new contacts, not Egypt. Dulles's statement had assumed that Egypt must be judged "solely" by whether "she is for us or for the Soviets." Byroade deplored the double standard whereby the United States welcomed warmer relations with the Soviet Union but Arab nations were held to a different standard. The ambassador said he feared that "before too long," the United States would be cast as "the unreasonable member" in the East-West contest.[43]

As before, the ambassador's plea would be ignored. By the time Byroade's letter arrived, Foster Dulles had already taken steps toward implementing his negative decision on assistance to the Aswan Dam, including his plan to replace Byroade with someone more attuned to his outlook.

Upon learning of the Egyptian ambassador's imminent return, George V. Allen informed Secretary Dulles in a memorandum that a decision regarding the Aswan Dam project could no longer be avoided. "To proceed with the December offer would be contrary to our entire policy towards Egypt," wrote Allen. It would reap "Congressional and public opposition at home" and concern among other nations in the region. Allen's recommendation was to finesse the issue, keeping the door open for future collaboration if Egypt responded with actions that demonstrated goodwill. Perhaps Allen hoped to stretch the matter out until after the November election, but Dulles was done with equivocation on Aswan. His handwritten notation at the bottom of Allen's memorandum read: "Not approved."[44]

On Friday, July 13, John Foster Dulles traveled to Gettysburg to hold his first truly substantial conversation with the president since his June 9 surgery.[45] The agenda was crowded. They discussed the trip to Panama and the limitations on Ike's activities there. Eisenhower approved Dulles's plan to travel on to Colombia, Ecuador, and Peru after the Panama conference. They discussed the Soviet Union's de-Stalinization process, the U-2 spy plane flights over the Soviet Union, and the British contribution to NATO force levels. Then Dulles turned to the Arab-Israeli conflict, asserting that, despite continuing tensions, "the prophets who had anticipated Israel being over-run in June were already proved wrong."

Finally, Dulles addressed the Aswan Dam with the convalescing president. Ike had been disengaged from the issue for weeks. Dulles did not want a thorough discussion; he had no intention of letting the president meddle with his plans. The secretary briefly summarized the situation. They had "sat tight" while Shepilov was in Egypt and, as it turned out, the Russian had not made a deal on the dam. Now the Egyptians were prepared to "take our proposal on the original terms and withdraw their own counterproposals." Dulles finessed his own position, saying that the State Department was "not in a position now to deal with this matter because we did not know of the legislative situation." He said that the department's view "on the merits of the matter" had been "somewhat altered," a statement to which Eisenhower appears not to have responded. Dulles said that the State Department was still deliberating and he would "consult" with Eisenhower the following week.

There had been a dozen items on the agenda for the meeting and Dulles had devoted only a few minutes to Aswan. This was a rapid-fire briefing for the recuperating president, not a real discussion. For Eisenhower, this discussion of Aswan must have sounded like something happening on another planet; he had no up-to-date information and did not seek any. Ike apparently felt that he had no choice but to trust his secretary of state. Dulles penciled on his agenda sheet that a final decision on Aswan would be formalized on July 19, the day of the next National Security Council meeting. He—apparently on purpose—did not inform the president that the Egyptian ambassador was returning to Washington and expecting a firm answer at that time.

Late on the afternoon of July 13, Dulles took another step in preparation for the upcoming confrontation with the Egyptian ambassador. After returning to Washington, he called in the British ambassador, Sir Roger Makins.[46] Dulles was more direct with Makins than he had been with the president. He said he had "mentioned" the matter to Eisenhower and "wanted to talk to the President further before reaching a final decision." Dulles raised the prospect that Congress might attach a rider to legislation prohibiting using foreign aid funds for Aswan. In any event, the amount likely to be approved would make it difficult to free up even $50 million for Egypt and "we would be obliged to steal from everyone else" to do that. He also expressed "increasing doubts regarding the benefits which would inure to the West."

With this introduction, Dulles then edged into his real agenda, which was "how the matter should be handled if we determined not to proceed." He told Makins that his inclination was to tell Nasser "what the situation is." He did not want the Egyptian leader to go to Moscow with an American offer "in his pocket." Dulles fantasized that "if we withdraw our offer beforehand, the Russians may overplay their hand and ask so much that it would react against them in the Arab world."

Two days later, Dulles cleared the diplomatic decks to deal with Egypt. The State Department announced that Henry Byroade would be reassigned to South Africa, making it impossible for him to influence policy toward Egypt. Raymond Hare, currently director general of the Foreign Service, would replace Byroade in Cairo. George V. Allen would be reassigned as ambassador to Greece. Deputy assistant secretary of state William Rountree would assume Allen's position as assistant secretary of state for Near Eastern, South Asian, and African affairs. "The purpose," the press story said, "was to strengthen the hand of the United States in Cairo and Athens."[47]

Meanwhile, late on Friday the 13th, Foster Dulles had received encouraging news from William Knowland. The day before, Dulles and Joint Chiefs chairman Admiral Radford had testified behind closed doors, urgently asking the Senate Appropriations Committee to restore the cuts in the foreign aid appropriation and provide at least $4 billion. The committee had just approved the Mutual Security bill and, in a close vote, restored some of the previous cuts, bringing the total recommended to $4.1 billion. Lyndon Johnson had voted with the administration. Dulles declared himself "gratified."[48]

In fact, however, the Senate Appropriations Committee had approved a report accompanying the bill that would be troublesome for the administration. The report, issued July 14, included this language: "The committee directs that none of the funds provided in this act shall be used for assistance in connection with the construction of the Aswan Dam, nor shall any of the funds heretofore provided under the Mutual Security Act as amended be used on the dam without prior approval of the Committee on Appropriations."[49]

Despite the president's decision to attend the Panama conference and his July 10 declaration of intentions to the legislators, Ike was still plagued with doubts about his physical condition. He had kept a light schedule the rest of the week, assigning the vice president to chair the NSC and cabinet meetings. He wrote Robert Woodruff, a Coca-Cola executive and Georgia golfing buddy, that he appreciated Woodruff's optimistic predictions about his health but "there have been times when I have had my doubts." Eisenhower was thinner than he had been for years; he was concerned that "it will be some weeks before I can regain my lost weight." On July 14, he tried to be upbeat with his grandson, David, writing: "I get stronger every day, and yesterday walked all the way to the gate and back, a distance of a mile." [50]

Eisenhower was determined, ready or not, to return to the Oval Office. He took a walk around the farm grounds on Sunday morning and spent forty minutes chipping and putting on his putting green. At 3:54, his motorcade departed the farm, arriving at the White House at 6:06. Once there, Ike began what Ann Whitman called "a limited schedule of office routine." Whitman noted in her diary that "there was evident still a great physical and psychological depression." Ike could not bring himself to plan for the San Francisco convention, writing a supporter on July 16 that "I am in a dilemma" and "my plans are still quite indefinite." One plan was set; he would leave for Panama on July 21, less than a week after his return to the White House. [51]

Two days after he returned to the White House, Tuesday, July 17, Ike got around to reading the Senate Appropriations Committee report, with its prohibition against aid to the Aswan Dam. Adams called Foster Dulles to tell him that the president was upset. While willing to engage in "consultation" with the committee, Ike believed that needing to seek its "approval" for presidential action was unconstitutional. Eisenhower, Adams said, had concluded that he "does not feel bound" by the report "and does not intend to be." Dulles immediately wrote Senator Carl Hayden (D-Arizona), the chairman of the committee, that "the Executive Department of the Government would not feel bound by the language in the Senate Appropriations Committee report." [52]

Later, Senator Knowland called Foster Dulles to tell him that his letter had been read to the committee. The objectionable language was in the committee report, not in the actual bill, but Knowland believed that the administration would proceed "at its peril" if it ignored the strong feelings in the committee. Dulles called it "a grave constitutional question" if a congressional committee demanded approval of the president's execution of foreign policy. Knowland suggested putting the exclusion of funding for the Aswan Dam in the legislation; Dulles replied that he hoped that would not be necessary "because we have just about made up our minds to tell the Egyptians we will not do it." Knowland said that the Senate would not deal with the bill before July 20. Dulles, anticipating his meeting with the Egyptian ambassador, said that "it might well be taken care of by then." [53]

Later that day, George V. Allen confirmed in a memorandum to the secretary of state that Ambassador Hussein would arrive in Washington on July 19 and seek an immediate appointment with the secretary. [54] While reinforcing Dulles's conclusion that the offer to assist with the Aswan Dam should be withdrawn, Allen and his staff in the Near East Office had been wrestling with the possible consequences of that decision. He warned that the Aswan Dam was of great symbolic importance to the Egyptian people. "Therefore," Allen concluded, "we should not underestimate the strength of Nasser's reaction to a withdrawal of the December 1955 offer."

Nonetheless, Allen's team did not think that Nasser's response would be catastrophic. He said they expected the Egyptian leader to lead an outcry over the West's "broken promises" and "betrayal" and make an approach to the Soviet Union. But the Egyptian people would see this as "his failure to deliver." In response, Nasser might "whip up the war fever against Israel to an increased pitch as a means of making disappointment on the Aswan High Dam more nearly tolerable." Nowhere in Allen's memo did he say his analysts contemplated the possibility that Nasser might consider a stronger reaction related to the Suez Canal.

DECISION ON ASWAN

Thursday, July 19, was a momentous day for the Eisenhower administration's Middle East policy. For the first time since his surgery, the president presided at a National Security Council meeting. [55] CIA director Allen Dulles reported that, in the Middle East, government officials were being assassinated via "parcel post bombs." Since only Arab officials had been killed, Arab leaders were blaming the Israelis. Eisenhower asked whether there was mail service between Israel and the Arab states. Dulles responded negatively; the bombs could be mailed from elsewhere. An Egyptian military attaché assigned to Jordan had been one of the assassination victims, but the CIA director informed the president that no one in Egypt had been assassinated by these bombs. Eisenhower then concluded the meeting by saying that it had been "the shortest and sweetest NSC meeting" he had experienced in three years in office.

John Foster Dulles was scheduled to meet with the Egyptian ambassador, Hussein, at four that day, and after the NSC meeting the secretary and Herbert Hoover remained to brief the president.[56] Dulles informed Eisenhower for the first time that the Egyptian ambassador was returning to Washington with instructions to accept the December 16 offer. He described how conditions had changed since December, pressing his now favorite argument—that the austerity imposed on the Egyptian people by the costs of the project would make its sponsors unpopular. Nasser, he said, was increasingly difficult to work with and this project would require close collaboration.

The conversation was a fait accompli. Eisenhower, so long disengaged from this issue, showed no inclination to pull the plug on the secretary's plans. Hoover's notes on the meeting reveal that Ike "concurred" with Dulles's intent to withdraw the American offer. Dulles showed the president a draft of a statement he planned to release following his meeting with the Egyptian ambassador. The minutes reflect that "the President approved its general line." This decision, with such momentous consequences, took all of twelve minutes.

Dulles immediately informed Sir Roger Makins of the decision. Makins was taken aback by its suddenness and complained that the British government would have preferred more consultation before a decision was reached. Dulles said his government had no choice. The Senate was scheduled to debate the foreign aid bill on Friday. Unless the matter were resolved before then, it was inevitable that opponents of the Aswan project would attach a rider to the legislation prohibiting funds for Aswan.[57]

Francis Russell, special assistant to the secretary, met in advance with Ambassador Hussein and confirmed to the secretary that Nasser was "hellbent" to go forward with the project, even though the Soviets had made no "firm offer." Egypt was reluctant to accept a Soviet offer but, if the West's offer was not fulfilled, Nasser would be justified in taking the Soviet deal. Foster Dulles called his brother Allen to relate Russell's news. The secretary told the CIA director that if the United States did not withdraw the offer, "Congress will chop it off tomorrow." Foster said he had concluded he "would rather do it himself." He clung obsessively to the perception, disputed by World Bank president Eugene Black, that the Egyptian people would rebel against the austerity the project would demand. "You don't get bread," he said, referring to the Egyptians, "because you are being squeezed to build a dam." The brothers agreed that the decision was "hazardous" but Allen thought it would prove wise "in the long run." Apparently, the CIA director had received no intelligence that would indicate that Nasser was planning any kind of extreme response.[58]

At 4:10, Dr. Ahmed Hussein entered the secretary of state's office alone. Undersecretary Hoover, George V. Allen, and William Rountree were present.[59] Without waiting to hear what the ambassador might say, Dulles plunged into a blunt announcement of his decision regarding the Aswan Dam. He "had reluctantly come to the conclusion that it was not feasible at present for the United States to go forward with this undertaking." Dulles recited his well-rehearsed reasons, in particular, "the long-range impact of the project upon relations with the Egyptian people and its government." Dulles suggested that "implementation would impose a period of 12 to 16 years of austerity on the part of the Egyptian people, and a major portion of Egyptian resources would have to be dedicated to this particular work."

Dulles emphasized that public opinion in the United States had turned against the Egyptian government in recent months; therefore, it was doubtful that funds could be obtained from Congress. No other project in the administration's mutual security program was "as unpopular today as the Aswan Dam." Dulles hinted at the possibility that the United States might assist with less ambitious projects in the future if Egyptian policies made that possible.

Hussein, finally getting a chance to speak, inquired whether this meant that "a final decision" had been made. Dulles responded affirmatively and handed the ambassador the press release he intended to put out later in the day. Hussein nonetheless tried to make his case. He said he had met numerous times with the Egyptian president and "had found Nasser anxious to reach an agreement on the basis of the December offer." Hussein refuted Dulles's paternalism about the Egyptian people, saying they believed so much in the project that they "would not resent the sacrifices which its implementation would entail." Dulles responded that the dam project should be "put on the shelf" until there were better relations between the two countries.

Hussein then played the only card he had left—the Soviet offer. He said he "sincerely hated to see the Russians take advantage of the present situation." They had made a "very generous" offer and his government had hoped that an agreement with the West could be achieved before Nasser traveled to Moscow. Dulles expressed his preference that Egypt not collaborate with the Soviets but said the American foreign aid program "had been injured more by the [administration's] proposal to assist in financing the Aswan Dam, in light of our relations with Egypt, than by anything else."

Dulles went on to say that some Arab countries believed that Egypt was intent on dominating them. Hussein responded that "Egypt had no intention of dominating other Arab states." The goal was "to get rid of colonialism." Nasser "had no intention of being friendly with the Soviet Union at the expense of friendship with the United States." As Hussein prepared to leave, he and Dulles agreed that Hussein would tell the waiting reporters that he would leave "to the Secretary" any comment on their meeting.

When William Knowland called, Dulles told him the deed was done. Dulles thought "it would be interesting to see what happens," anticipating that Nasser would go to Moscow and sign an agreement. Knowland confirmed that the vote on foreign aid would come on Friday morning. Secretary Dulles called his brother and reported that the ambassador "had handled himself surprisingly well and with dignity." [60]

Dulles's press release rehashed the themes he had struck with Hussein. After reviewing the history of negotiations, the third paragraph concluded, "Developments within the succeeding seven months have not been favorable to the success of the project, and the United States Government has concluded that it is not feasible in present circumstances to participate in the project." The release went on to say that the United States still sought "friendly relations" with the government and people of Egypt, and might consider other assistance at an appropriate time. [61]

Almost twenty years later, Eugene Black was still bitter over Dulles's rejection of the Aswan project. The World Bank president believed that the United States handled the issue "much more badly than Nasser did." Black was particularly cynical about Dulles's insistence that the project would force austerity on the Egyptian people. The Americans had gone from assuming, in December 1955, that the Egyptians could afford the project to deciding, in July 1956, that they could not. Black called that "an excuse." It was, he said, like being denied a loan by the bank and then being humiliated about it in public. "You don't put it in the newspaper that your credit's no good," he said. "That's what made Nasser mad as hell." [62]

On Friday, July 20, Dulles had lunch with Henry Luce, the publisher of *Time,* and C. D. Jackson, another publisher and former Eisenhower assistant. Dulles was, according to Jackson, "very happy over the Aswan Dam turndown." He thought that this was "as big a chess move as U.S. Diplomacy had made in a long time." Dulles said to Jackson, "Well, if we hadn't turned the Egyptians down yesterday, Congress would have turned them down today, which is another reason why I think it was a good move on our part." Dulles believed that Nasser was now "in a hell of a spot." If he said no to the Russians he would be in trouble, and if he said yes the United States would spread propaganda in the Soviet satellite nations, blaming the project for their poor living conditions.[63]

Later that day, Henry Byroade, who had lost the argument and would soon lose his job, dutifully wired the State Department that Nasser was not surprised—he had "expected all along" the Americans would not follow through. Nasser did not react immediately. The four-day Muslim Bairam holidays in Egypt had just begun, so no newspapers had appeared either Thursday or Friday. Byroade had uncovered "no indication" as to what "counter-move" Nasser might take. That evening, the British announced that they were joining the Americans in withdrawing their offer to assist with the Aswan Dam. Two days later, Ambassador Bohlen in Moscow reported that correspondents who heard Shepilov comment about the news got the impression that the Soviet government "was not at least at this time planning to undertake financing the project."[64]

The *New York Times* interpreted the decision on Aswan and the reassignment of Henry Byroade as the inauguration of a new "get tough with Egypt" policy. The *Times* recalled that, in 1953, President Eisenhower, only six weeks in office, had proclaimed a new Middle East policy designed to ameliorate the "deterioration in relations between the Arab Nations and the United States" and restore Arab "confidence and trust" in American leadership.[65]

The day after Dulles's withdrawal of support for Aswan—Friday, July 20—would be the president's last day in the White House before he departed for Panama. Ike was more focused on the challenge of traveling than the consequences of that action. The president's associates had been worried all along about his ability to withstand the trip, his first outside the United States since the heart attack. At the end of June, Attorney General Brownell and Secretary Dulles had discussed whether it would be "a mistake" for the president to go to Panama. Dulles raised the issue with Adams but Adams had replied that the president did not want to postpone the conference again. The chief of staff said that, while he expected the doctors to approve the trip, he was "not sure" the president should go.[66]

Ike himself was anxious. The evening of July 17, James Hagerty had called Foster Dulles to relay that the president had been wondering if former President Arnulfo Arias of Panama could be informed that Eisenhower was "still convalescing and that while the Secretary and others would stay at the receptions it would be necessary for the President to leave somewhat early." Hagerty said that Ike was "better" every day "but he gets tired." "The mornings are fine," Hagerty added, "but after his nap the afternoons are still a little rough."[67]

That Friday, Ike was tempted to cancel the trip to Panama. Eisenhower's son, John, stationed at nearby Fort Belvoir in Virginia, remembered that Ike was still wearing a surgical drain. Nixon recalled that, just prior to leaving, Eisenhower looked "like an invalid—sick, tired and in pain." Sherman Adams's assistant, Jerry Persons, later told speechwriter Emmet John Hughes that, on that day, the president was "a sorry sight." Ike had summed up his feelings about the trip to Persons: "If I don't feel better than this pretty soon, I'm going to pull out of the whole thing."[68]

Nevertheless, the president departed the White House at 9:50 P.M. and, seven minutes later, arrived at National Airport and boarded his aircraft. The *Columbine* was airborne at 12:05 A.M. on Saturday, July 21. After arriving in Panama, Eisenhower met at 11:00 A.M. with the attending presidents at Panama's presidential palace. Ceremonies continued until almost eleven that night. Eisenhower kept a busy schedule of appointments and meetings for the next two days. Ike cabled Mamie that he was feeling better: "Steady improvement continues. No distress of any kind."[69]

On Monday, Foster Dulles called Hoover to report that "things were going very well" in Panama. Citing Ike's heavy schedule, Dulles said the president "came through magnificently, although yesterday was a cruel day." Dulles pronounced himself "greatly reassured" about the problem he and Hoover had been discussing—undoubtedly whether the president would be up to handling any crisis that might arise. Dulles breathed a sigh of relief: "He can take it." President Eisenhower departed Panama that evening and arrived back in Washington at eight on Tuesday morning.[70]

Eisenhower had been energized by his experience in Panama. He was not as physically fragile as he had feared. Later, in a discussion with Nixon, Foster Dulles remarked that the Panama trip had done the president "a world of good—like a shot in the arm." Jerry Persons told Emmet Hughes that he was astounded at the transformation. "So he goes down to Panama, almost gets crushed by the mobs, meets God-knows how-many Latin American diplomats, suffers through all the damn receptions—and Tuesday, *Tuesday*, mind you, three days later, he comes waltzing back looking like a new man." [71]

Eisenhower recorded an upbeat assessment of the Panama meetings in his diary. He had relished "the chance to pay my respects, in a single conference, to each of the Republics lying to the South of us." He concluded: "All in all, I would class the meeting as a very successful affair in the promotion of good will." Eisenhower now knew that he was back—that he could cope with a tough schedule and serious issues. That was fortunate, as he was about to be presented with both. [72]

Contrary to his recent pattern after intense activity, the president did not take Tuesday, July 24, off. He arrived at the Oval Office just before nine and conducted a full day of meetings, capped off by a brief golf practice late in the afternoon. Most of the meetings were with key White House staff—Sherman Adams, appointments secretary Bernard Shanley, special counsel Gerald Morgan, Andrew Goodpaster, and Persons. A week after he had left Gettysburg, Ike was finally taking charge. With Secretary Dulles out of the country, the president held no meetings related to the Middle East.

"A HELL OF A SPOT"

But the Middle East ground was shifting beneath the president's feet. Henry Byroade sensed it coming. This was the day—July 24—when President Eisenhower formally sent his nomination as ambassador to South Africa to the United States Senate. In spite of his lame-duck status, Byroade faithfully reported to the State Department on Nasser's short speech that day, in which the Egyptian premier had angrily accused the Americans of "false and misleading announcements, without shame and with disregard for the principles of international relations, that the Egyptian economy is unsound." The Egyptian leader, Byroade reported, had "tensely" pledged to make a longer speech in Alexandria on July 26. Foreign Minister Mahmoud Fawzi asked Byroade to come to his office for a meeting at 7:00 P.M. on the 26th, approximately an hour after Nasser would begin his Alexandria address. Then Fawzi had canceled that meeting, saying that Byroade would be informed by special messenger when it would be rescheduled.[73]

By Wednesday, July 25, Herbert Hoover was beginning to worry. The State Department still had no solid information on what Nasser was going to do in response to the Aswan decision. He asked William Rountree, the incoming assistant secretary for Near Eastern affairs, "to consider urgently" the possible consequences. Rountree said that the Middle East Policy Planning Group that had been studying Egyptian and Aswan policy was still in existence, and would go to work on the problem. That day, Senate and House conferees finally agreed on a foreign aid appropriation of $3,766,570,000, which, when increased by reappropriated leftover funds, came to $4,006,570,000—less than the $4.9 billion Eisenhower had originally sought.[74]

The president was still not focused on the Middle East. He conducted a cabinet meeting that day dedicated to assessment of the Operation Alert civil defense exercise that had been conducted the first part of the week.[75] Ike reminded the cabinet that, however smoothly the imaginary war had gone, in the wake of a nuclear war, people would be "scared," perhaps "hysterical," some "absolutely nuts." Theirs would be "a completely bewildered population." Eisenhower recalled listening to an alleged expert before World War I who had tried to prove that no war could last more than sixty days because the adversaries would run out of money. Two world wars had demonstrated the folly of that analysis. "Money is not necessary to fight a war," he said. "All one needs is men, material and morale." The power of government orders could replace money. When the government said, "you will do something or get shot in the back, you do it." Ike warned that "not all of the casualties of such a war will be lives. Among those casualties will be justice." "War," he said, "is the antithesis of justice and fairness."

On Thursday, July 26, Gamal Abdel Nasser delivered an emotional, three-hour anti-American speech to a cheering crowd in Alexandria. Near the end, Nasser announced what no American government official had anticipated—a presidential decree nationalizing the Suez Canal Company. He planned to use the proceeds from the operation of the canal to fund the Aswan Dam project. "This money is ours and the Suez Canal belongs to us," the Egyptian leader declared. "The Suez Canal was built by Egyptians and 120,000 Egyptians died building it. Thus, we shall build the High Dam our own way."[76]

Immediately, Egyptian officials and a squad of police seized control of the Suez Company's headquarters in Cairo—ironically located across the street from the American embassy. John Foster Dulles had been wrong. It was not Nasser but the United States and its allies who were now "in a hell of a spot."

7

★★★★★★

A GROWING RIFT

July 27–August 23, 1956

> "I have given you my own personal conviction, as well as that of
> my associates, as to the unwisdom even of contemplating the use
> of military force at this moment."
>
> Eisenhower to Anthony Eden, July 31, 1956

IF THE Panama conference didn't jolt Eisenhower out of his post-surgical doldrums, Nasser's nationalization of the Suez Canal certainly did. With John Foster Dulles in South America, Ike was compelled to personally take charge of the situation. The morning of Friday, July 27, the president called a meeting in the Oval Office with Hoover, Allen Dulles, and Colonel Goodpaster. Hoover handed Eisenhower a cable from Andrew Foster, the chargé d'affaires at the American embassy in London, who had been summoned to an emergency meeting of the British cabinet at eleven the previous evening. The cabinet, Foster reported, took "an extremely grave view of the situation." The British leaders had grilled Foster as to whether the United States would support economic and military action against Nasser. Foster had pledged to seek clarification before he met with Prime Minister Anthony Eden and Foreign Secretary Selwyn Lloyd at 5:00 P.M. on the 27th.[1]

The British reaction to the nationalization decree bordered on hysteria. Britain and France had owned a controlling interest in the Suez Canal Company, including the hiring of its officials and operators, for decades. In the wake of the liquidation of the British Empire after World War II, the loss of the canal seemed to confirm beyond all doubt that the United Kingdom was no longer a world power. Suez was a lifeline for Britain. Nearly fifteen thousand British ships had passed through Suez in 1955, and sixty thousand British troops passed through the waterway annually. Above all, two-thirds of the Britain's oil supply came through the canal. Its closing would bring Britain to its knees.[2]

Therefore, it was no surprise that Foster reported the British government appeared to be preparing for war. Eden had placed British commanders in the Mediterranean on alert and ordered an assessment of the forces that would be required to seize the canal. As Foster's meeting with the cabinet ended, Foreign Minister Lloyd had told Foster that the "only solution lay in a Western consortium taking over and operating the Canal, establishing itself if need be by military force."

Eisenhower read the cable in silence. This president, who could react so emotionally over small things like interruptions on the golf course, was remarkably dispassionate at this moment. Ike noted analytically that Nasser's action was "not the same as nationalizing oil wells, since the latter exhausts a nation's resources and the Canal is more like a public utility, building them up."

Hoover feared that "the British will want to move very drastically in this matter." A cutoff of oil shipments through the canal would be devastating. The president, referring to the Suez Company's British employees, granted that "no nation is likely to allow its nationals to be held in what amounts to slavery." Eisenhower asked Hoover to prepare a statement, "the shorter the better," discuss it by phone with Secretary Dulles, and bring it back to him. "We should give no hint of what we are likely to do" and state that the United States regarded the matter "with utmost seriousness" and was consulting others. There should be "one sentence making clear that Nasser's speech was full of misstatements regarding the United States."

The next communication Eisenhower read was a starkly pessimistic message from Anthony Eden. The prime minister asserted that "we cannot allow Nasser to seize control of the Canal in this way, in defiance of international agreements." Britain had six weeks of oil reserves and Western European reserves were smaller. Eden believed that the Egyptians could not be trusted, nor did he deem them competent to operate the canal. Economic pressure would likely fail, so Eden was prepared "to use *force* to bring Nasser to his senses." The prime minister requested that Eisenhower send a representative, hopefully Secretary Dulles, to talk with the French starting Monday. "The first step," he wrote, "must be for you and us and France to exchange views."[3]

From Paris, U.S. ambassador Douglas Dillon reported that the French were equally ready to go to war. Foreign Minister Christian Pineau had asserted that occupying the canal "would not be too difficult an undertaking." The French wanted to send twenty-four more Mystère jets to Israel and were urging the Canadian government to provide Israel with F-86 fighter planes. Foster Dulles, in Lima, Peru, read this communication with trepidation. He cabled, "We should go slow about mixing up [the] canal problem with [the] Israel-Arab problem."[4]

The seizure of the Suez Canal dominated the agenda that morning at the president's cabinet meeting.[5] Hoover briefed the members, employing the president's metaphor of "an international public utility" and informing them that a statement would be released at noon. Attorney General Herbert Brownell made the simplest of points about the legality of Nasser's action: "The entire length of the Canal lay within Egyptian territory."

At noon, the State Department issued a statement that said just what Eisenhower wanted—nothing of substance: "The announcement of the Egyptian Government on July 26 with respect to the seizure of the installations of the Suez Canal Company carries far-reaching implications. It affects the nations whose economies depend upon the products which move through this international waterway and the maritime countries as well as the owners of the company itself. The United States Government is consulting urgently with other governments concerned."[6]

REFRAMING THE PROBLEM

At 5:00 P.M., Eisenhower met again with Hoover.[7] He shared Eden's message, including his request for a representative at the meetings in London. After some discussion, Ike selected a longtime associate, Robert D. Murphy, the deputy undersecretary of state. Murphy had been indispensable in helping Eisenhower with delicate matters of wartime diplomacy in North Africa and Italy. Later in his administration, Eisenhower used an award ceremony to praise Murphy as "a shrewd observer, a wise counselor, a strong leader, and a diplomat of skill and decision." That was the kind of man the president needed at this difficult moment. Foster Dulles, once he returned from South America, could possibly join in the talks.[8]

Eisenhower had already made a decision that might put him at loggerheads with the French and British. He said he would not employ force over the nationalization of the Suez Canal unless the Egyptians "attacked our people." Anything more, he believed, would require congressional approval. Aware that Congress was planning to adjourn that day, Eisenhower wanted congressional leaders notified "on a most secret and confidential basis that the situation might get so serious that they might have to be called back into session." Ike interrupted the meeting to call Nixon, described the situation as "pretty bad," and asked the vice president to inform Lyndon Johnson and William Knowland that the president might be forced to act if American nationals were endangered.[9] After he hung up, Eisenhower instructed Hoover to talk to the House leaders, Sam Rayburn and Joe Martin, and to brief the Joint Chiefs.

Then the president dictated a concise response to Eden's telegram, informing him that Robert Murphy was on his way to London.[10] Eisenhower expressed sympathy for Eden's situation but stated that "there are one or two additional thoughts that you and we might profitably consider." Eisenhower resorted to a favorite strategy for addressing a difficult problem—he enlarged it. The canal seizure was not just a British-French matter, he wrote the prime minister: "The maximum number of maritime nations affected by the Nasser action should be consulted quickly in the hope of obtaining an agreed basis of understanding." Ike had instinctively concluded that he could slow down the allied rush to war if he got more nations involved.

Ike's long day was not over. He held phone conversations at six with Hoover, at 9:57 with Joe Martin, and 10:55 with Knowland. Just before eleven, the president sent a message to Sherman Adams, telling him that the leaders of the House and Senate had informed him that they had adjourned.

At ten the next morning, Saturday, July 28, the president met with Hoover and Robert Murphy, who was preparing to leave for London. Hoover had talked with Foster Dulles, who had urged that they discourage military action by the allies. The president doubted that military intervention could be justified "in terms of world opinion."[11] Eisenhower's first strategic gambit for halting the rush to war had been his insistence on broadening the base of nations addressing the Suez problem. Now he set forth a second—to distinguish ownership of the canal from the competency of its operations. Ike considered aloud the Eden argument: if no action was taken now, the operations of the canal "may gradually deteriorate without giving a specific occasion for intervention at any later time." If the nationals of Western countries were seized, that would justify intervention. Ike was of two minds. He wanted to avoid war but did not believe "that the Western world could sit and do nothing, waiting to see whether the operation of the Canal deteriorates."

Eisenhower, Hoover, and Murphy agreed that the United States should avoid joining "in any precipitate action with the French and British." Ike argued again that any intervention should be supported by all the maritime powers. As for the Russians, Eisenhower thought it was "very clear that the Soviet Union was not going to get into a major war over a question of this kind." Ike succinctly summarized the second component of his reframing strategy: "Egypt was within its rights, and that until its operation of the Canal proved incompetent, unjust, etc. there was nothing to do."

It had been a tough couple of days for the recuperating president. After this meeting, tired and stressed, Ike made what Ann Whitman called "a hurried decision" and left for Gettysburg at 11:15 A.M., even though the weather was threatening.[12]

THE SECRETARY RETURNS

Foster Dulles arrived at National Airport at noon on Sunday. Hoover and Herman Phleger, the State Department's legal advisor, met him at the airport and then, in order to avoid reporters, went to Dulles's home to review the situation. Afterward, Dulles called the president. The secretary had not yet found his bearings on what to do. The French government had pleaded urgently for Dulles to come to London, but he was reluctant to go. Eisenhower, for the time being, concurred. He agreed with Dulles that the use of force was not justified at this point. Still, Ike said he was worried about the "danger of developing inefficiency in the operation of the Canal" and that "a progressive decline" might make action more difficult later.[13]

By now, Eisenhower had crystallized his twofold approach to the Suez crisis—broadening the base of nations involved and separating ownership of the canal from its operations. Such clearheaded logic was antithetical to the war of words across the Atlantic. On Monday, July 30, Anthony Eden told a cheering House of Commons that Britain would never accept placing the Suez Canal "in the unfettered control of a single power, which could, as recent events have shown, exploit it purely for purposes of national policy." Eden hinted at action by the Royal Navy.[14]

In spite of the public posturing by the prime minister, Eisenhower knew he had some leverage. The latest CIA intelligence bulletin had concluded that "Britain and France are reluctant to take military action without United States support." The initial response by the Soviet Union had been muted. Nikita Khrushchev, the Soviet Communist Party chairman, endorsed the Egyptian action but urged restraint, complimenting the "common sense, experience and political sobriety of the statesmen of Britain and France" in other postcolonial situations. He asserted that there was "no other way out" but for the Western nations to recognize that nationalizing the canal was "in the spirit of the times."[15]

Eisenhower spent from midday Saturday to Tuesday morning at Gettysburg. He tried to get in some recreation, spending time playing bridge with friends. At 8:21 on Tuesday morning, the president left Gettysburg, arriving back at the White House about an hour later. The restful time had been needed; Ike was about to be presented with even more serious developments.[16]

BREAKING NASSER?

In London, Robert Murphy did his best with a difficult assignment. He reported to Dulles that his opening statement to British and French leaders on July 29 had reflected Eisenhower's views that the primary question was "the maintenance and the operation of the Canal as it affects our shipping" and that discussions must move beyond the three nations to "the broadest possible base" in a manner that would receive "the benefit of an affirmative world opinion." Military force, Murphy argued on behalf of the president, "should be relegated to the background."[17]

Murphy's second report to Dulles was pessimistic. He doubted that political and economic pressures would work with Nasser. British and French military preparations were proceeding rapidly. The only hope was to convene a conference of affected nations as soon as possible. Murphy shared the French view that Nasser's action was a "direct consequence" of the American withdrawal of aid to the Aswan Dam project.[18]

On Monday, July 30, the London conferees floundered. To the foreign ministers of England and France, Murphy was an underling, without significant influence. Late that morning, Dulles and Eisenhower came to the

A GROWING RIFT ★ 139

realization that the London conference was spinning out of control. The secretary read a cable he proposed to send to Murphy, repeating that the United States could make no commitment to the use of force without congressional action and recommending a conference sponsored by three or more of the signatories to the Convention of 1888, which had guaranteed access for the European powers to the waterway. Ike responded, "That is our stand." "Egypt," he said, "should operate the Canal efficiently and carry out its promise to those affected—show that we are not indifferent but we are not going to war over it." The United States, Eisenhower asserted, was "not going to be hysterical and rush into it." Ike stuck to two themes—"insist on proper operation of the Canal and we must get a broader base for operating in the future." In response to his conversation with the president, Dulles instructed Murphy to relay to the British and French Eisenhower's view that Nasser should not be presented with "an ultimatum requiring him to reverse his nationalization action under the threat of force." Such an ultimatum would make war "inevitable."[19]

Two communications pushed Eisenhower and Dulles to take more drastic action. Ambassador Henry Byroade, still serving in Cairo in spite of his upcoming transfer to South Africa, held a private conversation with Nasser. The Egyptian president insisted to the ambassador that newspaper reports alleging that he plotted his action with the Russians were "not true." Still, Byroade reported, Nasser was "quite bitter" over the American rejection of aid for the Aswan Dam project. Nasser admitted to the ambassador that he had planned nationalization in advance if Ambassador Hussein was unable to convince the Americans to go forward. Now he wanted the United States government to understand that he had done so as an "alternative to accepting Russian assistance on the Dam."[20]

The most troubling communication was from Murphy. Based on private conversations, he had concluded that Eden and Macmillan had decided "to drive Nasser out of Egypt." They believed that military action was "necessary and inevitable." Murphy described Eden, Macmillan, and Lloyd as men who "act as though they really have taken a decision after profound reflection." Macmillan had expressed the fear that his country's loss of influence in the Middle East would turn Britain into "another Netherlands." The British leaders, Murphy said, expected that the president, their former supreme allied commander, would appreciate "the finality" of their decision.[21]

A RIFT?

Eisenhower called a meeting at 9:45 A.M. on Tuesday, July 31, with Secretary Dulles, Hoover, and State Department legal advisor Herman Phleger. After fifteen minutes, they were joined by Allen Dulles, Secretary Humphrey, deputy defense secretary Reuben Robertson, assistant secretary of defense Gordon Gray, and Admiral Arleigh A. Burke, the chief of naval operations.[22]

The agenda was Murphy's urgent message that the British had decided to "break Nasser." Eisenhower said it was "a very unwise decision" by the British, especially given they had not made a "counterproposal" to the Egyptians. Eisenhower forecast the consequences of military action: "The Middle East oil would undoubtedly dry up, and Western hemisphere oil would have to be diverted to Europe, thus requiring controls to be instituted in the United States."

Eisenhower then made a decision—Secretary Dulles must travel to London immediately "and make clear how impossible it would be to obtain Congressional authorization for participation by the United States in these circumstances." Eisenhower turned to Allen Dulles and asked what the Arab reaction would be to a British attack. The CIA director responded that, without any British counterproposal, an attack would "arouse the whole Arab world." The president enlarged that to "the whole Moslem world."

Foster Dulles said he hoped that a conference of maritime nations, unanimously backing international administration of the canal, might succeed in setting the stage for an agreement with Egypt. But he despaired that the British "seem to have dropped the idea of a conference in favor of an ultimatum." Allen Dulles suggested that Nasser probably would not attend a conference, but his brother was more hopeful if it were sponsored by the 1888 signatories.

Admiral Burke said that the Joint Chiefs agreed that "Nasser must be broken," but he said that it could be accomplished through economic and political means. If not, then the United States should support British military action. Eisenhower was reluctant to adopt that conclusion. The issue was not just Nasser, he said. "Nasser embodies the emotional demands of the people of the era for independence and for 'slapping the white Man down.'" Eisenhower foresaw that nationalism of this kind could "array the world from Dakar to the Philippine Islands against us."[23] Burke said that the key was to split Egypt from other Arab and Muslim nations. Eisenhower responded, with resignation, that "we have been trying to find means of doing just this for several months."

Secretary Dulles, frustrated by the failure of his policy, could not contain his feelings. He exclaimed, "Nasser must be made to disgorge his theft." Dulles painted an apocalyptic vision. War would cut off oil to Europe, force oil rationing in the United States, damage the automobile industry, and result in an economic recession. It could also probably trigger an Israeli attack on Jordan, "with the result of inflaming the whole Arab world." The British, he said, based on their experience in two world wars, were calculating that once war began, the United States would enter the fray.

Eisenhower asserted that the United States must "let the British know how gravely we view this matter, what an error we think their decision is, and how this course of action would antagonize the American people despite all that could be done by the top officials of the Government." He deemed it "essential" that other measures be tried.

Dulles worried aloud that his personal involvement in the talks in London would signal that "something serious" had happened to allied-American relations. Eisenhower did not shrink from that possibility. He used a loaded word—"rift"—heretofore unthinkable in describing British-American relations. "If Mr. Dulles can't persuade the British from their course," he said, "the news of the rift would come out right away." Humphrey asked what repercussions would flow from such a rift. Eisenhower replied that "such an event would be extremely serious, but not as serious as letting a war start and not trying to stop it." Foster Dulles accepted the necessity that he go to London; if a split developed with the allies, he said, the administration would be criticized for not having involved the secretary of state. Dulles thought that "there is a chance—just a chance" that he could "dissuade them, perhaps a bit at a time, gradually deflecting their course of action."

Eisenhower moved to conclude the meeting, ordering that there be "not a whisper about this outside this room."

As the harried secretary of state prepared to fly to London, he was handed a special National Intelligence Estimate that must have felt like a slap in the face. It concluded, "President Nasser has for the time being greatly strengthened his position, not only as leader of Egypt, but also as the spokesman and symbol of Arab Nationalism throughout the Middle

East." At 12:54 P.M. the president called to alert Dulles that he was sending over the message the secretary was to hand-carry to Eden. Twice in the next eleven minutes, Ike called Dulles to discuss revisions, barely delivering the final version to the secretary in time for his departure.[24]

The message that Eisenhower had labored over so frantically was designed to avoid any British misunderstanding of his intent.[25] He wrote Eden that he had been informed "on a most secret basis of your decision to employ force without delay or attempting any intermediate and less drastic steps." Eisenhower insisted that a conference of the signatories of the Convention of 1888 be convened "before such action as you contemplate should be undertaken." "I have given you my own personal conviction, as well as that of my associates," Eisenhower wrote, "as to the unwisdom even of contemplating the use of military force at this moment." He reminded Eden that the United States could join in military action only if Congress was called into special session. For Congress to approve intervention, "there would have to be a showing that every peaceful means of resolving the difficulty had previously been exhausted."

Eisenhower repeated his warning. If the British decision to take military action was "firm and irrevocable," then "the American reaction would be severe" and "great areas of the world would share that reaction." The United States would not be party to military action unless "every peaceful means" of solving the problem "had been thoroughly explored and exhausted." Once that was done and failed, "then world opinion would understand" that more drastic action was justified. Eden could not have misunderstood: Dwight Eisenhower was effectively shouting "Stop!" on British plans for military action.

The rest of the president's day was a whirlwind of meetings, mostly dealing with politics and planning for the Republican convention. Ike left the office at 5:35, saying "This has been quite a day." Ann Whitman observed that the president was worried he had overdone it. He had not exercised during the day so he walked briskly around the circle in back of the White House twice. Ike confessed to Whitman that he had gained some weight, and she noted he "was worried about his pulse and took it himself—but it was fairly low and not skipping."[26]

MISSION TO LONDON

John Foster Dulles, without much rest, touched down in London late in the morning of Wednesday, August 1. He knew he needed to deliver on one of the most delicate diplomatic missions of his career. The secretary went immediately to a noon meeting with Selwyn Lloyd, who emotionally labeled Nasser "a paranoiac like Hitler." Then Dulles raced to a luncheon with Anthony Eden, with whom he shared the president's letter. The secretary assured the prime minister that the message was pure Eisenhower, not drafted by anyone else, and "expressed his basic thinking on the subject." Undeterred, Eden argued that "prompt forcible action" was essential. If Nasser "got away with it," the outcome would be disastrous for British and French interests in the region. He did not expect the United States to participate militarily but hoped for economic support, oil, and an American effort "to neutralize any open participation by the Soviet Union."[27]

Dulles spoke plainly for the president: the United States was unwilling to back military intervention at this time. London and Paris needed to pursue other methods to get Nasser to "disgorge" what he had swallowed. Eden reluctantly agreed to sponsor an international conference, provided it happened quickly and did not constitute acceptance of Nasser's action. The prime minister opposed participation by the Soviet Union but, because Moscow was a signatory to the Convention of 1888, Dulles convinced him that it was unavoidable. After the meeting, Dulles was hopeful. He cabled Eisenhower, saying, "Matters are not going badly." But Hoover reported to the president that the French were leaking stories that the use of force was imminent.[28]

August 1 was the day for the president's news conference.[29] The members of the Washington press corps, unlike their European counterparts, were unaware of the allied threats to use military force to remove Nasser, and Ike did not intend to dispel their ignorance. Instead, he talked cheerfully about his experience at the Panama conference and fielded political questions. Finally, a French journalist, armed with information American reporters lacked, asked about the messages the president had received from Anthony Eden and the French premier, Guy Mollet, about Suez. Eisenhower coolly responded: "I never publicly mention the substance of messages received from heads of other states and governments or the substance of my replies." He said that the world confronted "a very grave issue, important to every country in the world that has a seacoast, and maybe even all the rest. So it is something to be handled with care, to make sure we are just and fair; but we must make certain that the rights of the world are not abused." Eisenhower had managed to say nothing of substance, not even mentioning Suez or Nasser.

On Thursday, August 2, Dulles reported to the State Department on his progress in persuading the British and French to sponsor a conference designed to seek "some treaty arrangement" incorporating the principles of the Convention of 1888, with a board of directors operating the canal as an "international public utility." Dulles naively hoped that such a proposal might "be difficult for Egypt to reject." [30]

Later, Dulles assessed for Eisenhower the British and French determination to take the canal by force unless Nasser accepted international control. "I am not sure from their standpoint they can be blamed," he wrote. Britain and France believed that their influence throughout the Middle East and North Africa was threatened. Dulles said he had persuaded them "that it would be reckless to take this step unless and until they have made a genuine effort to mobilize world opinion in favor of an international solution of the Canal problem." The secretary had tried to ensure that parties attending the conference would be broadly based, not "loaded" in favor of the Western nations. He had also sought sufficient time to prepare for such a complicated conclave. Eisenhower responded: "You are proceeding exactly in accordance with my convictions, and we can all hope you will achieve a program that can marshal world opinion behind it." [31]

Dulles had turned in a virtuoso diplomatic performance. Later that day, the three powers issued a statement that recognized "the right of Egypt to enjoy and exercise all the powers of a fully sovereign and independent nation, including the generally recognized right, under appropriate conditions, to nationalize assets" that were not primarily a matter of "international interest." The statement went on to say that nationalizing the Canal Company involved "far more than a simple act of nationalization." The Canal Company was "an international agency" and the seizure had been designed to "serve the purely national purposes of the Egyptian Government, rather than the international purpose established by the Convention of 1888." The statement called for a conference of the 1888 signatories and other nations concerned with the operations of the canal, to commence on August 16 in London. [32]

As Dulles winged his way back to Washington, Eisenhower meditated on the convergence of electoral politics and Middle East tensions in a letter to Swede Hazlett. [33] Ike took exception to the Democrats' decision to "view with alarm" his absences from the White House. "One man" (undoubtedly Adlai Stevenson) had alleged that the president had been absent from duty for 143 days after the heart attack and another forty-two after the surgery.

"Nothing is said," he wrote, "about the fact that in Denver, within five days of my initial attack, staff officers were in my room asking for decisions, while in my latest operation, I had to be functioning again in the space of three days." Eisenhower, like so many recovering patients, was rewriting the history of his illnesses to conform to his political situation.

"A satisfactory solution" for the Suez matter was not yet in sight, Eisenhower wrote to Hazlett. "In the kind of world we are trying to establish," he said, "we frequently find ourselves victims of the tyrannies of the weak." By committing to treat small and powerful nations equally, "we unavoidably give to the little nations opportunities to embarrass us greatly." He went on to say that the opponents of foreign aid failed to realize that "isolation is no longer possible or desirable" and that it was in the interests of the United States to help smaller nations "make a living." Ike recalled the fable teaching the moral that "the rich owner of a factory could not forever live on top of the hill in luxury and serenity, while all around him at the bottom of the hill his workmen lived in misery, privation and resentment." Eisenhower concluded: "We must learn the same lesson internationally."

Clearly, Eisenhower was thinking about Egypt and the Aswan Dam. Gone was his earlier disposition to diminish Nasser and elevate the king of Saudi Arabia. He was looking ahead, thinking about what he could do once the current predicament passed. "We must pursue a broad and intelligent program of loans, trade, technical assistance and, under current conditions, mutual guarantees of security," he told Hazlett. "We must stop talking about 'give aways.' We must understand that our foreign expenditures are investments in America's future." Then he added, in words that sound thoroughly modern, "No other nation is exhausting its irreplaceable resources so rapidly as is ours." Without friendly trading partners, "where do we hope to get all the materials that we will one day need as our rate of consumption continues and accelerates?" Ike concluded that "in the approach to such grave difficulties as the Suez crisis, there is a great need for keeping in the back of the mind the understanding of these broader, long-term issues in the international world."

At noon on Friday, August 3, a weary John Foster Dulles arrived back in Washington and plunged immediately into meetings at the State Department. Assistant press secretary Murray Snyder called to tell the secretary that arrangements had been confirmed for him to deliver a televised report to the nation at seven that night, introduced by the president. At 2:15, Foster called his brother Allen, who congratulated the secretary for his diplomatic success in a "tough" situation. The British and French, Foster stated, "are steamed up." He went on to say that the job was not yet finished—he had only achieved "a cooling-off period." About fifteen minutes later, Secretary Dulles and Hoover met with Eisenhower at the White House to plan Dulles's report to the nation.[34]

The president began the broadcast that evening by emphasizing "the tremendous importance of the Suez Canal" to the economies of the world, including the United States. "So all of us were vastly disturbed," he said, "when Colonel Nasser a few days ago declared that Egypt intended to nationalize the Suez Canal Company." Eisenhower emphasized that, "at my request," Secretary Dulles had left South America and flown immediately to London to confer with British and French leaders. Dulles, calling the Suez Canal "the world's greatest highway," then provided an overview of the consultations, resulting in the plan for the conference starting August 16 in London. Eisenhower closed the telecast by congratulating Dulles for upholding "the interests of the United States in the international field with due regard for fairness to every other nation, and with the objective of promoting peace in the world."[35]

A COMPLICATED CONFERENCE

Meanwhile, that same evening of August 3 in Cairo, President Nasser had requested another conversation with Ambassador Byroade, who found Nasser "relaxed and friendly," but insisting that he "could not accept international control." That would be colonialism in a new form, he said, and went on to say he would not participate in the London conference. According to Byroade, Nasser refused to attend "under threat of invasion and starvation"—referring to the threatened freezing of Egyptian assets by Western nations. Nasser claimed he was prepared to sign "with anyone" a new international agreement that would guarantee "freedom of passage and uninterrupted use of Suez Canal facilities."[36]

Eisenhower had his hands full with his angry allies. On August 5, Anthony Eden responded to the letter Foster Dulles had delivered, reluctantly agreeing to follow the American lead if it would help to "undo what Nasser has done and to set up an International Regime for the Canal." The British leader said his goal was still "the removal of Nasser, and the installation in Egypt of a regime less hostile to the West." Eden was skeptical that Nasser would accept the outcomes of the conference, and feared that Soviet support for Egypt would make a clear result impossible. The British and French governments "could not possibly acquiesce in such a situation." Eden insisted that "our people here are neither excited nor eager to use force. They are, however, grimly determined that Nasser shall not get away with it this time, because they are convinced that if he does their existence will be at his mercy. So am I." [37]

Monday was a frenetic day for the president in dealing with the Suez crisis. The press had begun to speculate that Eisenhower himself might attend the August 16 conference in London. The question had been fueled by an earlier Eisenhower press conference statement that he "would go anywhere, any time in the interest of peace." Eisenhower called Foster Dulles to see what he thought of the idea. Dulles was skeptical because the president's presence would pressure other heads of state to attend. Ike commented that if he went, and the crucial people did not attend, that would be "a terrible slap in the face." To complicate matters, the conference was scheduled to begin just prior to the Republican convention. Ike said he was willing to consider going "if there is a clear chance of doing good" and he could do something to "save the peace of the world." [38]

Dulles and Eisenhower decided to discourage any Soviet temptation to misuse the conference. Dulles coached Ambassador Chip Bohlen in Moscow to employ "a quite informal confidential approach to high Soviet officials." He should be candid about British and French intentions and warn the Soviets that, while the United States opposed force, they should not assume that the Americans would refrain from intervention "if the conference method breaks down." Soviet leaders should remember that, in the first and second world wars, the United States had become involved "when the chips are down." This should be said in "an appropriate informal way of chatting" and "without in any way formalizing the matter." [39]

Bohlen delivered a formal message from Eisenhower informing Premier Bulganin that he had instructed the ambassador "to let you know personally how seriously I regard the situation precipitated by the Egyptian Government's effort to seize the operations of the Suez Canal." The United States was trying to resolve the situation by means of "the peaceful conference method," and he hoped that the Soviet Union would support that approach. [40]

Bohlen reported that Bulganin had "listened attentively and appreciated the President writing him on this subject." The ambassador said he had pressed the Soviet leader to assist with persuading Egypt to be receptive to the conference. Bulganin agreed that "this matter must be settled by peaceful means," but the Soviet position was that "any international action in regard to the Suez Canal would constitute interference in Egyptian internal affairs." When pressed, Bulganin granted that "other countries had an interest, including the Soviet Union, in the free navigation through the Canal." In his report to Washington, Bohlen termed the conversation as "not satisfactory," but he said he hoped he had managed to communicate how seriously the United States viewed the matter.[41]

Ike ended the day with a meeting that mirrored the turmoil of his administration over Suez. He debated with Dulles and Dillon Anderson, the assistant to the president for national security affairs, whether to take the canal seizure to the National Security Council. Dulles was opposed, saying that the crisis should be handled with "decisions day by day by the President." Then, Anderson reminded them that the Joint Chiefs' analysis of military options had already gone out to NSC members. Ike stated that, in that case, "formal NSC action" should be avoided. "We should in no event," Eisenhower added, "indicate what our military course would be should other nations intervene militarily." Once the London conference ended, he concluded, the administration's position should be that "no affirmative U.S. military course of action would be determined except with the concurrence of Congress."[42]

The burdens of the day had left Ike in a foul mood. Ann Whitman recorded that Eisenhower "hit some golf balls," walked around the exterior of the White House, and was "still in bad temper," wondering aloud "why anyone would want such a job as that of the President."[43]

STONEWALLING THE PRESS

Eisenhower was apprehensive about his Wednesday, August 8, news conference. He knew that the reporters would not permit him to continue to evade the subject of Suez. He rehearsed possible responses in his diary, covering the history of the Suez Canal and the events leading up to Nasser's "very inflammatory speech" announcing nationalization "because of the United States refusal to help him build the Aswan Dam." The president, thinking on paper, crafted a rationale that would put the onus on Egypt. Nasser, he wrote, had "sent back to us a whole list of conditions that would have to be met" and "they began to build up their military forces by taking over equipment provided by the Soviets." Suddenly, in July, Nasser had "sent us a message to the effect that he had withdrawn all of the conditions that he had laid down, and was ready to proceed under our original offer." The situation had changed and, thinking the "whole project dead, we merely replied we were no longer interested."[44]

That morning, prior to the news conference, Eisenhower spoke twice with Secretary Dulles and Attorney General Brownell—the latter undoubtedly to clarify the legal authority of Egypt to nationalize the canal. With Dulles, Ike further rehearsed his planned remarks and pinned down details. He even wrote out a statement to read to reporters but, after reviewing it in his pre-conference briefing, decided not to use it. In spite of his intensive preparation, the president again decided to say as little as possible.[45]

At 10:30, Eisenhower strode into the room and invited the reporters to sit down. "Good morning," he said. "We will go directly to questions."[46] Immediately a reporter asked how the president felt "about the use or threat of force in the Suez dispute?" Ike tersely signaled his no-comment strategy: "I can't answer that question quite as abruptly and directly as you have asked it." He hoped for settlement "by peaceful means." He stood for "the conference method" as the best solution. Asked if the British would seek an agreement with the United States before taking military action, Eisenhower cited "delicate negotiations" and said, "I wouldn't undertake to reveal anything that goes on in the diplomatic communications between ourselves and any other country." Asked if a peaceful solution might be impossible, Eisenhower said that "there is good reason to hope that good sense will prevail." Would the United States become involved if war broke out? Eisenhower's response was the most evasive yet: "I am not going to speculate that far ahead. That is piling an if on top of an if, and I think I will not try to comment."

Afterward, meeting with Foster Dulles, the president said his news conference "had not been a very satisfactory one." The questions had been designed to "trap him" into revealing more than he should. Dulles struck a more positive note, informing the president that the London conference could go forward; a sufficient number of nations had agreed to participate. The secretary revisited the issue of whether the president should attend, noting how Woodrow Wilson had squandered his prestige at the Paris Peace Conference in 1919. Eisenhower said that he had already concluded that the conference "was no place for him." They then discussed the discouraging tone of Anthony Eden's response to the message Dulles had hand-delivered on August 1. Dulles suggested only "a cordial acknowledgment" of the letter. Ike agreed. He had no more stomach this day for deal-ing with British and French paranoia.[47]

The August 9 meeting of the National Security Council was the first since the nationalization of the Suez Canal and only the second for Eisen-hower since his surgery.[48] Foster Dulles painted a dark picture of Egyptian ambition. Nasser, he said, was "dreaming of a build-up of Arab power and a corresponding diminution in the power of the West." Dulles recounted his success in organizing a conference aimed at establishing "a public in-ternational authority to operate the Canal in accordance with the treaty of 1888." He admitted that it was uncertain whether Egypt would accept such a program.

Secretary Dulles then raised grim questions. What would the United States do "if the Conference fails to agree or if its proposals are rejected by Nasser?" The British and French would surely resort to force. Should the United States attempt to stop them from attacking? If the United States helped the allies, how much support should be provided? They would want moral support, economic support (mostly oil), and "making it clear that if the hostilities were enlarged by the overt participation of the USSR, we would move in full force." If the allies moved against Egypt, would Israel also attack? Since the United States was publicly committed to providing assistance to any victim of aggression, would the administration then be obligated to come to Egypt's aid? Only one proposition in this muddled situation was clear to the secretary of state: "We would be in the hostilities if the Soviets came in."

Eisenhower, citing Anthony Eden's letter, said that the prime minister was nurturing the "vain hope" that the oil pipelines would continue to function in the event of war. Allen Dulles agreed that the pipelines would be cut. The council discussed contingency plans for providing oil to Eu-rope in the event of war. Eisenhower ordered both the State and Defense departments to work "constantly" on contingency plans for each possible scenario and then allowed his temper to erupt over Nasser's action. Egypt, he said, "had gone too far." Europe could not be expected to survive "at the mercy of the whim of a dictator." "If Nasser is successful," the president concluded, "there will be chaos in the Middle East for a long time." On that dismal note, the meeting ended.

The next day, Eisenhower received a classified intelligence report from the State Department's Near East Office regarding "the probable effects of economic sanctions on the Egyptian economy." The upshot: economic sanctions, while imposing stresses on the Nasser regime, "would probably not be sufficient within a year's time or even longer to threaten its survival." Moreover, truly successful sanctions—difficult to implement—would result in "almost complete Egyptian economic dependence on the Sino-Soviet Bloc." That same day, the Soviet Union announced its readiness to attend the London conference on August 16, but its agenda was less than positive. Moscow openly opposed any effort to internationalize control of the Suez Canal and denied that the upcoming conference could take "any decisions whatever" affecting the waterway's governance.[49]

THINKING THE UNTHINKABLE

Eisenhower was back to working a seven-day week. John Foster Dulles arrived for an 8:30 A.M. meeting on Saturday, August 11, armed with a long agenda.[50] In spite of his preoccupation with the Middle East, Ike could not escape politics. Dulles and the president discussed the Republican Party platform, which the secretary worried was being written without adequate input from the State Department. Ike wanted the platform to be short but Dulles pointed out that the document needed to provide speakers at the precinct level with material that transcended "mere generalities." Eisenhower, unhappy with that conclusion, admitted that it was probably "inevitable."

On Sunday morning at 10:30, Eisenhower convened a meeting to prepare for the session with congressional leaders. It included, among others, Secretary Dulles, Admiral Radford, CIA director Allen Dulles, and NATO commander General Alfred Gruenther.[51] The agenda was to attempt to anticipate the issues the legislators might raise. They agreed that the urgent question would be: if the conference failed or Nasser refused to accept a reasonable proposal, would Britain and France then be justified in taking military action, and what would the United States do to support them? Dulles responded that if the British and French felt compelled to act, "it would seem to be clear that the United States should give them moral and economic support." Ike was not so sure about that. He had already, in effect, legitimized Egypt's nationalization of the canal. He was now contemplating something that, for the former supreme allied commander, he might have previously termed "unthinkable"—to refuse, in the case of war, to come to the aid of his World War II allies.

At noon, the president and key aides met with the bipartisan congressional leadership, led by Senate majority leader Lyndon Johnson, House speaker Sam Rayburn, and Republican minority leaders Senator William Knowland and Congressman Joe Martin.[52] Eisenhower admitted to the group that things were not going well in the Middle East. Secretary Dulles then reviewed the history of the situation, starting with the Convention of 1888.

Dulles called the situation "almost a life and death issue for Britain and France." Two-thirds of the oil for Europe traveled through the canal, with the remaining third transported by pipelines. The dreaded scenario was that "oil might be cut off entirely." Speaker Rayburn asked whether Nasser had "definitely said he will close the Canal." Eisenhower and Dulles agreed that he had not, but the French and British believed "that his words cannot be trusted." The secretary said that the allies, despite agreeing to the conference, still believed that "Nasser is a wild man brandishing an axe and they do not have to wait for the blow to fall."

After considerable discussion, Lyndon Johnson expressed the view "that we can't deal with the Colonel and shouldn't we face up to it and say so to our allies." LBJ saw only two options—the unlikely resolution of the situation by peaceful means, or "tell our allies that we *are* their ally and to support them." While American financial support would be temporary, "we should tell them they have our moral support and they should go on in."

Eisenhower chose not to reveal to the hawkish congressional leaders, especially the Democrats, how close he was to breaking ranks with the allies over Suez. He responded with a classic Eisenhower fog of words, finding the majority leader "perfectly right in one respect": the United States could not accept "an inconclusive outcome leaving Nasser in control." But, he added, "We can't resign ourselves to underwriting the European economy permanently." Johnson could have been excused for being unsure of what he had just heard. Later, Ike further confused the issues by assuring the legislators that "we do not intend to stand by helplessly and let this one man get away with what he is trying to do," and that "the US will look to its interests."[53]

Following the meeting, Eisenhower received more discouraging news. Nasser had formally announced that he would not attend the London conference. The *New York Times* reported the next day that Britain had launched "a major airlift to the Middle East," moving five thousand troops across the English Channel and through the Mediterranean to Cyprus, positioned for possible action against Egypt.[54]

TALKING INSTEAD OF FIGHTING

The London conference was scheduled to begin on August 16. On Tuesday, August 14, Foster Dulles held a final consultation with the president.[55] He told Eisenhower that "the decisive issue would be whether or not Egypt alone should have the right to hire and fire in terms of canal employees and also would have alone the right to fix the Canal tolls." Eisenhower, putting himself in Nasser's shoes, asked "how we would meet the situation that might arise if we were asked to accept the same control with reference to the Panama Canal?"—obviously referring to the unquestioned authority of the United States government over that canal at that time. Dulles argued that the Suez Canal more "decisively affected the very livelihood of a score of nations." Ike suggested a supervisory board, designated by the affected nations, that "would have a voice in the selection of a general manager" and "some right of arbitration on the question of tolls."

Eisenhower's doubts underlined what both he and Dulles knew—that this effort at diplomacy was probably doomed to failure. But talking was still better than going to war. As the burdened secretary rose to leave, the president looked up and said something that Foster Dulles relished hearing—that Ike "recognized how difficult the task was, but that he had confidence and wished me well."

The next day, Eisenhower shifted his attention to preparations for the Republican convention, scheduled for August 20–23 at the Cow Palace in San Francisco. The demands of juggling presidential politics with a foreign crisis would fully test whether Ike had adequately recovered from his illnesses of the past year. As Dulles flew toward London, Eisenhower worked with speech writer Arthur Larson on drafts of his address for accepting the nomination. Typical of Eisenhower, he labored over every sentence, every word.[56]

On Thursday, the London conference began. Of the twenty-four nations invited, only two had declined—one being Egypt. John Foster Dulles cabled the president about a "busy first day," crammed with meetings with British and French officials and the Russian foreign minister, Shepilov. Dulles delivered the keynote speech and informed Eisenhower that "it apparently made a good impression." Still, he somberly concluded, "I have no doubt the reception in the Arab world will be bad."[57]

On the day that the conference began, Dwight Eisenhower was micromanaging the content of the Republican platform. He pressed Senator

Prescott Bush of Connecticut, the committee chairman, to avoid language that was "a little too purple and flowery." A few days later, a cantankerous Eisenhower called Herbert Brownell about the platform's wording regarding civil rights, petulantly threatening not to go to San Francisco if he did not get what he wanted.[58]

Dulles reported to Eisenhower on August 17 that, "of the twenty-two participating countries, twelve can be counted on to back proposals along the lines we have in mind." Ike was too busy to respond, but Hoover cabled Dulles that the president had followed his communications "with great interest and asked me to express to you his confidence and appreciation."[59]

That day, Eisenhower the candidate was preoccupied with politics. He phoned Bill Robinson, a frequent golfing buddy, whose advice he sought on the content of his acceptance speech. According to Robinson, the Democratic convention, held in Chicago, August 13–17, had been a "pretty sorry experience." Adlai Stevenson had been nominated again, with Tennessee senator Estes Kefauver as his running mate. Robinson thought that Stevenson had conducted himself well but he did not think the Democrats as a party had inspired confidence. Ike was not so sanguine. He said that the White House staff thought the Democrats "had succeeded in inducing a fighting spirit—to get people out to really storm the country, to work hard."[60]

On Saturday the 18th, Eisenhower found time to pen a note to Dulles in response to the news that the secretary, in consultation with the British and French, had hammered out a draft proposal to be circulated. "You seem to be surpassing even your own unique capacity for bringing some order and sanity to confused situations," Ike wrote.[61]

That evening, Dulles had dinner with the man in charge of the British treasury, Harold Macmillan, the chancellor of the exchequer. Macmillan, Dulles told Eisenhower, saw three stark choices—Nasser accepts the proposal, the allies compel him to accept it, or they accept his refusal. "In the last event," Macmillan concluded, "Britain is finished and so far as I am concerned, I will have no part in it and will resign." This report sounded so ominous that Eisenhower took time out from politics to read the draft agreement and respond to Dulles. He worried that the description of the board of directors as actually "operating, maintaining and developing of the Canal" was something Nasser would find "impossible to swallow." The president suggested giving the board "supervisory" rather than operating authority, more like an American corporate board of directors.[62]

Dulles responded that the allies would never accept the agreement "if all the hiring and firing of pilots, traffic directors and other technicians and engineers is made by the Egyptians with only some right of appeal." That would mean that Egypt could still "use the Canal as an instrument of national policy." The British and French would view that as "abandonment" of their objectives. Eisenhower countered that if a board selected the general manager, then the hiring and firing of lower level officials would be "an administrative detail." Both men knew that, however they tweaked the provisions, Nasser was unlikely to accept the arrangement. Ike conceded: "I understand the box you are in." [63]

Eisenhower correctly sensed the great weariness that was consuming his secretary of state. Dulles despaired that the conference was dragging on. Moreover, Dulles reported that he found himself "subjected to very strong pressure" to head the delegation that would travel to Cairo to negotiate with Nasser. The night of August 20, following a reception hosted by Prime Minister Eden, Macmillan had taken Dulles aside and urged him "most strongly to take on the negotiation with Nasser." Macmillan did not believe "that anyone else could pull it off." Eisenhower supported Dulles's hesitance: "By no means should you become involved in a long wearisome negotiation, especially with an anticipated probability of negative results in the end." "It would be worse than embarrassing," he wrote, "if you should get tied into drawn-out conversations which would in the long run prove unsuccessful." Ike concluded: "I will approve your decision and support you in whatever action you finally decide you must take." [64]

Dulles reported to Eisenhower on August 21 that the conference was moving toward closure, with eighteen of the twenty-two nations set to approve the American proposal. The four dissenters were the Soviet Union, India, Indonesia, and Ceylon. Shepilov had delivered "a very inflammatory speech charging our plan as being a maneuver of colonialism and designed to reimpose Western rule on Egypt." Dulles was discouraged, concluding that the Soviet "purpose is to prevent a settlement and to become themselves dominant in the Arab world." [65]

ANOTHER CALL TO DUTY

Eisenhower understood the importance of staging his arrival in San Francisco so he would appear to be the picture of health and vitality. The early word had been that the president would not arrive in the convention city until August 22. Suddenly—not nearly as sudden as it appeared—Eisenhower decided to fly to San Francisco a day early. That evening—Tuesday, August 21, about seven o'clock—the presidential aircraft landed at the San Francisco airport. The president and Mrs. Eisenhower were greeted by six thousand cheering supporters. Eisenhower stated that, after reading about the convention in the newspapers, "I suddenly decided this was too interesting a place to stay away from until Wednesday night." Thousands more lined the fifteen-mile route to the St. Francis Hotel as the president passed by in a bubble top limousine. About six blocks from the hotel, Eisenhower ordered the caravan stopped and the canopy opened so he could stand and wave to the crowds.

The staging from that moment onward, undoubtedly shaped by Jim Hagerty, worked to perfection. *New York Times* reporter Russell Baker described the president as "three pounds heavier and somewhat ruddier" than before the Democratic convention the previous week. "He looked more like the grinning enthusiastic campaigner of 1952 and 1954," Baker wrote, "as he posed for picture after picture and stood waving to the throngs." A crowd of two thousand crowded in front of the hotel, chanting, "We want Ike, We want Ike," as the limousine came to a halt and a band began playing, "We Love the Sunshine of His Smile." [66]

Eisenhower's first full day at the convention, Wednesday, was a whirlwind of activity. The candidate endured a parade of GOP dignitaries to his hotel suite and still squeezed in time to review Foster Dulles's latest communications, commenting that "the Soviet tactics to stir up tension are certainly disappointing although not unexpected." The president praised the agreement that Dulles had molded, calling it "most impressive" and "a strong position on which to negotiate." [67]

Eisenhower probably did not see Dulles's message later that day. The secretary reported that he continued to be pressured to serve on the negotiating team that would meet with Nasser. One proposal before the eighteen-nation group was "that I alone should carry on the negotiations on behalf of them all, but I said I could not do that because of my broader responsibilities." He promised to send in his place an important State Department official—later identified as deputy undersecretary of state Loy Henderson, the former ambassador to Iran and a respected Middle East and Soviet expert. Dulles said he planned to stay in London through Friday to facilitate the first meeting of the negotiating committee. But he was fearful about where things would go from here: "If Nasser refuses to let his government even deal with this committee, there will be a serious crisis." Yet the secretary still indulged in wishful thinking: "If meetings and exchanges of views take place, then the chance of a peaceful settlement will, I think, be considerable."[68]

At 2:00 A.M. on Wednesday, August 22, Robert Menzies, the Australian prime minister, was awakened by a phone call from U.S. ambassador Winthrop Aldrich. The ambassador requested that Menzies come immediately to Aldrich's residence to meet with Foster Dulles and British Foreign Minister Selwyn Lloyd. Once he arrived, they pressed him to agree to chair the five-nation delegation that would travel to Cairo to meet with Nasser. After checking with his government, Menzies agreed. Dulles cabled the president from London: "The conference is now history."[69]

As expected, the Republican convention nominated Eisenhower and Nixon for a second term. The president and Mrs. Eisenhower arrived at the Cow Palace just before six on Thursday. "The most tumultuous roar of the convention," a reporter wrote, "went up when the President and Mrs. Eisenhower entered the hall."[70]

Ike's speech that evening was one of his best—well organized, efficiently delivered.[71] He barely alluded to the Democrats, contrasting the Republican Party as "the Party of the Future," focused on "long-range principle, not short-term expediency." Only near the end of the speech did the president discuss world peace. He pointed to his proposals for Atoms for Peace and disarmament and outlined "three imperatives of peace"—national strength, collective security, and building bridges to "the peoples under communist rule." Eisenhower praised people-to-people programs, with "interchange of ideas, of books, magazines, students, tourists, artists, radio programs, technical experts, religious leaders and governmental officials. My hope is that little by little, mistrust based on falsehoods will give way to international understanding based on truth."

The speech was noteworthy for what Eisenhower did not say. He did not rail against communist dictators. He did not denigrate his political enemies. The president said not one word about the crisis over the Suez Canal that, at that very moment, threatened his vision of a world at peace. But Eisenhower could not ignore what he had called in January a world "on the verge of an abyss."[72] In a world with nuclear weapons, he said, "war has become, not just tragic, but preposterous. With such weapons, there can be no victory for anyone." After such a difficult year, Ike surely experienced a feeling of exhilaration as he concluded: "The nomination that you have tendered me for the Presidency of the United States I now—humbly but confidently—accept."

The crowd roared and a demonstration began. Eisenhower called his family and the Nixons to the podium. After a few minutes of cheering, Eisenhower cut off the demonstration by announcing that Irving Berlin, the composer, would lead the crowd in singing "God Bless America." A last prayer was offered and, at 7:04, the Republican convention adjourned.[73]

Dwight Eisenhower had traveled a long road since September 24, 1955. So had Foster Dulles. In London, the exhausted secretary of state watched as the final plenary session of the Suez Canal conference established a five-nation committee to negotiate with Gamal Abdel Nasser regarding the future of the canal.[74]

The next phase in the Suez crisis was about to unfold.

8

★ ★ ★ ★ ★ ★

BETRAYAL OF TRUST

August 24–October 23, 1956

"The use of military force against Egypt under present circumstances might have consequences even more serious than causing the Arabs to support Nasser. It might cause a serious misunderstanding between our two countries."

Eisenhower to Anthony Eden, September 8, 1956

THE MISSION to Cairo that Australian prime minister Robert Menzies and his delegation were undertaking was almost certain to fail. Why would Nasser, his prestige so enhanced by his seizure of the Suez Canal, accept an agreement that would effectively return authority over its operations to the British and French? The delegation's inevitable failure was the main reason John Foster Dulles, aside from his exhaustion, did not want to go. So he had assigned undersecretary Loy Henderson to take on this thankless task.[1]

Following dinner on Thursday, August 23, British foreign secretary Selwyn Lloyd, under what Dulles called "obvious emotional strain," warned the secretary that there would be "a button pushed early in September and after that everything would happen automatically and be irrevocable." Dulles reaffirmed Eisenhower's opposition to military action to Prime Minister Eden the next morning. Eden responded that his government was "on the spot" and he intended to act "in a week or ten days unless the situation definitely clears up." Dulles countered with Ike's assertion that the only justification for military action would be Egypt blocking traffic through the canal.[2]

Eden wrote Eisenhower on August 27, praising Dulles's "remarkable achievement" in brokering an agreement among eighteen nations. But the prime minister saw no choice but to continue military preparations. Nasser might refuse to negotiate, he worried; they would not know for several days. "After that," he wrote, "we should be in a position to act swiftly." Eden called the situation "the most hazardous that our country has known since 1940." Henderson reported to Dulles that Eden, "obviously worried and perplexed" complained to him about the slow pace of the delegation's preparations for departure. "Oh these delays," Eden lamented. "They are working against us. Every day's postponement is to Nasser's gain and our loss."[3]

THE POST-CONFERENCE BLUES

On Wednesday, back in Washington, Dulles presented a somber assessment to Eisenhower. The British would be ready for military action by September 10 unless Nasser accepted the eighteen-nation plan, he said. That hardly allowed enough time for the delegation to effectively negotiate with Nasser. Eisenhower asked if he could do something to encourage Nasser to accept the proposals and Dulles suggested that the president issue a statement, which they drafted immediately.[4]

Ann Whitman called Thursday "a very busy day for the president." The National Security Council meeting that morning was one of the longest on record, lasting nearly three and one half hours.[5] Secretary Dulles reviewed at length the London conference for the NSC, emphasized the September 10 British-French target date for a decision on military action, and labeled the situation "very grave." If Britain and France attacked, he said, "the whole Arab world would be pitted against them, and obviously it would be easier to start a war than to finish it." Admiral Radford, reflecting the sentiment of the Joint Chiefs, said that if the allies went to war against Egypt, "the United States would have to provide them at least with logistic support."

Eisenhower broke his silence at Radford's invocation of "logistic support"—an act equivalent to war. He called the Suez situation "so grave that it must be watched hourly." At this point, he said, he intended to limit action to "the necessary steps to prevent the enlargement of the war if it actually breaks out." An action like that suggested by Radford, Ike went on, might mean "it would be necessary to consult with the Congress." When former Governor Stassen asked if an alternative might be for Israel to defeat Egypt, Eisenhower responded that "as quickly as that happened the United States would find all the Arab countries of the world united against us."

At such tense moments, the smallest matters get blown out of proportion. Eisenhower's August 29 statement, designed to encourage Nasser to accept the Menzies delegation's plan, had expressed the hope "that this waterway internationalized by the Treaty of 1888 will be operated so as dependably to serve its appointed purpose." Ike's use of the word "internationalized" elicited a howl of protest from the Egyptian government, contending that the president's phrasing denied the sovereignty of Egypt over the canal. Dulles called the president to tell him that the Egyptians "were making a big fuss over the words in his statement," a response he called "very silly." Nasser, he said, "was getting jittery." [6]

At his news conference on August 31, Eisenhower addressed the controversy. "We are, I think, talking at cross purposes," he said. Eisenhower said that his reference to the Suez Canal "as a waterway internationalized by the treaty of 1888" did not mean those nations owned the canal, only that Egypt could not jeopardize their rights to use the waterway. His August 29 statement had noted that Menzies's delegation would present a proposal to Nasser that "fully respected the sovereignty of Egypt." Nasser had managed to push the president of the United States, once again, into publicly recognizing Egyptian sovereignty over the canal. [7]

Ike was unaware when the next day, September 1, the French government sent a message through the Israeli military attaché in Paris asking the Israeli government whether it would join in developing an Anglo-French plan, code-named Operation Musketeer, for military action against Egypt; David Ben-Gurion immediately cabled a positive response. From this point forward, the French and the Israelis engaged in constant discussion about additional arms shipments and strategies related to the anticipated attack. [8]

Even without such knowledge, Eisenhower knew only too well the smell of war. On Sunday, Ike sent a sharply worded warning to Anthony Eden, asserting that British military preparations were only "solidifying support for Nasser." [9] "I must tell you frankly," Ike continued, "that American public opinion flatly rejects the thought of using force." He said he doubted that he could "secure Congressional authority even for the lesser support measures for which you might have to look to us." Eisenhower forecast a disaster if Eden continued on his present path. "I really do not see how a successful result could be achieved by forcible means," he wrote. The Western European economy would be devastated, oil shipments would be cut off, and the peoples of the region would be alienated, plus "all of Asia and all of Africa." "Seldom, I think, have we been faced with so grave a problem," the president wrote. He implored Eden to "put our faith in the processes already at work."

A DESPERATE IDEA

Foster Dulles knew the mission to Cairo was doomed. He would later tell Treasury Secretary George Humphrey that he "never expected the plan to work anyway." [10]

After the stresses of the London conference, Dulles escaped to his favorite retreat, Duck Island on Lake Ontario. However tired his body was, the secretary's mind was racing about what to do if and when Nasser rejected the eighteen-power proposal. On September 2, Dulles sketched out ideas that would eventually evolve into the Suez Canal Users Association (SCUA), an organization of the eighteen nations represented by the Menzies delegation, much like a union or trade association. The association would derive financial clout from the collection of transit tolls and negotiate with Nasser regarding access, operation, and governance of the canal. [11]

The good news from Cairo was that Nasser had met with the Menzies delegation at noon on Monday, September 3. Undersecretary Loy Henderson, with the delegation, described Nasser as "obviously nervous and ill-at-ease" but pledging no "hostile arguments" by the Egyptian government. But the sessions grew increasingly tense. By the third meeting, Nasser was characterizing the international board the delegation was proposing as "collective colonialism in regulated form." When Menzies tried to explain how upset the people of Great Britain and France were, Nasser interpreted the comment as a threat to use force, in which case, he said, he was "prepared to let it come at once. Egypt cannot give up its sovereignty because it feared trouble." Menzies desperately backpedaled, insisting he had implied no threat. [12]

The almost daily intelligence reports Eisenhower was receiving did not serve him well. The CIA had convened an interagency intelligence watch committee, subsidiary to the Intelligence Advisory Committee (IAC), normally chaired by the CIA director, Allen Dulles. The deputy CIA director, General Charles Cabell, chaired the watch committee, which was composed of senior intelligence representatives from the State Department, the three branches of the armed services, the CIA, the Atomic Energy Commission, and the FBI. Its September 5 report concluded that "military action by UK-French forces will almost certainly not be launched while discussions are under way in Cairo." But that would change if the British and French decided "that their objectives are not obtainable within a reasonable time by negotiations and by other non-military means." A special National Intelligence Estimate that same day assumed that the British and French would resort to military force only if Egypt denied their transit rights through the Suez Canal or attacked their nationals. The allies still appeared to be open to a negotiated compromise. Looking at the forces already mobilized, the NIE estimated that the allies "could probably attain their purely military objectives in Egypt within a very few days." But it was "highly unlikely," the NIE stated, that Israel would use British-French military action against Egypt as an excuse to launch an attack in Sinai or against other Arab states.[13]

Eisenhower held his weekly news conference at 10:30 that Wednesday morning. Asked whether the United States would support Britain and France if they refused to accept anything less than the eighteen-power proposal, Eisenhower dodged the question by saying he was "not going to comment on the contents of that proposal while it is being discussed in Cairo."[14]

The negotiations in Egypt were not going well. Loy Henderson's September 5 cable to the State Department reported that Nasser had "made it completely clear that Egypt would not accept any institutional arrangement which would provide for the operation of the Canal by an international body." The next day, Foster Dulles read Henderson's cable to Eisenhower. Ike, pondering this discouraging news, revived his previous suggestion that the board the Menzies delegation had proposed engage in "supervision," as opposed to actively operating the canal. Dulles argued that his idea of a users association was the best alternative. That approach, "based squarely on the rights under the Treaty of 1888," would provide a legal foundation for negotiation. Eisenhower, Dulles recorded in his notes, "recognized the bargaining value of such a position but expressed doubt as to whether it was practically workable."[15]

Meanwhile Henderson, to his dismay, had learned about Secretary Dulles's new ideas. In another cable, he opined that an "association of users" would prove even less acceptable to Nasser than the eighteen-power proposals and would "merely increase international tension and danger of resort to force." Most awkward for Henderson, Robert Menzies had been demoralized by Egyptian press reports that the United States did "not really have its heart" in the delegation's proposals and was "looking for other solutions more acceptable." [16]

That same day, Eisenhower was further disturbed by Anthony Eden's response to his previous letter. If the delegation in Cairo failed, Eden wrote, he wanted "some immediate alternative which will show that Nasser is not going to get his way." He called Nasser another Hitler and treated the seizure of the Suez Canal as "the opening gambit in a planned campaign designed by Nasser to expel all Western influence and interests from Arab countries." If Nasser withheld oil, Western Europe would soon be "on its knees before you." "We have many times led Europe in the fight for freedom," the prime minister declared. "It would be an ignoble end to our long history if we tamely accepted to perish by degrees." [17]

The next morning, Eisenhower discussed Eden's message with Dulles, who thought the letter "intemperate and ill-thought." Eisenhower complained that the British "have got themselves in a box in the Mid East because they have constantly been choosing the wrong things about which to be tough." No attack could be justified as long as the Egyptians ran the Canal efficiently, he said. The United States "could not really take a stand," Eisenhower grumbled; he was caught between the need to keep NATO strong and opposing the British and French "in their extreme attitude." The president said he wished that Western Europe would cease shifting toward "an oil economy." Eden's letter had forecast "a sorry end" to Britain's great history, he said. To Ike's ear, Eden was attempting to imitate Churchill's soaring rhetoric during World War II. Ike sighed: "This is where I came in." [18]

Eisenhower grasped at straws the rest of the day. He called Dulles about two ideas, one proposing that the major nations buy up the stock of the Suez Canal Company, and the other to send Robert Anderson, his personal envoy who had led a failed mission earlier in the year, back to the Middle East to negotiate with Nasser and offer financial inducements. Dulles shot down both proposals, reminding the president that, due to the Egyptian decree, the Suez Canal Company no longer existed and using Anderson to "go off on our own and negotiate" would undermine the Menzies delegation's efforts.[19]

After that, Ike calmed down. There would be no quick or simple solution. He returned to the task, in consultation with Dulles, of drafting a response to Eden's letter. Ike told Dulles he was convinced that an attack on Egypt would not only unify the Arabs against the West; it "would weaken and probably destroy the UN." He counseled that it was important "not to make mistakes in a hurry." Their best strategy at this point was to stall for time, to "go slowly."[20]

On Saturday morning, September 8, Eisenhower reviewed Dulles's blueprint for a users association. The plan called for the association to hire its own administrator who would have authority to control schedules, allocate pilots, employ personnel, make rules and regulations, maintain the canal, and collect fees for the operations of the association. The president was still skeptical; although it might be legally correct, he was "not sure it would work." Dulles argued that the United States "had to keep the initiative" because the British and French could not be restrained without an alternative. Eisenhower agreed that, however thin the proposal, "military measures should not be taken."[21]

Eisenhower's response to Prime Minister Eden's September 6 message was plainspoken.[22] "You are making of Nasser a much more important figure than he is," the president wrote, and he warned that an invasion of Egypt "might cause a serious misunderstanding between our two countries." "It seems to Foster and me," he continued, "that the result that you and I both want can best be assured by slower and less dramatic processes than military force." Ike then proposed the Dulles strategy, "a semipermanent organization of the user governments" that could work out "a de facto 'coexistence' " with Egypt and keep the canal functioning.

Eisenhower's approach was essentially an adaptation of the containment policy that had been the cornerstone of American policy toward the Soviet Union. The allies could contain Egypt, he suggested, by exploiting economic pressures and Arab rivalries, all the while exploring alternatives to dependence on the canal. "Nasser thrives on drama," Ike asserted, and they should "let some of the drama go out of the situation" and deflate Nasser through "slower but surer processes." This policy "would be less costly both now and in the future." There might eventually be no alternative to using force but doing it too soon, without more provocation, "could lead, in the years to come, to the most distressing results." By now, Anthony

Eden surely knew that, beyond all doubt, Dwight Eisenhower would not support an attack on Egypt. From this moment forward, the prime minister set out to deceive the president of the United States as to his real plans.

In Cairo, the disillusioning experience of the Menzies delegation was grinding to a halt. On Friday, September 7, Menzies sent Nasser a written summary of the eighteen-power proposal and then, according to Henderson, spent the next two days sick in bed. At 12:45 P.M. on September 9, Nasser's response was delivered, reaffirming Egypt's right to nationalize the canal, guaranteeing freedom of passage, equitable compensation, and a commitment to a peaceful solution—but declaring the delegation's proposals unacceptable. At 7:00 P.M., the delegation made a farewell call on Nasser. The mission had failed.[23]

Monday, September 10—the date the Americans thought the British had established for a decision on military action (the actual date was September 15)—was a day of frantic consultations at the White House. Foster Dulles called the president to review a statement saying "I am deeply disappointed about the rejection of Nasser of the 18-nation proposal." Dulles wondered if the president should release the statement but Ike, the wary presidential candidate, preferred that Dulles be the one associated with this failure. The president and the secretary consulted twice more, the last time concerning a new letter from Anthony Eden, who was planning to address Parliament on Wednesday and announce his acceptance of the idea of a users association.[24]

September 10 passed without war. Ike dared to hope he had convinced his ally once again to defer a resort to force. But he had no illusions; the crisis was not over. At 8:15 the morning of September 11, the president began a steady stream of meetings, including a review of options if Middle East oil were shut off to Europe. In his pre–press conference meeting, Eisenhower said that he could not continue to publicly ignore the "seriousness of the situation." The old canal authority had authorized its employees to leave their employment at the end of the week, "a serious mistake," he said, that would look like the Western powers were sabotaging the operations of the canal. That was precisely what the British and French were attempting to do, hoping that the withdrawal of the operators would precipitate a breakdown in canal operations that could be used as a pretext for war. They were, the president said, "sitting on a ke[g] of dynamite."[25]

Nonetheless, Eisenhower began his news conference that Tuesday without announcements.[26] When asked about the failure of the talks in

Cairo, Eisenhower praised Secretary Dulles and the delegation that had visited Nasser but said nothing about a users association. When asked if the United States would back Britain and France if they resorted to force, Eisenhower responded, "This country will not go to war ever while I am occupying my present post unless the Congress is called into session, and Congress declares such a war." He said he would sanction force only if Egypt did something aggressive to block traffic through the canal. "We are consulting with all our associates throughout the world on this," he added, "to see what is the very best next thing."

Eisenhower's decision not to mention the proposed users association left the announcement of that new gambit in the unstable hands of Anthony Eden. Foster Dulles called British ambassador Roger Makins and urged that the prime minister's remarks the next day "be reasonably conciliatory or at least not particularly bellicose." He noted that "Egypt is striking a note of sweet reasonableness." Dulles had reason to worry. Selwyn Lloyd had told Ambassador Aldrich that the British government was pleased with the secretary's plan for an association of users because it could be transformed into a "slap in the face" for Nasser.[27]

THE TROUBLED BIRTH OF SCUA

Prime Minister Eden's speech to the Parliament on September 12 fulfilled Dulles's worst fears. Eden presented the Suez Canal Users Association as a full-fledged mechanism for retaking the operations of the Suez Canal. The new organization, he said, would hire pilots, coordinate traffic, and generally oversee the operations of the canal. Most important, transit tolls would be paid to the association, not to Egypt. Eden bluntly stated that if the Egyptian government refused to cooperate, the British government would take other steps through the United Nations or, more ominously, "by other means." In spite of the tone of Eden's address, the State Department issued a statement indicating that the United States would participate in the users association "and would seek such cooperation with Egypt" as would uphold the users' rights as defined in the Convention of 1888.[28]

Eisenhower and Dulles knew they had only managed to buy a little more time. The intelligence watch committee report that day reinforced Eden's real intent—that Britain and France "may launch military action against Egypt in the event that their minimum objectives cannot be obtained by non-military means." A buildup of British and French forces in the Eastern Mediterranean was continuing and the two nations were conducting joint exercises off Malta. Inevitably, Eisenhower was distracted by his political obligations. That day, the Eisenhowers motored at midday to Gettysburg, where the Republicans kicked off the presidential campaign at the Eisenhower home.[29]

On Thursday, September 13, at 9:08 A.M., Ike called Foster Dulles, who was scheduled to hold a news conference that day. They discussed how belligerent Anthony Eden's speech had been. Ike worried that the press would not understand that the 1888 treaty was to be implemented "in cooperation" with the Egyptian government.[30]

Later that morning, Dulles informed Eisenhower that he had received an urgent message from Nasser, delivered by Ahmed Hussein, the Egyptian ambassador. It read: "The scheme which Prime Minister Eden wants to impose is an open and flagrant aggression on Egypt's sovereignty and its implementation means war. If the United States desires war, it may support the scheme, but if its desire is to work for a peaceful solution, the scheme has to be abandoned." Dulles had tried to calm Hussein, saying that Nasser's reaction was "based on a misconception" and the users plan "did not involve a violation of Egyptian sovereignty or anything else that should unduly disturb the Egyptian government." Nevertheless, the ambassador told the waiting press that the implementation of the users association plan would lead to war.[31]

At his news conference that day, Dulles tried to damp down this hysteria by espousing "cooperation with Egypt" and denying any intent "to impose some regime upon Egypt." When asked what the United States would do if the Egyptians prevented passage through the canal, the secretary said that he did not think that the British or the Americans would try to "shoot their way through the canal."[32]

Dulles met with British ambassador Makins that evening and proposed a meeting of the eighteen nations in London on September 19 for the purpose of launching SCUA. Then Dulles called Eisenhower for approval to go to London, saying his subordinates believed that no one else could handle Eden, Foreign Minister Lloyd, and French foreign minister Pineau. Ike, apparently concerned about his secretary of state's health, asked whether someone else could go. Dulles responded that Hoover had been ill and Robert Murphy was unavailable. Ike said he regretted that Dulles had "to do so much" but, he concluded, "If we can pull this off, it does not make any difference if they kick us out in January."[33]

It was not just Dulles's health that concerned Eisenhower, but his judgment under stress. It had been almost two months since the United States had withdrawn its offer of aid to the Aswan Dam project. Since July 26, when Nasser had nationalized the canal, Ike had pondered why relations with Egypt had gotten so out of hand. Barely back from surgery on July 19, he had signed off on Dulles's decision after only a superficial review of its implications. He and the secretary had since found no good opportunity to conduct a postmortem. But it troubled Eisenhower, even years later. In his memoirs, he wrote: "I never doubted the wisdom of canceling our offer but I was concerned, in view of the events of the following weeks, that we might have been undiplomatic in the way the cancellation was handled." [34]

Ike began to press Dulles about whether the withdrawal of aid to the Aswan project had been too "abrupt." On September 6, he had sent Dulles a letter based on a British subject's interview with Ali Sabri, the chief of Nasser's cabinet, who vividly described Nasser's response to America's withdrawal of aid. "The blow," Sabri had said, "was staggering." On September 17, following a consultation with Dulles prior to the secretary's departure for London, Eisenhower read a letter Dulles had brought to him, responding to his probing questions about the Aswan Dam decision. [35]

Dulles must have rewritten that defensive letter several times. He contended that the Egyptians knew by July 19 that the United States had lost interest in providing funds for the project. Congressional opposition had been ferocious. "If I had not announced our withdrawal when I did," he wrote, "the Congress would certainly have imposed it on us, almost unanimously." Egypt, by means of its "flirtations with the Soviet Union, had itself consciously jeopardized our sharing in this project, and they had tried to bluff us by pretending to Soviet 'offers.' " The outcome, he insisted, was not a "shock" or a "surprise" to the Egyptians. [36]

The second Suez Canal conference met in London, September 19–21. Eisenhower could not have been encouraged by the National Intelligence Estimate he received the day the new consultations began. "At least for the immediate future," it read, "the UK and France will almost certainly seek to keep the way open for the use of force." The NIE concluded that American opposition was the primary obstacle to war. [37]

In London, between meetings, Dulles continued to press Eden to keep the peace. Eden told him that the British had altered their military planning so they could maintain readiness without being bound to a fixed date, but they and the French were keeping their options open. Dulles did not know that, at that very moment, Shimon Peres, a member of the Israeli Defense

Ministry, was in Paris discussing arms purchases and confirming Israel's intention to join the French in a military operation against Nasser. Dulles reported to the president that he had made progress on organizing the users association and hoped to be done on September 21. "Perhaps," the weary diplomat wrote the president, "I shall stop at Bermuda Saturday morning for the swim I missed last time." [38]

Later on the 19th, Eisenhower made the first television and radio address of his presidential campaign, focusing on peace.[39] He claimed foreign policy successes for his administration in Korea, Iran, West Germany, Trieste, Austria, and Guatemala and cited the three locales where peace was threatened—"distant points on earth—a frontier in Europe [Germany], an island in the Pacific [Formosa], a canal in the Middle East [Suez]." The Suez Canal situation was, he emphasized, a "grave crisis." "We have spoken with care and with restraint," he said. "We cannot yet know whether the issue can be settled with justice and fairness to all. But we know that the world will know that America has spared no effort to save peace."

The next day, at a National Security Council meeting, General Charles Cabell, the deputy CIA director, reported on "the sharp increase in Arab-Israeli tension" and treated Israeli raids into neighboring states as an expression of the Israeli policy of "prompt reprisal."[40] Herbert Hoover expressed concern that the Israelis might "take advantage of the grave Suez Canal situation." Eisenhower shared his frustration: "The Israelis are of course well aware of how difficult it is for the United States to maintain its present policy of opposing aggression in the Middle East no matter which side commits it. What with the situation in Suez, the Israelis may feel that they have boxed the United States in."

The London conference issued on Friday, September 21, a statement formally recognizing Egypt's rejection of the eighteen-power proposals and a separate declaration establishing the Suez Canal Users Association. The meetings to formalize the SCUA organization were scheduled to begin October 1.[41]

A PROGRAM OF DECEPTION

On Sunday, September 23, the British and French did something totally unexpected. Without consulting Secretary Dulles—who was in flight back to the United States—they formally requested the U.N. Security Council to address the Suez situation. Dulles was infuriated at what he called the "utter confusion" precipitated by that decision. He complained to Arthur Flemming, the director of the Office of Defense Mobilization, that, in addition to the United Nations action, "they want us to stop letting our flag vessels pay Nasser" for transiting the canal. By impounding the transit fees, the allies could blackmail Nasser, withholding the funds the Egyptian leader needed to finance the Aswan Dam. If Nasser resisted the payment of tolls to SCUA, France and Britain could justify going to war. Dulles said he suspected that the Anglo-French petition to the Security Council was a sham; they knew very well that the Soviet Union would veto any anti-Egyptian resolution, providing another pretext for war. Dulles grumbled to Flemming that he was "anxious to play along with them but [it's] hard when we don't know what they are up to and they won't consult with us." [42]

The British were now committed to full-scale deception of Eisenhower, their World War II ally. Britain's chancellor of the exchequer, Harold Macmillan, arrived at the White House on Tuesday, September 25, with the apparent assignment of charming President Eisenhower. He succeeded to some degree. Ike told Foster Dulles that Macmillan "talked very much more moderately" about Suez than he had anticipated and had called the users association "a good thing." But these days, nothing was what it seemed. The Macmillan visit provided effective cover for a secret visit on September 26 by Prime Minister Eden and Foreign Secretary Lloyd to Paris to discuss a new target date in October for the invasion of Egypt. Three days later, an Israeli delegation, headed by Foreign Minister Golda Meir and chief of staff Moshe Dayan, arrived in Paris to commence serious planning for launching the war. [43]

Anthony Eden played his role in this deceptive charm offensive, writing the president after Macmillan had returned, to say he "was particularly delighted to hear from him that you were in such splendid form." Eden assured Ike that the British were "fully alive to the wider dangers of the Middle East situation. They can be summed up in one word—Russia." Nasser, he wrote, "is now effectively in Russian hands, just as Mussolini was in Hitler's." But Eden pledged "to do everything we can to make the Users' Club an effective instrument." That was dishonest; the British did not intend to use SCUA as anything but an excuse for war. The Egyptians could not have been encouraged when Selwyn Lloyd was selected as SCUA chairman—a sure sign of a lack of neutrality. [44]

By the end of September, British and French intent was accurately reflected in the buildup of forces in the Mediterranean—especially at Malta, Cypress, and Libya. The mobilization was impressive. The British and

French had gathered eighty thousand troops, pilots, and sailors and more than two hundred warships, in addition to merchant ships, landing craft, and thousands of vehicles; aircraft carriers and light bombers were not far away. One problem: both nations lacked significant numbers of battle-ready airborne troops. Without them, an invasion launched from Malta—a thousand miles from Egypt—would be cumbersome and slow, a logistical factor that would profoundly affect any attempt to launch a sudden, quickly victorious military operation.[45]

Eisenhower and Dulles took stock in a meeting on the afternoon of October 2.[46] Dulles said the British and French blamed the United States for "holding them back." Dulles wondered whether they really wanted "a peaceful solution." He described four contradictory strategies advocated by British factions—negotiation, overthrow through economic pressures, use of military force, covert coup. In response to the latter, Eisenhower declared: "We should have nothing to do with any project for a covert operation against Nasser personally." Ike did "not believe that the Canal issue was the one on which to seek to undermine Nasser." The United States, he said, had to maintain "an independent position as regards the British and French" until their intentions were clear.

Meanwhile, the CIA watch committee continued to misread British and French intentions. On October 3, the committee suspended publication of the so-called annex bulletin on the Suez situation because of "the preponderance of indications that the UK and France do not intend to resort to force at this time." In a remarkable failure of intelligence analysis, the report noted, in particular, "the absence of any evidence of British-French intentions to act against Egypt through Israel, despite various reported rumors to the contrary." A few weeks later, Eisenhower would fervently wish the CIA had followed up on those "rumors."[47]

AN ANGRY SECRETARY OF STATE

John Foster Dulles was out of patience with the Western European allies. At the Thursday, October 4, NSC meeting, he fumed about the British and French decision to take Suez to the United Nations, which had been done without his knowledge and against his advice.[48] Dulles feared that the move was "merely a cover for the ultimate use of force which seems to be the French position." He said that although he would attend the U.N. Security Council meeting in New York, the situation was "difficult" because the allies had kept the administration "so much in the dark." Eisenhower ended the discussion by forcefully repeating that "the United States would be dead wrong to join in any resort to force. We should instead hold out for honest negotiations with the Egyptians."

In New York on Friday morning, Dulles confronted the British and French foreign ministers, Selwyn Lloyd and Christian Pineau, about their sudden decision to appeal to the United Nations.[49] He raised questions "as to your real purpose" and quoted Eisenhower to the effect that "military measures would start a war which would be extremely difficult to bring to an end." In spite of the election campaign, Dulles said, the president's policies were "not swayed by political considerations."

Pineau responded that the United States government did not understand that "we risk much more than an economic difference over the Suez Canal. We are risking all of our influence in that part of the world." Nasser, he predicted, "will go farther and farther," and "Russia is back of him." Dulles pressed the diplomats to give negotiation more time: "If we are merely trying to clear the decks for the use of force," he asserted, "we will be condemned for having destroyed the UN, and that the US cannot agree to do." Lloyd countered that the British "can't get drawn into a long-term negotiation."

Dulles finally persuaded Lloyd and Pineau to commit their countries to participate in closed-door discussions with the Egyptians, outside the formal Security Council meetings in New York. Lloyd grudgingly agreed to participate in talks for "two or three days." Dulles replied in exasperation, "if you have ever argued in an Egyptian bazaar in Cairo, you will know that they don't work that fast." But he seized this small opening. "If Egypt will accept the heart of our proposal," he said, "that is, that the Canal be operated free from politics, then there are different ways of working it out." The fact was, the British and French were going through motions while preparing for war. Yet Dulles was a realist. Reporting to Eisenhower on his "heart-to-heart" talk with Lloyd and Pineau, he said both men believed a peaceful resolution was not possible, but they had agreed to private talks.

A NEW ROUND OF TALKS

Dulles frantically laid the groundwork for the closed-door talks. He told Eisenhower he had protested to Soviet foreign minister Shepilov that Soviet propaganda "was doing its best to sabotage our effort" and that the Russians were egging on the Egyptians "to greater excesses." Dulles had grumbled to Shepilov that he, the American secretary of state, "was today the most unpopular man in France and Britain" while Shepilov "was the most popular man in Egypt." Dulles also talked with Fawzi, the Egyptian foreign minister, who indicated a willingness to join the talks. The next few days, Dulles told the president, would be "make or break" as to whether significant talks could go forward.[50]

A pessimistic Foster Dulles joined C. D. Jackson, the publisher of *Fortune* magazine and former Eisenhower assistant in psychological warfare, and other friends for dinner the evening of October 5, after a long day of negotiation.[51] Jackson recalled the dinner as being "very interesting with Dulles pretty much on the defensive." The secretary confessed that the users association had been "a delaying action." He admitted that he "did not know how it would all end" and "did not even know what his next moves might be." He and the president might still have to invent "further SCUA's" to stave off war. Dulles had unwisely assumed it was safe to talk so candidly in the company of old friends. Brownie Reid, the publisher and editor of the *New York Herald Tribune*, had taken notes, and the next day Jim Hagerty called Jackson in alarm. Reid was planning to run an article on Sunday, saying that Dulles, in an exclusive interview, had said that "war would come in Suez within 7 or 8 days." Jackson assured Hagerty that the comments had been "off the record" and he succeeded in persuading Reid not to run the story.

To complicate matters further, Anthony Eden was struck with a fever the night of Dulles's dinner with Jackson, his temperature rising to a dangerous 106 degrees. The prime minister, who had been plagued with recurrent ill effects from earlier surgery, recovered sufficiently to return to work the following Monday, but colleagues found his conduct thereafter increasingly unpredictable and almost irrational, perhaps due to medication side effects.[52]

Between October 5 and 13, the United Nations Security Council met almost daily to discuss the British-French resolution on Suez, which called for affirmation of the Convention of 1888, negotiations based on the eighteen-power proposals that had been presented to Nasser, and Egyptian cooperation with SCUA. British and French deception was becoming more evident each day. The CIA's U-2 spy planes had discovered that, instead of there being twelve French Mystère jets in Israel, there were sixty. Meanwhile, Selwyn Lloyd had been assigned to placate Dulles. Meeting in the secretary's suite at the Waldorf-Astoria on Sunday evening, October 7, Lloyd feigned his "distress" that the newspapers were saying the United States and Britain "were divided on the Suez matter" when there was "an extraordinary degree of agreement." Dulles tried his best to be agreeable, saying he dared to hope that they had reached some agreement regarding the "ultimate," the use of force over Suez.[53]

THE HAGERTY PLAN

It was less than a month before the election and press secretary Jim Hagerty was worried. The Democrats were raising questions about the president's health, underlining the fact that Eisenhower had campaigned primarily on radio and television rather than submit himself to physically demanding trips around the country. "You can't be elected on radio or television," former President Truman had told reporters the previous week. "The people want to see what you look like, what the feel of you is." Eisenhower was planning a campaign trip to the West in mid-October, Truman said, because the president was "scared." Most important, Hagerty feared that his boss was appearing weak and indecisive in addressing the Suez Canal crisis. At the president's October 6 news conference, Hagerty had watched as Eisenhower refused once again to comment on Suez. Ike had declined to make a statement, the *New York Times* reported, "lest he upset the United Nations' handling of the problem."[54]

On Monday, October 8, Hagerty sent the president some "probably crazy" suggestions, granting that "the State Department will be horrified that I even put some of these thoughts down on paper."[55] Hagerty called for an approach that "would personally place the President of the United States in his proper role as the leader of world peace."

If the British and French were about to launch World War III, Hagerty wrote, "the American people and the people of the world expect the President of the United States to do something dramatic—even drastic—to prevent at all possible costs another war." This was "the number one question in the minds of the American people." Hagerty proposed that the president make a clear statement, "detailing step-by-step moves to keep the Suez peace" and warning the British and French "that the United States will not tolerate or support a war, or warlike moves, in the Suez area." The president should consider a personal meeting with Nasser; the idea that such a meeting would enhance the dictator's prestige was "an argument of the past." "Whether we or our Allies like it or not," Hagerty wrote, "Nasser *is* already a world figure." The press secretary urged the president to convene a summit conference after the election, including Egypt and Russia, and "take personal command in the sole interest of keeping the peace."

Then, Hagerty—citing "pure domestic politics in this year 1956"—unloaded a scenario guaranteed to grab Eisenhower's attention. "In 1952, with a war in Korea, you electrified our people and the people of the free world when you said, 'I shall go to Korea.' " What would happen if Adlai Stevenson publicly stated, "I shall call on Nasser" or "I shall call a Summit Conference on the Suez Canal."

Those words prodded Eisenhower into action. He phoned Hoover, concerned that the meetings in New York might fail. Quoting Hagerty's phrases without attribution, Ike wondered whether they should do something, "possibly dramatic, possibly even drastic" and opined that the Suez question "was probably [the] #1 question in the minds of the American people." Eisenhower said he had been persuaded that "we must do something more than talk," and even hinted at negotiating with Nasser.[56]

When Dwight Eisenhower wrote a subordinate a personal, same-day letter following a phone call, it unmistakably signaled that the chief wanted something done, and done quickly. Ike's letter to Hoover repeated Hagerty's proposal for "a White House statement outlining our position and detailing our step-by-step moves to keep the peace," and warning that the United States "will not support a war or warlike moves in the Suez area." Negotiation would continue until "a peaceful but just solution is reached—regardless of how long it takes"—words drawn directly from the press secretary's memorandum. He echoed Hagerty's assertion that Nasser was already "a world figure" and raised the possibility of the need for a summit meeting. Ike wrote that he was sending Hoover these ideas "as a clear indication of my readiness to participate in any way in which I can be helpful."[57]

Hoover was taken aback by his suddenly assertive president. He sent the letter to Dulles with a cover note, saying that "as a result of the political situation, the President may feel under some pressure to take a more direct part in the proceedings." The next day, after talking with Eisenhower, Dulles told Hoover he had concluded that he should return to address the president's concerns, even though returning to Washington in the middle of the closed-door talks "looks like a crisis." Dulles did not welcome this sudden activism on Eisenhower's part, just when he was trying to jump-start negotiations between the allies and the Egyptians. Dulles sent Eisenhower a detailed memorandum on Wednesday addressing his Hagerty-sourced ideas and saying he wanted "to personally discuss them with him." [58]

Dulles knew he needed to get to the president before he met with reporters. The next day, back in Washington, Dulles and Hoover briefed Eisenhower prior to his news conference. [59] The important news he shared was that Dag Hammarskjöld had arranged a meeting in his office with the British, French, and Egyptian foreign ministers—Lloyd, Pineau, and Fawzi. The secretary depicted Lloyd as "groping for some practical solution," Pineau as "unsympathetic," and Fawzi as "somewhat evasively disposed to move toward what might be an acceptable solution." Eisenhower repeated his adamant opposition to military action against Egypt.

Ike brought up the Hagerty plan without revealing its source. But Dulles was determined not to let the politically anxious president torpedo the secret negotiations going on in New York. He placated Eisenhower, assuring him that actions similar to what the president proposed were already in progress and that, if a real crisis arose, Dulles might "want to call on him to make some move."

Then Eisenhower asked about the alleged "differences" between the British and the United States, obviously seeking something to say to the reporters. Dulles either deliberately misled the president or, more likely, he was suggesting a political stance the president could take at his news conference: the secretary said he "was not aware of any, and on the contrary had been assured by both Lloyd and earlier by Eden of their great appreciation of my sticking with them." Dulles had given Ike what he needed, however contrary to the facts of the situation. Ike sounded reassured, saying he might mention Dulles's assessment to reporters.

At his news conference, Eisenhower departed from his usual reluctance to comment on the Suez crisis. [60] In contrast to previous sessions, his demeanor was decisive. When given an opening, he brought up the allegation that American policy "has not been clear and firm. This is an error." He reminded the press of four principles integral to the eighteen-power agreement that the delegation had carried to Cairo—respect for Egyptian sovereignty, "efficient operation of the Canal," avoidance of use of the canal for the political purposes of any country, and a "fair and increasing share of the profits to Egypt and profits to no one else."

When asked about anti-American sentiment in London and Paris, Eisenhower misled the press with Dulles's fabrication about the growing rift with the allies. He said he had asked the secretary of state that morning whether he had any indication that the British "were dissatisfied with our stand in this thing, or thought that we had been vacillating and not carrying forward as we started out. He hasn't and I assure you that I haven't." Ike amplified this extraordinary statement. "Our friendships with Britain are very, very important to us," the president said, "not only sentimentally but officially, politically, economically, and militarily.... The same goes for France," he said. "So," Eisenhower concluded, "I think these things arise out of misunderstandings, which I hope can be cleared up soon." This was a patently political performance, less than a month before the election; Ike had clearly decided that the electorate would not support an open break with the British and the French.[61]

Foster Dulles had rushed back to New York to make sure the tense private negotiations continued. The French were being difficult, he told Carl W. McCardle, the assistant secretary for public affairs. Pineau, "in a very unhappy mood," had been ordered "to have nothing to do with any negotiation at all." Due to Einsehower's strong statement at his news conference, there were rumors that the president would travel to New York to join in the negotiations. Later that day, Ike nurtured the fantasy of warm British-American relations in a letter to Anthony Eden, writing that "I deeply deplore the suggestions of the press both here and abroad that you and we are at cross purposes." Ike added, in a P.S., "I got a chance, at this morning's Press Conference, to say something on how much Britain & the British mean to us."[62]

"A POLITICIAN THESE DAYS"
The president was delayed for a few minutes at the beginning of the National Security Council meeting on Friday, October 12.[63] He walked into the room, apologized, and reminded council members that he was "a politician these days."

Even in the NSC, Ike and Dulles put a happy face on a bad situation. Hoover reported on the negotiations in New York, and that Secretary Dulles believed that "early agreement in principle was a possibility"; the British, unlike the French, "were showing a marked disposition to compromise with the Egyptians." Eisenhower candidly discussed his and Dulles's strategy of delay to drain the emotions of war. They had agreed that "if the United States could just keep the lid on a little longer, some kind of compromise plan could be worked out for a settlement of the Suez problem."

Ike concluded: "Time and time alone will cure the disease. The only question was whether we could be sure of the time."

At the United Nations Security Council meeting that same day, Secretary-General Hammarskjöld presented six principles for resolving the Suez issue: free and open transit through the canal, respect for Egyptian sovereignty, nonpolitical operation of the canal, tolls fixed in agreement between users and Egypt, allocation of a proportion of the revenue to developing the canal, and, in the case of disputes, a mechanism for arbitration. After the session, Dulles called Eisenhower to report that the British, French, Egyptians, and Russians had all endorsed the six principles. Dulles said this meant that "the status quo will be preserved for quite a while and there will be no use of force." He was naively hopeful about the intent of the European allies. "The British and French have done an awful good job here so far," he said. Dulles called Ike's press conference statements "perfect." [64]

That evening, Eisenhower appeared on a televised program, *The People Ask the President*.[65] Still following the Hagerty strategy, the president decided to make a big thing out of something he knew to be small. "I have an announcement," he began. "I have got the best announcement that I think I could possibly make to America tonight." Ike called the progress on the Suez situation at the United Nations "most gratifying." Egypt, France, and Britain had "agreed on a set of principles on which to negotiate; and it looks like here is a very great crisis behind us." The president said he had talked with Secretary Dulles just before the broadcast "and I will tell you that in both his heart and mine at least, there is a very great prayer of thanksgiving."

Eisenhower stuck to his script when asked about alleged British distress at the indecisiveness of American policy. He admitted to some British misunderstanding of American motives but "we were determined to pursue a course that would not lead to war." He called for "peace with justice," which required that his administration "be fair to our great allies in the West" and "equally fair to all the Arab world." That effort had been "a hard and weary row" with "many sleepless hours," but "we have taken one long step forward." He proudly asserted that "the steadfast adherence of this Government to one single policy has borne fruit."

On Saturday, October 13, the British and the French jointly introduced a draft resolution to the United Nations Security Council, designed to perpetuate the fraudulent appearance of their peaceful intentions. The resolution invoked the six principles, touted SCUA and its ability to collect tolls as a fulfillment of those principles, and invited the French, British, and Egyptian governments to continue discussions. The Soviet Union immediately cast a veto that killed the measure, apparently on the grounds that it was contrary to Egyptian interests and sovereignty.[66]

In spite of that news, on Sunday morning, Ike and Dulles expressed fragile hopes for the closed-door negotiations in New York. After church, Eisenhower remarked to a reporter that "it looked a little bad last night on the Suez thing, but things look better again today." At National Airport in Washington, the secretary said to reporters that, while the Soviet veto was a setback, there were "good grounds for hope" for a peaceful settlement and that negotiations would "go ahead just as though there had not been a veto."[67]

Later that day, Dulles called Eisenhower to congratulate him on his sixty-sixth birthday. Things had gone "fairly well" at the United Nations, the secretary reported, and closed-door negotiations were continuing under the auspices of Hammarskjöld. Ike was "relieved to hear this." He had heard a radio commentator allege that the negotiations were "in a state of collapse." Dulles guessed that such an assessment rested on the inevitability of the Soviet veto. Ike would have been more concerned had he known that Anthony Eden was secretly meeting that day with France's acting foreign minister, Albert Gazier, and deputy chief of staff General Maurice Challet at Chequers, the prime minister's country house, to review Anglo-French plans to seize control of the Suez Canal.[68]

SMOKE SCREENS

By Monday, October 15, the British, French, and Israelis had crystallized three strategies to deceive their American ally about what they were planning. That day, Dulles returned to Washington to meet with Eisenhower, Hoover, and assistant secretary Rountree to address smoke screen number one, the contrived appearance that Israel was preparing to make a major attack on Jordan.

That misperception was strengthened when, on October 10, the Israelis, in the dark of night, had launched a raid across the Jordanian border into the village of Qalqilya, northeast of Tel Aviv, killing forty-eight civilians. The Israeli government justified the raid as retaliation for the death of two citrus workers the day before—a rationale U.N. observers doubted. But as a maneuver to camouflage plans for attacking Egypt, it worked. Dulles told Eisenhower that he feared that Israel might take advantage of three circumstances—Jordan's virtual collapse, the preoccupation of Egypt and the Western powers with Suez, and elections in the United States, implying that Israel might be tempted to annex a segment of that unstable country.[69]

Eisenhower was disturbed by this news. After meeting with Dulles, Ike asserted forcefully in his diary that the Israelis "must stop these attacks." He had ordered Dulles to bluntly inform Israeli ambassador Abba Eban that "no consideration of partisan politics will keep this government from pursuing a course dictated by justice and international decency in the circumstances, and that it will remain true to its pledges under the United Nations." Eisenhower could not know that Israel's attack on Jordan was designed to reinforce the impression—smoke screen number one—that if Israel took military action anywhere, it would be against Jordan.[70]

Smoke screen number two involved the pretense that the allies intended to pursue SCUA as an alternative to war. Foster Dulles was deceived by that one in a meeting with Selwyn Lloyd on Sunday, the day before he met with the president. That conversation was so fractious that Dulles had chosen not to tell the president about it. No minutes of this meeting exist but the issues the two men had argued about were summarized in follow-up letters that crossed one another in the mail. Lloyd's letter expressed shock that Dulles, while willing to consider paying transit tolls to SCUA, had insisted that 90 percent of the revenues be transferred to Egypt.[71] "I cannot," Lloyd contended, "believe that is what you really intend." Lloyd insisted on the need for "some means of pressure as a counterpoise to Egypt's physical possession of the Canal." SCUA could provide that "bargaining power," he wrote. The British "have not admitted the validity of nationalization" and therefore did not admit Egypt's right to canal tolls after July 26. The foreign minister called this disagreement "a testing time for Anglo-American relations. . . . I am afraid that," Lloyd concluded, "if we cannot reach [an] agreement, SCUA will prove to have been stillborn, and the prospects of a peaceful settlement with Egypt will be gravely diminished."

In his letter, Dulles attempted "to straighten the matter out."[72] He wrote that the proposal to impound the tolls and pass nothing to Egypt was "quite contrary" to his original proposal. This would violate the American commitment to work cooperatively with Egypt. "What would happen," Dulles asked, "if, following the payment of dues to SCUA and their impounding, all our ships were denied access to the Canal?" He repeated his public assertion that the United States did not intend to "shoot its way through the Canal." Dulles must have felt like matters were coming unglued. He had encouraged the president to publicly state that there was no serious disagreement with the British. That fiction had been shattered. Dulles did not understand that the argument was a charade, but he knew one thing with certainty: he was rapidly running out of alternatives to war.[73]

Lloyd had fulfilled his assignment. He had shrewdly drawn Dulles into the quagmire of smoke screen number two—the British pretense that SCUA really mattered when his government was, in fact, preparing for war. Following Lloyd's meeting with Dulles, Eden directed the foreign minister to fly back to London to follow up with him on the prime minister's October 14 meeting with French officials at Chequers. On the 16th, Eden and Lloyd flew to Paris for a five-hour secret meeting with Mollet and Pineau, to work on the details of a war plan that included a role for the Israelis.[74]

The American intelligence community completely missed what was transpiring. On October 16, the very day that British and French officials were meeting secretly in Paris, CIA director Allen Dulles chaired a meeting of the Intelligence Advisory Committee.[75] The group reviewed a CIA working memorandum that, regarding the Arab-Israeli conflict, focused almost exclusively on the border tensions with Jordan, swallowing the allies' carefully contrived strategy to make the Americans believe that if Israel took aggressive action it would be against Jordan.

As for Suez, the memorandum showed that the CIA analysts had bought into smoke screen number three—British, French, and Egyptian acceptance of Hammarskjöld's six principles, and their commitment to additional face-to-face talks "in the next two or three weeks, or even earlier," as the memorandum stated it. While negotiations would "not be easy," the CIA analysts said they thought that additional concessions by the Western powers might "gain final agreement with Egypt."

Regarding the possibility of war, the memorandum read: "While the possibility of force by the UK and France has not been eliminated, we believe it does not constitute an immediate threat." The group, under Allen Dulles's leadership, concurred with the CIA's judgment that "revisions of the prior special estimates on the Suez Situation, or of the most recent estimative judgments of the IAC with respect to the likelihood of a major Arab-Israeli conflict, were not warranted at this time."

That day, Tuesday, October 16, President and Mrs. Eisenhower left in the morning for a campaign trip to the West, the longest and most demanding of the campaign. Ike would make appearances in Minnesota, Washington, Oregon, California, and Colorado before returning on Saturday. His agreement to undertake this stressful tour proved that his words to Swede Hazlett following the announcement of his candidacy on February 29 had been prophetic: "Politicians begin to get scared about the middle of October." [76]

But even on this campaign trip, Ike could not put the Middle East behind him. On Wednesday, he called Foster Dulles, asking if there was any news on Suez. Dulles grumbled that he had no news and that they had not been "fully posted about what was going on between the British and the French." Dulles belatedly confessed to Eisenhower that he had received "a rather disturbing letter from Selwyn Lloyd." Ambassador Lodge was to have lunch with Hammarskjöld and hoped to gain some new information. [77]

Then the allies nailed a date onto smoke screen number three. Lodge called Secretary Dulles to tell him that Hammarskjöld thought that Egypt, France, and the United Kingdom wanted another closed-door meeting and were considering October 29 in Geneva. This was a ruse; Dulles did not know that the allies had no intention of negotiating further with Egypt. Dulles dutifully informed Eisenhower that afternoon of Lodge's report and the possible resumption of talks. Eisenhower wondered, "Can't we get word to the Egyptians not to believe all they read but go on and negotiate?" [78]

On Thursday, a worried Foster Dulles called his brother Allen, complaining that the British and French "are deliberately keeping us in the dark." Others in the American government were equally jumpy. Yet American intelligence sources in London had failed to learn that Anthony Eden had hinted to the British cabinet that day that the conflict with Egypt might "be brought to a head as a result of military action by Israel against Egypt." At a Joint Chiefs–State Department meeting on October 19, Admiral Radford speculated that war was imminent because the British and French could not delay action much longer. Radford pointed to the financial costs of building up their forces in the Mediterranean and "the problem of keeping troops in a state of readiness over a long period." British and French leaders were, indeed, increasingly concerned about that reality, receiving reports that their troops, waiting in Malta, Cyprus, and Libya, were becoming bored and restless. [79]

The Middle East was not the only unstable spot in the international scene. In June, industrial workers in Poznan, Poland, had gone on strike for bread and freedom and the brutal repression of the riots by the pro-Soviet government generated concern in the Kremlin that the satellite nations were in danger of breaking away. Unrest had continued sporadically until, on October 19, Nikita Khrushchev had led a Soviet delegation to Poland and threatened to use the army to crush the rebellion, then backed away from that action. Meanwhile, the unrest in the Soviet satellites had spread to Hungary. Student protests erupted in Budapest and, from mid-October onward, Soviet control over Hungary was increasingly tenuous.[80]

MISLEADING THE AMBASSADORS

Ambassadors Aldrich in London and Dillon in Paris present a case study in ambassadorial misjudgment. They completely missed the signals that the allies had agreed upon a full-scale program of deception. On being informed of Dulles's argument with Selwyn Lloyd, Aldrich went to see the British foreign minister. Lloyd charmed Aldrich into believing that Washington was exaggerating a conflict over short-term tactics for pressuring Egypt by impounding canal tolls. Aldrich advised Dulles, "I believe the situation is fundamentally less divergent than the two communications so far exchanged would suggest, at least in relation to the long term." He continued, "I do feel that the govt is disposed to try to promote a solution through negotiations rather than the contrary." The ambassador could not have been more wrong.[81]

Douglas Dillon was no less gullible. He ran into the same ruse that Lloyd had used to mislead Aldrich—that the difference between the French and American positions "was one of time table." The French misled Dillon with smoke screen number two, that the impounding of canal dues in the interim would pressure the Egyptians to make a final settlement. SCUA would go fully into effect around November 1, with toll payments to the association beginning after the American election. Dillon took this to mean that the French did "not contemplate any military action prior to approximately Nov. 10." A high source within the French government had convinced him that the French "do not want military action and hope to avoid it."[82]

Neither Dulles nor his ambassadors understood that this dialogue was a hoax. Dulles, weary and frustrated, had swallowed the pretense that the administration of SCUA was a real issue, writing Lloyd again about how "disturbed" he was by the foreign minister's willingness to abandon the original idea of SCUA—an "on-the-spot" practical arrangement with

Egypt that would, "in fact, amount to an international participation in the operation of the Canal." U.N. Ambassador Lodge reported to Dulles that Secretary-General Hammarskjöld had learned that Nasser was open to SCUA becoming a useful negotiating body "without the taint of being a pressure device—if it were, he would not play with it." Lodge, along with the rest of the diplomatic corps, mistakenly concluded that "things are in good shape." [83]

Foster Dulles's anxieties were heightened when on October 19 a message arrived from Nikolai Bulganin. [84] The Soviet premier alluded to Adlai Stevenson's proposed ban on nuclear testing, called for an "unconditional prohibition" of nuclear weapons, impugned the integrity of the secretary of state, and accused the president of "bad faith." Eisenhower was campaigning in the West and could not deal with the message until he returned. Dulles was beside himself about it. The evening of October 20, he interrupted his attendance at the musical *Auntie Mame* at the National Theatre to call Hagerty and the president about the message. Dulles later told General Beetle Smith, the retired CIA director, that there had "never been a diplomatic note so crass as this one." Dulles hoped that Bulganin's endorsement would be "the kiss of death" for Stevenson because Soviet support "would be the last thing he would want." Meanwhile, Stevenson was on the attack, charging in a speech in Cincinnati that Eisenhower had misled the country with his optimistic statement on television on October 12 about the acceptance of the six principles by the parties to the Suez dispute. "Why didn't the President tell us the truth," Stevenson asked, instead of seeking to make "political capital out of a crisis that could engulf the world." [85]

Eisenhower, back at the White House after his Western trip, met with Dulles on Sunday morning. The secretary proposed returning Bulganin's message without an answer, which the Soviet leader would be bound to interpret as a diplomatic slap in the face. Eisenhower thought that such an action could be interpreted as "a break in relations." Ike wanted the response to sound more "surprised" than angry. Still, Ike's final letter was forceful. It deplored the Soviet premier's sending such a message during the presidential campaign. Eisenhower called the criticisms of the secretary of state "personally offensive" and regretted that Bulganin had seen fit "to impugn my own sincerity." [86]

A PHANTOM DATE

On Monday, October 22, there was a new, puzzling—at least to American leaders—development regarding the planned resumption of closed-door Suez talks in Geneva. Hammarskjöld informed Ambassador Lodge that the British and French had demanded a written proposal for protecting canal user rights from the Egyptian government before they would be willing to resume talks on October 29. This was a variation on smoke screen number three, designed to keep the Egyptians and the Americans focused on the minutiae of negotiations while Britain, France, and Israel prepared for war. Dulles told Ambassador Lodge that he was suspicious of the demand for a written proposal—he said it was contrary to "trading instincts." Lodge reported to Dulles that the secretary-general did not think "the situation had gone to pieces, but that it had slowed down a bit." Dulles said that his best information, based on Douglas Dillon's erroneous report, was that the French would stall until after the U.S. election and even then not be inclined to use force; but, he granted, "It is not over." Dulles cabled Dillon, asking him to inform the French that they were mistaken if they thought "our opposition to the use of force in connection with Suez results from an election situation and that we might not be as strongly opposed after the election." [87]

More signs of deterioration appeared on October 23. The British ambassador to the United Nations, Pierson Dixon, took Lodge aside to say that he was worried. The Egyptians had presented the requested proposal but the British did not like it and now the meeting on October 29 was in question. Lodge informed Dulles that Dixon claimed to be particularly concerned about Anglo-American relations. Dulles repeated to Lodge that he thought the British and French were "inclined to stall until after [the] election and with the feeling that probably we will be more disposed to back the use of force." Dulles told Lodge: "Of course we will not—the Pres. feels strongly against it." [88]

But now, Eisenhower and Dulles had more than the Middle East to worry about. The installation of a more liberal government in Poland had stimulated new protests in Hungary. The communist government of Hungary appealed for help from Soviet troops already stationed in that country. After riots escalated on October 23, Soviet tanks and soldiers moved into Budapest, preparing to put down the uprising. [89]

Unknown to Dulles and Eisenhower, on October 22, delegations from

Israel, Britain, and France had arrived under a shroud of secrecy at the secluded villa of the Bonnier de la Chapelles in Sèvres, just outside Paris. Christian Pineau, the French foreign minister, had gone home, and then driven his personal car to Sèvres to avoid being followed. The Israeli delegation, led by Prime Minister Ben-Gurion and chief of staff Moshe Dayan, had flown into a French military airport and had traveled to Sèvres in an unmarked car. Selwyn Lloyd, the British foreign secretary, arrived about 7:00 P.M., traveling, in his words, "incognito." [90]

Israel wanted all three powers to attack Egypt at the same time but the British refused, insisting on a more innocent-appearing pretext for intervention. Moshe Dayan suggested that Israel could make a raid near the canal, giving the British and French a reason to call for withdrawal of both Israeli and Egyptian forces to protect the traffic in the Suez Canal. When Lloyd proved reluctant, Pineau flew to London on October 23 and persuaded Eden to sign off on the Dayan plan. That arrangement would allow Eden and Lloyd to perpetuate the fiction, even in their memoirs, that they had not conspired with the Israelis. [91]

The stage was set for the signing of a formal agreement for launching an attack on Egypt.

9

★★★★★★

DOUBLE-CROSSING IKE

October 24–October 31, 1956

"Those who began this operation should be left to work out
their own oil problems—to boil in their own oil."

Eisenhower to Arthur Flemming, October 30, 1956

WEDNESDAY, OCTOBER 24

On Wednesday, October 24, three events caused the geopolitical landscape
to shudder beneath Dwight Eisenhower's feet. That afternoon, at Sèvres
outside Paris, Christian Pineau, the French foreign minister, Prime Minister
David Ben-Gurion of Israel, and Patrick Dean, the deputy undersecretary
of state for Great Britain, secretly signed a protocol providing that Israeli
troops would invade the Sinai Peninsula on October 29—ironically, the
date publicly set for resuming negotiations with the Egyptians. Anthony
Eden and Selwyn Lloyd had chosen not to attend, sending Dean so they
could maintain deniability and keep the conspiracy at arm's length. The
plan was that once the Israelis began to advance toward the Suez Canal
Zone, Britain and France would issue an ultimatum to Israel and Egypt to
cease fighting and accept Anglo-French occupation of the Canal Zone. If
Egypt, as expected, rejected the ultimatum, Britain and France would begin
bombardment on October 31, followed by troop landings.[1]

October 24 was also the day when Egypt, Syria, and Jordan signed a military agreement aimed at "the joint defense of the Arab front under a unified command to repulse any attack launched at any of the three states, on the consideration that such an aggression would be an attack against them all."[2]

Finally, October 24 was the day when, in response to protests in Hungary, the Soviet Union ordered ten thousand troops, along with tanks, artillery, and armored cars, into Budapest. That afternoon, when workers and students demonstrated in Parliament Square, the police and Soviet tanks opened fire, killing and wounding many of the protesters. The next day, the *New York Times* reported that an estimated 150 to 200 demonstrators had been killed.[3]

Eisenhower knew nothing of the secret meeting at Sèvres. The CIA failed completely to detect what was happening there. Chester Cooper, representing the CIA on the joint British-American intelligence committee, was good friends with the chairman of that group, Sir Patrick Dean. Cooper missed a clear hint of the conspiracy when he attended dinner at the Dean home on the 24th, only to be told by the British official's wife that "Pat has been called away suddenly." Dean was in Paris, substituting for Foreign Secretary Selwyn Lloyd in signing the secret agreement to attack Egypt. That day in Washington, the Intelligence Advisory Committee, chaired by Allen Dulles, gave Eisenhower no clues as to the emerging conspiracy among his allies. Assuming no imminent actions, the committee postponed further revision of intelligence estimates "at least for another week." The report noted, almost as an afterthought, that the FBI had picked up a rumor that an unnamed country "was considering the initiation of military action against Nasser," but the advisory committee failed to take it seriously.[4]

At 11:30 A.M. on the 24th—about the time that Chester Cooper was preparing to attend dinner at the Dean residence—Foster Dulles and Eisenhower met, both suspicious that danger was afoot. The secretary fretted that the French and British had instituted an almost complete communication blackout. Ambassador Winthrop Aldrich had reported that the British minister of defense, Walter Monckton, had resigned because he was unwilling to do what might be required if a decision was made to attack Egypt. The president and Dulles discussed the possibility of inviting Eden and Premier Mollet to visit Washington after the November election. That invitation, Ike told Dulles, "would not stand if in the meantime the British and French engaged in military action against Egypt." Dulles expressed his "great concern" that the British and the French would "commit suicide" by attempting to reimpose their rule on the Middle East and Africa. The president "fully shared" the secretary's concerns.[5]

Ike still had an election to win—now only two weeks away. That afternoon he answered questions in a televised program aimed at women voters. When asked about the Suez Canal, Ike launched into a historical dissertation that revealed little of substance. He endorsed Egyptian sovereignty, saying that "no one can challenge the legal right of Egypt to nationalize the Canal." The president reminded his audience of the importance of "this great waterway on which so much of the economy of the world depends" but waved off further discussion by calling this "a very complicated question" on which he "could talk all afternoon."[6]

THURSDAY, OCTOBER 25

As October 25 dawned, U.N. secretary-general Dag Hammarskjöld was valiantly trying to prevent war in Egypt. He had overseen the first phase of tense, closed-door talks among the British, French, and Egyptians in New York. He shared a draft summary of those discussions with the Americans, British, and French before transmitting it to Mahmoud Fawzi, the Egyptian foreign minister. Hammarskjöld's report envisioned the Egyptian-controlled canal authority negotiating with the new canal users organization on a framework for further talks. In Cairo, Ambassador Raymond Hare talked with Fawzi, who confirmed his government's willingness to continue negotiations on October 29. But Fawzi told Hare that he smelled a trap; he feared that the British and French demand for specific proposals from the Egyptians in advance was a ploy to justify torpedoing the negotiations.[7]

The American ambassadors in London and Paris were blind to what was happening under their noses. Convinced that war was not imminent, both men enthusiastically endorsed inviting the Anglo-French leaders to Washington after the election. Ambassador Douglas Dillon was confident that the French were prepared to let relations with the United States "coast" until the election was over. He thought that both Eden and Mollet would probably accept the invitation, "thus delaying any precipitate action which they might otherwise contemplate."[8]

Eisenhower arose early that Thursday, October 25, prepared for a long day of campaigning. The stresses of foreign crises mixed with political campaigning would have been significant if Eisenhower were a well man; he was not. During the month of October, he had experienced high blood pressure, bursitis, a stubborn upper respiratory infection, periodic heart irregularities, and almost continuous abdominal distress. On October 25, Ike would complain of abdominal pain, and the following day developed a case of diarrhea that lasted for most of a month.[9]

Eisenhower arrived at his office at 7:50 A.M., held two meetings, and a half hour later he and Mrs. Eisenhower departed for Union Station to board a train to New York for a day of campaigning, climaxing with a rally that night at Madison Square Garden. Before they embarked, the president had approved a statement calling the uprising in Hungary "a renewed expression of the intense desire for freedom long held by the Hungarian people." Eisenhower "deplored the intervention of Soviet military forces" whose purpose clearly was "to continue an occupation of Hungary by the forces of an alien government for its own purposes."

When the train reached Pennsylvania Station in New York, Ike and Mamie were met by a large crowd shouting, "I Like Ike!" Eisenhower later recalled how bizarre it felt to engage in the hoopla of campaigning when his thoughts were "absorbed with the international contests that had broken out in several parts of the earth."[10]

At 5:02, Foster Dulles called the president in New York. The convergence of Soviet intervention in Hungary with the Suez crisis had made relations awkward with America's traditional allies. Ike asked if Dulles had talked with the British and French about action on Hungary in the Security Council; Dulles said no, but he was preparing to initiate consultations that night. Dulles wanted to push ahead, even without the allies, because the issue was "hot and better understood now." Eisenhower was reluctant. "If you act in deliberate fashion," he said, "that may be better." Ike "would not do it alone" and was willing to accept even "a grudging assent" from the NATO allies. Both men worried that any action they took might be interpreted as "an election move." "The worst thing" Eisenhower said, "would be to be thought of as guilty of spurious interest."[11]

Eisenhower's speech at Madison Square Garden was a partisan address—dismissing the charges of his Democratic opponents and trumpeting his administration's accomplishments at home and abroad.[12] In foreign affairs, the president celebrated the fact that, on this night, there was no news "from any foreign battlefield calling our sons to danger and death." He extolled the people of Poland and Hungary who were willing to give their lives for freedom. These "are men and women whom America has never forgotten—nor ever will."

Ike did not mention the Middle East. He stated, "As your President, I cannot and will not tell you that our quest for peace will be simple, or its rewards swift. This quest may, in fact, cost us much—in labor and in sacrifice." At 9:35, the Eisenhowers departed Madison Square Garden for the return trip to Washington.[13]

FRIDAY, OCTOBER 26

On the morning of October 26, the U.S. Army attaché at the American embassy in Tel Aviv reported to Washington that the Israelis were mobilizing their armed forces on "a very large scale." In response to the embassy's query about the purpose of the troop call-up, Israeli authorities had resorted to their carefully planned smoke screen, citing the new Egyptian-Syrian-Jordanian military command and promoting the false impression that any Israeli military action would be against Jordan. The American ambassador, Edward Lawson, reported to the State Department that the Israeli press was speculating that "something big may happen."[14]

The National Security Council that morning addressed, in Eisenhower's words, "a scattering of reports from around the globe, all disquieting."[15] A rumor was discussed that the king of Jordan had been assassinated. Secretary Dulles feared that Jordan might disintegrate, leading to war between Israel and the Arabs. There were riots in Singapore and unrest in North Africa. But, Ike recalled, "the compelling news continued to be Hungary."

DCI Allen Dulles suggested that, due to the unrest in Poland and Hungary, Khrushchev, the Soviet Communist Party's first secretary, might be in trouble in the Soviet hierarchy. Eisenhower expressed concern that instability in the Soviet government might threaten world peace. He was concerned that if the Soviet leaders were losing control over the satellites, "might they not be tempted to resort to very extreme measures and even to precipitate global war?" Eisenhower called this "a situation which must be watched with the utmost care." He recalled that Hitler had known he was beaten in early 1945 but continued to fight, devastating Europe. "The Soviets might," he said, "even develop some desperate mood such as this."[16]

In mid-afternoon, Ambassador Winthrop Aldrich in London informed Foster Dulles that he had encountered Anthony Eden in a "mellow, relaxed mood" at dinner, a sharp contrast to the prime minister's usual agitated state. Eden's serenity was contrived; he told the American ambassador a bald-faced lie—that, in his view, the "Israeli-Jordan situation and Egyptian involvement therein is of more fundamental importance even than [the]

Suez problem." The prime minister complained about the lack of progress on negotiations with the Egyptians. Selwyn Lloyd almost stumbled into flagging the secret October 24 agreement, when he added that it was "still uncertain whether negotiations would take place [in] Geneva October 29." The American ambassador was remarkably naive about how the British leaders were deceiving him. He now believed that the previously hostile British attitude toward Egypt was "a temporary manifestation," and that Eden and Lloyd were embarrassed because they had overreacted to the seizure of the Suez Canal.[17]

None of this sounded right to Foster Dulles. He shared with Henry Cabot Lodge his "sense of foreboding" about what the British, French, and Israelis were planning. "It looks bad all along the line," he said. "They may be going in to fight." Later, Dulles cabled Aldrich about his suspicion that there was "a deliberate British purpose of keeping us completely in the dark as to their intentions with reference to Middle East matters generally and Egypt in particular."[18]

At such a moment, every public statement was precarious. Twice during the day, Dulles talked to Eisenhower on the phone about a speech the secretary was scheduled to deliver in Dallas, reviewing in particular his planned comments about Poland and Hungary. In the second discussion, Ike commented that the evening papers seemed to indicate that the Hungarian rebellion "is spreading." Eisenhower believed that British support was essential in the Security Council in order to discourage more drastic Soviet military actions. He wanted Dulles to tell the British that the Soviet repression was "so terrible we would be remiss if we did not do something." The president warned Admiral Radford, the chairman of the Joint Chiefs, and Allen Dulles, the CIA director, "to be unusually watchful and alert during the crisis occasioned by the Hungarian revolt."[19]

Press secretary Jim Hagerty was good at his job. He clearly understood his dual mission—to inform the press and, above all, to protect the president. His stellar achievement since September 24, 1955, had been the preservation of Eisenhower's image as a vigorous, essentially healthy man of action. With Stevenson making the president's health a campaign issue, the press secretary's nightmare would be another presidential illness—or even the rumor of one.

On that Friday morning, Hagerty stared down at an advance copy of columnist Drew Pearson's "Washington Merry-Go-Round," to be published the following day.[20] Pearson's column alleged that the president had suffered "a mild relapse" on his Western campaign trip the previous week; that driving back to the airport from an appearance in Minneapolis, Ike had suddenly turned to others in his limousine and said, "I can't take any more of this. Let's get out of here." The president's car, Pearson alleged, had been pulled out of the motorcade and rushed to his plane. When the president's party arrived in Seattle, Ike had reportedly refused to do anything for twenty-four hours. After his Portland speech, according to Pearson, the television microphones had picked up Ike reassuring Mamie, "I'm all right, I'm all right, I feel fine." Once back in Washington, Pearson wrote, Ike had canceled all major events—a press conference, an address to the United Nations on Atoms for Peace, and a motorcade through New York City. The president was scheduled for a "head-to-toe" physical examination at Walter Reed Hospital on Saturday, October 27—apparently, Pearson reasoned, the result of the incident on the Western trip. Pearson reported that Adlai Stevenson might call for an examination of the president by a bipartisan group of doctors.

Hagerty moved with lightning speed to ensure his rebuttal would be printed in the same papers that carried the Pearson column. At 10:30 A.M. on the 26th, the press secretary strode into the press room, waved the Pearson article at reporters, and called it "the most amazing document of falsehoods that I have ever seen." Hagerty insisted that the president's checkup had been scheduled for months. "At no time," Hagerty fumed, "did the President's car leave the motorcade" in Minnesota, nor had he failed to bid farewell to local dignitaries. Instead of being closeted in his hotel room in Seattle, the president had greeted Republican leaders and had gone to the twelfth floor to speak to 125 members of the state Republican Finance Committee. The president had gotten some confetti in his eye and Ike's statement about being "all right" to Mrs. Eisenhower was probably about his bloodshot eye. The canceled events were explainable, including the United Nations speech, due to "a certain amount of unrest in the satellite nations."

"I am trying not to get mad," Hagerty exclaimed, "but I think this is about as worse a job of reporting as I ever saw." When a reporter asked again, "Did the President, at any time on that trip, have a relapse—a mild relapse?" Hagerty replied: "Absolutely and categorically NO."

Actually, Pearson had much of the story correct, with some exaggeration. The core charge was that Ike had "closeted" himself in his suite in Seattle for twenty-four hours, seeing no one except his physician and family. Hagerty tried to confuse the reporters with the dates, implying that Ike's activities in Seattle before he retired permanently to his suite at the Olympic Hotel at 6:15 P.M.—greeting his brother Edgar and others at a reception at the airport and speaking briefly to a group of Republicans on the hotel's twelfth floor—were performed in the midst of Pearson's alleged twenty-four hours of isolation. In fact, Eisenhower did not leave his suite, nor did he have any meetings, from 6:15 P.M. on October 16 until 7:25 P.M. on the 17th—clearly twenty-four hours—when he departed for the Civic Auditorium to give his address. Dr. Howard Snyder's notes confirm that "the President and First lady spent the entire day in the Hotel."

That night, after motoring to Tacoma, Ike was highly agitated and did not get to sleep until 1:00 A.M. He was, Snyder observed, "quite exhausted" and his blood pressure and pulse were elevated. In the early afternoon the next day, the presidential party flew to Portland and arrived at the Multnomah Hotel about 3:20. Snyder again noted that Ike had endured "a fatiguing experience" in Tacoma. "The President," Snyder recorded in his log, "was emotionally upset because of exhaustion of these three days and at the prospect of the requirements for the days to come." Two hours later, Ike's pulse, the doctor noted, "was 100 and irregular." It remained as high and irregular just before he delivered what Snyder called "a splendid speech." Eisenhower finished the Western trip with stops in Los Angeles and Denver without further problems. But, Hagerty's protestations to the contrary, the president had endured two difficult days on the trip.[21]

SATURDAY, OCTOBER 27

On Saturday, October 27, Eisenhower arrived at his office shortly after eight, and conferred with speechwriters on the addresses he planned to make on a campaign trip to Miami and Jacksonville, Florida, and Richmond, Virginia—all to be delivered on Monday the 29th. The signals from Britain, France, and Israel continued to be contradictory. Selwyn Lloyd deceptively led Winthrop Aldrich to believe that the British were continuing to discuss negotiating with the Egyptians with Hammarskjöld. Edward Lawson, the American ambassador to Israel, wired Secretary Dulles that the Israeli mobilization had "continued beyond [a] point reached at any time during previous crises." A U-2 flight over British bases in Cyprus revealed large numbers of bombers and transport planes, and another U-2 pilot photographed a squadron of French fighter-bombers on an Israeli airfield.[22]

At 11:00 A.M., Eisenhower met with Foster Dulles, Herbert Hoover, and William Rountree.[23] Dulles reported that the issue of Hungary was scheduled to be placed on the Security Council agenda. "The revolt," Dulles continued, "has become widespread." Segments of the Hungarian armed forces had joined the rebels. Eisenhower said he was "happy" that he had made a statement about the Hungarian rebellion.

On the Middle East, Dulles reported that Israel's mobilization increased "the danger that they might make some substantial move." Both Dulles and Rountree assumed, erroneously, that Jordan would be the probable target of any Israeli military action. Dulles suggested that Eisenhower send a letter to Ben-Gurion, which they composed immediately. In the letter, Eisenhower focused on Jordan, imploring the prime minister to end the mobilization and signaling to the Israeli leader that the smoke screen had worked with the Americans. "These are days of great strain," the president wrote, calling for "statesmanship of a high order and self restraint by all parties."[24]

That evening, a worried Foster Dulles dispatched a telegram to embassies in the Middle East urging each mission to "be on alert" regarding the safety of American citizens. Events could move so rapidly that the embassies might need to "take urgent action" before they could be ordered to evacuate by the State Department. In this communication, Dulles perpetuated the hoax that the Israelis had so skillfully propagated, repeating that the "greatest danger lies in Jordan."[25]

Meanwhile, at 2:10 P.M., accompanied by General Snyder, Ike had left the White House to drive to Walter Reed Hospital for his overnight physical examination—his final checkup before the election.[26]

SUNDAY, OCTOBER 28

On Sunday, in London, while Eisenhower was at Walter Reed, Chester Cooper, the CIA liaison with British intelligence, picked up more clues that something was up. His friend, Patrick Dean, was Foreign Secretary Selwyn Lloyd's top aide, the chairman of the joint British-American intelligence committee on which Cooper served, and the man who, unknown to Cooper, had signed the secret agreement on behalf of the British government on October 24 at Sèvres. The Deans and the Coopers were planning to take their families for a drive in the country. Dean, according to Cooper, phoned and, sounding "distraught," said that he had been called to an urgent meeting with the foreign minister. After Dean's meeting ended, the couples belatedly motored into the English countryside. Cooper recalled that Dean's mood was "so morose, so preoccupied." When he pressed his friend as to whether his upset related to Hungary or the Middle East, Dean tersely replied, "You and I are in for much trouble, and it won't be because of Hungary." Cooper pursued this lead the rest of the day but without results. At bedtime, he later recorded, he was "a little worried," but "I slept well—the last night that would happen for quite a while."[27]

At the hospital, Ike read with delight the account of Secretary Dulles's comments upon returning to National Airport from his speaking engagement in Dallas. Reporters had asked the secretary's reaction to a Soviet charge that the United States had provoked the Hungarian uprising. Dulles responded with one word—"Tommyrot"—adding wryly that he did not know if that word would translate into Russian.[28]

Eisenhower could not escape the travails of the Middle East, even at Walter Reed. Hoover came to the hospital to update the president on the latest intelligence. The Israeli mobilization had intensified, reaching 80 percent of maximum, with 170,000 troops on active duty. This put the Israelis, a U.S. Army communiqué had informed the State Department, on the path to "maximum mobilization." The Intelligence Advisory Committee had confirmed major troop and matériel movements and "a state of alert in the Israeli Air Force." Some kind of action was expected in the next twenty-four hours. Eisenhower approved a new cable to Ben-Gurion, urging the Israeli prime minister "to do nothing which would endanger the peace." The White House released a statement by the president that contained similar comments and deplored Israel's mobilization as a threat to peace.[29]

Eisenhower's physical examination was completed by mid-afternoon on Sunday. As anticipated, the doctors found the president to be in good health. In particular, the tests regarding the sources of his two major illnesses—heart and intestine—revealed no problems. There was, the doctors noted, "a well-healed heart muscle scar which had been present since recovery from the attack last year."[30]

Leaving Walter Reed, Ike was energized by his positive checkup. Regardless of the chaos in Hungary and the Middle East, the election beckoned. He returned to his office, called in his speechwriters, and made changes in his planned remarks in the South, including two paragraphs on civil rights that Ann Whitman characterized as "much stronger than anyone around here had dared suggest." This was Eisenhower the master juggler at his best—confronting foreign crises while coping with politics and domestic issues. With a good report from his doctors, the old general was ready to do battle on all fronts, carrying a civil rights message into the South and issuing a clarion call for peace in the Middle East and Europe.[31]

Still, the turmoil in the Middle East left the president, in Emmet Hughes's words, "dismayed, baffled, and fearful of great stupidity about to assert itself." More than once, as he and Hughes worked on speeches, Eisenhower considered calling off his trip to the South. But if he canceled, Hughes recalled Ike saying, "There'd be political yapping all around that the doctors yesterday *really* found I was terribly sick and ready to keel over dead." He fumed about the Israeli mobilization and was particularly infuriated by indications that the British, his close friends, appeared to be conspiring with the French to encourage Israel's aggressive plans. "I can't believe," he said, "they would be so stupid as to invite on *themselves* all the Arab hostility to Israel." Ike sighed as he rose to leave the Oval Office: "Well, I better get out of here or—despite all these doctors—these things will have my blood pressure up to 490."[32]

Later that afternoon, deputy undersecretary of state Robert Murphy and Near East assistant secretary Rountree met with the French ambassador, Herve Alphand, and two British embassy representatives, Sir John E. Coulson and R. W. Bailey. Murphy shared the president's concerns "regarding the imminent danger of an outbreak of hostilities in the Middle East." The envoys claimed to know very little; they may well have been in the dark about their governments' plans. Murphy told them that Eisenhower "takes a very serious view of this evolution of the situation in the Middle East. The President assumes that Paris and London will take a similarly serious view." Then the group reconvened in Foster Dulles's office, so the secretary could apply another layer of pressure.[33]

Dulles called the timing of the Israeli mobilization "very ominous." The French ambassador insisted that he had "no information" regarding the Israeli mobilization. Dulles, reinforcing the red herring of a possible Israeli attack on Jordan, pressed Coulson on whether Great Britain would stand by its treaty obligations to protect Jordan. Coulson had no hesitation on that question and responded affirmatively.[34]

After that meeting, Dulles met with Hoover, Murphy, Rountree, and Phleger, the State Department's legal counsel. He called the president and reported that the French and British representatives "profess to know nothing about this at all." There were fresh signs of a British and French buildup in the Mediterranean. Ike said that he "just cannot believe Britain would be dragged into this." Dulles recommended that American citizens be evacuated from the potential war zone, including Syria, Israel, Jordan, and Egypt. The president wondered if evacuation would "exacerbate the situation." Ike was tempted to wait until morning before issuing an evacuation order, but Dulles quoted the Joint Chiefs to the effect, "If there is an attack, it would really be too late afterwards." Dulles noted that the French and British "have gotten all their people out." Eisenhower reluctantly concurred and said, with resignation, "It will be a world-shocking thing." [35]

Abba Eban was waiting to see Dulles. At seven that evening, Eisenhower called the secretary to find out what the Israeli ambassador had said. Eban had insisted, despite Dulles's doubts, that the Israeli mobilization was "purely defensive." Ike wondered again if he should cancel his trip to Florida. He finally decided against cancellation, hoping for news before his scheduled departure at 8:30 the next morning. Later, Dulles called Eisenhower to share some reassuring news—that the Israelis had made no significant withdrawals on their bank balances in New York. [36]

At 7:45 P.M., Dulles learned from Lodge that Hammarskjöld had received reports of "abnormal military activity" in Israel, including "very heavy troop movements." Ambassador Lawson cabled from Israel: "Military action on a large scale expected in very near future, perhaps within next 24 hours." When Lawson had delivered the president's message to Ben-Gurion at his home, the prime minister had continued to insist that his country's mobilization was a "precautionary measure imposed on us by events." Later, Lawson transmitted an announcement by the Israeli cabinet justifying mobilization, citing the renewal of activities by Egyptian Fedayeen raiders, the new tripartite Arab military alliance, and the presence of Iraqi troops on the Jordanian border. [37]

MONDAY, OCTOBER 29

Eisenhower was in the office by 7:30 on Monday, preparing for his campaign trip to the South. When Foster Dulles called to report that there had been no Israeli military action overnight, Eisenhower dared to hope that the fragile peace could be maintained, noting that events in both Hungary and Israel "seemed a little better this morning than last evening." Ike wondered whether the Soviet Union "might be willing to talk sense now more than at any time since [this] administration has been in power." He told Dulles that Ambassador Bohlen should quietly seek common ground with Soviet leaders because "things are not going the way any of us would want." This, Eisenhower believed, was the time to discuss "reducing tensions in the world." Dulles cautioned against doing anything "that would look to the satellite world as though we were selling them out." Ike told Dulles that the secretary could reach him through Colonel Goodpaster anytime during the day.[38]

After Eisenhower departed, Dulles called his brother Allen and said that there were "a lot of pieces" of evidence that "fitted into a pattern which suggest a high degree of cooperation between the French and the Israelis." "The evidence is almost conclusive," the secretary said. The CIA director had received a report that the Israelis planned to force a ship through the Suez Canal and use its rejection as "an excuse for force." He was concerned that "a spark" in the Middle East "could give the Soviets a shield to do things they can't do now" and that "the clock might be turned back in Central Europe."[39]

Foster Dulles's ambassadors in London and Paris were no help. Winthrop Aldrich, after a two-and-a-half-hour discussion with Selwyn Lloyd, reported that the foreign secretary claimed ignorance of Israeli plans and had identified Jordan as the mostly likely arena for action. Lloyd had stated "categorically," Aldrich reported, that he had "no reason" to believe that the French were conspiring with the Israelis. The bamboozled ambassador was convinced that Lloyd's protestations "carried sufficient conviction for me to conclude that any UK complicity in such a move is unlikely."[40]

By now, Foster Dulles knew better. He cabled Aldrich that "bits of evidence" were mounting that the French government was conspiring with the Israelis to start a war with French and British participation. Dulles shared the president's worst fear—"If [the] French and British allow themselves to be drawn into a general Arab war they will have started something they cannot finish" and thereby drive Arab and African states into the Soviet orbit. He implied that the president had decided that past alliances would not dictate the future. "It is unlikely," Dulles wrote the ambassador, "that [the] US will come to aid of Britain and France as in case of [the] first and second World Wars."[41]

At 11:56 A.M., the president's plane, the *Columbine*, touched down at the airport in Miami. In this first stop in the South, he addressed civil rights, recalling his promise four years earlier "to promote for all citizens equality before the law." Regarding issues abroad, Eisenhower asserted that "the United States cannot exist as an island of prosperity in a world of poverty." But, he somberly added, "Even as we speak this day of our hopes and strivings for peace and justice in the world, we know that there persists real and present danger to that peace. This danger rises in various places; none more critical at this moment than at the ancient crossroads of the world, the Middle East, where whole civilizations meet." Remarkably, Eisenhower did not mention Soviet repression in Hungary as an equivalent threat to world peace.[42]

The president did discuss Hungary at 2:30 when he spoke to a crowd at the Jacksonville airport. Ike deplored what was happening in Hungary, where "we see a once proud people being trampled down by marching regiments." Keeping the peace was Eisenhower's high calling. "Every phrase of our national effort—our economy—our prosperity, our opportunities for education—everything we want—depends upon progress in this reach for peace," he said. "We must move ever forward. We must not let anything tire us. We must never let anything wear out our patience—no matter how serious the problem. We must simply say, 'Then we work the harder.' "[43]

About that time, William Rountree was meeting with Eban trying to pry out of him the purpose of the Israeli mobilization. The ambassador assured Rountree that Israel had no intention of invading Egypt and that, in Rountree's words, "Israeli mobilization has been purely precautionary and protective." Suddenly, an aide handed Rountree a United Press ticker tape: "FLASH-FLASH-FLASH, MAJOR ISRAELI FORCES HAVE INVADED EGYPT AND HEAVY FIGHTING IS UNDERWAY." Rountree handed the flash to Eban, who appeared "flabbergasted." Rountree added, with considerable sarcasm: "I'm certain, Mr. Ambassador, that you will wish to get back to your embassy to find out exactly what is happening in your country."[44]

Eisenhower was boarding his plane for Richmond when Colonel Goodpaster handed him a note stating that the Israeli army had begun an assault on Egypt and that Israeli troops had already progressed to within twenty-five miles of the Suez Canal. The message said that Secretary Dulles wanted to talk with the president when he landed.[45]

The State Department's top diplomats were shocked by the news on the wire services. "I was taken completely by surprise," undersecretary Loy Henderson recalled. The impact on John Foster Dulles, Henderson recounted, was devastating: "I have never seen him more affected by any development. For a time he was a really broken man."[46]

Dulles told Lodge that he intended to call in the British and French ambassadors and "smoke them out to see where they stand." Meanwhile, Dulles heard from Ambassador Hare in Egypt that he had delivered Eisenhower's October 28 statement on the Israeli mobilization to Nasser—a message now drastically out of date. The Egyptian leader, returning from a four-day vacation, had been mystified and wondered out loud to Hare if Israel "really wanted war?" When Hare informed him that the United States was evacuating citizens, Nasser was "at a loss to understand why such action on our part should be felt necessary." Nasser did not know that, at that hour, Israel's forces were already rolling across the Sinai.[47]

In Washington, Secretary Dulles convened his "smoking out" session with the British and French envoys. Both ambassadors were suspiciously unavailable and so he was forced to settle for the second-level ministers, Sir John Coulson and Charles E. Lucet. Dulles urged that the Tripartite Declaration of 1950 be implemented by all three nations—the United States, Britain, and France—and that they take the issue of Israel's invasion to the Security Council. The diplomats either pretended ignorance or were truly in the dark. Coulson said he was "without instructions" but asserted that his government viewed the Tripartite Declaration as inoperative and would not take military action against Israel. Lucet concurred on behalf of the French and echoed Coulson, saying he had "no instructions." Dulles had his answer—the British and French were not going to collaborate in derailing the Israeli invasion; they were not even ready to sign on to something as mild as taking the issue to the Security Council.[48]

On Dulles's orders, Hoover called Lodge to instruct him to seek an urgent meeting of the Security Council the next day. Lodge later called Dulles to report that his conversation with Pierson Dixon, the British ambassador to the United Nations, had been "one of the most disagreeable and unpleasant experiences" he had ever endured. The British ambassador had been "virtually snarling." When Lodge raised their obligations under the Tripartite Declaration, Dixon had said, "Don't be silly and moralistic. We have got to be practical." According to Lodge, the British would not sanction any move against Israel in the Security Council.[49]

The *Columbine* landed in Richmond at 5:49. Ike descended the steps in a somber mood. He had considered canceling his appearance but decided against it, choosing instead to tell the crowd that he would speak "briefly" due to "the lateness of the hour." Jim Hagerty had already called Foster Dulles to tell him the president's party would return to Washington "as fast as we can" and meet at the White House.[50]

A distracted Eisenhower rolled through the obligatory statements of praise for every Republican candidate present, but his mind was elsewhere;

he forgot a congressional candidate and corrected the mistake at the close of his remarks. Afterward, Hagerty issued a statement to the press, drafted by Dulles and edited by the president, citing "disturbing news from the Middle East" and stating the president's intention to consult with the secretary of state as soon as he returned to the White House.[51]

Foster Dulles was agitated as he prepared to meet with the president: he had exhausted himself and damaged his health in a heroic effort to prevent war over the Suez Canal. Now he realized that he and American intelligence had been duped by the British, French, and Israelis. He lamented to William Knowland, the Senate minority leader, that the Israeli action had been "worked out with the French at least and possibly with the British." While he and the president had nursed suspicions about Israeli intentions, he said, "We thought they would attack Jordan."[52]

The Joint Chiefs reacted rapidly to the new situation. They accepted the Intelligence Advisory Committee's conclusion that "the scale and nature of the Israeli attack was sufficient to precipitate war with Egypt," not just a cross-border raid. It was unlikely that the Israelis would pull back. The chiefs placed Army units in Europe and the United States on alert, and ordered the repositioning of the ships of the Sixth Fleet in the Mediterranean, canceling all previously scheduled exercises and establishing a command headquarters on the *Pocono*.[53]

At 7:10, Eisenhower was back in the White House, angrily ordering Dulles to send a message to the Israelis: "Foster, you tell 'em, God-damn-it, that we're going to apply sanctions, we're going to the United Nations, we're going to do everything that there is so we can stop this thing."[54] They were joined by undersecretary of state Herbert Hoover, Secretary of Defense Charles Wilson, Joint Chiefs chairman Admiral Arthur Radford, and CIA director Allen Dulles. Israeli troops had penetrated seventy-five miles into Egyptian territory and were only about twenty miles from the Suez Canal.

The president recalled that the Tripartite Declaration of 1950 stated that America, Britain, and France "would support any victim of aggressions in the Middle East." Secretary Dulles predicted that the Israeli attack would disrupt the canal's traffic and that oil pipelines might be destroyed—an apparent reference to the administration's ongoing concern that, in the event of an Israeli-Egyptian war, pro-Nasser factions might sabotage the pipeline through Syria. Given Europe's dependence on Middle East petroleum, that prospect made British and French intervention inevitable. Dulles suggested that the French and British believed that "we have to go along with them." Eisenhower angrily asked: "What would they think if we were to go in to aid Egypt to fulfill our pledge?" Ike heatedly complained that "nothing justifies double-crossing us." With the election eight days away, Eisenhower insisted that he did "not care in the slightest" whether he was reelected or not. "We must make good on our word," he said. America could not afford to appear like "we are a nation without honor." If the British intervened, "they may open a deep rift between us."

In the midst of the meeting, Eisenhower dispatched a message demanding that Sir John Coulson, the British chargé d'affaires, come to the White House immediately. Coulson raced over and arrived at the Oval Office just as the meeting with the president, the Dulles brothers, Hoover, Wilson, and Radford was breaking up and the group was departing the office to pose for pictures. Coulson greeted a visibly irate President Eisenhower and then had to wait with Goodpaster until the president and the secretary of state returned about 8:15.

Ike was in no mood for small talk with Coulson.[55] The president warned the British diplomat: "If we do not now fulfill our word Russia is likely to enter the situation in the Middle East." He informed Coulson that he intended to take the Israeli invasion to the Security Council "the first thing in the morning—when the doors open—before the USSR gets there." Eisenhower insisted to Coulson that he "would not betray the good word of the United States" and, if necessary, he would call the Congress into special session "to redeem our pledge." In this angry moment, Eisenhower apparently contemplated that he might be compelled to do something extraordinary—intervene on behalf of Egypt and against Israel. The president left no doubt as to his position in the statement issued after the meetings; his and prior administrations had pledged "to assist the victim of any aggression in the Middle East. We shall honor our pledge."[56]

TUESDAY, OCTOBER 30

Tuesday, October 30, was a frantic day at the White House. Ben-Gurion's response to Eisenhower's message had arrived at 4:39 A.M., repeating the now familiar Israeli justifications for action against the "ring of steel" surrounding his country. Four hours later, Sherman Adams called Foster Dulles, who urged Adams to encourage the president to make a report to the American people. Adams shared that recommendation with Eisenhower

1

On October 31, 1956, in the Oval Office, a solemn President Eisenhower contemplated the gravity of the Suez crisis as he prepared for a televised report to the nation. Two days earlier, Israel had launched a military assault against Egypt across the Sinai Peninsula. At midday on the 31st, a British-French ultimatum to end the fighting had expired and Eisenhower received reports that allied planes had begun bombing raids on Egyptian airfields, ports, railways, and communication centers.

2

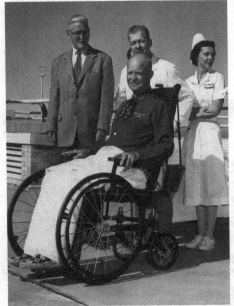

On October 25, 1955, a month after his heart attack, Eisenhower's doctors permitted him to sit in a wheelchair and soak up sun on the deck at Fitzsimons Army Hospital in Denver. In 1955, the standard treatment for a major heart attack was complete bed rest and severely limited activity. As a result, Ike was only marginally involved with the administration's response to a Soviet arms deal with Egypt that was confirmed the day of his heart attack.

3

On November 11, 1955, Veterans Day, after seven weeks in the hospital, Eisenhower returned to the White House prior to departing to Gettysburg for continued convalescence. Crowds cheered his motorcade along the route from the airport. Ike was upset when his doctors ordered his driver not to open the limousine's bubble top so he could stand and wave.

On July 26, 1956, in response to the American decision to withdraw an offer of aid for the construction of the Aswan Dam, President Gamal Abdel Nasser of Egypt decreed the nationalization of the Suez Canal Company, operated at the time by the British and French. On August 1 in Cairo, he was cheered by tens of thousands of his fellow citizens—the same day that Eisenhower ordered Secretary of State John Foster Dulles to fly to London to attempt to dissuade the British and French from going to war against Egypt.

In London, Dulles persuaded the British and French to convene a conference of maritime nations, the users of the Suez Canal, to address Nasser's nationalization. On August 3, when Dulles returned to Washington, he and Eisenhower delivered a televised report to the nation, announcing that the leaders of twenty-two nations would meet in London beginning on August 16.

When a delegation from the London conference went to Cairo, negotiations with Nasser broke down. Eisenhower and Dulles persuaded the allies to convene a second conference, September 19–21, to organize a Suez Canal Users Association (SCUA) to bargain with the Egyptians. Shortly thereafter, French foreign minister Christian Pineau, British prime minister Anthony Eden, French president Guy Mollet, and British foreign secretary Selwyn Lloyd met in Paris to consult about a secret plan to invade Egypt.

7

David Ben-Gurion, the Israeli prime minister, pictured here with Eisenhower, joined with the French and British in developing the secret plan for attacking Egypt. The final agreement, signed by representatives of the three governments on October 24 in Paris, called for an initial Israeli assault, Britain and France to issue a sham twelve-hour ultimatum to end the fighting, and the bombing of Egyptian ports and airfields once that deadline expired.

A prelude to the Suez crisis was the Soviet Union's arms deal with Egypt in September 1955, coinciding with Eisenhower's heart attack. John Foster Dulles dispatched diplomats to negotiate with Nasser, including assistant secretary for Near Eastern affairs George V. Allen (on the left). In the months to come, the American ambassador to Egypt, Henry A. Byroade (on the right), urged Dulles repeatedly, without success, to adopt a more positive attitude toward Nasser.

Allen W. Dulles was the CIA director and brother of the secretary of state. His agency failed to foresee Nasser's nationalization of the Suez Canal in response to the American withdrawal of an offer of aid for the Aswan Dam project, and failed to uncover the plot by Britain, France, and Israel to attack Egypt.

During the Suez crisis, Eisenhower met repeatedly with Secretary of State John Foster Dulles and Under Secretary Herbert Hoover, Jr. (shown here with another advisor on the right). When Eisenhower learned of the Israeli assault on Egypt on October 29, he rushed back to the White House from campaign events and angrily ordered Secretary Dulles to send a message to the Israelis: "Foster, you tell 'em, God-damn-it, that we're going to apply sanctions, we're going to the United Nations, we're going to do everything that there is so we can stop this thing."

After the British and French began bombing Egypt on October 31, Nasser's troops sank a 320-foot-long ship, loaded with rocks and cement, in the Suez Canal, blocking it to traffic. In all, the Egyptians scuttled thirty-two ships in the canal, obstructing the delivery of desperately needed strategic goods, including oil, to Western Europe.

On October 31, Eisenhower delivered a televised address about the invasion of Egypt by Israel, Britain, and France. "The United States was not consulted in any way about any phase of these actions," he said. "Nor were we informed of them in advance." Eisenhower said his opposition to the invasion was not intended "to minimize our friendship with these nations." But, the president concluded: "There will be no United States involvement in these present hostilities."

13

On November 5, 1956, British landing craft, flanked overhead by helicopters, landed troops at Port Said at the mouth of the Suez Canal. The British forces initially routed the Egyptian army but rumors of Soviet intervention stiffened resistance. The Soviet Union, already ruthlessly suppressing a revolt in Hungary, sent threatening messages to Israel, Britain, and France and proposed joint Soviet-American military action in Egypt to Eisenhower. In response, Eisenhower publicly warned the Soviets against intervention and placed American forces on alert.

14

The Eisenhowers and the Nixons respond to the crowd at the Sheraton Park Hotel in Washington on election night, November 6. Despite the Suez crisis, Eisenhower had won reelection by a landslide. Earlier that day, after voting in Gettysburg, Ike had rushed back to the White House to review disturbing intelligence from Moscow and to confirm by telephone with British prime minister Anthony Eden that he had agreed to a cease-fire in the Suez war.

15

Eisenhower and Nasser met in New York on September 26, 1960, during the annual meeting of the United Nations. Ike later described Nasser as "impressive, tall, straight, strong, positive." While Nasser reminded Eisenhower that the withdrawal of the offer of support for the Aswan Dam had been "an affront to Egypt's dignity," the Egyptian president thanked the United States "for its great help during the 1956 aggression against his country" and commended Eisenhower's "courage" in opposing his closest allies.

in a meeting a few minutes later. "No, I'd rather avoid that," Eisenhower said. He cursed "this damn FCC principle," the Federal Communications Commission's equal time requirement that would give Adlai Stevenson free air time to respond. The president was inclined to just put out a statement instead because an address to the nation would lead to "just the sort of public discussion we *least* need at this time." Later that day, Dulles and Adams would persuade him otherwise. Meanwhile, Ike agreed to cancel campaign events that had been scheduled for Texas, Oklahoma, and Tennessee, and to issue a press release to that effect. Emmet Hughes, observing the president during this meeting, recalled "his face drawn, eyes heavy with fatigue, worry or both."[57]

Shortly after 10:00 A.M., Eisenhower presided over a tense, hectic meeting with Foster Dulles, Hoover, Herman Phleger, Adams, Hagerty, and Colonel Goodpaster.[58] Ike read aloud a message he had drafted to send to Prime Minister Eden. Ike was still ignorant of Britain's role in the conspiracy with Israel, and nurtured faint hopes that he could persuade Britain to stay out of the conflict. The president and Dulles revised the message and sent it off. The president's frustration was evident in the cable. The Israeli incursion had left their governments "in a very sad state of confusion." If the United Nations labeled Israel an aggressor, Egypt might seek Soviet assistance and "then the Mid East fat would really be in the fire." That would confront the allies with circumstances "that would make all our present troubles look puny indeed."[59]

Lodge interrupted the meeting with a call to report that the British would only support a cease-fire resolution in the Security Council labeled "The Palestine Question."[60] That version, according to Lodge, would remove "all reference to measures to bring to an end the operations of Israeli forces in Egypt." The French were unwilling to support even that. At Eisenhower's insistence, Dulles instructed Lodge to proceed with the original resolution calling for a cease-fire, changing only one word—substituting language that spoke of Israel's attack "in" rather than "against" Egypt.

Eisenhower seethed with anger. "The French and the British do not have an adequate cause for war," he growled. "Egyptian action in nationalizing the Canal was not enough to justify this." The group agreed that the British and French had hoped to force the United States to choose—that, in Dulles's words, "the U.S. could not sit by and let them go under economically," referring to the allies' fragile finances and their near total dependence on access to Middle East oil. Ike's response was that he "did not see much value in an unworthy and unreliable ally and the necessity to support them might not be as great as they believed."

A message from Anthony Eden arrived. Ike stopped the proceedings to read it. There were no surprises in the prime minister's communication. He continued his deception, insisting that Britain had urged restraint on Israel and had elicited a commitment not to attack Jordan. Eden charged that Egypt's own actions had "brought this attack on herself." [61]

Secretary Dulles called the president just before noon to report that Eden was making a statement in the House of Commons that probably would announce British military action. [62] Eisenhower's anger had cooled; the United States needed to take a "hands off" posture, he said, making it clear "that we have not been, and are not now, associated with the French and the British in their activities." The president said that his first message to Eden had been "impatient" in tone, so he would send a short response to acknowledge Eden's new cable. Eisenhower took a deep breath: "After all, we will not fight them."

Still, Ike was determined not to fulfill the allies' expectations of a bailout. He would "let them stew in their own juice for a while. . . . They are our friends & allies," he grumbled, "& suddenly they put us in a hole & expect us to rescue them. . . . We are a Government of honor," he said to Dulles, "& we stick by it."

Eisenhower sent a cable acknowledging Eden's message and explained that "we here felt very much in the dark as to your attitude and intentions with respect to the Mid East situation." He noted their differing interpretations of the Tripartite Declaration of 1950, saying the United States had never modified its interpretation and "we find it difficult at this moment to see how we can violate our pledged word." [63]

Eisenhower and Dulles soon received disturbing news. The British and French had launched the second phase of the plot they had signed on October 24 in Paris. At 4:45 P.M. London time, 11:45 A.M. in Washington, Ambassador Winthrop Aldrich had been summoned to the British Foreign Office. He was handed copies of an ultimatum the British and French had delivered to Israel and Egypt only a few minutes earlier. It called on both nations to cease military actions, withdraw their forces a distance of ten miles from the Suez Canal, and accept temporary occupation of the Canal Zone by Anglo-French forces in order to ensure that canal traffic would not be interrupted. The parties were given twelve hours to comply—by

6:30 A.M. Cairo time. If they did not, British and French forces would intervene. Anthony Eden had announced the ultimatum to the House of Commons, echoed by Premier Guy Mollet before the French National Assembly.[64]

Two hours later, Foster Dulles called Eisenhower, read the ultimatum aloud, and called it "about as crude & brutal" as anything he had ever seen. Ike agreed it was "pretty rough." Dulles called it "utterly unacceptable." Eisenhower worried about Soviet reaction. He now felt trapped by his own rhetoric about aiding the victims of aggression; the aggressors this time would be the nations who, with him, had fought the Nazis. He was feeling more than a little wounded. "After all," the president muttered, "they haven't consulted with us on anything."[65]

At 3:00 P.M., Dulles called Eisenhower with a draft of a message protesting the ultimatum. Ike said the ultimatum was "a complete slap in the face"; he initially wanted a tough statement, not "a prayer that would not be answered." The president eventually acquiesced in a moderate message expressing "my deep concern at the prospect of this drastic action." "At least," Eisenhower rationalized to Dulles, "it establishes us before the Arab world as being no part of it."[66]

Anthony Eden's second cable of the day to Eisenhower was unrepentant. He contended that the ultimatum, aimed at both Israel and Egypt, sought "physical guarantees in order to secure the safety of the Canal." As expected, Eden hoped the president would "support what we have done, at least in general terms." Eisenhower searched for hints of moderation, telling Dulles that "at last he acts like he wants us to try to understand." The White House issued a statement informing the American people that the president's "first knowledge" of the ultimatum had come through "press reports."[67]

By late afternoon, Ike was tired and cranky. At 4:25, he reviewed the impact the Israeli attack on Egypt would have on European oil supplies with Arthur Flemming, the director of defense mobilization. Eisenhower also anticipated that the allies would run short of funds and "present us with a fait accompli, then expecting us to foot the bill." The president described himself as "extremely angry." "Those who began this operation," he told Flemming, "should be left to work out their own oil problems—to boil in their own oil."[68]

A few minutes later, Ike was still arguing with himself whether to be tough or diplomatic with the allies who had double-crossed him. He called

Secretary Dulles to read a draft of his response to Eden's second cable. This, the president quipped, was turning into a "trans-Atlantic essay contest." To Emmet Hughes, Ike ranted: "I've just never seen great powers make such a complete *mess* and *botch* of things!" There was no one, he said, "I'd rather have fighting along side me than the British.... But—*this* thing! My God!"[69]

In Moscow, Chip Bohlen tiptoed through a diplomatic jungle, trying to gauge Soviet reaction to the Israeli assault on Egypt and simultaneously discern the USSR's next moves in Hungary. The former Soviet foreign minister, Vyacheslav Molotov, had complained to Bohlen at a reception that the United States had not used its "great influence in Israel" to prevent the attack; in general, he said, the United States "had been in cahoots with England and France." On Hungary, Bohlen wrote that Eisenhower's wartime ally, Defense Minister Marshall Georgy Zhukov, was making statements that were a mixture of "untruths, half truths, and possibly some elements of real fact." Zhukov had characterized Soviet intervention in Hungary as a police action, an internal matter that should not have been taken to the Security Council.[70]

At 5:44 P.M., two weary men—Sherman Adams and Foster Dulles—discussed the long day. Dulles said the press should be told to go home—there would be no further announcements. Adams said the humiliating fact, especially for the president, was that "we got trapped by people in whom we had great faith." With the election imminent, Adams was concerned about how President Eisenhower looked "to this country and to the world." Finally, Dulles and Adams agreed, for both substantive and political reasons, that they needed once again to try to persuade the president to make an address to the American people.[71]

That night the British and the French vetoed the American-sponsored Security Council resolution calling for a cease-fire between Israel and Egypt. Ironically, the Soviet Union supported the measure. The council adjourned at 11:05 P.M. without action. The *New York Times* noted "the increasingly evident divergence between the United States on one side and Britain and France on the other." The next morning, in response to the vetoes, Eisenhower would take the unprecedented step of ordering that the issue be placed on the agenda of the General Assembly.[72]

Less than a half hour later, the deadline for the French-British ultimatum expired. The *Times* reported sightings of "the largest naval concentration seen in the eastern Mediterranean since World War II."[73]

Eisenhower received one bit of hopeful news that day. As the Hungarian government pledged to establish a multiparty system and hold free elections, the Soviet Union had issued a statement saying that "socialist nations can build their relations only on the principle of full equality, respect of territorial integrity, state independence and sovereignty, and noninterference in one another's domestic affairs." Eisenhower cautiously hoped that this announcement might foreshadow more moderate actions by Russian leaders in confronting uprisings in satellite states, a hope that would be brutally dashed in a few days.[74]

Just as he was preparing to retire for the night, Eisenhower received another cable from Eden. The prime minister, arrogantly assuming that Eisenhower would not object, wrote that he intended to quote some of Eisenhower's comments to the House of Commons "to justify British action and policy." At 10:52 P.M., a weary Eisenhower effectively threw up his hands and responded, "By all means use any part you see fit." Perhaps Eden did not appreciate the irony of Eisenhower's abrupt response. At this point, Ike knew that there was no use talking to the British.[75]

WEDNESDAY, OCTOBER 31

On Wednesday morning, October 31, Eisenhower was disconsolate after a night of fitful sleep. He continued to work on the letter to Eden that he and Dulles had discussed the previous day. The draft still simmered with presidential anger. "I must say," he began, "that it is hard for me to see any good final result emerging from a scheme that seems certain to antagonize the entire Moslem world." Ike hoped that "we shall not witness any such spectacle as the Soviets have on their hand in Hungary." He later decided against sending the message, partly due to the rush of events and his communications with Eden the previous evening.[76]

The morning papers broadcast the news of the British-French ultimatum, Eisenhower's "emphatic protest" about it, and reports that the administration was considering a cessation of economic aid to Israel until its government withdrew troops from Egyptian soil. James Reston, in the *New York Times,* concluded that the rift in the Western alliance "overshadowed even the grave events in the Middle East." The Egyptians had rejected the Anglo-French ultimatum, so war was imminent. Reston wrote that the nation's capital was awash with charges of "collusion" between Israel and France, perhaps involving the British.[77]

American leaders closely monitored the Soviet news media. By midday, the Soviet news agency, Pravda, was charging that the Israeli invasion of Egypt had been orchestrated by England, France, and the United States. American involvement, Pravda claimed, was proven by the fact that the American State Department ordered the evacuation of its citizens the day prior to the attack. The American embassy in Cairo cited similar reports in Egyptian newspapers, which called the Israeli invasion "an imperialist conspiracy closely linked to Suez and Algeria." [78]

At 8:35 A.M., Richard Nixon called Foster Dulles from Detroit for some coaching on what he could say on the campaign trail, especially because he was acting as the president's surrogate. Dulles urged the vice president to be careful about attacking the Israelis too directly because "they may have been used." Nixon, the secretary counseled, should also speak cautiously regarding Britain and France. Nixon's concern was that the papers overseas were charging that "we are to blame." He doubted the Republican ticket would lose many Jewish votes in the election as a result of opposing the Israeli invasion. The American policy was "still one that has kept American boys out and at such a time you don't want a pipsqueak for Pres." Dulles spoke warmly about "how wonderful" Eisenhower had been, trying "to do what is right regardless of the election—he will not sacrifice foreign policy for political expediency." [79]

A few minutes later, Dulles received a message from Ambassador Hare in Cairo, forwarding a plea from Nasser that the Sixth Fleet intervene to protect his country from a British-French invasion. Hare later recalled that he had bluntly asked Nasser if he already knew the answer would be no, so he could justify turning to the Soviet Union for aid. "No," Nasser said, "I really mean it." The ambassador added, "He wishes urgently to know President Eisenhower's reaction" and "he is not asking Russian help, at least for the present." Eisenhower was in no position to respond to Nasser's plea. He was stuck; he had pledged to defend any Middle East nation that was the victim of aggression, yet he could not attack the British and French, who were integral to NATO's defense against the Soviet Union. The word from the State Department to Hare, surely disappointing to Nasser, was that the United States "would do everything we can in the United Nations." [80]

Senator Knowland was worried. He first called Foster Dulles from Sacramento to find out if the president was thinking of calling Congress into special session. Dulles responded negatively. So far, there had been no reports of Anglo-French troop landings. The secretary said that, in the face of "unjustifiable action" by the British, the president was "doing everything he can." [81]

Unsatisfied, Knowland called the president to confirm what he had heard from the secretary of state. Eisenhower reassured the minority leader that he had no present plans to reconvene the Congress but said, "Keep in touch." Knowland expressed shock at the actions of the British and French. Ike said, as much to himself as to Knowland, that they should not be too bitter—"it is difficult for us to put ourselves in their shoes." But he could not mask his despair: "I am about to lose my British citizenship." He sighed. "I have done my best. I think it is the biggest error of our time, outside of losing China. I am afraid of what will happen." [82]

Eisenhower was heartened by the morning's news from Hungary. The American legation in Budapest confirmed the withdrawal of Soviet troops from the city; the Hungarian revolution appeared to be a "fact of history." Even more important, Pravda had published the Soviet government's declaration that it would observe "complete equality" with the satellites and "non-interference in one another's internal affairs." The statement admitted "downright mistakes" and affirmed that troops should be stationed in other socialist countries "only with the consent" of the hosting state. Allen Dulles told the president, "This utterance is one of the most significant to come out of the Soviet Union since the end of World War II." Ike was less trusting: "Yes, if it is honest." [83]

By mid-morning, Foster Dulles was planning with Lodge to implement Eisenhower's order to take a cease-fire resolution to a special meeting of the General Assembly. Lodge reported enthusiastic support for the president's policy at the United Nations, and Dulles suggested that the ambassador call Eisenhower with that news because Ike "was blue this a.m." Lodge followed up, telling Eisenhower that, in his experience at the United Nations, "never has there been such a tremendous acclaim for the President's policy." It was, the ambassador exclaimed, "absolutely spectacular." Ike remarked that it was "too bad this story couldn't be given to the press for all the United States to hear." [84]

At 11:30, Dulles called a meeting of the State Department's top staffers to confirm that he and the president were considering asking for a special session of the General Assembly. Hoover reported that the British Admiralty had warned all shippers to stay away from the Suez Canal. This meant a possible shutoff of oil shipments to Western European countries, whose reserves would last only fifteen to thirty days. [85]

During the day, the Soviet Union escalated its rhetorical attacks. Soviet radio carried reports from Cairo that the Israeli attack was "all part of a British-American plan to take over Suez." The Soviets began to make noises about intervention, accusing Britain, France, and Israel of "aggression" and warning of "dangerous consequences" if the invading powers did not withdraw.[86]

By late in the day on October 31, U-2 flights over Egypt confirmed for the president that British planes had begun bombing raids on airfields, ports, railways, and communication centers. The following morning, a U-2 pilot filmed neatly parked rows of aircraft at the main Egyptian airbase at Almaza; minutes later, his photography showed only burning, smoking wreckage. Eisenhower found something to cheer his dark mood in this technical achievement: "Ten-minute reconnaissance, now that's a goal to shoot for!" The spy plane's photographs of the British-French armada steaming toward Egypt were not encouraging.[87]

A week before the presidential election, the press had begun to question if Eisenhower was up to managing this deteriorating situation. James Reston, in an article entitled "Washington Loses Grip," opined: "The United States has lost control of events in areas vital to its security." The president, Reston asserted, "could no longer speak as keeper of the peace and leader of a unified alliance."[88]

Given such speculation, Eisenhower accepted the need to make a report to the nation. A military man who preferred action to rhetoric, Ike sometimes found such occasions stressful. But at those moments he manifested a talent for blending politics with patriotism. Eisenhower's great mission, from his first moments in office, had been the prevention of nuclear war. Seasoned by his searing experience in World War II, he had cast himself as the world's premier peacemaker. Now that mission was in peril.

Eisenhower was angry at the allies, but Ike had learned long ago that, however angry he might be, he must not show his rage in public. He decided to make a measured public response in two stages. First, he would deliver his television address to the nation that night—Wednesday, October 31. When Foster Dulles called that morning, Sherman Adams had assigned the secretary the task of writing the first draft of the speech. He briefed Dulles on the kind of talk Ike had decided he wanted to deliver—a fifteen-minute recitation of the facts, nothing more.[89]

Second, Eisenhower canceled all remaining campaign events before election eve except the address in Philadelphia the following evening—

where he planned to deliver a more substantial address on the crisis and the quest for peace. In the birthplace of the republic, Eisenhower could wrap his rhetoric in the flag and simultaneously make his case for peace and reelection.

As the time approached for the president's address from the Oval Office, the news from Egypt worsened. While French and British bombs continued to fall on Egypt, Nasser's troops had sunk a 320-foot ship, loaded with rocks and cement, in the Suez Canal, blocking it to traffic. In the days to come, the Egyptians would sink thirty-two ships and blame the blockage of the canal on the British.[90]

Adlai Stevenson knew he was an underdog in the election, but the trouble in the Middle East gave the Democratic candidate an opening. On October 31, Stevenson braved a frustrating day campaigning in New York in the rain. In four speeches, he mounted a sharply worded attack on the administration's policies in the Middle East. At an event sponsored by New York's Liberal Party, Stevenson lamented that "in a few months the Russian Communists have acquired a bridgehead in the Middle East which the Czars sought for centuries." The governor deplored the split with "our oldest, strongest allies," and now, "worst of all, the fate of mankind hangs in the balance in this seed-bed of human civilization." The Eisenhower administration, Stevenson contended, had been consistent in only one regard: "It has not told us the truth."[91]

Boarding his plane for Pittsburgh, Stevenson sought to detract from Eisenhower's televised remarks by releasing a telegram to the president. The candidate appealed to fears that the president's commitment to stand by the 1950 Tripartite Declaration's pledge "to aid the victims of aggression in the Middle East" might drag the United States into war. He urged Eisenhower "to reassure the nation that you will not commit us to any precipitate military action." Stevenson alleged that the rift with America's traditional allies "would aid the long held plans of Communist Russia to split the free world."[92]

At the White House, Emmet Hughes was at the epicenter of what he called a "total crisis" over the preparation of the president's television address.[93] The talk was scheduled for 7:00 P.M. Foster Dulles, sick and exhausted, had labored over a draft that did not reach Hughes until 3:15. Ike read it in the Cabinet Room because his office was crowded with television personnel and cables. The president quickly concluded that Dulles's draft was a disaster, and an hour later he ordered a new speech to be written.

Hughes described the next two hours as "fearfully tense." After six, he and the staff were still dictating and typing. Dulles, "ashen gray, heavy-lidded, strained," reviewed each page with little comment. The speechwriter took the draft to the president in his bedroom; Ike, reading the script while changing his suit, made one change. Hughes raced back to get the manuscript typed in the large print Eisenhower required, with certain phrases underlined for emphasis. A half hour later, Hughes was feeding the president the speech a page at a time across a table. At four minutes to seven, Ike read the last page and clutched the stack, saying, "Boy this is taking it right off the stove, isn't it?"

When the hour arrived in the Oval Office, Hughes marveled as the president, "looking trim in gray," sat down behind his desk under bright lights, and seemed "the most calm man in the room." The *New York Times* described the president's face as "grave" as he began to speak, never once flashing his famous smile. In spite of the hubbub surrounding the speech's preparation, the president's remarks came off as remarkably coherent and incisive.

Eisenhower told the nation that he hoped for "the dawning of a new day" in Eastern Europe, especially since the Soviets had just issued a statement suggesting more moderate policies.[94] The president was less optimistic about the Middle East. He laid bare the rift with his old allies: "The United States was not consulted in any way about any phase of these actions. Nor were we informed of them in advance." Eisenhower backed away from his earlier insistence that the United States would defend any nation that was a victim of aggression. The reason, although unstated, was obvious; the aggression was being perpetrated by staunch American allies. He softened his criticism of Britain and France by reciting the Egyptian actions that preceded the crisis, including Nasser's July 26 seizure of the Suez Canal Company and his rearmament with weapons from the Soviet bloc. Eisenhower's dissent from the allied invasion, he said, was intended "in no way to minimize our friendship with these nations—nor our determination to maintain those friendships." But, he solemnly concluded, "There will be no United States involvement in these present hostilities." As the *Times* noted, that pledge "ruled out the kind of help that Egypt could most use."

The president found a silver lining in the Middle East cloud—an opportunity for the United Nations to fulfill its potential. "I am ever more deeply convinced," he said, "that the United Nations represents the soundest hope for peace in the world." Because France and Britain had vetoed Security

Council action, he said he had taken the unprecedented step of submitting the issue to a special session of the General Assembly. "The peace we seek and need," Eisenhower concluded, "means much more than mere absence of war. It means the acceptance of law, and the fostering of justice, in all the world." In that quest, "we must stand fast."

Stevenson, en route to Pittsburgh, listened to the president's address on his plane's radio. Later, he sarcastically revived John Foster Dulles's language from the controversial *Life* interview, saying the world was "on the brink of war again." The candidate expressed appreciation that the president had "assured he has no present intention of calling Congress into special session or involving the United States in hostilities."[95]

Arthur Krock, of the *New York Times*, put the final touches on his column to be published the next morning.[96] Krock opined that whoever took office as president in January would be dealing with a "shattering responsibility," embracing the dual crises due to "the uprisings in the Soviet satellite states and today's British-French act of war against Egypt." The Democrats were positioned to argue, Krock wrote, that "the Administration has great culpability for the Middle East explosion and deserves no credit at all for the civil and armed demonstrations in Eastern Europe." He noted that numerous foreign governments blamed the crisis on Secretary Dulles, "on whom the President has heavily relied." That perception, Krock concluded, could be used to reinforce Adlai Stevenson's contention that Eisenhower "is not in charge of the store."

10

★ ★ ★ ★ ★ ★

DAYS OF CRISIS

November 1–November 3, 1956

"We believe that the power of modern weapons makes war not only perilous—but preposterous—and the only way to win World War III is to prevent it."

President Eisenhower at Convention Hall,
Philadelphia, November 1, 1956

THURSDAY, NOVEMBER 1

Ann Whitman described Thursday, November 1, 1956, as "another day of great crises." Sherman Adams recalled that, except for the president's illnesses, these days constituted "the worst week that Eisenhower experienced in all of the years I worked with him at the White House." In addition to the election campaign, the president, Adams remembered, had been harassed by numerous domestic issues, "the worst of which was the threatened oil shortage" due to the crisis in the Middle East. A cutoff of oil from that region could paralyze Western Europe, leading to demands on the United States that would impose strains on the American economy.[1]

The French and British were continuing their bombardment of Egyptian airfields in the Suez Canal Zone. The canal itself was blocked by the ships scuttled by the Egyptians. Israeli forces were still advancing in the Sinai, and Nasser had recalled most of his forces to defend the Canal Zone.[2] With the Anglo-French armada steaming toward Egypt, the days to come would present an avalanche of new problems. Small wonder that, on this day, Eisenhower and Foster Dulles would be in constant, harried consultation.

Dulles had become involved in a dispute within the government about how to head off the British-French invasion force. Noting that the Sixth Fleet was in position to obstruct the landings, the secretary had asked the chief of naval operations, Admiral Arleigh Burke, if the fleet could do that. Burke, more sympathetic to the allies than Dulles, recalled that he exploded, saying, "Mr. Secretary, there is only one way to stop them. But we will blast the hell out of them." Dulles had responded, "Well, can't you stop them some other way?" Burke's retort was an emphatic "No! If we're going to threaten, if we're going to turn them, then you've got to be ready to shoot. . . . And we can do that," Burke roared. "We can defeat them—the British and the French and the Egyptians and the Israelis—the whole goddam works of them we can knock off, if you want. But that's the only way to do it." Burke ordered the Sixth Fleet to stay near Egypt and be ready for *any* eventuality. "I didn't know who the damned enemy was because we were still having that discussion," he recalled telling his commanders. The controversy inside the administration leaked to the press and Joseph and Stewart Alsop reported in the November 2 *New York Herald Tribune* that "the highest American policy-makers actually played with the astonishing idea of ordering the American Sixth Fleet to oppose the Anglo-French landings on the Egyptian Coast."[3]

Ike and Dulles had no choice but to focus their efforts on action in the United Nations. Secretary Dulles called the president at 8:35 A.M. about the resolution the Americans planned to present that day to the U.N. General Assembly. The measure would call for an immediate cease-fire, the withdrawal of troops behind the armistice lines, a ban on military shipments to the region, and actions to open the Suez Canal. The previous afternoon, Dulles and his staff, after anguished discussion, had concluded that, in spite of the British and French attacks, they would recommend sanctions against only Israel.[4] These would include a cessation of economic, technical, and military assistance along with limiting U.S. exports and financial transactions with Israel. Ann Whitman noted that the president and Dulles did "not see eye to eye" on sanctions. Ike was appalled that the State Department would consider limiting the sanctions to Israel, excluding Britain and

France. He said he did not want it to look like he was trying to "pick on Israel," especially the week before the election. Dulles agreed but thought that Israel's aggression could not go unpunished. They planned more discussion at the upcoming National Security Council meeting. The need was to hammer out a position by five, when the General Assembly was scheduled to meet in New York.[5]

A few minutes later, Eisenhower took the question of the content of the United Nations resolution to the National Security Council. The result was a long, contentious meeting that featured, in Foster Dulles's understated language, "a great divergence of views."[6]

First, Allen Dulles briefed the council members on Hungary, calling what had happened there "a miracle." After assuming that a popular uprising could not succeed against Soviet weapons, the "impossible" had taken place. The CIA director called the Soviet statement of October 30 pledging improved relations with the satellite states "one of the most important statements to come out of the USSR in the last decade."

Then, Foster Dulles presented the issue of United Nations action regarding the Middle East. He asserted that if the United States did not seize leadership in the General Assembly, the Soviet Union would, assuring condemnation of Britain, France, and Israel as aggressors. Secretary Dulles shared the "mild sanctions" against Israel that he and his staff had approved the day before—mild because they did not propose freezing Israeli assets overseas or suspending remittances from Israelis and Jews in the United States. Eisenhower called it "a complete mistake for this country to continue with any kind of aid to Israel, which was an aggressor." The sanctions outlined in the proposed resolution were, he thought, "a little mild."

But Britain and France presented a tougher issue, even though they were bombing the Egyptians. Dulles expressed his concern that if the United States appeared to side with the old colonial powers it might drive former colonies into the Soviet Union's orbit. The war over Suez constituted "the death knell" for Britain and France as colonial powers, he said. The question was whether the United States would support "a policy of reasserting by force colonial control over the less developed nations, or whether we will oppose such a course of action by every appropriate means."

Harold Stassen, the president's assistant for disarmament, had listened to Dulles's presentation with growing agitation. He spoke up, contending that the United States should seek a cease-fire without condemning *any* of the three powers. Eisenhower said that he did not want to let the British and French off the hook, especially when, until the allies attacked Egypt, "transit through the Canal has increased rather than decreased since the Egyptians took over." Stassen granted that the British had "committed a terrible error," but he said that Britain was "a vital friend" and America's "real enemy was the Soviet Union."

Foster Dulles, exhausted and unwell, heatedly reminded Stassen that "it was the British and French who had just vetoed the proposal for a cease-fire." What the British and French had done, the secretary said, was "nothing but the straight old-fashioned variety of colonialism of the most obvious sort."

Stassen pressed his case, saying that American public opinion would be divided if the administration continued to oppose Britain, France, and Israel. He warned the president that he would risk losing congressional support for his policies. "How could we possibly support Britain and France," Ike asked, "if in doing so we lose the whole Arab world?" Eisenhower pointed out that Secretary Dulles was seeking only a mild sanctions resolution in the United Nations. When Stassen pressed again for a resolution calling for only a cease-fire, the president responded that "we could scarcely call for a cease-fire and continue to send supplies and assistance to Israel." The complication was the need to continue to supply war matériel to Great Britain and France to meet NATO requirements. Eisenhower expressed his "firm belief that we should state clearly that we are going to suspend arms shipments to the whole Near Eastern region while the UN is considering this crisis."

Eisenhower raised a politically explosive possibility. If the United Nations branded Israel as an aggressor, he said that what he really feared was "the prospect of imposing a blockade against Israel." Although he did not elaborate, the implication was plain: only the United States' Sixth Fleet would be capable of implementing a blockade that could effectively prevent the delivery of goods and military equipment to Israel. A U.N. resolution demanding such action would place the United States in an untenable position. Secretary Dulles responded that if the president did not seize leadership—if the United States confined itself to calling for a cease-fire as Stassen advocated—the General Assembly would call for such a blockade against not only Israel but also Britain and France. Eisenhower turned to Foster Dulles and ordered him to draft "the mildest things we could do" in order to block any "really mean and arbitrary resolution in the U.N. General Assembly."

Eisenhower was grappling with one of the most wrenching dilemmas of his presidency. "We do not want the British and French to be branded aggressors," he said. Dulles argued again for the minimum of suspending economic assistance to Israel. Eisenhower responded that "we would find plenty of Americans who think the Arabs are every bit as much aggressors as anyone else."

Stassen refused to back off and defended Israeli actions "in the face of so many provocations and fears." Exasperated, Foster Dulles escalated his rhetoric: "We do not approve of murder. We have simply got to refrain from resort to force in settling international disputes." Stassen was adamant, calling again for a resolution seeking a cease-fire alone. Eisenhower asked whether "we should not, as a precautionary measure, state that we are stopping all military, strategic, and governmental shipments from the United States to all nations involved in this mess at this time." He excused Secretary Dulles to leave to work on the resolution.

After Dulles left, Ike turned back to the group. These were men who, like him, had lived through the dark days of World War II, working closely with the nations who were now their adversaries in this crisis. Stassen had voiced the fear of others in the room that the president's commitment to principle would shatter the alliance that was essential to opposing Soviet expansionism. Ike tried to reassure them. He would do nothing, he said, "to break off our long alliance with Great Britain and France. We must not permit ourselves to be blinded by the thought that *anything* we are going to do will result in our fighting with Great Britain and France. Such a course of action is simply unthinkable, and no one can possibly believe that we will do it."

Eisenhower then raised the specter of direct Soviet military assistance to Egypt. He asked Admiral Radford whether the Russians could have "slipped" the Egyptians some atom bombs. Radford doubted that had happened. Eisenhower underlined the group's consensus—if the United States did not assert leadership, the Soviets would. He repeated the warning he had communicated to Anthony Eden: if the Russians intervened in the Middle East, "the fat would really be in the fire."

At 11:10 A.M., Secretary Dulles called and read a draft of the proposed statement on sanctions, which the president again called "mild." Ike urged Dulles to get the resolution to the United Nations before the five o'clock meeting. "The important thing," he said, "is not to let the Soviets get the initiative." Ike signaled that he was privately pondering what steps he could take to put genuine, behind-the-scenes pressure on the allies. While a cease-fire was the first objective, the president told Dulles, "You are not going to get a cease-fire by saying everybody please stop." Subsequent events suggest that Eisenhower was contemplating the fragile finances of the British government that he had discussed with Anthony Eden in January during the prime minister's state visit.[7]

Dulles read to Eisenhower a cable from Douglas Dillon in Paris, who had been given a detailed description of events in the conspiracy by Foreign Minister Pineau, including the planning that led to the October 24 secret agreement in Paris. Dillon had asked how the Israeli concern about Iraqi troops and Jordan figured into this; Pineau had replied that the focus on Jordan was "primarily a smokescreen to divert attention from the decision to undertake a joint operation against Egypt."[8]

Eisenhower and Dulles met at 12:50 P.M., just before Dulles was scheduled to depart to New York, to finalize their approach to the U.N. resolution. If the president knew he was sending a sick man to the United Nations, there is no indication in the meeting records or his diary. According to Chester Cooper, the CIA liaison in London, it was already rumored in the bureaucracy that "Dulles had been feeling ill all that week." Ike was focused on the crisis, not the health of his secretary of state. To Eisenhower and Dulles, beating the Russians to the punch at the United Nations was imperative; the press was speculating that the trigger for Soviet intervention in Egypt could be a resolution comparable to the one that had legitimized United Nations military action in Korea in 1950.[9]

About two, just as Foster Dulles was preparing to leave for the airport, Attorney General Brownell called him. Brownell, regardless of his title, was one of Eisenhower's trusted political advisors; he had been talking to the president about the political fallout of his dilemma with the British and French. Foster Dulles informed Brownell that a decision had been made: "We are going to do a few things quietly but not make any announcement." Brownell called that "a swell decision." He said that such an approach would be helpful "as far as the immediate project is concerned"—meaning the election. There was significant public sentiment, the attorney general concluded, "against casting aside the friendship we have with Britain."[10]

The secretary then called Allen Dulles to share about a brief meeting he had just held with Ambassador Abba Eban to warn him that the United States was reconsidering its existing programs of assistance to Israel. Eban, he said, was in "a very jubilant mood," claiming Egyptian forces had been defeated in the Gaza area. The CIA director commented that the American position would benefit generally if the president "called for a cease-fire and offered mediation." [11]

That was the essence of what Ike and Dulles had decided. With Dulles on his way to New York, Ike worked on two messages, neither of which he sent—but they provide insight into his thinking. He composed a follow-up note to the secretary that reflected their agreement—emphasizing the paramount need to achieve a cease-fire to keep the war from spreading and provide time to illuminate the adversaries' objectives so a final settlement could be negotiated. The United States was obligated, Eisenhower wrote, to lead because "a harshly worded resolution" would embarrass the administration. The Soviets, he wrote, "must be prevented from seizing a mantle of world leadership through a false but convincing exhibition of concern for smaller nations." Stassen had apparently won the argument he had made in the NSC meeting. American actions, Ike wrote, "must *not* single out and condemn *any one nation*—but should serve to emphasize to the world our hope for a quick cease-fire." [12]

The second message that Eisenhower drafted was to Eden. [13] His intent had been to send Eden a copy of his speech the previous night, and to affirm his government's friendship with Britain and France, even though the allies had made "a serious error." The draft focused on the U.N. secretary-general's six principles, which, by this time, had been integrated into the American resolution at the United Nations. These called for an immediate cease-fire, withdrawal of parties behind armistice lines, refusal by U.N. members to send arms into the area, and reopening the canal as soon as possible. The fifth and sixth points requested the secretary-general to report to the General Assembly regarding compliance with the resolution.

In this draft message, Ike urged four steps on the prime minister: "One—instantly call for a cease fire in the area; two, clearly state the reasons you entered the Canal Zone; three, announce your intention to resume negotiations concerning the operation of the Canal, on the basis of the 6 principles agreed by the United Nations; four, state your intention to evacuate as quickly as the Israelites return to their own national territory, and Egypt had announced her readiness to negotiate in good faith on the basis of the six principles." While Ike later decided, due to the rush of events, not to transmit this message, these organized thoughts would provide the foundation for his leadership in the days to come.

Meanwhile, Anthony Eden's government confronted escalating protests in the United Kingdom against its Middle East policy. London's major newspapers, including the normally pro-Eden *London Times*, were critical, especially over the rift with the Americans. Oxford University personnel, including ten heads of colleges, signed a statement saying that the British action against Egypt was "morally wrong." Dr. Geoffrey Fisher, the archbishop of Canterbury, told the House of Lords that "the United States thinks we have made a grave error, that world opinion on the whole—almost entirely—is convinced we have made a grave error." Protests had begun to spread to the streets. Selwyn Lloyd, the British foreign secretary, was greeted with shouts of "warmonger" outside a Conservative Party rally, where the demonstrators carried signs saying "Eden must go" and "Stop this Tory war." Students were arrested at Oxford University and protesters were arrested outside Parliament when mounted police broke up a demonstration.[14]

Eden faced a barrage of criticism in the House of Commons, where a vote of no confidence could bring down his government. Labour Party leaders raised insistent questions about the government's decision to go to war, and went so far as to lobby the American ambassador on the issue. Ambassador Aldrich reported to Secretary Dulles that Hugh Gaitskell and other Labour leaders had implored him to urge the United States to maintain its strong opposition to the "Eden-Mollet folly" in the Middle East. Gaitskell had contended to the ambassador that "more than half if not three quarters of [the] British nation" opposed Eden's "monstrous" policy.[15]

The feeler from the Labour Party may have been, in part, a response to press reports that morning. Buried on page 22 of the *New York Times* was a story that the administration had "pigeonholed plans to supply Britain and France with oil in the event their supplies from the Middle East are cut off." Without fanfare, Eisenhower had suspended the weekly meeting of the group charged with making such plans—the special Middle East Emergency Oil Committee—and another meeting on such matters at the Interior Department had been canceled. Oil importers, accustomed to receiving weekly bulletins that helped them make tankers available on short notice, were now being advised to "wait and see" what happened. This was a critical component of the Eisenhower-Dulles strategy to "do a few things quietly." Indeed, Eisenhower apparently had decided, in the words of his comment to Arthur Flemming on October 30, to let the allies "boil in their own oil."[16]

The possibility of the Soviets intervening, even covertly, was always on

Eisenhower's mind. After Secretary Dulles left for New York, Ambassador Bohlen reported from Moscow that the Soviets had issued a statement condemning the three powers for attacking Egypt but so far had mentioned the United States only as a signatory to the 1950 Tripartite Declaration. Bohlen interpreted Soviet policy as "official non-involvement at this stage," but he believed that the statement did not "preclude any clandestine assistance to Egypt." That concern became more concrete about 5:00 P.M., when Douglas Dillon reported from Paris that the loquacious Pineau had shared with him intelligence reports indicating that the Soviet Union was planning to station aircraft on Syrian bases and the foreign minister had urged quick action by the General Assembly to head off such an initiative. "The vital matter," Pineau had argued, "was to prevent [the] Soviets from turning [the] present action into general war." Hoover conveyed this information to Secretary Dulles, but discounted it because Admiral Radford had cited significant obstacles to intervention by the Soviets—the necessity for overflights of Turkey or Iran, and the significant exposure of Syrian bases to sneak attack by the Israelis. Hoover said that he and Allen Dulles agreed that "Pineau is desperately trying to stall for time." [17]

The Soviet Union confronted a dilemma of its own. In August, Khrushchev had stated that "the Arabs will not stand alone" if war broke out over the Suez Canal. Such a war, he said, "would be a just war." But Khrushchev had his hands full managing problems with satellite states: the Hungarian government had announced its intention to withdraw from the Warsaw Pact, declare its neutrality, and appeal to the United Nations for assistance. Moreover, Radford was correct; the logistical impediments to Soviet intervention in the Middle East were significant. [18]

Still, Eisenhower's principled opposition to British and French intervention presented Khrushchev with an opportunity to justify Soviet intervention because the West's anticommunist alliance was in disarray. But while he might relish the chance for a geopolitical victory by aiding Egypt against the Western powers, Soviet intervention without United Nations sanction could lead to war with Britain and France. Khrushchev knew that he could not count on the neutrality of the United States in such circumstances. Ike and Dulles had outflanked the Soviets with their sudden decision to take a cease-fire resolution to the General Assembly. That made it difficult, if not impossible, for the Soviet Union to propose U.N. military action in Egypt comparable to what the Security Council had authorized in Korea in 1950.

Eisenhower never allowed his subordinates to forget that, however unlikely, sliding into a nuclear war with the Soviet Union was a real possibility. Ike had been haunted by the Net Evaluation Subcommittee's report on January 23, describing the horrific impact of nuclear war on American life. In response, he had pushed the Joint Chiefs to review the implications for military capabilities following an attack. On November 1, with the Middle East in turmoil, Joint Chiefs chairman Radford received a staff report concluding that a surprise attack by the Soviet Union would result in 60 to 70 percent casualties among military personnel in the United States. The national government, the staff group's report said, would be "virtually wiped out." Transportation, energy, manufacturing, labor forces, and financial structures would be in complete chaos, with a devastating effect on any military response to the attack.[19]

Such matters preyed on Ike's mind as, fatigued, he shifted his energies to preparing for a major political address that evening—his last prior to the election. He had considered canceling the speech, but he wanted to say something more substantive than was possible in his bare-bones television report of the previous night. The speech was scheduled for the Convention Hall in Philadelphia—an ideal setting for the president to apply the founding principles of the republic to the greatest foreign crisis of his administration.

Due to the burdens of the day, by mid-afternoon, the speech had not been written. At just past 2:40, Eisenhower started working with Emmet John Hughes and others, including White House counsel Gerald Morgan, Sherman Adams, Colonel Goodpaster, and Jim Hagerty. Hughes left the president about five o'clock to write a draft, the very hour that the General Assembly was convening in New York. Ann Whitman called the preparation of the speech "as difficult as the preceding night, almost" and that "the typewriters had to go to the train," which departed Union Station at 6:30.[20]

In Philadelphia, the New York Times reported, an "overflow crowd of several thousand" waited "outside in a steady rain" for a chance to see the president enter the Convention Hall. Once on stage, Ike looked out at an auditorium packed with eighteen thousand partisans prepared to cheer his every word. After refuting his opponent in moderate tones without naming Stevenson, Eisenhower launched into what Russell Baker of the Times called "a high-level speech" by a man who had spoken "not as a Republican partisan, but as President of all the country."[21]

Eisenhower expressed his "deep dismay" at "the crack of rifle-fire and the whine of jet-bombers over the deserts of Egypt." He celebrated the anticolonial sentiments of the founding fathers. In a rare rhetorical flourish, he expanded the core principle of the Fourteenth Amendment, "equal protection of the laws," to apply to international affairs: "As there can be no second-class citizens before the law of America," he asserted, "there can be no second-class nations before the law of the world community." While hopeful about Hungary, Ike called the Middle East "a less hopeful—a much sterner—test of our principles." He said the nation had pursued "a path of honor" by standing against the use of force in both cases. The United States "cannot and will not condone armed aggression—no matter who the attacker, and no matter who the victim. We cannot—in the world any more than in our own nation—subscribe to one law for the weak, another law for the strong; one law for those opposing us, another for those allied with us. There can be only one law or there will be no peace."

The dilemma about the allies that had so riled the National Security Council that morning was still on the president's mind. Eisenhower bowed to "those great nations, those great friends, with whom we now so plainly disagree," but insisted that America would "continue to practice the peace that we preach." He solemnly concluded: "We believe that the power of modern weapons makes war not only perilous—but preposterous—and the only way to win World War III is to prevent it."

The speech lasted twenty-nine minutes. Eisenhower was completely drained by four days of unrelenting crisis. He drank two Scotches before dinner on the train and three highballs after dinner, arriving at Union Station at 12:29 A.M., November 2.[22]

FRIDAY, NOVEMBER 2

When Eisenhower arose on the morning of Friday, November 2, he learned that the General Assembly had endured one of its most difficult meetings ever. When the emergency session had convened at 5:00 P.M. the previous day, Secretary Dulles introduced a draft resolution calling for an immediate cease-fire in Egypt, withdrawal of forces behind armistice lines, a ban on the shipment of military goods into the region, and steps to reopen the canal. The session continued for two and a half hours and, after a break, resumed at 9:50 for five more hours of debate. At long last, the body adopted the American resolution by a vote of 64–5, with the Soviet Union voting in the affirmative, and six nations abstaining. Predictably, the negative votes included Britain, France, and Israel in addition to Britain's loyal Commonwealth nations Australia and New Zealand. This was another diplomatic triumph for the American secretary of state, who was surely suffering from fatigue and severe stomach discomfort. The General Assembly adjourned at 4:20 A.M.[23]

When the British House of Commons convened, Labour leader Hugh Gaitskell immediately asked Eden whether the government would honor the U.N.'s call for a cease-fire. Eden responded ambiguously that he would have to study the resolution. The resulting uproar in the House of Commons was such that the body scheduled an extraordinary Saturday session for the purpose of continuing debate.[24]

Meanwhile, the fighting in Egypt continued. The Egyptian air force had been destroyed by British bombing; Israel now controlled the Sinai Peninsula and the Gaza Strip. Thirty thousand Egyptians reportedly had been killed, captured, or forced to desert their posts.[25]

When Hoover called Eisenhower at 11:05 A.M., he mentioned Stevenson's harshly critical speech on television the night before, delivered as a response to the president's Wednesday evening address to the nation. Hoover said that Vice President Nixon and deputy attorney general William Rogers thought that Stevenson's address was "the most effective thing he has done in the campaign." Oveta Culp Hobby, the former secretary of health, education, and welfare, had called Ike to assert that Stevenson's increasingly effective campaign theme was, "Have we thrown away our Western allies for Russia?"[26]

Stevenson had delivered a scathing attack on Eisenhower. He had requested equal time on television to respond to the president's October 31 address but had been unable to secure an answer until late in the day on November 1. The candidate arrived at the television studio in Buffalo, New York, furiously editing his manuscript six minutes before he was to go on the air. Once he began, the Illinois Democrat fully exhibited his renowned oratorical skills. He accused the administration of trying to "conceal the truth from the people." "Had the Eisenhower Administration taken a firm stand in the Middle East," Stevenson declared, "had it aided Israel with arms and territorial guarantees, we might, I believe, have been able to prevent the present outbreak of hostilities." The candidate charged: "We have alienated our chief, our ancient and strongest European allies. We have alienated Israel. We have alienated Egypt and the Arab countries. And in the United Nations our main associate in Middle Eastern matters now appears to be the Soviet Union—in the very week when the Red army has been shooting down the brave people of Hungary and Poland." Stevenson concluded with a sweeping accusation: "I doubt if ever before in our diplomatic history has any policy been such an abysmal, such a complete and such a catastrophic failure."[27]

Not long after Hoover briefed Eisenhower, Ambassador Raymond Hare reported from Cairo with news that must have heightened Eisenhower's fears that the crisis threatened the viability of the United Nations. Egypt had severed diplomatic relations with Britain and France and was contemplating withdrawal from the United Nations, citing its failure "in thwarting the ambitions of great imperialist powers." Later in the day, Dulles and Eisenhower learned from Hare that he had visited Nasser and delivered a message from the president urging him to avoid drastic actions. Nasser had expressed his appreciation and confessed that he had previously believed that the British and French would not embark on a policy that had not been cleared with Eisenhower. "Now," Hare wrote, "he recognized he had been wrong."[28]

Ever the strategic planner, Eisenhower began to think about exploiting the crisis to craft a comprehensive settlement in the Middle East. Ike was frequently impatient when situations spun out of his control. He had been forced to sit and wait for U.N. action in New York. At such moments, Eisenhower was tempted to draft strategies too complex for messy circumstances—just as he had done the previous year by insisting that aid to the Aswan Dam be linked to a comprehensive Arab-Israeli settlement.

At noon, Eisenhower called Hoover to say he was anxious to meet with Dulles as soon as the secretary returned from New York. In light of the American success in the General Assembly, Ike wanted to "keep up the momentum" and submit another resolution establishing an arbitration commission to examine the entire Middle East situation. The president thought that Prime Minister Nehru of India might collaborate with him on such a proposal; if so, he thought that the result could be "spectacular."[29]

When Dulles returned, he and Hoover met with a president hell-bent on turning the Middle East crisis into something constructive and permanent.[30] Ike had long viewed the conflict between Israel and its Arab neighbors as the linchpin of any plan for a general reduction of Western-Arab tensions. He talked loosely about a far-fetched scheme to establish a "neutral strip" of land around Israel, ignoring the fact that establishing such a buffer zone would require hostile neighbors to give up land.

Ike's more immediate concern, once a cease-fire took place, was to establish a process aimed at molding a more permanent peace within the context of the United Nations. He wanted two United Nations committees—one addressing the Suez crisis and the other the Arab-Israeli conflict. These would refer recommendations to a higher-level panel comprised of heads of state that might include Eisenhower and Nehru, among others. Hoover tried to slow the president down, wisely suggesting that, with bloodshed still ahead, proposing this process might be premature. Ike was in no mood for delay. Because the United Nations had ordered a cease-fire, he insisted "there must then immediately be machinery for straightening out the situation." Regardless of the election campaign, he said, the State Department should not be concerned "about preempting too much of his time."

Tired and sick though he was, John Foster Dulles always tried to be responsive to the president when he was in this kind of damn-the-torpedoes mood. Dulles phoned Near East assistant secretary William Rountree from the president's office about names of prospective statesmen and diplomats to serve on Eisenhower's proposed committees. He and Ike discussed Dillon's cable about his meeting with Pineau detailing the "whole unmitigated story" about the conspiracy to attack Egypt. Apparently Eisenhower was still finding it difficult to accept that the British had been full partners in the conspiracy. Dulles, in the president's presence, asked a question he surely knew the answer to—were the British involved? Rountree responded, "Oh, yes." [31]

Later, Dulles called Ambassador Lodge and quickly discovered that pushing the president's new proposal would be difficult, if not impossible, in the present chaos. [32] Lodge was dealing with British and French envoys who were, he said, "in a very emotional condition." The two allies had decided to push a resolution condemning Soviet intervention in Hungary, partly to derail further action by the General Assembly on their intervention in Egypt. Secretary Dulles acidly commented that "it is a mockery for them to come in with bombs falling over Egypt" and rail against the Soviet Union "for perhaps doing something that is not quite as bad." He personally wanted "no part of it."

Regarding Eisenhower's proposal, Dulles told Lodge that the president was "anxious to have it done." They grappled with the question of calling the General Assembly back into session to address the president's proposals. Finally, Dulles chose a strategy of delay, telling Lodge to wait because the General Assembly might need to be called into session when British and French troops landed in Egypt. Then Dulles called in Arnold Heeney, the Canadian ambassador to the United States, to enlist his assistance in promoting the president's proposal for two committees—one to address the future of the Suez Canal and the other to address the issues regarding Palestine. Dulles could now report to Eisenhower that he had done his duty, while quietly finessing the president's demand for immediate action.[33]

After a virtually sleepless night and a difficult day, Foster Dulles summoned the energy to talk twice that evening with his brother Allen.[34] In the first call, the CIA director described his brother's triumph in the General Assembly as a "wonderful result." Foster shared that the British and French were angry because the United States would not join them in promoting a resolution on Hungary. Allen struck a somber note; he was, he said, "worried about Hungary." The news there was "pretty bad." The CIA director was alluding to the reports that demonstrations had erupted again across the country. The Hungarian government had withdrawn from the Soviet-sponsored Warsaw Pact and appealed to the United Nations for assistance. In response, the Soviet Union had closed the Hungarian border with Austria and Soviet tanks were advancing on Budapest but had not yet moved into the city.[35]

In his second call, Allen Dulles updated that information, telling his brother that CIA agents had intercepted a Moscow broadcast that claimed that the protesters in Hungary were spreading terror, thus providing a rationale for a buildup of Soviet forces. The CIA director also said he had a message from Cairo regarding "the seriousness of the situation." Foster Dulles responded that he had seen the message from Ambassador Hare. That cable had described the "thunder of bombings" on the outskirts of Cairo, and the "continuous rattle of anti-aircraft fire." The British had knocked out radio communications but a mobile transmitter had announced, referring to the General Assembly resolution, that sixty-four nations were supporting the Egyptians.[36]

Lodge, still up at 11:00 P.M., wired Secretary Dulles about unconfirmed reports of Anglo-French troop landings in Egypt and warnings that other Arab states were preparing to declare war. It was evident that Britain and France intended to ignore the General Assembly's resolution and proceed with landings. Lodge urged that they reconvene the General Assembly "at once" and the United States "manage this matter ourselves" rather than leaving the door open for a Soviet resolution.[37]

John Foster Dulles would not see these latest reports on the war zone. He had already gone to bed. The secretary was at war with his body. He woke up later with a severe pain in his stomach—pain so racking that his wife, Janet, called for an ambulance to transport him to Walter Reed Hospital.[38]

That night, in Detroit, Adlai Stevenson outlined his own plan for peace in the Middle East, proposing a cease-fire, a restoration of the "grand alliance" with Britain and France, security for Israel, international oversight of the Suez Canal, and a new initiative regarding Arab refugees and economic assistance to the region. Stevenson reminded the crowd that, only a few days earlier, the president had proclaimed "good news from Suez"—a comment that drew a chorus of boos. "Today," Stevenson continued, "there is war in the Middle East. Only a few days ago, the President told the American people that he knew of no disputes with our European allies." Boos and hisses interrupted the candidate. "Today," Stevenson resumed, "the Soviet Union has achieved a major victory by splitting the coalition of free nations; and we find ourselves in bed with Communist Russia and the dictator of Egypt." The *New York Times* reported "more boos and more displays of antagonism toward General Eisenhower, Mr. Dulles and Vice President Richard M. Nixon in the hall tonight than in most of the rest of Mr. Stevenson's campaign addresses."[39]

Eisenhower dispatched Nixon to serve as his political surrogate on the campaign trail, with the assignment of answering Stevenson's charges. In Hershey, Pennsylvania, Nixon—armed with a telegram anointing him as the president's spokesman—hailed the American break with the British and French as a "declaration of independence that has had an electrifying effect throughout the world." Nixon assailed Adlai Stevenson's charge that the president could have avoided the Middle East crisis. The General Assembly vote, with only five nations opposing the American resolution, gave "the lie" to Stevenson's "preposterous charge" that America stood alone in the world.[40]

Freed from campaigning, Eisenhower took time that evening to dictate letters. Through the years, Ike had often relieved his stress at difficult moments by thinking on paper with friends whose discretion he could trust, especially Swede Hazlett. To Hazlett that evening, Ike called the Middle East situation "a terrible mess." The Arab-Israeli dispute, he said, was "the underlying cause of the unrest and dissension" in the region. "Everybody in the Moslem and Jewish worlds is affected by it," he wrote; any action against an Arab state would always be regarded as "a Jewish plot." France and Britain, Eisenhower wrote, "have made a terrible mistake." The president confessed to Hazlett that the possibility of Soviet intervention "does not make sleeping any easier." [41]

That same evening, Ike also wrote to NATO commander General Alfred Gruenther: "Life gets more difficult by the minute. I really could use a good bridge game." [42] He shared that "sleep has been a little slower to come than usual. I seem to go to bed later and wake up earlier." The situation in the Soviet satellites caused him "just as much concern." "I have finished campaigning," the president informed Gruenther, adding that his speech in Philadelphia "had almost no allusions in it whatsoever to the political campaign." The president admitted that "as election day approaches, everybody gets the jitters."

Ike was bone tired, both physically and emotionally. He wrote Gruenther that, if he lost the election, "you can be sorry for anyone you want in this world *except me*!" Eisenhower fantasized about retirement: "raising prize cattle, going shooting two or three times a year, fishing in the summer, and intersper[s]ing the whole thing with some golf and bridge, doing it with abandon and no sense of responsibility whatsoever—maybe such a life wouldn't be so bad. A man could pretend to have an office, establish his hours as twelve to one—and take an hour off for lunch!"

Retirement was not yet an option for Dwight Eisenhower. That night, the newspapers were reporting "large-scale Soviet troop movements across Poland." [43]

SATURDAY, NOVEMBER 3

Whatever hopes Eisenhower may have had that the passage of the United Nations cease-fire resolution would change the situation in Egypt had been quickly dashed. On Saturday morning, November 3, the news was increasingly dismal. Syrian saboteurs had reportedly blown up the British oil pipelines running through their country to the Mediterranean. There were reports from Cairo that Egyptian troops were pouring into the city to defend the capital, while Anglo-French air strikes were heavier and increasing in frequency. The entire Egyptian air force had been destroyed on the ground. According to U.S. Army sources, Anglo-French troop landings appeared "imminent." [44]

Yet the British and French ships were moving at a snail's pace toward mounting their land assault, the result of Anthony Eden's determination that Britain appear to be a peacemaker, not an invader. This delay caused consternation among administration personnel who favored supporting the British. In London, just after dawn, CIA liaison Chester Cooper's phone rang, ordering him to come to the American embassy for a conversation on a secure phone with Robert Amory, Jr., the CIA deputy director. "Tell your friends," Amory barked at Cooper in a loud voice, "to comply with the goddamn cease-fire or go ahead with the goddamn invasion. Either way, we'll back 'em up if they do it fast. What we can't stand is their goddamn hesitation waltz while Hungary is burning." [45]

That "hesitation waltz"—the plodding progress of the Anglo-French armada toward Egypt—fulfilled one of Eden's objectives: it temporarily convinced Eisenhower that such a bumbling military strategy surely indicated that the British had joined the conspiracy only at the last moment. Amory probably reflected Allen Dulles's outlook, but there is no evidence that Eisenhower intended to back the British, no matter at what speed they proceeded—unless, of course, the Soviets intervened.

More bad news awaited Ike as he entered his office that Saturday morning. He learned that Secretary Dulles had been rushed to the hospital during the night with severe abdominal pain, at first thought to be a kidney stone. Ann Whitman recorded that the White House had been informed that the secretary had been operated on for "a perforated intestine." In fact, the surgeons at Walter Reed Hospital had removed a cancerous tumor from the secretary's colon. [46]

Chester Cooper's reaction to the news of the secretary of state's surgery reflected how little CIA operatives understood about Dwight Eisenhower's grip on decision making. The men in the ranks erroneously assumed that the Dulles brothers were running American foreign policy. "And so," Cooper stated years later, "at the most critical moment of crisis in both Hungary and the Middle East, John Foster Dulles was taken out of action. Responsibility now rested with a well-meaning, but basically uninterested President and an unimaginative, relatively inexperienced, reportedly anti-British acting secretary, Herbert Hoover, Jr." [47]

By the time State Department officials, led by Acting Secretary Hoover, gathered in the Oval Office during the eleven o'clock hour, Eisenhower was in a dark mood. [48] Ike complained that, on Friday, a State Department spokesman had failed to make clear that the suspension of shipments of arms and matériel to the Middle East applied to all nations in the region. The rest of the news would not improve the president's mood. Hoover worried that Egyptian soldiers fleeing the Sinai might start riots in Cairo.

William Rountree responded that the State Department had sent a message to Nasser, urging him to prevent mob action. Nasser, he said, had been "very appreciative and said that for the first time he realized that the United States was not just playing the British game in the area."

Hoover placed a new statement by Anthony Eden in front of the president. The declaration was designed to perpetuate the fraudulent impression that Great Britain's motive was to play the peacemaker in Egypt. Eden had rejected the United Nations cease-fire resolution, characterized the British-French bombardment as a "police action," and set conditions that he knew would not be welcomed by Israel and Egypt. The French and British would cease military operations, the prime minister announced, only after the Israeli and Egyptian governments had consented to the deployment of a United Nations peacekeeping force. Until that force was constituted and on the ground, Israel and Egypt would need to accept "forthwith limited detachments of Anglo-French troops to be stationed between the combatants." Translation: British and French forces would occupy the Suez Canal Zone.[49]

Eisenhower's ill-conceived plan for two United Nations committees— one on Suez and one on the Israeli-Arab conflict—was complicated by Eden's rejection of the cease-fire. Eisenhower granted that "interim action" would be necessary, "such as a neutral zone around Israel" and "clearing the Canal and operating it." Hoover noted that the British and French were harassing the U.S. delegation at the U.N. to join them in a resolution condemning the Soviet Union's actions in Hungary. Eisenhower acidly retorted that "such a thought was almost absurd."

Jim Hagerty urged that the administration announce an American position immediately; "otherwise we will get ourselves mixed up in the proposals of others." Eisenhower agreed but he was in no mood to compromise with the British and French. He grumbled that "there is no cause for the UK and the French to go into the Canal area." He wanted it communicated that "we are not waiting for or accepting the entry of the French and the British." Following Hagerty's advice, Eisenhower approved a White House statement for the press secretary to issue following the meeting. It praised the General Assembly for its overwhelming approval of the American resolution ordering a cease-fire in the Middle East. It went on to say that the United States would propose to the General Assembly "two additional resolutions with respect to the critical Middle Eastern situation," establishing committees that would separately address Arab-Israeli tensions and the Suez conflict.[50]

Meanwhile, Robert Murphy, assuming some of Foster Dulles's diplomatic duties, and Herman Phleger, the State Department's legal counsel, met with Arnold Heeney, the Canadian ambassador, to ask his assistance in passing a resolution authorizing a United Nations peacekeeping force. Phleger underlined the importance of Egyptian agreement with the proposed resolution; otherwise the U.N. force would appear to be only a substitute for Anglo-French troops. The United States' dual motives were apparent: to head off strong General Assembly condemnation of Britain and France and encourage them to hold off on troop landings. There was still slim hope for the latter because the Anglo-French naval forces were almost two days distance from the coast of Egypt. Heeney said the Canadians were ready to help by proposing such a resolution and that the Canadian foreign minister, Lester Pearson, was in New York with his "pencil in the air."[51]

At 7:00 P.M., Henry Cabot Lodge, who normally would have called Secretary Dulles, phoned the president.[52] After Lodge reported on the difficulties of promoting the new resolutions the president wanted, Ike did most of the talking, barking rapid-fire orders at the ambassador. He firmly endorsed the resolutions establishing his two-committee process as "the next step" and said he thought they "provided a very definite method by which problems might be settled." The point, Eisenhower said, was "to attack the basic causes." Still, he understood the need for preliminary steps, especially the organization of a United Nations police force to separate the belligerents, before he could move forward on his grand design. It would be "a great tragedy," Ike concluded, if British and French forces landed in Egypt. He ordered Lodge to involve the secretary-general in constituting the United Nations force because Hammarskjöld "could act more freely" than a committee. All the parties to the conflict, he said, must accept the plan for the United Nations force, organized by the secretary-general. Lodge was instructed to see Hammarskjöld and Pearson and sell them on this simpler, more direct method.

At the request of the Egyptian government, the General Assembly reconvened at 8:00 P.M. The United States had already circulated its resolutions promoting the two-part Eisenhower plan to address the Arab-Israeli dispute and the status of the Suez Canal. But Dulles and Lodge had agreed previously that this was not the moment to push for the president's big plan. Lodge, on behalf of the United States, agreed to delay action on resolutions establishing the two committees so that the Canadians could introduce a resolution to order the secretary-general to submit a plan within forty-eight hours for the composition of a United Nations force, in time to possibly head off the landing of French and British troops on the Egyptian mainland. The assembly voted to adopt that resolution 57–0, with nineteen abstentions, and passed another resolution to reinforce the call for a cease-fire, again with Britain, France, and Israel voting in opposition. The meeting adjourned at 3:00 A.M. on Sunday, November 4.[53]

Meanwhile, William Rountree's Joint Middle East Planning Committee had reported to the Joint Chiefs of Staff on the critical question of possible Soviet actions in response to the crisis. The committee noted that, thus far, the Soviet government had confined its opposition to diplomatic activity, mostly at the United Nations, in spite of Khrushchev's August 23 statement that "Egypt, if attacked, will not stand alone." At this time, Soviet military action seemed unlikely partly because it "would incur unacceptable risks of general war."[54]

Once again, Ike relieved his tensions by writing a confidential letter, this time to Lewis Douglas, the ambassador to the United Kingdom under Truman. Eisenhower admitted that "in spite of all that has happened, Britain must continue to be our best friend—so I have no intention of using the British Government as a whipping boy." Still, he fumed, "they have been stupid." The British and French had "allowed their distrust and hatred of Nasser to blind their judgment and they have used the wrong vehicle for carrying on their fight to deflate him."[55]

Ike may have felt that the political opposition in the United States was similarly "stupid." Eleanor Roosevelt was quoted in the press as saying that Israel had acted in self-defense, and she accused the administration of favoring the Arabs. Mrs. Roosevelt claimed that Britain and France had been "brought to the point of desperation" by American policy. "It leaves us in the very strange position," she said, "of supporting the Kremlin and an Egyptian dictator against our oldest and strongest allies. It is an ironic, strange, and horrible situation."[56]

Eisenhower had prided himself on working effectively with the Democratic leaders of Congress on foreign policy. But six of the eight Democratic members of the Senate Foreign Relations Committee had issued a statement attacking Eisenhower's policies. The senators' names read like a Who's Who of Senate foreign policy leaders—the acting chairman, Theodore Green of Rhode Island, J. William Fulbright of Arkansas, John Sparkman of Alabama, Hubert Humphrey of Minnesota, Mike Mansfield of

Montana, and Wayne Morse of Oregon. The only names missing were the outgoing chairman, Walter George of Georgia, and Russell Long of Louisiana. The senators called the situation in Egypt the country's "worst diplomatic disaster in memory." "We wholeheartedly agree," they said, "with Adlai Stevenson that President Eisenhower's Middle East policy has failed and that it has reached an absolute dead end." They charged that the president had presided over "four years of indecision, tactlessness, timidity, and bluster." [57]

That night of November 3, two events, thousands of miles apart, symbolized Eisenhower's seemingly intractable problems, entangling politics with an international crisis. In his last major address prior to the election, Stevenson raised more insistently the issue of the president's health, asserting that the president "now lacks the energy" to cope with the crisis in the Middle East. Americans, he contended, were burdened with "part-time Government in Washington." "Every consideration," Stevenson continued, "the President's age, his health and the fact that he cannot succeed himself make it inevitable that the dominant figure in the Republican Party under a second Eisenhower term would be Richard Nixon." He asked the crowd if they wanted Nixon "as Commander in Chief to exercise power over peace and war? Do you want to place the hydrogen bomb in his hands?" [58]

On the other side of the globe, in Moscow, Soviet officials hosted Shukri al-Kuwatly, the president of Syria. Kliment Voroshilov, the chairman of the Soviet Presidium, publicly declared: "The Soviet Union is ready to supply Syria with the necessary assistance to overcome as rapidly as possible the vestiges of colonialism and to reinforce its complete independence." The Syrian leader enthusiastically embraced Soviet support "against the yoke of tyranny," charging that "aggression unleashed in our area is being used by some people with the aim of starting a world conflict." [59]

Once again for Dwight Eisenhower, untroubled sleep would be impossible.

11

★ ★ ★ ★ ★ ★

A PERFECT STORM

November 4–November 6, 1956

"We have given our whole thought to Hungary and the Middle
East. I don't give a damn how the election goes."

Eisenhower to Anthony Eden, Election Day, November 6, 1956

SUNDAY, NOVEMBER 4

President Eisenhower fervently hoped for a quiet Sunday, just three days
before the presidential election. Ike planned to attend services with Mamie
and his son, John, at the National Presbyterian Church. But the Suez crisis,
mixed with the growing crisis in Eastern Europe, was about to turn into a
perfect storm.[1]

Ike had been encouraged when, following the violence in Budapest on
October 24, Soviet troops had withdrawn and the Soviet government had
issued a statement on October 30 pledging improved relations with the satellites. But in subsequent days, tensions had worsened between the Hungarian government and the Soviet Union, and Soviet forces were once again
moving toward Budapest. On November 2, Allen Dulles had described the
evolving situation in Hungary to his brother Foster as "pretty bad." On
November 4, at 3:13 A.M., the Soviet Union vetoed an American resolution
in the U.N. Security Council calling on the Soviet government to withdraw

its forces from Hungary. About 4:00 A.M., the Soviets delivered a four-hour ultimatum to the Hungarians stating that if their government did not capitulate, Soviet forces would bomb Budapest. Later that day, the Russians sent 200,000 troops and four thousand tanks into Hungary.[2]

In the Middle East, Israel had seized nearly all of the Sinai Peninsula and the Gaza Strip and had taken five thousand Egyptians prisoner. The State Department feared that Israel might launch a preventive attack on Syria. With John Foster Dulles in the hospital following cancer surgery, Acting Secretary of State Herbert Hoover disrupted his sleep at 4:30 A.M. to cable the American ambassador in Tel Aviv that the United States "cannot condone any steps" leading to further military action. The British and French armada, numbering a hundred ships, was approaching the Egyptian coast.[3]

At 9:30 A.M., mobilization director Arthur Flemming convened a group that included Secretary of Defense Charles Wilson, Hoover, and the Joint Chiefs chairman Admiral Radford. The agenda, in light of the destruction of three oil pipelines in Syria and the blocking of the Suez Canal, was whether the United States should provide oil to Britain and France. Flemming, from his discussions with the president, knew that Eisenhower preferred to let the allies "boil in their own oil" for a while. Ike did not want even the appearance of collaboration with the British and French. The minutes of the meeting reflect that, after much discussion, the group had agreed that "nothing would be done today and no initiative would be taken." In the spirit of Ike's hard-nosed approach, Flemming concluded that the United States should "play hard-to-get" and resist "giving away a vital card."[4]

The Eisenhower family departed for church just before eleven. While sitting there, the president's thoughts must have raced over the deteriorating situation in Europe and the Middle East. Eisenhower understood all too well that the two previous world wars had begun incrementally, one step at a time, until the participants careened down the proverbial slippery slope to global conflict. Ike's Cold War strategy, even his rhetorical reliance on massive retaliation, had been built around containment of those small steps that could escalate into a nuclear holocaust. Now, with violent conflicts in both Europe and Egypt, Eisenhower's goal of preventing another world war was clearly in jeopardy.

In his memoirs, Ike recalled his anxious thoughts that day. The Soviet offensive in Hungary raised the issue, three days before the election, of whether the United States would use force to oppose "this barbaric invasion." The Soviet action was hauntingly similar to Hitler's aggression that had precipitated World War II. But Eisenhower knew from experience—bedrock doctrine for him—that wars are won by employing overwhelming force. His primary allies, Britain and France, were mired in conflict in Egypt. Hungary was inaccessible by air, sea, or land without violating the territory of neutral or communist states. Ike knew he had no choice; unilateral American action was not an option: "Unless the major nations of Europe would, without delay, ally themselves spontaneously with us (an unimaginable prospect), we could do nothing." The United Nations General Assembly would never authorize military intervention to dislodge the Soviets from Hungary. "So," he concluded, "as a single nation the United States did the only thing it could: We readied ourselves in every way possible to help the refugees fleeing from the criminal action of the Soviets, and did everything possible to condemn the aggression." [5]

After church, the president and his son drove to Walter Reed Hospital to see Dulles. Then Ike returned to the White House, where, without taking time for a formal Sunday dinner, he convened an emergency meeting about Hungary with Hoover, CIA director Allen Dulles, and other advisors.[6] Hoover informed the president that, given the Soviet veto in the Security Council, the United States would submit a resolution on Hungary to the General Assembly at 4:00 P.M. A Canadian resolution, authorizing Secretary-General Hammarskjöld to organize a peacekeeping force in Egypt, had passed about 3:00 A.M. in the Assembly by a vote of 57–0. Hoping to head off the landing of troops on Egyptian soil, Hammarskjöld immediately moved to organize and deploy a token force that the British and French dared not attack.[7]

Regarding Hungary, Hoover handed Eisenhower a draft of a proposed letter to Soviet premier Nikolai Bulganin. Eisenhower edited the draft, telling Hoover that it was important to offer options to Bulganin "by which he could reduce the shock and dismay the world has felt at Soviet actions in Hungary." This was standard Eisenhower doctrine, to give an opponent an escape hatch from a confrontation that could escalate into great conflict.

Eisenhower's letter expressed his "profound distress" at the news from Hungary. He recalled the Soviet leader's statement of October 30, pledging nonintervention in other states, a posture that appeared to be "an act of high statesmanship." The president was, he said, "inexpressibly shocked by the apparent reversal of this policy." "I urge," he continued, "in the name of humanity and in the cause of peace that the Soviet Union take action to withdraw Soviet forces from Hungary immediately and to permit the Hungarian people to enjoy and exercise the human rights and fundamental freedoms affirmed by all peoples in the United Nations charter." Then Eisenhower offered the escape hatch option, suggesting that the Soviet representative to the United Nations announce that his government was withdrawing its forces from Hungary. The letter contained no hint of any planned American action except to take the issue to the General Assembly.[8]

The White House issued a statement regarding the results of the emergency meeting. It repeated the president's "shock and dismay at the Soviet attack on the peoples and government of Hungary" and called for Soviet withdrawal and self-determination for Hungary. Eisenhower referred to his message to Bulganin, although he waited to release it to the public until the following day, ensuring it would reach the Soviet leader before it appeared in the press. The statement also noted that, in the meeting, the participants had conducted "a thorough review of the Middle East situation."[9]

The press searched for reasons for the sudden shift in Soviet policy. The *New York Times* raised the possibility that Khrushchev, the Communist Party chairman, who had led the de-Stalinization movement, had lost out to the hard-line Stalinist wing of the party, repeating speculation making the rounds in Washington—that the British-French assault on Egypt had provided a "moral smoke screen behind which the Soviet leaders found it convenient to operate."[10]

In New York, Hammarskjöld scrambled to fulfill his instructions from the General Assembly to secure a cease-fire and put together a peacekeeping force. Ambassador Lodge informed Hoover that the secretary-general had sent a message to the British cabinet stating that Eden's conditions for agreeing to a cease-fire, designed to give the Anglo-French forces control of the Canal Zone, were "out of the picture." If London and Paris did not accept the U.N. directive, Hammarskjöld had said, they would be responsible for "preventing the cessation of hostilities between Israel and Egypt." Hammarskjöld had said to Lodge that he hoped the British were beginning to understand "the predicament they were in."[11]

In contrast, the word from Cairo was sweet reason. Ambassador Hare reported that he had heard indirectly that Nasser would welcome designation of the American Sixth Fleet as an interim United Nations police force in the Suez area, that he was pleased with the American role in the General

Assembly, and that the United States had won support in the region "without firing a shot." Hare urged caution in response since "drowning men grasp at straws."[12]

The assembly's resolution had called for a cease-fire within twelve hours. The secretary-general—knowing that the British cabinet was in session and that French premier Guy Mollet and Foreign Minister Christian Pineau were scheduled to arrive in London—shrewdly moved the deadline from 8:00 P.M. to midnight to give those leaders more time to consider their situation. But the hourglass was running out on Hammarskjöld's heroic efforts. By morning, the British and French would be ready to launch the second phase of their assault on Egypt by landing ground forces.[13]

MONDAY, NOVEMBER 5

At dawn on November 5, British and French paratroopers landed in Egypt; Washington learned of the invasion at about 8:00 A.M. Hammarskjöld's hopes for deploying a United Nations force before the landings took place had been dashed.[14]

Eisenhower had received two messages from British prime minister Anthony Eden during the night. The second was the more substantive.[15] Eden expressed his "great grief" that the events in Egypt "have placed such a strain on the relations between our two countries." The prime minister reminded Eisenhower that he had made clear to Khrushchev, when the Soviet leader had visited London in April, that the Middle East "was an issue over which, in the last resort, we would have to fight." The British and the French had concluded that they "had to act at once to forestall a general conflagration throughout the Middle East. . . . This is the moment," he wrote, "to curb Nasser's ambitions." If they failed, "everything will go up in flames in the Middle East."

Eden rejected the General Assembly's resolution calling for a cease-fire within twelve hours, before any peacekeeping force could be deployed on the ground. His rationale: "We cannot have a military vacuum while the UN force is being constituted and is being transported to the spot." He complained that the British and French were "being pilloried as aggressors" while the Soviet Union was brutalizing Hungary and "no voice is raised in the United Nations in favour of intervention there." Eden beseeched the president for understanding regarding "the terrible decisions that we have had to make. I remember nothing like them since the days when we were comrades together in the war."

This day before the election, Eisenhower met with Vice President Nixon, Acting Secretary Hoover, State Department legal counsel Phleger, and press secretary Hagerty.[16] Reports of the Anglo-French landings hung like a cloud over the meeting. The important news, according to Phleger, was some indication that Eden "now wants to join in with the other free nations to settle this matter." Eisenhower mentioned the two letters he had received from Eden and said he would try to move the prime minister toward a cease-fire. Calmly in command, Eisenhower urged that the United States "stick with the plan developed thus far in spite of the UK and French landings." Ike was alluding to the two-pronged strategy he had evolved—one public, the other private. The public component, approved by the General Assembly, linked a cessation of hostilities with the landing of a token United Nations force. The behind-the-scenes strategy involved the prohibition Eisenhower had put in place denying American financial assistance or petroleum to the allies as long as they were still fighting in Egypt.

Hoover worried aloud about the possibility that the Soviet Union might send forces into Syria. Eisenhower requested that Allen Dulles, who was not present, keep a close watch on the Syrian airfields, obviously referring to U-2 spy plane flights over the area. Also, oil supplies from the Middle East had been largely disrupted, raising the possibility that NATO forces in Western Europe would be adversely affected. Eisenhower advocated quietly and swiftly putting American heavy tankers and oilers into readiness, including those normally used for nonmilitary purposes. Still, Ike wanted to maintain the pressure on the British and the French. He ended the meeting, stating that "the purposes of peace and stability would be served by not being too quick in attempting to render extraordinary assistance."

Eisenhower tried to write Anthony Eden after the meeting, but he never sent the letter.[17] Still, the draft shows his thinking at this critical stage of the crisis. Eisenhower was "saddened," he wrote, by "the temporary but admittedly deep rift that has occurred in our thinking as respect of the Mid East situation." Although the British and French troops had landed, Eisenhower hoped they would not engage in serious fighting and allow the cease-fire to take effect. Eisenhower mentioned his club in the closet—his awareness that Britain's "financial problem is going to be a serious one, and this itself I think would dictate a policy of the least possible provocation."

Later, Ann Whitman noted that the president had concluded that "events had gone too swiftly" to make this message appropriate for transmission. After British and French paratroopers landed in Port Said in

Egypt, efforts to arrange a cease-fire had failed. The Anglo-French forces initially subdued the city with relatively little bloodshed and the Egyptian governor was prepared to surrender. Suddenly loudspeaker vans had broadcast the news that Russian assistance was on the way. In response to that unfounded rumor, the governor reversed his decision to cease fighting and decreed that combat should continue.[18]

Although Eisenhower had canceled further campaigning, it was election eve and he had political obligations. In the afternoon, he traveled to Republican National Committee headquarters, where he expressed his appreciation to 250 campaign workers. Ike was in no mood for the usual presidential get-out-the-vote exhortation, saying that, "no matter what happens, I think we should not think of it too much as the time for rejoicing. Friends of ours, people in Eastern Europe, are enslaved and suffering, and there are still threats to the peace existing in Egypt."[19]

Suddenly, the leaders of the Soviet Union poured more fuel on the international fire: Premier Bulganin sent messages to Prime Minister Eden and Premiers Guy Mollet of France and David Ben-Gurion of Israel, warning that the conflict in the Middle East could escalate "into a third World War." The Soviet leader, implying a nuclear threat, equated the attacks on Egypt with a hypothetical attack on Britain and France by "more powerful states possessing all types of modern weapons of destruction," including "rocket weapons." Bulganin pronounced a dark ultimatum that may have sounded even harsher in translation: "We are full of determination to crush the aggressor and reestablish peace in the [Middle] East by using force."[20]

The Soviet delegation to the United Nations engaged in more saber rattling, asking that Bulganin's warnings be circulated at the General Assembly. The Soviet foreign minister, Dmitri Shepilov, demanded an immediate meeting of the Security Council to discuss "the non-compliance" of Britain, France, and Israel with the cease-fire resolutions of November 2. His draft resolution called for planning for military assistance to Egypt, especially by the United States and the Soviet Union, if the British and French did not cease military operations within twelve hours and withdraw their troops from Egyptian soil within three days. More ominous, Shepilov confirmed in writing the Soviet Union's readiness "to contribute to the cause of curbing the aggressors, of defending the victims of aggression, and of restoring peace, by sending to Egypt the air and naval forces necessary for the achievement of this purpose."[21]

That was not all. Ike had his own message from Bulganin. Late in the day, Eisenhower read Ambassador Bohlen's translation of that message, issued simultaneously with the warnings to Israel, Britain, and France.[22] Bulganin called the situation in Egypt an "alarming and responsible moment"; a week had passed since Egypt had been attacked "without any cause, causing death and destruction, inhuman bombardments by English and French aviation." The landings of Anglo-French paratroopers had resulted in "human sacrifices" when the Egyptians were only "defending their freedom and independence."

Bulganin made an extraordinary proposal to Eisenhower—that the United States and the Soviet Union join forces "to restore peace and tranquility" in the Middle East. The United States and the USSR, he contended, should issue an ultimatum to the combatants, announce a readiness to intervene, and jointly mobilize their naval fleets "to stop aggression and terminate further blood-shed." Bulganin concluded with a statement guaranteed to command Eisenhower's attention: "If this war is not stopped, it is fraught with danger and can grow into [a] third world war."

Ike interpreted Bulganin's pledge to work through the United Nations as window dressing. If he rejected Bulganin's scheme—as Soviet leaders surely knew he would—the implied threat was unilateral intervention by the Soviets. Ambassador Bohlen confirmed Eisenhower's judgment that the Bulganin messages were primarily a ploy to divert attention from Hungary. But, he warned, "it would be imprudent to dismiss this merely as an empty propaganda gesture."[23]

The Suez crisis had reached a treacherous tipping point. At 5:00 P.M., Eisenhower called a meeting to address Bulganin's warnings with Adams, Hoover, Hagerty, Phleger, Hughes, and Goodpaster.[24] Ike did not, under any circumstances, intend to permit Soviet troops on the ground in the Middle East. Hughes recalled that the president was in a somber mood. "You know," he said, "we may be dealing here with the opening gambit of an ultimatum. We have to be positive and clear in our every word, every step. And if those fellows start something, we may have to hit them—and, if necessary with everything in the bucket."[25]

Eisenhower told the group that he wanted a public statement in response to Bulganin that would constitute "a clear warning—a passage that would make it unmistakably clear that the United Nations, including the United States, would oppose with force any attempt to violate the U.N. plan for getting a cease-fire." America should say to the Arab states in the United Nations, "Do you want the Soviets in the Middle East doing what they are now doing in Hungary?" Recalling Hitler's last days, the president described the Soviet leaders as "scared and furious" about the growing unrest in the satellite nations, "and there is nothing more dangerous than a dictatorship in this state of mind." Events were pushing Eisenhower closer to his ultimate nightmare—World War III. He intended to be ready. Eisenhower instructed Sherman Adams to request congressional leaders to meet with him on Thursday or Friday for a preliminary consultation in case he was forced to ask Congress for a declaration of war.

Eisenhower edited the White House statement issued after the meeting. The crisp, clear, military-style language was designed to communicate without equivocation how seriously he would view Soviet military intervention in the Middle East. It was "unthinkable"—a favorite Eisenhower term— "unthinkable" that the United States would join with Soviet military forces to intervene in Egypt. He implied that the Russian proposal was merely an attempt to divert attention from Hungary. Eisenhower called for support of the current United Nations resolutions, pointing out that the Soviet Union, by abstaining, had failed to vote in favor of deploying a United Nations force in Egypt. Then came Eisenhower's "clear warning": "Neither Soviet or any other military forces should now enter the Middle East area except under United Nations mandate." Any unilateral action "would violate the United Nations Charter, and it would be the duty of all United Nations members, including the United States, to oppose any such effort." [26]

The president issued this public statement without a personal reply to Bulganin. Ike understood that this pregnant silence, broken only by the public statement, would alert Soviet analysts that the old general's dander was up. The *New York Times* got the message. While Eisenhower's statement had not directly said that the United States would use its armed forces to oppose Soviet action in the Middle East, "that was the implication that leading Western diplomats immediately discerned." [27]

On Eisenhower's orders, the Joint Chiefs of Staff met and agreed to alert commanders in the region "as a result of a Soviet note to the President and subsequent Soviet comments in the press." The Joint Chiefs not only took steps to provide airlift capacity and support for the United Nations force but, in the Mediterranean, placed the Sixth Fleet, which included aircraft with nuclear capabilities, on full alert. The chiefs viewed the situation as the closest they had come to war with the Soviet Union since World War II, so the entire Navy was directed to "maintain readiness to implement emergency war plans." Simultaneously, the chiefs moved Sixth Fleet ships into a position where they would be interspersed with the British and French navies—a move designed to say to the Soviet Union, in the words of a subsequent top secret study by the Navy, that "an attack on one would be an attack on all." [28]

At the United Nations, there were rays of light in the gloom. Britain and France, while not yet agreeing to a cease-fire, indicated a willingness to consider one if Egypt and Israel accepted the insertion of a United Nations force between the belligerents. Later, Secretary-General Hammarskjöld received word that Egypt had accepted the resolution providing for a United Nations force. Israeli ambassador Abba Eban forwarded a cable from his government saying that Israel had agreed "unconditionally" to a cease-fire and, "since this morning, 5 November, all fighting has ceased between Israel and Egyptian forces on land, sea and air and full quiet prevails." At 8:00 P.M., the United Nations Security Council met to debate the Soviet resolution transmitted earlier in the day in the wake of Bulganin's warning messages, demanding that Britain, France, and Israel implement a cease-fire within twelve hours and withdraw from Egypt within three days or be faced with the prospect of American and Soviet Union military assistance to Egypt. The United States exercised its veto to ensure that the Soviet resolution would not be approved for consideration. [29]

This was election eve, so Ike's day was not yet over. The stresses—both physical and psychological—were taking a toll on the president. After the tense meeting over the Bulganin message, Ike had called in his doctor, Howard Snyder, who found the president's blood pressure elevated and his heartbeat irregular, "with an average of 8 skips per minute." Ike lay down on his bed but developed a headache, possibly because he had eaten only a dish of carrots and a glass of yogurt since breakfast. He called Snyder an hour later and the doctor found that the president's abdomen was distended and he was in considerable discomfort. The president was severely agitated and undoubtedly profane, as was his habit at such moments. His upset, the doctor recorded, was "due to what he termed an ultimatum that had been served upon him by Bulganin." Ike growled to his physician that "if he were a dictator, he would tell Russia if they moved a finger, he would drop our entire stock of atomic weapons on them." [30]

Ike took some aspirin and Snyder gave him Serpatilin—a mood stabilizer of the day—and then the president ate dinner. At 8:55, Eisenhower pulled himself together and addressed a crowd in Boston via closed-circuit television from the White House library. He delivered a short, upbeat campaign talk, but with solemn overtones. At one point, the weary president sighed that "there is so much to do. Many things yet unfinished." Toward the end, he spoke about his preoccupation—"world peace." Eisenhower cited the "many crises" of recent days and reaffirmed his readiness "to stand by principle." "Justice," he continued—"justice is a necessary part of world peace, because without justice there will be no peace." Obviously thinking about the Middle East and his old allies, the president concluded, "There must be one law for all, not just one for us and one for the others. We must have one law that rules us all." [31]

Ironically, the Democratic candidate, Adlai Stevenson, was also addressing a Boston crowd in his final speech of the campaign. In a last attempt to pull out a victory, the governor escalated his rhetoric about the president's health. Fortunately for Ike, no Stevenson spy had been in the room a couple of hours earlier when the president's doctor had been ministering to him. Eisenhower's foreign policy, Stevenson charged, "is in disarray in all parts of the world." His Middle East policy was "in ruins and has furthered the Soviet design to penetrate this strategic area, to the great damage of the cause of freedom." If the president served another term, he would be over seventy years of age. Stevenson reminded his audience of William Henry Harrison, who was elected at age sixty-eight and died a month later. A vote for Eisenhower, Stevenson asserted, was a vote for Richard Nixon to become president "within the next four years." Stevenson characterized Eisenhower as "isolated, uninformed and uninterested," a leader whose "negligence on questions of peace and war may plunge the whole world into the horror of hydrogen war." [32]

About 11:45, at the end of an hour-long television broadcast sponsored by the Republican National Committee, Eisenhower made remarks to the nation, televised live from the White House library. He avoided specific comment about Hungary and Egypt. Instead he returned to the theme of his previous campaign addresses—the need for the rule of law in the world. The president noted the troubles of recent days—"our tensions, our anxieties, our concerns for people that are downtrodden, people that are being ruthlessly exploited, even killed for their love of freedom." While that was an oblique reference to Hungary, the Egyptians might have found hope in Eisenhower's repetition of one of his favorite themes. "We have a very large stake in the freedom of every people," he said, "wherever they may be, just as we do in our own. We do not believe in second-class citizens. And there can be no second-class nations. Before the law all are equal; let us remember that."[33]

After what seemed an interminable day, Ike requested "a tall glass" of Scotch and water. The president retired a little after 1:00 A.M.[34]

TUESDAY, NOVEMBER 6—ELECTION DAY

Ike rose on Election Day to a Middle East that seemed in greater turmoil than the day before. He had slept until about 6:30 although Mamie later told Dr. Snyder that the president had been restless a few hours earlier. At eight, Ike called Snyder at his home to say there was a "bulging" in the abdominal scar from his surgery in June. A half hour later, when the president was already in his office, the doctor confirmed that the scar was infected. He carefully monitored the president's health the rest of the day, accompanying him even when he left the White House to vote. Later that day, Snyder summoned Dr. Leonard Heaton from Walter Reed Hospital to examine the president's infected abdominal scar, which was red, swollen, and tender.[35]

Ike had more than physical reasons to be agitated. Additional British and French assault forces had landed in Egypt and the fighting had intensified. Following Snyder's examination, Eisenhower met with Sherman Adams and Allen Dulles, who were later joined by Hoover and Flemming.[36] The CIA director reviewed a special National Intelligence Estimate that had been approved at 1:30 A.M., and was already out of date.[37] That document concluded it was unlikely that the Soviets would risk a general war. Still, Soviet forces were capable of inflicting small-scale attacks by air or submarine against British-French forces in the Mediterranean. One worry was whether the Soviets might, in a more general war, use "rockets" they had developed. These were medium-range ballistic missiles with nuclear warheads, possibly deployed in the satellite states, and possessing an eight-hundred-mile range, meaning they could reach France, Britain, or Israel. As for Egypt, the estimate concluded that it appeared that the French and British were now planning to limit their military operations to the Suez Canal area, partly in response to growing popular opposition to the war in Britain.

There were worrisome new developments since the NIE had been drafted. The CIA director showed Eisenhower intelligence indicating that the Soviet Union had told the Egyptians that they intended to "do something" to end the hostilities. Ike ordered Dulles to continue U-2 reconnaissance flights over Syria to see whether the Soviets were deploying aircraft at Syrian airbases, but he confirmed a previous order to avoid any flights over Russia at this time.

The president brooded over the slide toward a larger war. "Our people should be alert," he said. "If the Soviets attack the French and British directly, we would be in war, and we would be justified in taking military action even if Congress were not in session." If reconnaissance disclosed Soviet planes on Syrian bases, he said, "there would be reason for the British and French to destroy them." Eisenhower stared directly into the abyss of nuclear war; he inquired whether American naval units in the Mediterranean were equipped "with atomic anti-submarine weapons." The minutes provided no answer to that question.

This being Election Day, the American people expected to see pictures of their president and his wife casting their ballots. At 9:13, Ike, Mamie, and Dr. Snyder departed by car for Gettysburg, where the Eisenhowers, as Pennsylvania residents, were obligated to vote.

Meanwhile, the Soviet warnings had thrown French leaders into a state of near panic, resulting in an emergency cabinet meeting. U.S. ambassador Douglas Dillon reported that Premier Mollet and Foreign Minister Pineau were anxiously awaiting the American response to Bulganin's communications. Dillon said French leaders had told him that they would consider a cease-fire once all their troops were ashore, but not in response to Soviet pressure. They did not plan to withdraw until United Nations troops were in place and still wanted French troops integrated into that force.[38]

After President and Mrs. Eisenhower had departed for Gettysburg, Acting Secretary Hoover received the French ambassador, Hervé Alphand, who insisted he be permitted to deliver an urgent message to the president about the possibility that the Soviet Union might attack British and French forces.[39] Hoover, usually a patient man, did not mince words. He told Alphand that "the only way to get the situation back on the tracks was for the French and British Governments to accept unequivocally and unconditionally the UN resolution calling for a cease fire, with the withdrawal of forces, and the acceptance of a UN police force." Alphand insisted that this was a separate matter, an argument Hoover angrily swatted down. Hoover was so scathing in his statements that Alphand later called William R. Tyler, the deputy director for West European affairs, who had been in the meeting, anxiously asking if Hoover had meant that the United States might abrogate its obligations under NATO to come to France's defense. Tyler reassured the stressed diplomat that his fears were groundless. What he did not say was that Hoover's approach reflected a clear Eisenhower strategy—to project ambiguity to the British and French about American willingness to invoke NATO as long as they were making war in Egypt while, behind the scenes, fully preparing to come to the allies' defense if the Soviet Union acted against their forces.[40]

The British were suffering their own anxiety attack, but theirs was rooted more in their finances than in the Soviet warnings. The British pound was pegged to the American dollar at a rate of $2.80, so the maintenance of adequate reserves was essential to prevent the government from being forced to devalue the currency, an action that would damage the British economy. The United Kingdom had lost $50 million in reserves the first two days after beginning the bombing in Egypt. Suddenly, as British paratroopers were landing, speculation accelerated against the pound in the currency markets. Harold Macmillan, the chancellor of the exchequer, was increasingly apprehensive about a precipitous loss of dollar reserves. Macmillan had anxiously asked the International Monetary Fund to return the British quota—the funds his government had previously paid into the fund. While the British cabinet was in session the morning of November 6, Macmillan learned that the American Treasury Department—no doubt following Eisenhower's orders—had vetoed the return of the IMF funds until Great Britain agreed to a cease-fire. It was evident later that Macmillan had exaggerated the extent of the drain on British reserves but his gloomy report to the cabinet had a profound impact on its deliberations about whether to continue the fighting in Egypt.[41]

In his memoirs, British foreign minister Selwyn Lloyd bitterly recalled that Anthony Eden was "emotionally affected when he was told that the administration of his close wartime friend, Eisenhower, through the mouth of George Humphrey, the American Secretary of the Treasury whom Macmillan also regarded as a friend, was obstructing our drawing from the International Monetary Fund what was our own money." Lloyd confirmed that the denial of that request nurtured suspicions among British leaders that the rampant speculation on the pound "was being stimulated by the United States Treasury." Macmillan recalled in his memoirs that the run on the pound was centered in New York, spearheaded by the Federal Reserve, which was selling pounds at a rate that was "far above what was necessary as a precaution to protect the value of its own holdings."[42]

Not long after the president left for Gettysburg, Ann Whitman recorded that the news from the Middle East "looked so bad at one point that they contemplated asking him to turn around and come back." Rumors were rampant that Soviet intervention was imminent—that the Russians were recruiting "volunteers" to send to Egypt; new intelligence reports indicated that Russians were arriving in Egypt carrying "special weapons" and that Soviet troops were massing on the border with Turkey, a NATO ally. While intelligence sources did not expect an attack on Britain and France proper, they recognized that, in the Black Sea area, the Soviet Union had two thousand jet fighters and five hundred bombers. In response to what appeared to be a deteriorating situation, the Joint Chiefs extended the alert already ordered for the Sixth Fleet to the U.S. Atlantic Fleet.[43]

Some of the bad news came directly from Moscow. Ambassador Bohlen had cabled at 10:44 A.M., Washington time, that the Soviet mood had become "more ominous." Bohlen interpreted Bulganin's messages the previous day to the French, British, and Israelis "as close to [an] ultimatum." The Soviets, he said, had concluded that continued fighting in the Middle East was "making it increasingly difficult for them to maintain complete inaction." The ambassador believed that the Soviet impatience transcended any attempt to distract world opinion from their repression in Hungary. Russian leaders, he had concluded, were "motivated by conviction that Middle East fighting might spread and that sooner or later [the] Soviet Union would have to take some definite position." Bohlen hoped that the Russians would settle for a cessation of hostilities. It was imperative, he said, that American leaders convince the Kremlin that military action against Britain and France would result in armed resistance from the United States. "This warning would be very much more effective," Bohlen continued, "if it could be accompanied by some official communication from [the] U.S. government as to when all hostilities would cease against Egypt."[44]

This news unsettled the leadership of the White House staff. Someone (probably staff secretary Andrew Goodpaster) called Admiral Radford to ask if the president should turn his car around and return to the White House. Radford cautioned against doing anything that would attract unwanted attention. Still, everyone agreed it was essential to ask the president, without fanfare, to come back as quickly as possible. As a result, Colonel Goodpaster arranged for the president to be flown back to Washington.[45]

That morning, the Joint Chiefs had already been frantically defining the steps they would recommend to the president to improve readiness for a general war. If the president approved, they would "dispatch to the commanders of unified and specified commands an alert message." Such an alert would involve recalling personnel from leave, increasing the number of interceptor aircraft on alert, deployment of tanker squadrons, and, above all, "preparations to reinforce the Sixth Fleet" and "improve U.S. military readiness in the Persian Gulf area."[46]

The Eisenhowers voted, then were driven to their farm, where they were greeted by Ike's brother Milton. Almost immediately, the president went into the house to take a call from the White House. Whitman noted in her diary that, apparently because the staff feared communications leaks, "the President did not know, until his return, the reason he was called back." Goodpaster met Ike at the airfield in Washington and, while they motored to the White House, reviewed developments, including the prospects for a cease-fire and reports of unidentified jet aircraft, possibly Soviet, overflying Turkey. Goodpaster had one piece of good news; U-2 photography had confirmed that there were no Soviet aircraft in Syria. The United States would continue U-2 flights over Syria for most of the next two weeks.[47]

Eisenhower arrived back at the White House at 12:38 P.M. and was briefed in his office by Hoover and Phleger about a message from Ambassador Aldrich in London that Anthony Eden had informed him of his intent to declare a cease-fire. Ike ordered that a call be placed to Eden to confirm that report.[48] Then the president went into an emergency meeting in the Cabinet Room. There were eighteen men present—the vice president and the top leadership of both the State and Defense departments, including the Joint Chiefs. This was nothing less than a council of war. Despite renewed hope for a cease-fire in Egypt, the danger of Soviet military intervention dominated the meeting.[49]

Admiral Radford informed the president that the Joint Chiefs had assessed American readiness for a major war, and he read the list of steps the military leaders had agreed upon. Eisenhower, cool under fire, urged careful and deliberate implementation: "These should be put into effect by degrees—not all at once, in order to avoid creating a stir. Units can be put on alert, and the number of ships and aircraft on ready status should be increased." Ike was reluctant to visibly move forces into the waters near the conflict, but he wanted steady progress toward achieving "an advanced state of readiness, starting the next morning." He suggested that recalling personnel from leave would be "an action impossible to conceal which would let the Russians know—without being provocative—that we could not be taken by surprise." Later, Ike changed his mind about taking this step.

Radford placed the situation in military perspective. Admitting that "it is very hard to figure out Russian thinking," he believed it would be militarily difficult for the Soviets to attempt operations in the Middle East. While the Soviets had the aircraft to deliver troops, Radford said, he doubted they would take that course. "The only reasonable form of intervention," he stated, "would be long-range air strikes with nuclear weapons—which seems unlikely." Eisenhower had already reached a similar conclusion. Robert Murphy, a favorite Eisenhower diplomatic troubleshooter, had heard the president say earlier, "Look at the map. Geography makes effective Soviet intervention in Egypt difficult, if not impossible." [50]

Then the sun broke through the war clouds. Word came that Anthony Eden was now available and Eisenhower left the meeting to talk with him. "I can't tell you how pleased we are that you found it possible to accept the cease-fire," Ike told his old wartime ally. "We are going to cease firing tonight," Eden tersely replied. Ike asked whether British compliance with the cease-fire would be "without condition?" Eden said, almost resentfully: "We cease firing tonight at midnight provided we are not attacked." [51]

Eisenhower had thought a great deal about what he would say when this moment came. "I am talking off the top of my head," he said, but he was not. Ike understood that a potentially contentious issue—clearing the canal of its sunken ships—could unravel the cease-fire. The British and French had technical troops with the skills to clear the canal. If they ordered those troops into action, the allies could convert that process into a de facto occupation of the Canal Zone.

Eisenhower headed off this possibility by insisting that Eden keep the cease-fire as simple as possible and put aside, for the time being, the issue of clearing the canal. Eden countered that with "the long cease fire, the cessation of hostilities, that is more complicated." But Eden was not in a strong bargaining position with the president, and he reluctantly agreed to include technical troops in the cease-fire. Ike, still gracious in tone, said, "If I may make a suggestion, I would offer them"—meaning the technical troops—"to Hammarskjöld—but I would not insist that he take them." That would take the matter out of Eden's hands. Eden grumbled about the difficulty of working such things out. Eisenhower's tone took on an edge: "The point I want you to have in your mind is that the cease-fire tonight has nothing to do with technical troops. You cease anyway." Eden spit out the words: "Unless attacked."

Eisenhower started to address "the more permanent affair," a longer term settlement of the crisis over the canal, but Eden muttered that he was due in Parliament "in five minutes," seeking a vote of confidence over the cease-fire. He asked Eisenhower what he could say about their talk. Ike responded, "You can say that I called to say how delighted I was you found it possible to cease fire tonight so that negotiations could start." Eden asked the president to repeat his words, so he could write them down.

Eisenhower turned to a critical issue they had not discussed—the necessity for a rapid withdrawal of foreign troops from Egypt. He told Eden he did not want "to give Egypt an opportunity to begin to quibble so that this thing can be drawn out for a week." Once Hammarskjöld got his U.N. force there, "you people ought to be able to withdraw very quickly." He shrewdly preempted any Eden plan for including British and French troops in the United Nations contingent. "I would like to see none of the great nations in it," Eisenhower said. "I am afraid the Red boy is going to demand the lion's share. I would rather make it no troops from the big five," referring to the permanent members of the Security Council at the time— France, Great Britain, the United States, Nationalist China, and the Soviet Union. Eden, unhappy at that prospect, commented that unless the U.N. had "a good force," large enough to be effective, keeping the peace would not be easy. Eisenhower replied that if the Egyptians or anyone else "attacked the United Nations and its whole prestige and force—then everyone is in the thing." In other words, if such circumstances arose, the United States would intervene. Still a man of few words, Eden said, "May I think that one over?"

Ike urged Eden to call him anytime. Eden, preparing to go the House of Commons for a vote of confidence, replied, "If I survive here tonight, I will call you tomorrow." The first hint of warmth in the conversation came when Eden asked about Foster Dulles and how things were going for the president on Election Day. Ike replied: "We have given our whole thought to Hungary and the Middle East. I don't give a damn how the election goes."

Eisenhower had correctly suspected that Eden was scheming to camouflage a de facto occupation of the Canal Zone. Ambassador Aldrich communicated to the State Department that Eden's first indication of his willingness to accept a cease-fire had assumed that British and French troops would clear the canal—what Ike had called "technical issues." Eisenhower immediately reinforced his phone call, cabling to Eden his "urgent" concern that the cease-fire be accepted "without condition," and putting off until later the possible use of "technical troops" to clear the canal. He urged that "no excuse be given for Soviet participation in the UN force," and that none of the "big five" nations should provide troops for this force. In response the next day, Eden wrote that, while his government had not made the use of its technical troops a condition for the cease-fire, "we are on the spot and [we are] the only people who can do it quickly." He was willing to consider Eisenhower's premise that none of the Big Five should be in the peacekeeping force but, he added, this was "a matter on which there are very deep feelings here." [52]

Eisenhower cabled Guy Mollet with the same argument, flattering the French premier for joining in "an act of high statesmanship" while pushing his clearheaded proposal—a cease-fire without conditions, involving only nonpermanent members of the Security Council in the United Nations force, and leaving the clearing of the canal for later. [53]

Eisenhower did not view the crisis as over. Late in the day, State Department officials were still worrying about Soviet intentions. At 3:31 P.M., Ambassador Bohlen identified six methods the Soviets might employ to intervene in the Middle East, ranging from covert transportation of volunteers to submarine attacks on British and French ships and the deployment of bomber and fighter aircraft to Syrian bases. [54]

A little later, the reports of Eden's presentation to the House of Commons arrived. Eden had read aloud his communication to the secretary-general indicating his government's agreement to the cease-fire and a willingness to proceed with removing the barriers to traffic in the Suez Canal. Eden also read his reply to the warning from Bulganin, refuting the Soviet leader's charges and reminding Bulganin that "in the past three days Soviet forces in Hungary have been ruthlessly crushing the heroic resistance of a truly national movement for independence." [55]

At 5:45 P.M., Hoover called a meeting of key State Department officials to implement the president's orders arising out of this dramatic day. They agreed that a cease-fire would be useless unless linked to British, French, and Israeli withdrawal of forces. They discussed the meeting the president wanted with congressional leaders, tentatively scheduled for Friday. Hoover, taking nothing for granted, sent an urgent message to Ambassador Hare in Cairo, asking him to ensure that Nasser was aware that the British and French had accepted a cease-fire that would go into effect at 2:00 A.M. Cairo time and that the president had rejected the Soviet proposal for joint intervention. Hare was instructed to counsel Nasser that his interests would be served by working with the United Nations and that Egypt should "leave no doubt that it would not welcome unilateral Soviet intervention." [56]

Subsequent communications from the American embassies in Britain and France showed that Eisenhower's pressure for a cease-fire without conditions was making progress, although with considerable foot-dragging. After receiving Eisenhower's cable, Mollet had called Eden and asked whether Eisenhower wanted immediate withdrawal of their forces. They finally agreed they would refuse to withdraw troops until the United Nations force was in place and ready to function; the two leaders reluctantly accepted the arrangement whereby neither British nor French forces would be part of the U.N. contingent. [57]

Eisenhower knew that the peace was fragile and Soviet intentions were still unclear. So he gave the green light to implement most of the steps for increased readiness that were discussed at his noon meeting. Ike decided to defer two recommendations—to improve the readiness of the Strategic Air Command and to recall personnel from regular leave. At 11:56 P.M., orders went out from the Joint Chiefs to implement the remainder of the president's orders, effectively putting the Sixth Fleet and the Atlantic and Pacific fleets on battle-ready alert, deploying additional ships, submarines, and tactical air resources, and placing heavy troop carrier wings on a twelve-hour alert. [58]

About ten that evening, the Eisenhowers, friends, and family traveled to the Sheraton Park Hotel, where a suite had been reserved for watching the election returns. Even though it had become apparent earlier in the evening that the president had won reelection by a huge margin, Eisenhower did not go downstairs to address supporters until 1:45 A.M. Ike had insisted on waiting for Stevenson to make his concession speech, something the defeated candidate seemed loath to do. The president concluded his brief remarks to campaign supporters with a pledge: "With whatever talents the good God has given me, with whatever strength there is within me, I will continue—and so will my associates—to do just one thing: to work for 168 million Americans here at home—and for peace in the world." [59]

Meanwhile, hours earlier—approximately 2:00 A.M. Cairo time, 7:00 P.M. in Washington—the fighting had ended in the Middle East.

12

★ ★ ★ ★ ★ ★

A RELUCTANT WITHDRAWAL

November 7–December 24, 1956

"I am quite certain that unless we can restore very soon the Mid
East as the principal source of oil supply, there is nothing we can
do to save Western Europe."

Eisenhower to Lewis Williams Douglas, November 30, 1956

THE WEDNESDAY, November 7, *New York Times* headline read: "Eisenhower
by a Landslide," followed by, "Suez Warfare Stopped Under British-French
Cease-Fire." Ann Whitman noted in her diary that the White House staff
were in their offices "with far too little sleep—two to three hours at the
most."[1]

At 8:43, Anthony Eden called the president in the White House living
quarters before Ike could get to the Oval Office.[2] Eden and Premier Mollet, claiming intelligence revealing new Soviet designs on the Middle East,
wanted to immediately fly to the United States to see the president. At first,
Ike was enthusiastic at the chance to reconcile with his old allies. "After
all," he said to Eden, "it is like a family spat." But he soon realized that his
response had been premature. Eisenhower hastily convened a meeting with
Adams and Goodpaster, soon joined by Acting Secretary of State Hoover
and Treasury Secretary Humphrey. They told the president that a state visit

at this time might, in Hoover's words, "give the impression that we are teaming with the British and French." Secretary Dulles, Hoover said, was "very much opposed to the visit at this time." [3]

The sticking point was the withdrawal of Anglo-French forces from Egypt. Eisenhower had been unable to trust what the British and French were telling him for many weeks, so why could he trust them now? He called Eden back. [4] "I have some problems," he said, exaggerating that he had just held "a partial Cabinet meeting" whose members thought "our timing is very, very bad." Eden, nonplussed, resorted to brusque, one-sentence responses. "Will you be sending Mollet a message?" he asked. Eisenhower said, "I think you better call him." Eden tersely snapped, "He will speak in a half hour," alluding to Mollet's impending announcement of the trip. Eisenhower responded, "You'd better call him right away." This was bad news for the beleaguered British leader; it would soon become widely known that the president of the United States had refused to see him.

Afterward, Eisenhower and Hoover went to see Foster Dulles at Walter Reed. Ike informed Dulles that Eden was "quite concerned about the Russians moving into the Middle East" and had sought a meeting to discuss "what the Bear will do and what we would do in the face of the Bear's acts." Dulles responded that unless the British and French withdrew within a week's time, the "fire will go on burning" and might prove impossible to put out. Ike and Dulles agreed that a meeting with the allies should be "contingent on the British and French having previously gotten their troops out of Egypt." Eisenhower later cabled Eden to that effect, suggesting that compliance with the U.N. resolution "would permit us to meet here by the end of next week"—a clear hint that the British had better get moving on withdrawal. [5]

ISRAELI INTRANSIGENCE

In this cauldron of troublesome protagonists—Britain, France, Egypt, the Soviet Union, and Israel—the latter would eventually prove to be the most intransigent. When the fighting stopped, Israeli forces controlled the Sinai Peninsula, the Gaza Strip, and the entry to the Gulf of Aqaba. In his November 7 address to the Knesset, the country's legislative body, Prime Minister Ben-Gurion rejected the General Assembly's resolution calling for U.N. troops to replace Israeli forces and declared the Israeli-Egyptian armistice agreement of 1949 "dead and buried." [6]

In a 5:30 P.M. call, Hoover asked Eisenhower if he had seen Ben-Gurion's statement. Ike said he had and called it "terrible." Hoover hand-delivered the president's response to Israel's chargé d'affaires, Reuven Shiloah, and administered his own stern verbal reprimand. If Israel refused to withdraw, Hoover told Shiloah, his nation could be charged with "gravely endangering world peace," resulting in resolutions "calling for strict sanctions" and a movement to expel Israel from the United Nations.[7]

Eisenhower's letter to Ben-Gurion was equally blunt. He urged the Israeli leader "to comply with the resolutions of the United Nations General Assembly" and "to make your decision known immediately." Ben-Gurion responded ambiguously, ignoring the occupation of Gaza and Aqaba, and stating that "we have never planned to annex the Sinai Desert." He wrote that Israel, "upon conclusion of satisfactory arrangements with the United Nations," would withdraw its forces from "the Suez Canal area." Ike chose to interpret Ben-Gurion's letter broadly, saying he appreciated the prime minister's message "informing me that you will withdraw your forces from Egypt."[8]

In Cairo, Nasser had not yet formally accepted the cease-fire, but he told Ambassador Hare that the United States "need not worry" about Soviet involvement with Egypt. His country, he asserted, would continue its "long struggle" to get rid of foreign domination. "I don't trust any big power," he said.[9]

"KEEPING THE POT BOILING"

By the morning of November 8, a myriad of rumors regarding Soviet intentions convinced American authorities that the Suez crisis was not really over. A Soviet MiG fighter reportedly had shot down a British Canberra reconnaissance aircraft over Syria at 45,000 feet, fueling speculation that Soviet volunteers were piloting the planes. Communist China and the Soviet Union had announced that they were signing up large numbers of volunteers to send to Egypt. Four Soviet aircraft were reported to be stationed at the Aleppo airfield in Syria, and a Soviet submarine and other warships were rumored to have been sighted in the Turkish Straits.

Eisenhower was calmer about the prospect of Soviet intervention than others, especially the British. Still, he ordered the American military to be prepared for any contingency. The Atlantic Fleet was instructed, according to a secret Navy study years later, to "detect, report, track Soviet or Satellite forces including merchantmen" using "defensive armament only." Naval forces off the American East Coast were instructed, in the event of attacks by Soviet bloc vessels, to "counter attack using every available means to destroy." The U.S. Sixth Fleet was shifted to an operating area southwest of Crete "in order [to] improve readiness posture for general emergency." Two U.S. aircraft carriers were moved to the eastern end of the Mediterranean.[10]

The National Security Council met for two and a half hours the morning of November 8 to assess the situation.[11] Oil was the first issue on the agenda. Ike brought in Robert Anderson, his personal envoy, who had been consulting with the oil companies and, by implication, with the Middle East's oil-producing nations, especially Saudi Arabia. He reported that the canal was blocked by eight or nine ships and that the Iraq pipeline had been sabotaged and its pumping stations destroyed. Aramco's Trans-Arabian Pipeline (informally called the Tapline) through Saudi Arabia was still intact, but it was uncertain how long it would remain in operation.

Eisenhower asked Anderson if American oil production could be increased without appearing to the Arab nations to be "bailing out the British and the French." Anderson thought that it would be difficult if the government was visibly involved. "If we really get the Arabs sore at all of us," Ike said, "they could embargo all oil," with disastrous consequences for Europe. Eisenhower approved the movement of U.S. Gulf Coast oil to the East Coast in foreign-flag tankers, a move designed to camouflage preparations for sending it to Europe.[12]

Eisenhower then surveyed the perfect storm of the past few days. Still smoldering with anger, Ike said he wanted "a complete history of this cabal with which the British and French were involved." While he had opposed the invasion, Eisenhower, as a military man, was harshly critical of the Anglo-French military operations, saying that "there was no excuse for the long delay in the landing of British and French troops in the Suez Canal area once they had made the decision to do so."

Eisenhower called the Soviet repression of Hungary "a bitter pill for us to swallow," but, he added, there was little the United States could do about it. By this time, thousands of Hungarians had died and more than 200,000 refugees were pouring across Hungary's borders into neighboring states. Ike had concluded that breaking off diplomatic relations with Moscow would accomplish nothing. He shared that the Soviet premier, Nikolai Bulganin, had sent him a message that morning saying, in effect, that "what was going on in Hungary was none of the business of the United States."

Soviet intent in the Middle East was the urgent matter. DCI Allen

Dulles framed the question: "How far will the Soviets go in this situation and what will they do?" The CIA, he said, believed that, for the time being, the Soviet "emphasis would be on keeping the pot boiling," rather than taking actions that would lead to a larger war. However, one intelligence source had informed the CIA that the Soviets had asked Turkish permission to send five Soviet warships through the Turkish Straits. Other possibilities included a Soviet-sponsored coup in Syria or landing technicians or MiG aircraft there. Admiral Radford argued that the Soviets were already "in Syria" and that the Syrian air force was incapable of having shot down the British reconnaissance aircraft. Eisenhower countered that he believed "the Russians would play their game short of anything which would induce the United States to declare war on them."

Hoover clarified the immediate steps. First, get the United Nations peacekeeping force established in Egypt. Second, British and French forces must withdraw. Third, Israel must return to the 1949 armistice lines. Finally, the United States could begin to deal with the oil situation. If the Soviets dared to attack the U.N. police force, he said, that "would be tantamount to a Russian attack on the whole world." Eisenhower reinforced Hoover's conclusion, saying that "the main thing now was to get the UN police force into Egypt and the British and French forces out of Egypt. This action would pull the rug out from under the Soviet psychological offensive."

THE EISENHOWER STRATEGY

Eisenhower had settled on his strategy for winding down the Suez crisis. If the British and French did not commit themselves to withdrawal, he was prepared to endure a firestorm of criticism in Europe and the United States for withholding financial aid and oil from the Europeans, who were facing the onset of winter weather.

Eisenhower's approach operated on three levels. The first was his residual anger at his old allies for double-crossing him. The second was his commitment to principle, upholding the United Nations resolutions requiring withdrawal from Egypt. The third factor was immensely practical, focused on the long haul. Eisenhower explained it later in a letter to a critic, former ambassador Lewis Douglas."[13] Douglas had alleged that the president was requiring the equivalent of unconditional surrender from the British and French before providing "desperately and urgently needed supplies of oil."

Eisenhower responded that "the oil supply of Western Europe, a vital necessity, depended in the long run upon the *readiness of the Arab world to sell to Western Europe*." He had warned the allies that the sure way to cut off oil supplies "would be the employment of force in the Suez," an action certain to create "a situation where the Arab populations would support Nasser fanatically." Anglo-French leaders had ignored the fact "that in the long run Western Europe's economy could be sustained only by Mid East oil."

Eisenhower revealed to Douglas that he had made an implicit bargain with Saudi Arabia, probably mediated through Robert Anderson. "After the invasion and when the larger pipelines were destroyed," he wrote, "we were able to keep operating the [Saudi Arabian] Tapline—with a capacity of 330,000 barrels a day—only on the promise that, for the moment, none of that oil should go to the British and the French." Ike painted a stark vision of reality: "I am quite certain that unless we can restore very soon the Mid East as the principal source of oil supply, there is nothing we can do to save Western Europe. *The fuel requirements of the entire Western world cannot possibly be permanently supplied from North America and Venezuela.*" Eisenhower summarized his case: "We must remain true to our friends, but we must likewise remain on a friendly status with the Mid East oil suppliers. The only other alternative would be a gigantic occupation of the Mid East by military force."

WHY A CEASE-FIRE?

Amid the flurry of activity during the two days following the cease-fire, there is little evidence that Eisenhower spent much time and energy trying to ascertain why, after months of clandestine planning, the three nations, especially Britain, had agreed so quickly to a cease-fire. The Soviet threats of intervention on November 5 certainly played a role, although they were not as pivotal as the Soviets claimed. Anthony Nutting, a member of the British cabinet who had resigned in opposition to the Suez war, argued in his memoirs that the Soviet warnings "had no more influence on the decision of Britain and France to stop fighting than had our intervention in Egypt upon the Russian decision to crush the Hungarian revolt at all costs." Nutting listed items he considered "far more decisive." One was the growing political opposition in Britain, not only from the opposition Labour Party but from the public. Even more critical were the economic factors: "the closing of the Canal and stoppage of Middle East oil shipments" and, above all, "the run on the pound."[14]

Christian Pineau, the French foreign minister, later insisted that he had overheard a call from Eden to Mollet. According to Pineau, the British prime minister said that he had received a call from Eisenhower, "who told me if you don't get out of Port Said tomorrow, I'll cause a run on the pound and drive it to zero." [15] Neither Eisenhower nor Eden confirmed this call in his memoirs. Pineau may have confused this alleged call with the one Eisenhower made to Eden on November 6, just after the cease-fire was announced. If it took place as Pineau described, Eden, who often shaded the truth, may have exaggerated in order to shift the blame for his cease-fire decision.

One thing was certain: Eisenhower's opposition to the invasion was central to the outcome. It would have been uncharacteristic of Eisenhower to make a direct threat, such as the one reported by Pineau, to a foreign leader. Still, the financial pressures visited on the British clearly bore Ike's imprint, mediated through Treasury Secretary Humphrey. Early on, Eisenhower had decided to hold both funds and oil hostage until the British and French fully agreed to withdraw from Egypt.

BIRTH OF A DOCTRINE

Eisenhower was more focused on the future than the details of what had caused the British-French venture to collapse. He was ready to use the Suez crisis to shape a new American commitment to stability and security in the Middle East. After the November 8 NSC meeting, Ike dictated notes to his diary, partly in preparation for a meeting with congressional leaders the next day. [16] These notes outlined what would later come to be known as the Eisenhower Doctrine.

The United States must "be promptly ready to take any kind of action that will minimize the effects of the recent difficulties and will exclude from the area Soviet influence," Ike wrote. Once foreign troops were withdrawn, the immediate steps were obvious—restoration of the pipeline and canal operations, negotiations regarding the operations of the canal, and the provision of surplus food and other aid to relieve suffering.

But Eisenhower's primary concern was long-range. "We must lay before the several governments information and proposals that will establish real peace in the area and, above all to exclude Communist influence from making any headway therein." Historians have often emphasized the portions of the Eisenhower Doctrine, as finally passed by Congress in 1957, that justified American military intervention in the Middle East. But Eisenhower's focus on November 8, 1956, was not military but "the constructive things" that the United States could do.

Eisenhower laid out a sweeping agenda. "In return for an agreement that it will never accept any Soviet offer," the United States could "provide Egypt with an agreed-upon amount of arms—sufficient to maintain internal order and a reasonable defense of its borders," including training missions, technicians, and economic assistance for postwar reconstruction. Similar aid could be provided to Israel. Ike envisioned translating "the tripartite statement of May 1950 into a bilateral treaty with each of the countries in the area." The new policy would move beyond Israel and Egypt, providing assistance to Iraq, Jordan, Saudi Arabia, and Lebanon, and cementing economic "and friendly ties" with each of these countries.

Ike even revisited the troublesome project that had triggered the Suez crisis. "We can make arrangements for starting the Aswan Dam," he dictated, "on a basis where interest costs would be no higher than the money costs ourselves. This, of course, would be contingent upon Egypt negotiating faithfully on the Suez Canal matter and in accordance with the six principles laid down by the United Nations." Eisenhower later called Humphrey, stating his willingness to "go back in the Aswan Dam" and provide $75 million to Egypt as a means of demonstrating "that we will be friends with them." [17]

By the time he met with bipartisan congressional leaders the morning of Friday, November 9, Eisenhower had decided to defer, for the time being, a detailed presentation of such dramatic initiatives. While he had won a second term with 57 percent of the vote and 457–73 in the Electoral College, Ike still faced a Democratic Congress with a two-seat majority in the Senate and a thirty-three-seat margin in the House. So he chose to tread carefully, both in terms of the Soviet threat and proposals for the future.

Eisenhower stated to the congressional leaders that the meeting had not been prompted by "a crisis situation," but "for the general purpose of catching up with the world situation" after weeks of distraction due to the election. Still, he reminded them that in a nuclear age they all needed to remember that "either we achieve peace or we face extinction." He left it to Allen Dulles to report that the Soviet Union's warning notes of November 5, in the light of the brutal repression in Hungary, had been "sufficiently vague to leave open the possibility of unilateral action" in the Middle East. Admiral Radford added that the armed forces were ready for "any eventuality." [18]

Eisenhower outlined the principles of his emerging doctrine, emphasizing "the great importance of the Middle East in the cold war." But his focus was more economic than military. The efforts of the United States, he said, "ought to be concentrated to a greater degree on helping these nations strengthen their economies" as a means of preventing Soviet penetration of the region. He wisely said nothing about the Aswan Dam or Egypt.

When asked what would happen if the Soviets intervened militarily in the Middle East, Ike responded that "the U.S. would have to meet the issue like men." He expressed his hope that the U.N. efforts to secure the withdrawal of foreign forces from Egypt and establish a peacekeeping force "could be carried through in timely fashion." [19]

Eisenhower had presented himself to congressional leaders as a self-confident, fully in charge president—camouflaging how exhuasted, physically and mentally, he was. Afterward, Hoover urged him to go to Gettysburg for the weekend for some rest. Ike said that he did not want "to stay away that long at this time." Later that afternoon, Foster Dulles, obviously briefed by Hoover, called from Walter Reed Hospital to encourage the president to go to Gettysburg to recuperate from "election strain & all this"; however, Ann Whitman recorded, "the President won't." Ike later told his brother Edgar that "our problem in the Mid East continues at such a critical stage that I cannot contemplate leaving Washington at this time." [20]

With Soviet threats in the air, Eisenhower and Dulles chose this moment to finally respond to Bulganin's message of November 5 proposing joint intervention in Egypt. Ike sharply rejected the proposal as if it were still on the table, calling it contrary to United Nations resolutions and its charter. It was, he wrote, "difficult to reconcile your expressed concern for the principles of morality and the objectives of the United Nations with the action taken by Soviet military units against the people of Hungary." The Soviet Union, Eisenhower concluded, should "comply with the Resolutions of the U.N. on the subject of Hungary." That "would be a great and notable contribution to the cause of peace." [21]

The rumors were still flying. On Saturday November 10, the Soviets again threatened to send trained "volunteers" to join the Egyptian armed forces unless the "aggressors" withdrew from Egypt. Ambassador Bohlen in Moscow reported that Bulganin and Khrushchev had told visiting Greek mayors that the Soviet government "intended" to seek permission to overfly Greek territory to transport volunteers to the Middle East. That day, Allen Dulles presented Acting Secretary Hoover with intelligence that Syria "is in a critical condition where a Communist coup might be pulled off." As a result, the Navy issued an order mandating "increased readiness in the Atlantic Fleet." Naval forces off the East Coast of the United States were ordered to "be ready for any emergency but no publicity [should] be given to the state of readiness."[22]

On Monday, November 12, Eisenhower again visited Foster Dulles at Walter Reed.[23] He told Dulles that he still wanted to believe that "the British had not been in on the Israeli-French planning until the very last stages when they had no choice but to come into the operation." Eisenhower's weariness must have been apparent. The next day, Hoover, undoubtedly coached by Dulles, called again to urge Ike to get some rest. The president jested that "if it didn't look like all the world was breaking loose," he would go to the golf course that day.

Ike complained to Hoover in that phone conversation about "the alarming messages from Britain & France about our not agreeing to [a] meeting." The allied leaders were saying that "we are missing the point"—that the Soviet Union was "moving in, with a much stronger & heavier transfer of power than we anticipated." He ordered Hoover to institute a study, "as a matter of urgency," to investigate the needs of Iraq, Jordan, Saudi Arabia, Libya, and even Egypt "by holding out the carrot as well as the stick." "I am very anxious," Eisenhower concluded, "to see the constructive side of what we are going to do out there."[24]

The news conference on November 14 was Ike's first since October 11. He limited his comments about the Middle East because "the last thing we must do is to disturb any of the delicate negotiations now going on under the leadership of Secretary General Hammarskjöld." Eisenhower noted that "for the first time in history," the United Nations machinery for settling international disputes was "receiving a thorough test." He placed the threat of Soviet intervention in the context of a world where "men can develop weapons that are so terrifying as to make the thought of global war include almost a sentence for suicide." Eisenhower then alluded to his emerging doctrine for aid to the Middle East. "Our help will be given," he said, "without any conditions attached" and with "no strings of economic or political imperialism." "We are trying to be friends with both sides," he said. Unlike the Soviet Union, "every move we make must be balanced by a consideration of justice for both sides."[25]

By the morning of November 15, White House anxiety over possible Soviet intervention in the Middle East had begun to fade. Ann Whitman noted in her diary that "tensions seem to be lifting somewhat." The United Nations had landed a token peacekeeping force in Egypt, a landmark event. Late in November, Soviet foreign minister Dmitri Shepilov insisted to reporters that he had evidence of "new plans of aggression" and "incontestable information" that the British, French, and Israelis intended to attack other Middle East countries. But by then, inflammatory Soviet statements no longer caused a stir.[26]

EDEN IN TROUBLE

Eisenhower visited Foster Dulles's hospital room on Saturday, November 17, the day before the secretary was scheduled to depart for Key West, Florida, to continue his recuperation. The fate of Anthony Eden was on the president's mind. In an extraordinary revelation, Ike shared with Dulles that two British generals had told him they perceived "an increasing lack of confidence in the British Prime Minister." By talking to those generals, Eisenhower was perilously close to meddling in British politics. Ike commented to Dulles that "one of the most pleasant things in life was to find one's estimate of a man increased each time he had dealings with him." But, he continued, "one of the most disappointing things was to start with an exceedingly high opinion of a person and then have continually to downgrade this estimate." Eden, he said, "fell into the latter category."[27]

The politicians in London had reached a similar conclusion. By November 19, rumors abounded that Anthony Eden was ill. In the prime minister's absence, R. A. "Rab" Butler, the Conservative Party's leader in the House of Commons, and Chancellor of the Exchequer Harold Macmillan began jointly to run the government. Ambassador Winthrop Aldrich reported from London that Macmillan had told him that the "British Government may be faced within the next few days with the terrible dilemma of either (a) withdrawing from Egypt," replaced by a token United Nations force that could not secure the Suez Canal or clear it of wreckage, or (b) "renewing hostilities in Egypt and taking over the entire Canal in order to remove the obstructions." Macmillan knew that the latter was not an option. He told Aldrich that he was willing to go to Washington as "Eden's deputy" because "Eden might not be well enough to come." This, Aldrich wrote, indicated "that some sort of movement is on foot in the Cabinet to replace Eden."[28]

A couple of hours later, Aldrich called Eisenhower directly to confirm that Eden would be forced to step down.[29] Hoover reported to the president that the "guess" was that the British cabinet "is completely to be re-shuffled, and that Eden is going out because of sickness."[30]

About 10:00 P.M., Aldrich informed Hoover that Eden had suffered a "physical breakdown" and was leaving for a vacation in Jamaica "immediately." Macmillan had told Aldrich that, once Eden departed, he was confident he could get the cabinet to vote for withdrawal "if you can give us a fig leaf to cover our nakedness."[31]

On Tuesday evening, November 20, Eisenhower met with Hoover, Humphrey, and Goodpaster to discuss the crisis in the British government.[32] Humphrey expressed the hope that Butler, rather than Macmillan, would be the new prime minister. Ike countered that Macmillan was "a straight, fine man" and "the outstanding one of the British" he had served with during World War II.

With Eden on the way out, the moment had arrived for the United States to consider financial assistance to Britain. Secretary Humphrey explained how the United States could provide the "fig leaf" that Macmillan sought by clearing the way for withdrawal of British funds from the World Bank, setting the stage for a loan from the United States, and asking the Export-Import Bank to extend credit to allow the British to pay for exports from the United States. Eisenhower was still cautious, saying that he wanted to confirm that it would be acceptable to the Saudis and the Egyptians if the United States announced in advance that "we would help out as soon as the French and British agree to start getting out of Suez at once."

Ike laid out three steps to move matters forward. First, inform the British that "we are ready to talk about help as soon as the pre-condition is established"—meaning the "initiation" of withdrawal, not its completion. Second, talk with the Arabs "to obtain the removal of any objections they may have regarding the provision of oil to Western Europe." Third, prepare to discuss "American money assistance." But, Ike said, he required a firm public statement from the British about withdrawal, not just private hints.

With that agreed, Eisenhower put in a call to Aldrich and ordered the ambassador to inform Macmillan and Butler "informally" that "we are interested and sympathetic, and, as soon as things happen that we anticipate, we can furnish 'a lot of fig leaves.' " On November 21, Aldrich cabled Hoover that he had learned that the British decision on withdrawal of troops would be made in the next two days, although it actually took several days longer.[33]

At four that afternoon, Eisenhower convened a meeting, in his words, "for the purpose of gaining an understanding of the sequence of actions planned in the Middle East, and the means of dovetailing actions in the fields of oil and finance."[34] In attendance were Hoover and his top State Department lieutenants, in addition to DCI Allen Dulles, Secretary Humphrey, Admiral Radford, Arthur Flemming, Goodpaster, and C. D. Jackson, his former assistant on psychological warfare.

Hoover presented a sixteen-page document outlining the president's proposed new policy for the Middle East, a result of the study Ike had ordered on November 13.[35] Its objectives included protection of access to oil reserves and rights of passage through the Suez Canal, preservation of both the state of Israel and independent Arab states, and, above all, the "exclusion of Soviet military power or control." The document's central premise was historic: "United States objectives are best served by peace, political stability and economic and social progress in the Middle East." In other words, the United States would assume the burden, previously the province of the United Kingdom, of guaranteeing the stability and security of the Middle East.

Eisenhower read through the document in the presence of the group, making comments. Because his highest priority was to ensure the availability of Middle East oil to Europe, he repeated his desire to build up King Saud as an alternative to Nasser, stressing "the importance of restoring Saud's oil markets in Western Europe." He emphasized the need to get the British to withdraw from the oil-rich Al Buraimi Oasis, where they had landed troops in October 1955, as a means of appeasing Saudi Arabia.[36] Eisenhower's overall question was: "What *must* we do in Europe and then the question, how do we square this with the Arabs?" Ike said that "the moment troops start out of Suez we should tell the Arabs that we are starting to confer with the Western Europeans on how we can restore Middle East oil markets in Western Europe."

At noon on Friday, November 23, Eisenhower met with Hoover, Douglas MacArthur II, the acting secretary's assistant, and Goodpaster.[37] Hoover reported that the oil situation for Europe was getting critical and "the psychological factor"—European fears that the United States would not come to their aid—was "assuming major importance." Hoover advocated doing something within twenty-four hours, but Ike was not ready to jump that quickly. He instructed Hoover to tell the new British ambassador, Sir Harold Caccia, that the United States "must stay 4-square with the UN, so Britain must take some preliminary actions."

Two days later, Hoover resumed his plea to the president for action on oil for Europe but Ike stuck with his hardnosed policy.[38] He restated his intent to withhold assistance until the invading powers "accepted"—that was his carefully chosen word—"immediate withdrawal of their troops." If that signal came through, Ike was ready to issue a statement emphasizing humanitarian motives, "with winter coming on, and in order to prevent widespread suffering in Europe."

Hoover raised the larger question, based on a conversation with Secretary Dulles: what would happen once the British announced they were prepared to withdraw? He said he thought it "might be necessary for us to approach the British and say that it looks as though they are 'through' in the area, and ask if they want us to try to pick up their commitments." Ike was reluctant to state it that baldly. He said he still wanted to give the British "every chance to work their way back into a position of influence and respect in the Middle East." Yet Eisenhower surely knew that Hoover was correct: the United States was taking over from the British in the Middle East.

HOLDING THE LINE

On Monday morning, November 26, three weeks after the election, Eisenhower was finally ready to get away from Washington for a "working vacation" in Georgia. He arrived at the office at 7:40 and, after meeting briefly with Hungarian refugees, departed for the airport. By mid-afternoon, Ike was playing golf at the Augusta National Country Club.

The aftermath of the Suez war still harassed the president in Georgia. The morning of the 27th, Ike was on the phone to Foster Dulles in Key West. He had just heard from his old friend, Lord "Pug" Ismay, the chief military assistant to Churchill during World War II, who had echoed the complaint of many Europeans that "we deserted our two friends in their hour of trial, and now won't even help them out with oil and gas." Douglas Dillon had reported that, in France, service stations were refusing to fill American cars with gasoline, and taxis were declining to pick up Americans. Ike said that he had received hints that the British were almost ready to announce their withdrawal but needed a little more time. Dulles advocated holding the line; Ike agreed but expressed his willingness to change directions "the second they gave just an indication." When Eisenhower contemplated issuing a statement, Dulles was concerned that a press release expressing sympathy for the plight of the Europeans might make it appear that the president was applying public pressure to Britain and France. Ike said he would draft a short statement and have Jim Hagerty read it to Dulles for his approval. Dulles complained that "it was they who double-crossed us and now they are trying to put the blame on us. Nothing," he said, "has been stronger or clearer than your letters to Eden." [39]

Eisenhower was fending off criticism from other prestigious sources. Winston Churchill wrote him: "To let events in the Middle East become a gulf between us would be an act of folly on which our whole civilization may founder." If the allies did not act to restore their relationship, the former prime minister wrote, "we must expect to see the Middle East and the North African coastline under Soviet control and Western Europe placed at the mercy of the Russians." [40]

In response, Eisenhower recited the history of his warnings to Eden and how British and French leaders "had deliberately excluded us from their thinking." [41] The British action had been, he wrote, "in violation of the basic principles" of the United Nations, and the invasion of Egypt "could not be judged as soundly conceived and skillfully executed."

Eisenhower agreed with Churchill that "the Soviets are the real enemy" and asserted that "we want to help Britain right now, particularly in its difficult fuel and financial situation, daily growing more serious." He plainly stated the requirement: "a British statement that it would conform to the resolutions of the United Nations." "Nothing saddens me more," Ike concluded, "than the thought that I and old friends have met a problem concerning which we do not see eye to eye. I shall never be happy until our old time closeness has been restored."

DECISION IN LONDON

The word finally came from London on the afternoon of November 29. Ambassador Aldrich had encountered British cabinet members in a state of "acute depression" following what they called "the most terrible meeting." The cabinet had agreed that, on Monday, December 3, Foreign Secretary Selwyn Lloyd would announce to the House of Commons that the government would comply with the United Nations resolution for withdrawal from Egypt. Some cabinet members were certain that this meant "the fall of the government" because more than a hundred Conservative members of Parliament had signed a motion deploring the positions of the United Nations and the United States. Aldrich reported that Rab Butler, in his position as the Conservative leader in the House of Commons, was more optimistic, believing he could line up a sufficient number of votes by Monday "to insure the government's survival."[42]

Eisenhower quickly sent the signals the British needed. At noon on November 30, Arthur Flemming's Office of Defense Mobilization released a statement that, "with the approval of the President," the Interior Department had been requested to authorize fifteen American oil companies to coordinate efforts to provide oil to compensate for shortages "resulting from the closing of the Suez Canal and some pipelines in the Middle East." The plan called for shipping 500,000 barrels more a day than normal and expressed concern for "both consuming and producing countries"—reflecting Ike's sensitivity to Middle East oil markets, especially Saudi Arabia's. Almost simultaneously, the Augusta White House issued a statement authorizing this action by the ODM.[43]

Also on that day, the White House issued a statement authorizing the entry of 21,500 Hungarian refugees into the United States.[44]

On Sunday, Eisenhower and Foster Dulles put on a show of optimism for the press. Ending his recuperation in Key West, Dulles flew to Augusta, attended church with the Eisenhowers, and consulted for two hours with the president over lunch. Afterward, Dulles expressed to reporters his and the president's continuing concern over Soviet repression in Poland and Hungary. Dulles said that he and Eisenhower were agreed that the chances for peace in the Middle East had improved during the last month. After talking with reporters, Dulles flew back to Washington to resume his duties for the first time since his surgery.[45]

The countdown to the British announcement was tense. On Monday morning, December 3, Ambassador Aldrich informed Hoover that, as instructed, he had pressured Butler to ensure that Lloyd's announcement to the House of Commons would include a specific date for withdrawal, without which the United States would find it difficult to persuade the Egyptians to expedite the clearing of the canal. Butler had assured Aldrich that the British intended to withdraw within two weeks, give or take a day or two, and complete the evacuation by December 18. But Lloyd's statement to Commons said only that the withdrawal would take place "without delay," pledging to work with the U.N. commander on a timetable for complete withdrawal "in a short time."[46]

Eisenhower called Dulles, concerned about the ambiguity of the Lloyd statement. Dulles countered that the British and French intentions were clear, even though their statements lacked "a precise date or time period."

He told Eisenhower that Humphrey was poised to take actions that would free Chancellor of the Exchequer Macmillan to announce that IMF withdrawals and Export-Import Bank loans would be permitted. The next day, Macmillan informed the House of Commons that the American Treasury would recommend to Congress that it immediately waive $143 million in interest payments on a World War II loan, due December 31.[47]

In response to the British announcement, the State Department issued a statement, approved by Eisenhower and Dulles, that welcomed the British-French commitment to withdrawal and asserted that, in response, the early clearance of the canal had become "imperative" and should not be delayed until the British and French completed their withdrawal.[48]

Anthony Eden was still officially prime minister and would be for another month. On December 14, like a ghost from the past, Eden stepped off his plane in London, looking tanned and rested from his Jamaican vacation. Still determined to justify going to war over Suez, he seemed oblivious to the fact that his power was gone all but in name. "I am convinced, more convinced than I have been about anything in all my public life," he said to reporters at the airport, "that we were right, my colleagues and I, in the judgments and decisions we took and that history will prove it so." On December 20, Eden falsely insisted to the House of Commons that "there was not foreknowledge that Israel would attack Egypt—there was not."[49]

On December 22, forty-eight days after their invasion, the last of the British and French forces departed from Egypt as allied jets screamed overhead. In Port Said—the north entrance to the Suez Canal where the British had first landed on November 5—crowds of Egyptians celebrated for days with parades and demonstrations. On December 24, demonstrators dynamited the eighty-foot statue of Ferdinand de Lesseps, the Frenchman who had completed the construction of the canal in 1869.[50]

Back in Washington, Dwight Eisenhower had ordered Emmet Hughes to begin work on his inaugural address by rereading the final chapter of *Crusade in Europe*, the president's memoir of World War II. Perhaps that was a measure of Eisenhower's assessment of the importance of the Suez Canal crisis. He told Hughes that he wanted to build the address around the theme of the "price of waging peace."[51]

CONCLUSION:
WAGING PEACE IN THE MIDDLE EAST

"The United States never lost a soldier or a foot of ground during my administration. We kept the peace. People ask how it happened—by God, it didn't just happen."

Eisenhower Quotation inscribed on the wall of the
Eisenhower Museum, Abilene, Kansas[1]

A TEST of leadership is what a president does following a crisis to shape the future. Two days after the cease-fire in Egypt, Ike had outlined in his diary a Middle East strategy, eventually called the Eisenhower Doctrine. He was prepared to radically reorient American policy and employ American power to defuse other threats to world peace that might arise in the region.[2]

A MIDDLE EAST STRATEGY

As 1957 dawned, Eisenhower launched a legislative offensive that, by any measure, was breathtaking. On New Year's Day, he convened a four-hour marathon meeting with congressional leaders of both parties. In that meeting, Eisenhower outlined the content and rationale for a resolution he planned to ask Congress to adopt.

The resolution contained three interrelated components. The first two concerned economic and military assistance to friendly Middle East states. The third was the sword in the closet, authorizing in advance the use of American military forces to thwart aggression or head off communist subversion. Eisenhower told congressional leaders that their endorsement of his groundbreaking proposal would "put the entire world on notice that we are ready to move instantly if necessary."[3]

On January 5, Eisenhower addressed a joint session of Congress and submitted his resolution, reinforcing the request five days later in his State of the Union address. Ike had already enlisted House speaker Sam Rayburn and Senate majority leader Lyndon Johnson in his cause, and fought off all efforts to limit the resolution to military measures without provision for economic assistance. By January 16, victory in the House was assured when, according to the *New York Times*, Rayburn "passed the word that Congress should quickly and decisively grant President Eisenhower's request for stand-by authority to use troops in the Mideast." On January 30, Ike welcomed Saudi Arabia's King Saud to Washington, eliciting from the Arab leader a statement that Israel "is now an historical fact and must be accepted as such." That day, the House of Representatives passed the resolution 355–61.[4]

The Senate was a tougher challenge. Israel still controlled the Gaza Strip and the entry to the Gulf of Aqaba, which Egypt had previously closed to Israeli shipping. As a result, Egypt was threatening to shut down its salvage operation clearing the Suez Canal. Eisenhower warned Israel that he might support United Nations sanctions; that ignited a storm of protest in the staunchly pro-Israel Congress. On February 20, Eisenhower met with congressional leaders but failed to persuade them to support his position. That evening, he went over their heads to the nation on radio and television, imploring Israel to comply with U.N. resolutions calling for withdrawal. Privately, Ike warned Israeli prime minister David Ben-Gurion that he would consider supporting a cutoff of private contributions from Americans to Israel. Eventually, Eisenhower's pressure paid off and, on March 1, Israel announced its intention to withdraw.[5]

That cleared the last major obstacle to passage of the Eisenhower Doctrine. The Senate passed the resolution 72–19 on March 5 and Eisenhower signed it four days later. In just two months, the president had persuaded a Congress controlled by the opposition party to expand the American commitment to the Middle East and grant him unprecedented authority to respond to threats in the region.[6]

Eisenhower's new strategy also required that he heal the rupture in the Western alliance. In late March, he met in Bermuda with Harold Macmillan, the new British prime minister, who had succeeded Anthony Eden in January. Their first day's discussion focused almost exclusively on the Middle East. Eisenhower called that session "the most successful international meeting I have attended since the close of World War II."[7]

Meanwhile, Egypt resumed clearing the Suez Canal and the United States brokered secret negotiations securing an agreement on the operation of the canal acceptable to the West. On March 29, the first major convoy of nine freighters transited the canal, and by April 29 the last sunken wreck had been removed.[8]

Episodes of instability erupted during 1957 in Jordan, Oman, and, most seriously, in Syria. Twice during 1957, Eisenhower moved the Sixth Fleet to the eastern end of the Mediterranean in a show of force designed to calm potential rebellion in friendly states. When Syria appeared to be coming under communist control, Eisenhower successfully restrained Turkey and Iraq from taking military action until the crisis passed.[9]

In July 1958, in response to a coup in Iraq, Eisenhower sent fourteen thousand troops to Lebanon to shore up the shaky, pro-Western government in Beirut. Fears that Nasser might retaliate by restricting access to the Suez Canal or that the Soviet Union might respond aggressively did not materialize. Eisenhower withdrew the remaining troops in October.[10]

A COLD WAR CONTEXT

Many of the troubles that Eisenhower confronted in the Middle East remain with us. We still wrestle with on-again, off-again negotiations between Israel and its Arab neighbors and twenty-first-century anxiety about Western dependence on Middle East oil. While the continuity is striking, we should resist the temptation to lay seminal responsibility for present difficulties at Eisenhower's door. His was a very different era.

The context for the Eisenhower Doctrine was the strategic vision Ike had brought to the White House in 1953. Unequivocally committed to containment of the Soviet Union and Soviet-inspired communism, he saw the globe as a mosaic of tension spots, with the Middle East increasingly significant as the years passed. To assess his leadership, we must see the world as Eisenhower saw it—fragile, dangerous, only a few years removed from a bloody world war, confronting the real possibility of a new war with an adversary armed with nuclear weapons.

Two decades after the end of the Cold War, Eisenhower's anticommunist rhetoric may sound archaic, but Ike believed that war with the Soviet Union would destroy the American way of life. He peered into that atomic "abyss" and insisted that those around him do so as well, making civil defense exercises a recurrent feature of American life.

Ike had ample reason for his apocalyptic vision. The Soviet Union had conducted its first successful test of a hydrogen bomb in August 1953. The unpredictability of nuclear war had been demonstrated when, in March 1954, an American nuclear test in the Pacific had spun out of control, producing three times the expected explosive power, 750 times the magnitude of the bomb dropped on Hiroshima in 1945. In early 1956, Ike had received a report that indicated that 65 percent of the American people would be casualties in a nuclear exchange.[11]

This nuclear-haunted Cold War was the prism through which Ike viewed Middle East issues. To him, the region was a "keg of dynamite" that, in the right circumstances, could explode into a nuclear confrontation.[12] A Middle East split into two armed camps, one committed to the West and the other to the Soviet Union, could set the stage for Armageddon. To Eisenhower, this meant heading off any Soviet effort to gain a significant foothold in the region. But, in September 1955, at the moment that the Soviet Union made an arms deal with Egypt, Eisenhower was taken out of action with a heart attack.

Although he was, in so many respects, a "Cold Warrior," Eisenhower was, as General Andrew Goodpaster remembered, "slow to pick up the sword." He repeatedly sought negotiations with the Soviets on the reduction of arms. Ike avoided involvement in "brushfire wars" that could escalate into a nuclear confrontation. He ended the war in Korea in 1953, declined to intervene militarily in Indochina in 1954, and, above all, refused to support his World War II allies in their attack on Egypt in 1956. Eisenhower was the least interventionist of any modern president, although he approved covert operations in places like Iran and Guatemala. The only time he landed troops on foreign soil was in Lebanon in 1958, in a virtually bloodless show of force.[13]

Any inadequacies in the Eisenhower approach to the Middle East are largely the consequence of his commitment to this big Cold War picture.

In a troubled postwar world, Ike skillfully positioned American power to contain communism, presided over the demise of European colonialism, sought to preserve Western access to scarce resources, and championed some degree of justice for smaller nations through the United Nations. His management of that wide-ranging agenda confirms John Lewis Gaddis's conclusion that Dwight Eisenhower was at once "the most subtle and brutal strategist of the age." [14]

THE TROUBLE WITH OIL

Discussion of the Middle East inevitably comes back to oil. It is the foundation of the strategic importance of the region. In 1956, two-thirds of Western Europe's oil came through the Suez Canal. What Eisenhower wrote to Lewis Douglas in November 1956 was indisputable: without Middle East oil, there was, he wrote, "nothing we can do to save Western Europe." Therefore, Western access to oil was at the root of the Suez crisis. [15]

While at the time the United States had sufficient oil to meet its needs, Eisenhower foresaw a less certain future. In September 1956, as the Suez crisis moved toward war, Ike reviewed a report showing that the United States confronted an "increasing dependency on foreign oil"; the American percentage of imported oil had increased from 5 to 20 percent since the end of World War II. Eisenhower was surely thinking of oil, among other resources, when he recorded in his diary that "the material resources of the world are constantly being depleted and at an accelerated pace. The time is bound to come when some of these items will begin to mount sharply in price. Some may even become almost completely exhausted." A few days after the nationalization of the Suez Canal, Ike wrote to his friend Swede Hazlett that "no other nation is exhausting its irreplaceable resources so rapidly as is ours." [16]

On January 1, 1957, oil was the first issue Eisenhower addressed with congressional leaders when he presented his proposal for a Middle East resolution. Protecting access to Middle East reserves was critical, he said, not just for Europe but for "the future importance of oil to us directly." The day that American soldiers landed in Lebanon—July 15, 1958—Eisenhower wrote in his diary: "The true issue in the Middle East is whether or not the Western world can maintain its rightful opportunity to purchase vitally needed oil supplies peaceably and without hindrance or payment of blackmail." [17]

Access to oil was a major reason that Eisenhower cultivated King Saud of Saudi Arabia as a counter to the Arab leadership of Nasser. In the midst of the Suez crisis, he negotiated the continued flow of Saudi oil to the non-belligerent nations. When Eisenhower welcomed King Saud to the United States in early 1957, he laid the foundation for a strategic relationship with Saudi Arabia that survives to this day.

EISENHOWER AND ARAB NATIONALISM

Given his Cold War priorities, it would be easy to jump to the conclusion that Eisenhower was insensitive to the legitimate aspirations of emerging nations like Egypt. The reality is more complex. Certainly Ike was ambivalent, at best, about Nasser and whether the Egyptian president wanted to ally himself with Soviet leaders. More than once, Eisenhower's penchant for complex plans led him to place strings on offers of military and economic aid to Egypt—conditions that Nasser believed he could not accept.

To some extent, Eisenhower's ambivalence toward Nasser reflected John Foster Dulles's negative view of the Egyptian leader. Henry Byroade, the American ambassador to Egypt, pleaded repeatedly with Dulles for a fresh approach to Nasser, who he believed did not want to ally himself with the Soviets. Dulles perceived Byroade as too friendly with Nasser, brushed off his protests, and eventually reassigned him elsewhere.

Eisenhower bears some personal responsibility for his isolation from Byroade's insights. The president disliked reading long diplomatic dispatches, preferring short reports directly from the secretary of state. Byroade's appeals for a more enlightened policy probably never reached Ike's desk or were filtered through Dulles.

On the other hand, Eisenhower, more than any other Western leader, recognized that the era of imperial rule was finished. He implored his European allies to bury the corpse of colonialism and move on. From the moment he took office, Eisenhower pressured the British to remove their troops, stationed in the Suez Canal Zone for decades, and succeeded in securing an agreement in 1954 for their eventual withdrawal from Egypt.

An ironic outcome of that achievement is noteworthy. When the last of the British troops withdrew from the Canal Zone in June 1956, it became more feasible a month later for Nasser to nationalize the canal. One fact is undeniable: if Eisenhower had joined with the British and French in an attempt to topple Nasser, his government would not have survived. But Ike understood that the aftermath of deposing Nasser would be tumultuous. The point is that, in both circumstances, Eisenhower chose to support the aspirations of the Egyptians to rid themselves of European rule.

In spite of the obstacles, in a distant, awkward way, Ike and Nasser understood each other. Eisenhower believed that his intervention in Lebanon led to "a definite change in Nasser's attitude toward the United States" and concluded that, by 1959, Nasser was "progressively less aggressive." Ike gave the Egyptians credit for operating the Suez Canal "in a way satisfactory to all users." [18]

The two men finally met in New York on September 26, 1960, during the annual meeting of the United Nations. [19] Ike described Nasser as "impressive, tall, straight, strong, positive." The Egyptian president thanked the United States "for its great help during the 1956 aggression against his country." Ike reminded Nasser that in spite of the presidential election and political pressures on behalf of Israel, he "had given all-out support to the UN in causing the withdrawal of British, French, and Israeli forces." Nasser warmly commended "the courage of the U.S. in standing up against the wishes of its closest allies," while Ike placed the Suez conflict in global perspective, telling Nasser that "war has taken on a new dimension since Hiroshima." Not all of the discussion was positive. Nasser reminded Eisenhower that "it was an affront to Egypt's dignity when the word came suddenly from Washington that the U.S. had withdrawn its offer to build the Aswan Dam." But mostly the two men discussed the United Nations and the needs of emerging nations.

Eisenhower's fervent support for the United Nations is a salient factor in evaluating his approach to Arab nationalism. When the Security Council blocked his effort to halt the warfare over Suez, Ike took the issue to the General Assembly, where the small nations each had a vote. With their support, he and John Foster Dulles achieved a cease-fire resolution and authorization for a U.N. peacekeeping force. When Soviet premier Nikolai Bulganin proposed that Soviet and American forces jointly end the war in Egypt, Eisenhower warned the Soviet leader that any unilateral action "would violate the United Nations Charter." Later, when Israel resisted pressure to evacuate its forces, Eisenhower declared to the American people that "the United Nations must not fail." [20]

In spite of his efforts, Eisenhower would leave office with major issues unresolved among the emerging states in the Middle East. In 1960, the continued Arab-Israeli conflict still angered Nasser and Ike expressed his regret that he had been unable to resolve it. Although the Alpha plan was rejected by the protagonists, Eisenhower and Foster Dulles deserve some credit for making the effort. A measure of the difficulty of the task is that, a half century later, we are still pursuing that elusive peace.

SETTING THE STAGE FOR CRISIS

The impact of Eisenhower's two major illnesses on American policy in the Middle East is undeniable. Without Ike to moderate his secretary of state's impulsive tendencies, John Foster Dulles floundered over what to do about the Soviet arms deal with Egypt, as did the National Security Council. Ironically, Eisenhower's dominance in policymaking contributed to the disorder. Ike had always made the decisions—not the NSC, not Dulles.

What happened in Eisenhower's absence should put to rest, once and for all, the myth that John Foster Dulles dominated the shaping of American foreign policy; while his influence was significant, the only time Dulles was truly in charge was when Ike was out of commission. Left to his own devices, Dulles was contradictory, initially threatening Nasser, then backing off and arguing to the British that the West should "not take any threatening or drastic step at this time." [21]

In some measure, the Eisenhower administration had dug this hole for itself by insisting that any American arms deal with Egypt meet strict American conditions, including cash rather than credit transactions. In the Alpha plan, Eisenhower and Dulles tied military assistance and aid to the Aswan project to a demand that Nasser make peace with Israel. That complicated approach, mixed with Nasser's inclination to play one side against the other, led to a breakdown in negotiations.

Once Eisenhower resumed some responsibilities after his heart attack, he recognized the altered geopolitical landscape. He recommitted the United States to assisting Egypt in the funding of the Aswan Dam, resulting in an American offer of aid in December 1955.

However, in the following months, the administration stumbled through a series of misjudgments and miscues related to Aswan. Ike paid little attention to the ongoing negotiations with Egypt during the first half of 1956. He was preoccupied with his health, his decision about running for a second term, and, once he made that decision, beginning to campaign for reelection. Secretary Dulles became concerned that Eisenhower, responding to political pressures, might approve the premature sale of arms to Israel and upset delicate negotiations in the Middle East. In late March, Dulles proposed a policy shift designed to provide the president with political cover—blaming Nasser for continuing conflict, delaying completion of the negotiations of aid to Aswan, and removing roadblocks for American allies providing arms to Israel. With some qualms, Eisenhower signed off on a policy that set the stage for later difficulties.[22]

The timing for Eisenhower's second illness—his intestinal surgery—could not have been worse. By the time he returned to the White House on July 15, 1956, Dulles had already decided to renege on the offer of aid to the Aswan project, largely because Congress refused to support it. He had talked with the president vaguely and briefly two days earlier, giving Ike the misleading impression that he had not made up his mind.

Then, on July 19—the day that Dulles was scheduled to meet with the Egyptian ambassador—Dulles, in a twelve-minute meeting, obtained Eisenhower's assent to his decision to withdraw aid to the Aswan project. Only later did Ike express regret about how that important action was handled. That afternoon, Dulles justified his decision to the ambassador on the paternalistic grounds that the Egyptian people would resent the austerity forced upon them by the project. Then the secretary of state issued a press release announcing the withdrawal of the offer of aid.[23]

What followed represents a colossal failure of intelligence. Eisenhower, a master at spinning out strategic contingencies, failed to foresee the possibility of Nasser's nationalization of the Suez Canal. In fairness, neither did the State Department, the CIA, or Ike's European allies. Foster Dulles bears special responsibility. In an April 1956 briefing for congressional leaders, Dulles had noted that "the Suez Canal can be blocked." Eugene Black, the World Bank president, had warned Dulles that if he withdrew the offer of aid to Aswan, "all hell will break loose," but Dulles plowed ahead. The one man who could have stopped him—Dwight Eisenhower—was not paying close attention.[24]

Once Nasser seized the canal and the British and French began preparing for war, Eisenhower recovered his equilibrium and, from that moment onward, worked tenaciously to head off war. In his conversation with Anthony Eden about the seizure, he brilliantly reframed the issue, making it more difficult for the allies to go to war. He argued that the issue involved a number of nations—not just Britain and France—and he upheld Egypt's right to nationalize the canal and be judged on the effectiveness of its management.

CRISIS LEADERSHIP

Eisenhower's confrontation with his World War II allies, Britain and France, over Suez remains the dramatic centerpiece of the story. A half century later, it is hard to fathom the courage that Eisenhower summoned in opposing his wartime partners, especially in the face of fierce criticism from the Democrats in the midst of a presidential election campaign.

Ike believed that any attempt to restore quasi-colonial authority in Egypt was unacceptable. There is little doubt that, without his principled opposition, the British and French would have gone to war soon after Nasser nationalized the canal. Throughout the crisis, Eisenhower played a major role in ushering in the post-imperial era in the Middle East.

Eisenhower's perspectives on the global Cold War, the West's growing dependence on Middle East oil, and his responses to Arab nationalism are important, but a narrower, important question remains: how well did Eisenhower manage the crisis that erupted over Suez on October 29, 1956?

By mid-October, Eisenhower and Dulles were running out of options. Again, the intelligence failure was palpable. On October 16, at the very moment that British and French officials were in Paris planning their invasion of Egypt, the Intelligence Advisory Committee, chaired by CIA director Allen Dulles, accepted a smoke screen the allies and Israel had brilliantly contrived—that if Israel attacked anywhere, it would be in Jordan.[25] An even more embarrassing intelligence misadventure was the failure of American officials to find out about the secret meeting in Paris on October 24 to formalize the plot.

Eisenhower recalled in his memoirs that "October 20, 1956 was the start of the most crowded and demanding three weeks of my entire presidency." During this period, Eisenhower embodied the wisdom of his preachment that "plans are worthless but planning is everything," enabling him to "do the normal thing when everyone else is going nuts." Ike had long ago done his policy homework on the Middle East. In spite of his anger at his betrayal by people he had saved from the Nazis, Eisenhower was prepared to navigate the crisis with a rich mixture of high principle and tough-minded diplomacy.[26]

The allies apparently thought that, once they were fighting, Eisenhower would come to their aid; they were sorely mistaken. For a short time, he even contemplated the "unthinkable" option of intervening on behalf of

Egypt against the British, French, and Israelis. Once he cooled off, he solemnly stated to Foster Dulles, "After all, we will not fight them." [27]

But neither would he give in to them. When the allies issued an ultimatum designed to justify force, Ike said they could "boil in their own oil." [28] He defied intense public criticism and denied oil and financial assistance to the allies both before and after the cease-fire, until the British and French publicly committed themselves to withdrawing from Egypt.

When one strategy failed during the crisis, Eisenhower improvised another. When the British and French vetoed a cease-fire in the United Nations Security Council, he went to the General Assembly. When Foster Dulles went to the hospital for cancer surgery, Ike moved undersecretary Herbert Hoover, Jr., Robert Murphy, and other subordinates into Dulles's roles. In some cases, he took on Dulles's duties himself, issuing direct orders to U.N. ambassador Henry Cabot Lodge, Jr., to take essential shortcuts to organizing a United Nations peacekeeping force.

The most difficult period began on November 4 when the Soviet Union intervened massively in Hungary. Again, Eisenhower was prepared. With his allies tied down in Egypt, Ike pragmatically recognized the limits to what he could do. He offered assistance to refugees but, in spite of the ferocity of the Soviet action, Ike rejected the politically attractive option of breaking diplomatic relations.

On November 5, Soviet premier Bulganin's threatening messages to Israel, Britain, France, and the United States placed Eisenhower in a seemingly impossible position. He responded by treating Bulganin's message as an ultimatum, putting American forces on alert, and clearly communicating that unilateral Soviet intervention in Egypt would be opposed by the United States. Simultaneously, Ike maintained the pressure on the allies for a cease-fire.

Although feeling sick and under enormous stress, Eisenhower never wavered. On Election Day, when the White House staff panicked over rumors from Moscow, Ike returned from Gettysburg to preside over a calm and reasoned meeting regarding American readiness for a big war. When the British accepted the cease-fire, he was two steps ahead of Anthony Eden, anticipating that the prime minister would try to exclude his technical troops from the cease-fire and seek to include British and French forces in the United Nations force—options that Eisenhower immediately shot down.

Following the cease-fire, Ike understood the crisis was not really over. There were still rumors of possible Soviet intervention, and the British, French, and Israelis were dragging their feet about committing to withdrawal. Eisenhower was relentless, coaxing his allies to act on principle and applying continued financial and resource pressures. In some respects, Eisenhower did not close this chapter of the Suez Canal crisis until the Eisenhower Doctrine was passed on March 5, 1957, and he was reconciled with the British a few weeks later in Bermuda.

By any standard, his was a virtuoso presidential performance—an enduring model for effective crisis management.

SUEZ AND WORLD PEACE

Eisenhower's historic contribution following the Suez crisis was the commitment of the United States to maintaining the stability and security of the Middle East. For more than a half century, that responsibility has lain on the desk of every new president. After Suez, another decade passed before another Middle East war broke out. How much Eisenhower contributed to that temporary peace is open to debate, but his successors have not been notably successful in stabilizing the region or resolving its most fractious controversies.

Ike's paramount concern was that a Suez-type crisis might escalate into a nuclear holocaust. If that happened, Eisenhower foresaw that Americans would be "digging ourselves out of ashes, starting again." In the midst of the Suez Crisis, with bombs falling on Egypt, that horrific scenario was on his mind. In his final campaign speech on November 1, 1956, he said: "We believe that the power of modern weapons makes war not only perilous—but preposterous." "The only way to win World War III," Eisenhower declared, "is to prevent it." [29]

Ike did not mention the Middle East or the Suez crisis in his January 1961 farewell address.[30] Still, Suez, as his administration's greatest foreign crisis, was a backdrop to what he described as the need "to carry forward steadily, surely, and without complaint the burdens of a prolonged and complex struggle." "Crises," he added tersely, "there will continue to be." Eisenhower still worried that "another war"—meaning a nuclear war—"could utterly destroy this civilization which has been so slowly and painfully built over thousands of years." After eight years, he happily concluded: "I can say that war has been avoided."

Dwight Eisenhower had avoided "that war" over a canal named Suez. One can imagine him wanting to remind his listeners: "By God, it didn't just happen."

ACKNOWLEDGMENTS

★ ★ ★ ★ ★ ★

MY MOST important acknowledgement is to Dwight D. Eisenhower himself, who insisted on the meticulous record keeping that allows me to take the reader right into his hospital room or the Oval Office. Ike resisted pressures to build his library in a metropolitan center or attach it to a university, placing it in his hometown of Abilene, Kansas, a three-hour drive from my home. The Eisenhower Library's staff members in Abilene are the ongoing custodians of those records, so I am especially indebted to Director Karl Weissenbach, Deputy Director Tim Rives, Chalsea Millner, Catherine Cain, Kathy Struss, and Chris Abraham. I especially revere legendary archivists David Haight (who was instrumental in declassifying hundreds of documents essential to this book) and Jim Leyerzapf, both recently retired.

Three Eisenhower organizations have supported my work, including the Eisenhower Library Foundation, the Eisenhower Institute, and the Eisenhower Memorial Commission, whose director, Brigadier General Carl W. Reddel, has been particularly supportive.

Susan Eisenhower, Ike's granddaughter and a scholar in her own right, called the neglect of the Suez story to my attention. John S. D. Eisenhower, Ike's son and Susan's father, provided insights about his father's personality and ways of addressing issues. Daun van Ee at the Library of Congress, editor of the published Eisenhower papers, knows more about Eisenhower than any human being and always finds time to answer questions and provide provocative interpretations. Irwin F. Gellman, working on a multivolume biography of Richard Nixon, reviewed my work, alerted me to important sources, and offered sage advice. Dr. Michael Birkner at Gettysburg College has been an advisor and supportive colleague. George Colburn of Starbright Media Corporation has inspired my research with his videotaped interviews of Eisenhower-era personalities. Jeffrey Barlow at the Naval History and Heritage Command in Washington, D.C., advised me concerning naval maneuvers during the Suez crisis and Tim Frank facilitated my obtaining a copy of an important declassified study of the naval history of the Suez crisis.

No historian can function without the dedicated assistance of libraries and librarians. Beyond the Eisenhower Library, Nan Myers at Wichita State University's Ablah Library provided me with special access to the *FRUS (Foreign Relations of the United States)* volumes; Veronica McAsey, the director of the Southwestern College Memorial Library, afforded similar access to the *Public Papers of the Presidents* and other services; Princeton University's Seeley Mudd Library and the Dartmouth College Library provided copies of documents that saved me from time-consuming and expensive travel.

My agent, Will Lippincott of Lippincott, Massie and McQuilkin, and Roger Labrie, my editor at Simon & Schuster, have been my partners once again in producing the book. Their working relationship is something special. Labrie, a skilled wordsmith, is unusually knowledgeable about Eisenhower and a master at both supporting and prodding anxious authors to finish their tasks. I thank the Simon & Schuster leadership team who took a chance on an unknown author with my first Eisenhower book and dared to invest in another one. A special thank you to Simon & Schuster's publisher, Jonathan Karp, who selected the title and has provided support to position the book to appeal to a broad audience.

Special friends include Rev. Tom Wallrabenstein, who read early drafts; the Rev. Dr. Allen Polen who freed me repeatedly from lay pastor responsibilities at Prairie View United Methodist Church (a congregation that has enthusiastically supported my work); David Seaton, the publisher of the *Winfield Daily Courier*, who provided sage observations that have shaped my understanding of politics; and David H. Swartz, the former ambassador to Belarus and fluent in Russian, who translated a critical message from Soviet premier Nikolai Bulganin to Eisenhower. Dr. Carl E. Martin, my former president and college classmate, has been an enthusiastic advocate for my post-retirement career as a historian and Dr. W. Richard Merriman, Jr., current president of Southwestern College, helped me set the stage for that career and has been consistently supportive.

Above all there is Grace, the most devoted and helpful partner a man could hope for. She has proofed hundreds of drafts of the manuscript, contributed creative ideas, caught my mistakes, and provided the emotional support indispensable to the challenging task of telling the story of the Eisenhower presidency.

NOTES

ABBREVIATIONS

ACW	Ann C. Whitman
AWD	Allen W. Dulles
CF	Central Files (Eisenhower Library)
CREST	CIA Records Search Tool, National Archives
DDE	Dwight D. Eisenhower
DDEP	*The Papers of Dwight David Eisenhower* (published)
D-H	Dulles-Herter Series
DP	John Foster Dulles Papers
EL	Eisenhower Library
FRUS	*Foreign Relations of the United States*
HH	Herbert Hoover, Jr.
HP	James Hagerty Papers
JFD	John Foster Dulles
LC	Library of Congress
MILLER CTR., UV	Miller Center of Public Affairs, University of Virginia
NA	National Archives (Archives II, College Park, Maryland)
NSC	National Security Council
NYT	*New York Times*
OF	Official File (Eisenhower Library)
OH	Oral History
OSANSA	Office of the Special Assistant for National Security Affairs
PC	Press conference
PPP	*Public Papers of the Presidents*
RG	Record Group
S-M-P	Seely Mudd Library, Princeton University
WH	White House
WHOSS	White House Office, Office of the Staff Secretary

INTRODUCTION

1 Fred I. Greenstein, in *The Hidden-Hand Presidency: Eisenhower as Leader* (Baltimore: Johns Hopkins University Press, 1982), is often credited with launching the reinterpretation of the Eisenhower presidency.

2 Dwight D. Eisenhower, *The White House Years: Waging Peace, 1956–61* (Garden City, New York: Doubleday, 1965), p. 20.

3 For a detailed study of British actions and intentions, see Keith Kyle, *Suez: Britain's End of Empire in the Middle East* (London: I. B. Tauris, 2003); for background on the Soviet intervention in Hungary, see Aleksandr Fursenko and Timothy Naftali, *Khrushchev's Cold War: The Inside Story of an American Adversary* (New York: W. W. Norton, 2006), and William Taubman, *Khrushchev: The Man and His Era* (New York: W. W. Norton, 2003).

4 The primary American studies are Donald Neff, *Warriors at Suez* (New York: Linden Press/Simon & Schuster, 1981) and Cole C. Kingseed, *Eisenhower and the Suez Crisis of 1956* (Baton Rouge: Louisiana State University Press, 1995). Examples of diplomatic studies include Douglas Little, *American Orientalism: The United States and the Middle East Since 1945* (Chapel Hill: University of North Carolina Press, 2004), pp. 77–87; Peter L. Hahn, *Caught in the Middle East: U.S. Policy Toward the Arab-Israeli Conflict, 1945–1961* (Chapel Hill: University of North Carolina Press, 2004); and Diane B. Kunz, *The Economic Diplomacy of the Suez Crisis* (Chapel Hill: University of North Carolina Press, 1991).

1. THE MAN AND THE MOMENT

1 Video interview, Elliot Richardson, *The Eisenhower Legacy: Dwight D. Eisenhower's Military and Political Crusades,* Part 3: "Politician and President, 1953–1961," Starbright Media Corp., eisenhowerlegacy.com.

2 "Abroad: As a Solemn President Took the Oath," *NYT,* Jan. 21, 1953; "Footnotes to History," *NYT,* Jan. 21, 1953; "President's Plan," *NYT,* Jan. 21, 1953; *Public Papers of the Presidents* (PPP): *Dwight D. Eisenhower, 1953* (Washington, D.C.: U.S. Government Printing Office, 1960), no. 1, pp. 1–8.

3 James Reston, "Inaugural Is Held to Extend U.S. Commitments to World," *NYT,* Jan. 21, 1953.

4 Eden to DDE, Sept. 6, 1956, *Foreign Relations of the United States* (FRUS), *1955–57,* Vol. XVI, "Suez Crisis" (Washington, D.C.: U.S. Government Printing Office, 1990), no. 181, pp. 400–403.

5 For more about Eisenhower's decision to run, see William B. Pickett, *Eisenhower Decides to Run: Presidential Politics and Cold War Strategy* (Chicago: Ivan R. Dee, 2000); Herbert Brownell, Jr., *Advising Ike: The Memoirs of Attorney General Herbert Brownell* (Lawrence: University Press of Kansas, 1993), p. 98.

6 Eisenhower commented on the dangers of limited wars upon receiving a Net Evaluation Subcommittee report on January 23, 1956, detailing the devastation that would result from a nuclear war; Memorandum for Record, Jan. 23, 1956, *FRUS, 1955–57,* Vol. XIX, "National Security Policy," no. 54, pp. 188–92.

7 John Lewis Gaddis, *The Cold War: A New History* (New York: Penguin, 2005), p. 64; General Andrew J. Goodpaster, Interview with the author, Jan. 20, 2004: Goodpaster was promoted from colonel to general in 1968.

8 DDE Diary, Jan. 6, 1953, Louis Galambos and Daun van Ee, eds., *The Papers of*

Dwight David Eisenhower (DDEP), (Baltimore: Johns Hopkins University Press, 1996), no. 1034.

9 Douglas Little, *American Orientalism: The United States and the Middle East Since 1945* (Chapel Hill: University of North Carolina Press, 2004), pp. 125–63.

10 Dwight D. Eisenhower, *The White House Years: Mandate for Change, 1953–56* (Garden City, NY: Doubleday, 1963), p. 197; "Cairo Forms Liberation Front," *NYT*, Jan. 24, 1953.

11 Dwight D. Eisenhower, *The White House Years: Waging Peace, 1956–61* (Garden City, NY: Doubleday, 1965), pp. 20–23.

12 Convention Respecting the Free Navigation of the Suez Maritime Canal, Oct. 29, 1888, *The Suez Canal Problem* (Department of State Publication 6392, Oct. 1956), pp. 4–9.

13 For background on the Arab-Israeli war and U.S. recognition of the state of Israel, see Little, *American Orientalism*, pp. 77–87, and Peter L. Hahn, *Caught in the Middle East: U.S. Policy Toward the Arab-Israeli Conflict, 1945–1961* (Chapel Hill: University of North Carolina Press, 2004), pp. 44–63.

14 Tripartite Declaration Regarding the Armistice Borders, May 25, 1950, Department of State Bulletin, June 5, 1950, p. 886, http://unispal.un.org/UNISPAL.NSF/0/3EF2BAA011AD818385256C4C0076E724.

15 Cabinet Meeting, July 27, 1956, B 7, EL; DDE Diary, B 16, Misc. (1), EL.

16 Dwight D. Eisenhower's Papers as President (Ann Whitman File), National Security Council Series (NSC), 133rd Meeting, Feb. 24, 1953, B 4, EL; DDE to Churchill, Feb. 24, 1953, International Series, *DDEP*, no. 54.

17 Goodpaster, Interview with the author, Jan. 20, 2004.

18 *History of the National Security Council* (Office of the Historian, Bureau of Public Affairs, United States Department of State, 1997), p. 6; State of the Union Address, Feb. 2, 1953, *PPP*, no. 6, p. 18 (entire address, pp. 12–34).

19 Dwight D. Eisenhower, "Some Thoughts on the Presidency," *The Reader's Digest* (November 1968), p. 54. Eisenhower reinforced this view of presidential decision making, contending that he would advise any president that "on important matters, in the end, you alone must decide"; see Eisenhower, "The Central Role of the President in the Conduct of Security Affairs," in Colonel Amos A. Jordan, Jr., ed., *Issues of National Security in the 1970's* (New York: Frederick A. Praeger, 1967), p. 214. Ann Whitman, Ike's secretary, wrote his brother Milton that, of all the president's duties, the National Security Council "seems to be the most time consuming, from the standpoint of the number of hours *in* the actual meeting, the briefing before the meeting that has seemed to become a routine, and the time that the President must give, occasionally, to be sure that the minutes of the meetings reflect exactly the decisions reached"; Whitman to M. Eisenhower, Aug. 28, 1956, DDE Diary Series, Dwight D. Eisenhower's Papers as President (Ann Whitman File), B 17, Aug. '56 Misc. (1), EL.

20 Remarks at the National Defense Executive Reserve Conference, Nov. 14, 1957, *PPP*, no. 235, p. 818; Conference, April 19, 1956, White House Office, Office of the Staff Secretary (WHOSS), Subject Series, Alpha Subseries, B 23, President and Seaton, EL.

21 The detailed minutes of the 344 NSC meetings during the Eisenhower years, so long classified, are now available. While the essential content is there, the sanitized minutes don't always reflect the heated, sometimes salty character of the exchanges, especially with the president. Because the meetings were secret, even

former staff members were reluctant to talk about them. But Ike's style of leadership was similar in other settings. He was, everyone agreed, a good listener who welcomed disagreement and freewheeling discussion. But the moment would come when, after listening intently, Eisenhower might make a comment that crystallized the entire discussion. On occasion, if truly irritated, he could erupt with a curse. Roemer McPhee, Jr., a former legislative aide, recalled a meeting with congressional leaders addressing how many nuclear weapons they should seek in the proposed budget. Ike listened silently for a long time. Suddenly, a presidential hand slammed loudly down on the table. "God dammit!" McPhee recalled Ike saying. "How many times can you kill a man!" Interview with the author, Jan. 9, 2004.

22 Brownell, *Advising Ike,* pp. 288, 297–98; Hagerty Interview, OH-91, Vol. IV, pp. 504–5, EL; Goodpaster Interview with the author, Jan. 20, 2004. A detailed analysis of Eisenhower's approach to delegation is found in Fred I. Greenstein, " 'Centralization Is the Refuge of Fear': A Policymaker's Use of a Proverb of Administration," in Robert T. Golembiewski and Aaron Wildavsky, eds., *The Costs of Federalism: Essays in Honor of James W. Fesler* (New Brunswick, N.J.: Transaction, 1984), pp. 117–39.

23 Interview with Eisenhower, July 28, 1964, Dulles Oral History Project, OH-14, EL; Eisenhower, *Mandate for Change,* pp. 122–23; Interview with James Hagerty, Oct. 14, 1965, Hagerty Papers (HP), B 129, re John Foster Dulles, EL; Brownell, *Advising Ike,* p. 134; Townsend Hoopes, *The Devil and John Foster Dulles* (Boston: Little, Brown, 1973), pp. 135–37; Thomas G. Paterson et al., *American Foreign Relations: A History,* Volume 2: *Since 1895,* 7th ed. (Belmont, CA: Wadsworth, 2010), p. 279.

24 Richard H. Immerman, *John Foster Dulles: Piety, Pragmatism and Power in U.S. Foreign Policy* (Wilmington: Scholarly Resources, 1999), pp. 44–45.

25 Eisenhower Interview, July 28, 1964, OH-14, EL; the account of the speech episode is confirmed in Sherman Adams, *First-Hand Report: The Story of the Eisenhower Administration* (New York: Harper & Brothers, 1961), p. 81; Keith Kyle, *Suez: Britain's End of Empire in the Middle East* (London: I. B. Tauris, 2003), p. 46; Eisenhower Interview with Walter Cronkite, May 23–29, 1961, DDE Papers, Post-Presidential, B 24, EL.

26 Brownell, *Advising Ike,* p. 134; James Srodes, *Allen Dulles: Master of Spies* (Washington, D.C.: Regnery, 1999), pp. 431–32; "The Administration: Hoover for Smith," *Time,* Aug. 30, 1954; the August 1953 coup in Iran remains the most controversial legacy of Eisenhower's early policies in the Middle East, largely because Iranian-American relations continue to be difficult. Once again, oil was the issue. In 1951, the Iranian government had failed to ratify an agreement with the British-dominated Anglo-Persian Oil Company, effectively nationalizing the country's oil industry. Dr. Mohammed Mossadegh, the Iranian prime minister, led the drive to end British involvement. The British government persuaded the Eisenhower administration that Mossadegh was moving closer to the communists. Eisenhower authorized the CIA to cooperate with the British in an operation that was actually a countercoup because the Mossadegh government had forced the Shah of Iran to abdicate. The CIA operation in August 1953 restored the Shah to his throne, only to be overthrown again in the 1979 Islamic revolution. See Kermit Roosevelt, *Countercoup: The Struggle for the Control of Iran* (New York: McGraw-Hill, 1979); Stephen Kinzer, *All the Shah's Men: An American Coup and the Roots of Middle East Terror,* 2nd ed. (Hoboken: Wiley & Sons, 2008); Interview, Loy Hen-

derson, ambassador to Iran at the time, Columbia University Oral History Series, OH-191, EL. For U.S.-U.K. covert operations plans to render Nasser ineffective—Operations Omega and Mask—see Douglas Little, "Mission Impossible: The CIA and the Cult of Covert Action in the Middle East," *Diplomatic History*, Vol. 28, no. 5 (Nov. 2004), pp. 679–82.

27 Interview with James Hagerty, Oct. 14, 1965, HP, B 129, re John Foster Dulles, EL; Richard H. Immerman, "Eisenhower and Dulles: Who Made the Decisions?," *Political Psychology* (Autumn 1979), pp. 21–38.

28 Brownell, *Advising Ike*, pp. 287–90, 301.

29 Interview, Eugene R. Black, May 13, 1975, OH-341, EL; "World Bank Head in Cairo," *NYT*, Feb. 20, 1953.

30 Osgood Caruthers, "Egyptian Dam to Dwarf Pyramids," *NYT*, Feb. 6, 1956; Donald Neff, *Warriors at Suez* (New York: Linden Press/Simon & Schuster, 1981), pp. 124–25.

31 Address, "The Chance for Peace," April 16, 1953, *PPP*, no. 50, pp. 179–88.

32 "Text of Secretary Dulles' Address to U.S. Newspaper Editors," *NYT*, April 19, 1953; "Arabs Prepare for Dulles," *NYT*, May 9, 1953; C. L. Sulzberger, "Suez Deadlock Spurs Fears for West's Aims in Mid-East," *NYT*, May 10, 1953.

33 DDE Diary, May 14 1953, *DDEP*, no. 188; Herbert Brownell, Jr., confirms some of these concerns in *Advising Ike*, pp. 266–67, saying that Dulles often "gave the impression of preaching to his conferees and often painted those who disagreed with him as unintelligent," although Brownell respected Dulles as "a skillful negotiator" with "a great mental capacity and a fine analytical mind."

34 Eisenhower, *Mandate for Change*, pp. 201–2.

35 Walter H. Waggoner, "Dulles Back, Cites Gains in Near East," *NYT*, May 29, 1953; Eisenhower, *Mandate for Change*, p. 203; Little, *American Orientalism*, pp. 166–67.

36 Kennett Love, "U.S.-British Stand on Suez Awaited" & Ann O'Hare McCormick, "Abroad," *NYT*, March 16, 1953; DDE to Eden, March 16, 1953, *DDEP*, no. 82.

37 Churchill's letter is quoted in Eisenhower, *Mandate for Change*, pp. 198–99.

38 DDE to Churchill, March 19, 1956, *DDEP*, no. 95.

39 Eisenhower, *Mandate for Change*, pp. 202–5.

40 Little, *American Orientalism*, p. 167; Steven Z. Freiberger, *Dawn over Suez: The Rise of American Power in the Middle East* (Chicago: Ivan R. Dee, 1992), pp. 70–71; Osgood Caruthers, "Egyptian Dam to Dwarf Pyramids," *NYT*, Feb. 6, 1956.

41 Raymond A. Hare, Interview, July 22, 1987, Foreign Affairs Oral History Collection of the Association for Diplomatic Studies and Training, Library of Congress, American Memory, loc.gov.

42 Anglo-Egyptian Agreement Regarding the Suez Canal Base, Oct. 19, 1954, *The Suez Canal Problem* (Department of State Publication 6392, Oct. 1956), pp. 20–23; Robert C. Doty, "Suez Pact Signed for Britain's Exit," *NYT*, Oct. 20, 1954; Freiberger, *Dawn over Suez*, p. 76; Eisenhower, *Waging Peace*, pp. 26–27.

43 Little, *American Orientalism*, pp. 125–32; Hahn, *Caught in the Middle East*, pp. 152–57; Freiberger, *Dawn over Suez*, pp. 63–66, 83–106.

44 Kenneth W. Condit, *History of the Joint Chiefs of Staff*, Vol. VI, "The Joint Chiefs of Staff and National Policy, 1955–56" (Washington, D.C.: Historical Office Joint Staff, 1992), pp. 152–56; Freiberger, *Dawn over Suez*, pp. 83–106.

45 Freiberger, *Dawn over Suez*, pp. 101–3. For a detailed account of the raid and the

events surrounding it, see Kennett Love, *Suez: The Twice-Fought War* (New York: McGraw-Hill, 1969), pp. 1–20, 83–125.

46   Neff, *Warriors at Suez*, pp. 74–77, 182–83; Freiberger, *Dawn over Suez*, p. 100.

47   Khrushchev's memoirs reveal that he underestimated Eisenhower. He remembered that, in Geneva, he viewed the president as "a run-of-the-mill politician" who was "relying totally on Dulles," a man Khrushchev viewed as "lacking in common sense, intoxicated and paralyzed by hatred." Khrushchev's outlook guaranteed that the hopeful "spirit of Geneva" would be short-lived; Sergei Khrushchev, ed., *Memoirs of Nikita Khrushchev* (University Park, PA; Pennsylvania State University Press, 2007), p. 41.

48   Memorandum for the Record, Jan. 23, 1956, *FRUS, 1955–57*, Vol. XIX, "National Security Policy," no. 54, pp. 188–92.

49   Statement of Policy by the National Security Council, July 23, 1954, *FRUS, 1952–54*, Vol. IX, "The Near East and Middle East," pt. 1, no. 219, pp. 525–36; also found in White House Office, Office of the Special Assistant for National Security Affairs (OSANSA), Policy Papers, B 12, NSC 5428 (1), EL.

50   Hahn, *Caught in the Middle East*, pp. 182–93: Freiberger, *Dawn over Suez*, pp. 107–32.

51   Russell to ambassadors, July 22, 1955, *FRUS, 1955–57*, Vol. XIV, "Arab-Israeli Dispute," no. 169, pp. 310–18; Editorial Note, *FRUS, 1955–57*, Vol. XIV, no. 164, pp. 303–4; JFD & DDE Conversation, Aug. 5, 1955, *FRUS, 1955–57*, Vol. XIV, no. 182, pp. 338–39.

52   Russell, Memo for File, Aug. 12, 1955, *FRUS, 1955–57*, Vol. XIV, no. 190, p. 349; JFD to DDE, Aug. 19, 1956, *FRUS, 1955–57, 1955–57*, Vol. XIV, no. 202, pp. 368–69.

53   Editorial Note, *FRUS, 1955–57*, Vol. XIV, no. 262, pp. 448–49; Neff, *Warriors at Suez*, pp. 84–85.

54   Press Release, JFD Speech, Aug. 26, 1955, John Foster Dulles Papers (DP), Subject Series, B 1, Alpha Speech (4), EL; "Text of Dulles Talk on Arab-Israeli Affairs" *NYT*, Aug. 27, 1955; Leo Egan, "Dulles Proposes Peace Guarantee for Israel, Arabs," *NYT*, Aug. 27, 1955; Harrison E. Salisbury, "Political Overtone Noted in Dulles' Mid-East Plan," *NYT*, Aug. 28, 1955.

55   Neff, *Warriors at Suez*, p. 85; Russell Baker, "President on Holiday," *NYT*, Aug. 21, 1955; "President Fishes, then Cooks Catch," *NYT*, Aug. 27, 1955.

56   Dana Adams Schmidt, "Dulles Gets Hint Arabs Are Armed by Soviet Union," *NYT*, Aug. 31, 1955; Editorial Note, Meeting, Sept. 20, 1955, *FRUS, 1955–57*, Vol. XIV, no. 286, p. 483.

57   Russell Baker, "Eisenhower Goes to Fishing Camp," *NYT*, Sept. 21, 1955.

2. CRISES OF THE HEART

1   "Despideda" means "goodbye" in Cebuano, an Austronesian (Malayo Polynesian) language spoken in the Philippines, where Eisenhower had served under General Douglas MacArthur. A detailed description of Eisenhower's Colorado vacation and the events surrounding his heart attack is found in the Howard Snyder Papers, Book Draft, B 11, EL.

2   Ann C. Whitman notes, Sept. 29, 1955, DDE Diary, B 9, Personal Diary EL, the times and comments on schedule in this book are based on the president's daily appointment schedules. While the DDE Diary and ACW Diary occasionally have copies of these schedules, they are all available in the White House Office, Of-

fice of the Staff Secretary (WHOSS), Appointment Schedule Series, EL, or online, Dwight D. Eisenhower Daily Appointment Schedule, Miller Center of Public Affairs, University of Virginia (Miller Ctr., UV), http://millercenter.org/scripps/archive/documents/dde/diary.

3 Snyder Book Draft, B 11, EL; Dwight D. Eisenhower, *The White House Years: Mandate for Change, 1953–56* (Garden City, NY: Doubleday, 1963), p. 636.

4 ACW Diary, Sept. 29, 1955, Dwight D. Eisenhower's Papers as President (Ann Whitman File), B 6, EL; Statement by Secretary of State Dulles before U.N., *NYT*, Sept. 22, 1955; Peter L. Hahn, *Caught in the Middle East: U.S. Policy Toward the Arab-Israeli Conflict, 1945–61* (Chapel Hill: University of North Carolina Press, 2004), pp. 182–93. The Soviet side of the arms deal with Egypt is examined in detail in Aleksandr Fursenko and Timothy Naftali, *Khrushchev's Cold War: The Inside Story of an American Adversary* (New York: W. W. Norton, 2006), pp. 57–82.

5 JFD to DDE, Sept. 23, 1955, DP, Telephone Conversation Series, B 11, WH, EL; Dulles had revealed on Aug. 30 that the Soviets had possibly made an offer to Egypt, but the deal had not been confirmed until now; Dana Adams Schmidt, "Dulles Gets Hint Arabs Are Armed by Soviet Union," *NYT*, Aug. 31, 1955.

6 Snyder Book Draft, B 11, EL.

7 JFD to AWD, Sept. 24, 1955, DP, Tel. Conv., B 4, Tel. Conv. Gen., (5), EL.

8 Snyder Book Draft, B 11, EL.

9 DDE Diary, Sept. 29, 1955, B 9, Personal, EL; Snyder Book Draft, B 11, EL.

10 Robert J. Donovan, *Confidential Secretary: Ann Whitman's 20 Years with Eisenhower and Rockefeller* (New York: E. P. Dutton, 1988), p. 93; DDE Diary, Sept. 29, 1955, B 9, Personal, EL.

11 Sherman Adams, *First-Hand Report: The Inside Story of the Eisenhower Administration* (New York: Harper & Brothers, 1961), p. 149; Herbert Brownell, Jr., *Advising Ike: The Memoirs of Attorney General Herbert Brownell* (Lawrence: University Press of Kansas, 1993), p. 273; James A. Hagerty Diary, Sept. 24, 1955, HP, B 1a, EL; the file contains two versions of the diary entries on the president's heart attack, one unedited with the wrong date (Sept. 21) and a later, more carefully edited version. This account blends the two.

12 DDE Diary, Sept. 29, 1955, B 9, Personal, EL.

13 For details of Paul Dudley White's career and treatment regimen for Eisenhower, see Clarence G. Lasby, *Eisenhower's Heart Attack: How Ike Beat Heart Disease and Held On To the Presidency* (Lawrence: University Press of Kansas, 1997), pp. 83–129.

14 Hagerty Diary, Sept. 24, 1955, HP, B 1a, EL.

15 DDE Diary, Sept. 29, 1955, B 9, Personal, EL.

16 Hagerty Diary, Sept. 25, 1955, HP, B 1a, EL. For a detailed critique of Howard Snyder's response to the heart attack, see Lasby, *Eisenhower's Heart Attack*, pp. 85–112, and Robert H. Ferrell, *Ill-Advised: Presidential Health and Public Trust* (Columbia: University of Missouri Press, 1992).

17 Adams, *First-Hand Report*, p. 156.

18 Burton Crane, "Stock Prices off Sharply; Loss Is Put at $14 Billion," *NYT*, Sept. 27, 1955; William M. Blair, "Cabinet Meeting Called by Nixon," *NYT*, Sept. 27, 1955.

19 John S. D. Eisenhower, *Strictly Personal* (Garden City, NY: Doubleday, 1974), p. 181.

20 Hagerty Diary, Sept. 25–26 1955, HP, B 1a, EL; Press Conference by Paul Dudley White, Sept. 26, 1955, Press Conference (PC) Series, Dwight D. Eisenhower's Papers as President (Ann Whitman File), B 4, Illness, EL; Lasby, *Eisenhower's Heart Attack*, pp. 113–15.

21 Snyder Book Draft, B 11, EL; Robert E. Gilbert, *The Mortal Presidency: Illness and Anguish in the White House* (New York: Basic Books, 1992), pp. 90, 94. Lasby, *Eisenhower's Heart Attack*, pp. 118–21, has the main setback occurring on Sunday, Oct. 2, and provides additional detail on the "armchair" method of treatment.

22 Snyder Book Draft, B 11, EL.

23 JFD & Nixon, Sept. 25 & 26, 1955, DP, Tel. Conv., B 4, Tel Conv. Gen. (5), EL.

24 Donald Neff, *Warriors at Suez* (New York: Linden Press/Simon & Schuster, 1981), p. 111; JFD & Hoover, Sept. 27, 1955, DP, Tel. Conv., B 4, Tel. Conv. Gen., (5), EL; Harry Gilroy, "U.S. Hint of Arms Heartens Cairo," *NYT*, Sept. 27, 1955.

25 Conversation, foreign ministers, Sept. 27, 1955, *FRUS, 1955–57*, Vol. XIV, "Arab-Israeli Dispute," no. 317, pp. 529–32.

26 JFD to AWD, Sept. 28, 1955, DP, Tel. Conv., B 4, Tel. Conv. Gen., (5), EL.

27 "Nasser Criticizes West," & Thomas J. Hamilton, "Egypt to Obtain Arms of Soviet," *NYT*, Sept. 28, 1955; "Israel Asks Arms," *NYT*, Oct. 3, 1955.

28 JFD to Hoover & JFD to George V. Allen, Sept. 28, 1955, DP, Tel. Conv., B 4, Tel Conv. Gen. (5), EL; Elie Abel, "U.S. Speeds Envoy to Question Cairo, *NYT*, Sept. 29, 1956.

29 JFD to Nasser, Sept. 27, 1955, DP, Chronological Series, B 12, JFD Chrono. (1), EL; Neff, *Warriors at Suez*, pp. 94–97; "Egypt Is Angered by Allen Mission," *NYT*, Oct. 1, 1955.

30 Sherman Adams Memoirs Draft, Article II, "The Eisenhower Illnesses," Adams Papers, Dartmouth College, ML-8, B 14:30; Brownell, *Advising Ike*, pp. 273–74; Adams, *First-Hand Report*, p. 154.

31 NSC 259th Meeting, Sept. 29, 1955, B 7, EL.

32 Cabinet Meeting, Sept. 30, 1955, Cabinet Series, Dwight D. Eisenhower's Papers as President (Ann Whitman File), B 5, EL.

33 Conversation, Oct. 3, 1955, *FRUS, 1955–57*, Vol. XIV, no. 323, pp. 543–49.

34 Letter presented at Press Conference, Oct. 3, 1955, PC Series, B 4, Illness, EL.

35 Press Conference, Oct. 4, 1955, PC Series, B 4, Illness, EL.

36 NSC 260th Meeting, Oct. 6, 1955, B 7, EL.

37 Press Conference, Oct. 7, 1955, PC Series, B 4, Illness, EL.

38 DDE to Hazlett, Oct. 6, 1955, *DDEP*, no. 1596; DDE to Blaik, Oct. 10, 1955, *DDEP*, no. 1598; Lasby, *Eisenhower's Heart Attack*, pp. 130–31.

39 Whitman notes, DDE Diary, October 10, 1955, B 9, Personal, EL; Russell Baker, "President Better but Doctors See a 'Long Way to Go,' " *NYT*, Oct. 9, 1955, p. 1.

40 DDE Diary, Oct. 10, 1955, B 9, Personal, EL.

41 Oct. 11, 1955, DP, WH Memoranda, B 3, Meetings with President (2), EL.

42 DDE to Bulganin, Oct. 11, 1955, *DDEP* Nos. 1599 & 1600; Russell Baker, "Eisenhower Takes Active Role Again on Foreign Policy," *NYT*, Oct. 12, 1955.

43 NSC 261st Meeting, Oct. 13, 1955, B 7, EL.

44 DDE Diary, Oct. 12, 1955, B 9, Personal, EL; JFD to Humphrey, Oct. 17, 1955, DP, Tel. Conv., B 4, Tel. Conv. Gen. (3), EL.

45 Press Conference, Oct. 14, 1955, PC Series, B 4, Illness, EL; DDE to LBJ, Oct. 14, 1955, *DDEP*, no. 1602; DDE to Stephens, Oct. 16, 1955, *DDEP*, no. 1603.

46 "Soviet Fiscal Offer to Egypt Confirmed," *NYT,* Oct. 14, 1955; Dana Adams Schmidt, "U.S. Ready to Aid 2 Arab Projects," *NYT,* Oct. 21, 1955.

47 Conv. with President, Oct. 19, 1955, DP, WH Memo., B 3, Meetings with Pres. (2), EL; DDE to RN, Oct. 19, 1955, DP, WH Memo., B 3, Meetings with Pres. (1), EL; also *DDEP,* no. 1607 & *PPP,* Oct. 23, 1955, no. 226, p. 832.

48 NSC 262nd Meeting, Oct. 20, 1955, B 7, EL.

49 Report on Deterrence of Major Armed Conflict, *FRUS, 1955–57,* Vol. XIV, no. 340, pp. 592–603, summary on pp. 602–3.

50 NSC 5428 was first signed by Eisenhower on July 23, 1954, but went through several revisions: National Security Council, July 23, 1954, *FRUS, 1952–54,* Vol. IX, pt. 1, no. 219, pp. 525–36.

51 Bulganin to DDE, Oct. 20, 1955, *FRUS, 1955–57,* Vol. XIV, no. 349, pp. 636–38; also Dulles-Herter Series (D-H), Dwight D. Eisenhower's Papers as President (Ann Whitman File), B 6, JFD Oct. 1955, EL; DDE to Bulganin, Oct. 24, 1955, *DDEP,* no. 1611; Walmsley to State Dept., Oct. 26, 1955, *FRUS, 1955–57,* Vol. XIV, no. 356, pp. 648–49.

52 DDE Diary, Oct. 25, 1955, B 9, Personal, EL; Statement by President, Oct. 26, 1955, *PPP,* no. 227, p. 833; Conversation, Oct. 26, 1955, DDE Diary, B 9, Personal, EL.

53 ACW Diary, Oct. 26, 1955, B 7, EL.

54 Hazlett to DDE, Oct. 21, 1955, Name Series (Ann Whitman File), B 18, EL; DDE to Hazlett, Oct. 26, 1955, *DDEP,* no. 1613.

55 NSC 263rd Meeting, Oct. 27, 1955, B 7, EL; for a detailed account of the Al Buraimi dispute, see Daniel C. Williamson, *Separate Agendas: Churchill, Eisenhower, and Anglo-American Relations* (London: Lexington Books, 2006), pp. 75–105.

56 DDE Diary, Oct. 29, 1955, B 9, Personal, EL.

57 JFD to State Department, Oct. 30, 1955, *FRUS, 1955–57,* Vol. XIV, no. 370, pp. 680–85.

58 U.S. Delegation to State Department, Oct. 31, 1955, *FRUS, 1955–57,* Vol. XIV, no. 371, pp. 683–84.

59 DDE Diary, Nov. 1, 1955, B 9, Personal, EL.

60 NSC 264th Meeting, Nov. 3, 1955, B 7, EL.

61 "The Battle of Auja," *Time,* Nov. 14, 1955.

62 DDE to White, Oct. 31, 1955, *DDEP,* no. 1616; Ike apparently had asked Dr. Thomas Mattingly, his Walter Reed Hospital cardiologist, to seek out other opinions about the program of complete rest that Dr. White had prescribed. The president wrote White that Mattingly claimed to have canvassed 150 cardiologists at a meeting in New Orleans, and they had cast a "unanimous vote in favor of your program of treatment for one slightly (hopefully) damaged President."

63 Donovan, *Confidential Secretary,* p. 98; John Eisenhower, *Strictly Personal,* p. 183; Russell Baker, "Eisenhower Takes Walk in the Sun," *NYT,* Nov. 4, 1955, p. 13.

64 DDE to White, Nov. 6, 1955, *DDEP,* no. 1621.

65 ACW Diary, Nov. 7, 1955, B 7, EL; DDE to JFD, Nov. 7, 1955, *DDEP,* no. 1622.

66 DDE to JFD, Nov. 8, 1955, *DDEP,* no. 1623; Plans for Departure, Nov. 8, 1955, WHOSS, Subject Series, Alphabetical Subseries, B 1, Governor Adams (1), EL; Meeting, Nov. 9, 1955, D-H, B 6, EL.

67 Conversation, Nov. 9, 1955, *FRUS, 1955–57,* Vol. XIV, no. 391, pp. 720–23.

68 Statement, Nov. 9, 1955, *PPP*, no. 234, p. 839; Russell Baker, "Appeal Indirectly Aimed at Supply of Weapons by the Soviet Bloc," *NYT*, Nov. 10, 1955.
69 ACW Diary, Nov. 7, 1955, B 7, EL; Plans for Departure, Nov. 8, 1955, WHOSS, Subject Series, Alpha Subseries, B 1, Governor Adams (1), EL.
70 Joseph A. Loftus, "President Flies Back to Capital; Shows No Fatigue," *NYT*, Nov. 12, 1955; Howard Snyder Medical Diary, Howard Snyder Papers, Nov. 11, 1955, B 7 (2), EL; DDE to Nixon, Nov. 16, 1955, *DDEP*, no. 1628; Remarks on Arrival in Washington, Nov. 11, 1955, *PPP*, no. 236, p. 841.
71 Loftus, "President Flies Back to Capital," *NYT*, Nov. 12, 1955.
72 Snyder, Medical Diary, Nov. 11, 1955, B 7, EL.
73 DDE to Pollock, Nov. 12, 1955, DDE Diary, B 11, Nov. 1955 (2), EL.

3. BACK IN THE SADDLE AGAIN

1 DDE Diary, Nov. 14, 1955, B 11 (2), EL.
2 DDE to George Merle Powell, Nov. 16, 1955, *DDEP*, no. 1629. For Eisenhower's schedule for the period covered by this chapter, see Eisenhower Appt. Schedule, Miller Ctr., UV, millercenter.org.
3 Medical Diary, Nov. 14–16, 1955, Snyder Papers, B 7, EL; W. H. Lawrence, "Stevenson Seeks Nomination in '56," *NYT*, Nov. 16, 1955.
4 DDE to Silver, Nov. 15, 1955, *PPP*, no. 239, pp. 843–44.
5 NIE, Nov. 15, 1955, *FRUS*, *1955–57*, Vol. XIV, "Arab-Israeli Dispute," no. 411, pp. 750–71.
6 DDE Diary, Nov. 15, 1955, B 11, (2), EL.
7 DDE to White & DDE to Mattingly, Nov. 17, 1955, DDE Diary, B 11, (1), EL (White also in *DDEP*, no. 1631); DDE to Knox, Nov. 19, 1955, *DDEP*, no. 1632; DDE to Griffin, Nov. 21, 1955, DDE Diary, B 11, (1), EL.
8 "Dulles Defers Comments," & Allen Drury, "Eisenhower Gets Report by Dulles on Geneva Talks," *NYT*, Nov. 18, 1955; Harrison Salisbury, "Eisenhower Pledges Drive to Establish 'Just Peace,' " & "Text of Dulles Report to Nation," *NYT*, Nov. 19, 1955.
9 DDE to Eden, Nov. 19, 1955, *DDEP*, no. 1633.
10 NSC 267th Meeting, Nov. 21, 1955, B 7, EL.
11 Medical Diary, Nov. 21, 1955, Snyder Papers, B 7, EL; Cabinet Meeting, Nov. 22, 1955, B 6, EL.
12 Dwight D. Eisenhower, *The White House Years: Mandate for Change, 1953–56* (Garden City, NY: Doubleday, 1963), p. 646; Medical Diary, Nov. 22, 1955, Snyder Papers, B 7, EL.
13 ACW Diary, Nov. 23, 1955, B 7, EL.
14 Eden to DDE, Nov. 27, 1955, *FRUS*, *1955–57*, Vol. XIV, no. 429, pp. 808–9.
15 DDE to Hoover, Nov. 28, 1955, *FRUS*, *1955–57*, Vol. XIV, no. 430, pp. 809–10; also in DDE Diary, B 11, Phone Calls, EL.
16 JFD to DDE, Nov. 29, 1955, Dulles Papers (DP), Tel. Conv., B 11, White House (WH), EL.
17 NSC 268th Meeting, Dec. 1, 1955, B 7, EL.
18 Policy on Financing Aswan Dam, Dec. 2, 1955, *FRUS*, *1955–57*, Vol. XIV, no. 433, pp. 818–19.
19 DDE to JFD, Dec. 5, 1955, DP, WH Memos, B 3, WH Corres.-Gen. (1), EL; *DDEP*, no. 1652.
20 Medical Diary, Dec. 6, 1955, Snyder Papers, B 7, EL.

21 Conversation, Dec. 8, 1955, DP, WH Memos, B 3, Meetings with Pres. (1), EL; *FRUS, 1955–57*, Vol. XIV, no. 442, p. 837.

22 NSC 270th Meeting, Dec. 8, 1955, minutes dated Dec. 9, B 7, EL.

23 Luncheon Conversation, Dec. 8, 1955, DP, WH Memos, B 3, Meetings with Pres. (1), EL.

24 Hagerty Diary, Dec. 11, 1955, HP, B 1a, EL.

25 Footnote no. 3, DDE to Powell, *DDEP*, no. 1658; Legislative Meetings Series, Dec. 12–13, 1955, Dwight D. Eisenhower's Papers as President (Ann Whitman File), B 2 (5), EL.

26 Elie Abel, "Dulles Confirms Plan to Increase Foreign Aid Fund," *NYT*, Dec. 21, 1955.

27 Hagerty Diary, Dec. 13–14, 1955, HP, B 1a, EL.

28 Editorial Note, *FRUS, 1955–57*, Vol. XIV, no. 453, pp. 854–56.

29 Hoover to JFD in France, Dec. 15, 1955, *FRUS, 1955–57*, Vol. XIV, no. 458, pp. 863–64.

30 DDE Diary, Dec. 16, 1955, B 11 (2), EL.

31 Dwight D. Eisenhower, *The White House Years: Waging Peace, 1956–61* (Garden City, NY: Doubleday, 1965), pp. 30–31; State Dept. to Embassy in Egypt, Dec. 16, 1955, *FRUS, 1955–57*, Vol. XIV, no. 461, pp. 868–70; "West Will Help Egypt Build Dam," *NYT*, Dec. 18, 1955.

32 Cabinet Meeting, Dec. 16, 1955, B 6, EL; Hanes to Barnes, Dec. 22, 1955, DP, WH Memos, B 3, Meetings with Pres. (1), EL.

33 NSC 271st Meeting, Dec. 22, 1955, B 7, EL; Peter L. Hahn, *Caught in the Middle East: U.S. Policy Toward the Arab-Israeli Conflict, 1945–1961* (Chapel Hill: University of North Carolina Press, 2004), pp. 76–79.

34 JFD to Allen, Dec. 23, 1955, DP, Chronological Series, B 13, JFD Chronology, Dec. 1955 (3), EL.

35 JFD to American Embassy in Israel, Dec. 29, 1955, *FRUS, 1955–57*, Vol. XIV, no. 471, p. 889; Russell to JFD, Dec. 28, 1955, *FRUS, 1955–57*, Vol. XIV, no. 470, pp. 888–89.

36 DDE to Hazlett, Dec. 23, 1955, DDE Diary, B 11 (1), EL; also *DDEP*, no. 1670.

37 DDE to White, Dec. 27, 1955, DDE Diary, B 11 (1), EL; ACW Diary, Jan. 10, 1956 (recalling Dec. 26), B 8, EL.

38 Medical Diary, Dec. 28, 1955, Snyder Papers, B 7, EL.

39 State of the Union Message, Jan. 5, 1956, *PPP*, no. 2, pp. 1–9.

40 Secret Service logs, Jan. 8–9, 1956 (doc. dated. Jan. 12), DDE Diary, B 12, Jan. 1956 Misc. (5), EL; JFD-Allen phone call, Jan. 8, 1956, DP, Tel. Conv., B 5, Tel. Conv. Gen., (8), EL.

41 ACW Diary, Jan. 10, 1956, B 8, EL.

42 DDE Diary, Jan. 10, 1956, B 9, Personal (2), EL; also in *DDEP*, no. 1681.

43 Adams Interview, June 19, 1970, OH-162, no. 3, EL.

44 ACW Diary, Jan. 11, 1956, B 8, EL; also in DDE Diary, B 9, Personal, (2), EL.

45 DDE to Hazlett, Jan. 23, 1956, DDE Diary, B 12, Misc. (3), EL.

46 DDE to Ben-Gurion & DDE to Nasser, Jan. 9, 1955, DDE Diary, B 12, Misc. (5), EL; DDE Diary, Jan. 11, 1955, B 9, Personal (2), EL; also in *DDEP* no. 1684.

47 Conversation, Jan. 11, 1956, DP, WH Memos, B 4, Meetings with Pres. (6), EL; *FRUS, 1955–57*, Vol. XV, "Arab-Israeli Dispute," no. 14, pp. 20–22.

48 Knowland to JFD, Jan. 12, 1956, DP, Tel. Conv., B 5, Tel. Conv. Gen. (7), EL.

49 NSC 272nd Meeting, Jan. 12, 1956, B 7, EL.

50 Eisenhower expressed similar sentiments in his diary, Jan. 11, 1956, *DDEP*, no. 1684.

51 Undated but almost certainly the meeting of Jan. 13, 1956, Hagerty Papers, B 8, Personal, Mr. Hagerty, EL.

52 Sherman Adams, *First-Hand Report: The Story of the Eisenhower Administration*, (New York: Harper & Brothers, 1961), p. 184; Milton to DDE, Jan. 16, 1956, DDE Diary, B 12, Misc. (4), EL.

53 Annual Budget Message, Jan. 16, 1956, *PPP*, no. 12, pp. 102–7.

54 Anderson to State Department, Jan. 19, 1956, *FRUS, 1955–57*, Vol. XV, no. 21, pp. 28–36.

55 JFD to Anderson, Jan. 23, 1956, *FRUS, 1955–57*, Vol. XV, no. 28, pp. 50–51.

56 Anderson to State Department, Jan. 23, 1956, *FRUS, 1955–57*, Vol. XV, no. 29, pp. 51–56.

57 James Shepley, "How Dulles Averted War," *Life*, Jan. 16, 1956; Elie Abel, "Dulles Redefines War Risk Policy for Saving Peace," *NYT*, Jan. 18, 1956.

58 "Democrat Shocked," *NYT*, Jan. 15, 1956; William S. White, "Rayburn Assails Stand by Dulles," *NYT*, Jan. 17, 1956.

59 Elie Abel, "Dulles Stands on Assertion," *NYT*, Jan. 14, 1956; Elie Abel, "Dulles Redefines War Risk Policy," & "Transcript of Dulles News Conference," *NYT*, Jan. 18, 1956; Richard J. H. Johnston, "Stevenson Bids President Repudiate or Oust Dulles," *NYT*, Jan. 18, 1956.

60 Pre–Press Conference Briefing, Jan. 19, 1956, DDE Diary, B 12, Misc. (4), EL.

61 News Conference, Jan. 19, 1956, *PPP*, no. 16, pp. 160–71; Telegram to N.H. Secretary of State, Jan. 19, 1956, *PPP*, no. 15, pp. 159–60.

62 DDE to McCrary, Jan. 23, 1956, DDE Diary, B 12, Misc. (3), EL; DDE to Hazlett, Jan. 23, 1956, DDE Diary B 12, Misc. (3), EL.

63 Memorandum for Record, Jan. 23, 1956, *FRUS, 1955–57*, Vol. XIX, "National Security Policy," no. 54, pp. 188–92.

64 DDE Diary, Jan. 23, 1956, B 9, Personal (2), EL; also *DDEP*, no. 1708.

4. THE CANDIDATE

1 Conversation, Jan. 23, 1956, DP, Chrono., B 13, JFD Chrono. (1), EL; William S. White, "President Meets George in Effort to End Policy Rift," *NYT*, Jan. 24, 1956. For the president's schedule during the period covered by this chapter, see Eisenhower, Appt. Schedules, Miller Ctr., UV, millercenter.org.

2 DDE to John Eisenhower, Jan. 24, 1956, *DDEP*, no. 1717; John S. D. Eisenhower, *Strictly Personal: A Memoir* (Garden City, NY: Doubleday, 1974), pp. 386–88; Susan Eisenhower, *Mrs. Ike: Memories and Reflections on the Life of Mamie Eisenhower* (Sterling, Va.: Capital Books, 1996), pp. 294–95; Marilyn Irwin Holt, *Mamie Doud Eisenhower* (Lawrence: University Press of Kansas, 2007), pp. 115–16; Sherman Adams, *First-Hand Report: The Story of the Eisenhower Administration* (New York: Harper & Brothers, 1961), p. 182.

3 Pre–Press Conference Briefing, Jan. 15, 1956, DDE Diary, B 12, Misc. (3), EL.

4 News Conference, Jan. 25, 1956, *PPP*, no. 20, pp. 182–95.

5 Meeting with Zaroubin, DDE Diary, Jan. 25, 1956, B 12, Misc. (3), EL; Bulganin's letter, dated Jan. 23, 1956, is found in the same source (1); JFD to DDE, Jan. 25, 1956, DDE Diary, B 12, Misc. (3), EL; DDE to Eden, Jan. 26, 1956, *DDEP*, no. 1721.

6 DDE to Bulganin, Jan. 28, 1956, DDE Diary, B 12, Misc. (1), EL; also *DDEP* no. 1723.

7 "Text of Statement on Arms for Israel," *NYT,* Jan. 29, 1956.

8 "Eban Asks Britain and U.S. for Arms," *NYT,* Jan. 31, 1956; "Stevenson Asks Arms for Israel," *NYT,* Feb. 5, 1956.

9 Elie Abel, "Eden Opens Talks with Eisenhower," *NYT,* Jan. 31, 1956, p. 1.

10 Conference, Jan. 31, 1956, DDE Diary, B 12, Goodpaster, EL; Dwight D. Eisenhower, *The White House Years: Waging Peace, 1956–61* (Garden City, NY: Doubleday, 1965), p. 23; Elie Abel, "Eden, Eisenhower Weigh U.N. Force on Israel Border," *NYT,* Feb. 1, 1956.

11 Joint Statement, Feb. 1, 1956, *PPP,* no. 26, pp. 214–15.

12 Naval Demonstration Order, Feb. 2, 1956, *FRUS, 1955–57,* Vol. XV, "Arab-Israeli Dispute," no. 70, p. 131.

13 See Diane B. Kunz, *The Economic Diplomacy of the Suez Crisis* (Chapel Hill: University of North Carolina Press, 1991), pp. 47–57, for the context of this situation.

14 DDE to JFD, Feb. 1, 1956, DDE Diary, B 12, Tel. Calls, EL.

15 Adams to JFD, Feb. 2, 1956, DP, B 11, Tel Conv. WH (5), EL. Javits missed seeing the president because, on February 2, Ike had departed for Gettysburg to recuperate from the meetings with the British. Adams later told Secretary Dulles that he gave Javits "hell" and said, "We will not permit people to come in here and talk like that." Adams also gave Pennsylvania congressman Hugh Scott "a piece of his mind." When other congressmen sought a White House audience, Adams bluntly told them that the issue "does not belong here," but with the secretary of state. Adams said that "the last thing" he would do was to say whether the White House was opposed to arms for Israel; JFD to Congressmen, Feb. 6, 1956, DP, Chrono., B 13, JFD Chrono. (4), EL; Dana Adams Schmidt, "Dulles Hints Further Delay in Sale of Arms to Israel," *NYT,* Feb. 7, 1956.

16 Embassy to Anderson, Feb. 4, 1956, *FRUS, 1955–57,* Vol. XV, no. 74, pp. 138–40; Embassy to State Dept., Feb. 7, 1956, *FRUS, 1955–57,* Vol. XV, no. 103, pp. 185–87.

17 ACW Diary, Feb. 13, 1956, B 8, EL.

18 DDE Diary, Feb. 7, 1955, B 9, Personal (2), EL.

19 Pre–Press Conference Briefing, Feb. 8, 1956, DDE Diary, B 13, Misc. (5), EL.

20 News Conference, Feb. 8, 1956, *PPP,* no. 32, pp. 227–39.

21 ACW Diary Entries, Feb. 13, March 8, 1956, B 8, EL.

22 Cabinet Meeting, Feb. 13, 1956, B 6, EL; ACW Diary, Feb. 13, 1956, B 8, EL.

23 Press Conference, Feb. 14, 1956, Cabinet Series, B 4, EL; *NYT,* Feb. 14, 1956, p. 20; James Reston, "Open Door on 2d Term," & W. H. Lawrence, "Eisenhower Fit to Run," *NYT,* Feb. 15, 1956.

24 DDE to Milton Eisenhower, Sept. 12, 1955, *DDEP,* no. 1583.

25 James Reston, "President Goes South This Week," *NYT,* Feb. 13, 1956.

26 Lawrence E. Davies, "Stevenson Cites Burden of Office," *NYT,* Feb. 17, 1956.

27 Arthur Krock, "Party Struggles Hinge on Eisenhower's Word," *NYT,* Feb. 18, 1956.

28 Nasser to DDE, Feb. 6, 1956, Dwight D. Eisenhower's Papers as President (Ann Whitman File), International Series, B 9, Egypt (1), EL.

29 Ben-Gurion to DDE, Feb. 14, 1956, *FRUS, 1955–57,* Vol. XV, no. 70, p. 131.

30 Osgood Caruthers, "Egypt and World Bank in Accord," *NYT,* Feb. 10, 1956; "Egypt to Ask Bids on Dam," *NYT,* Feb. 17, 1956.

31 "U.S. Bars Tanks for Saudi Arabia," *NYT*, Feb. 17, 1956; "The World," *NYT*, Feb. 19, 1956; "Georgia Vacation," *NYT*, Feb. 18, 1956.

32 "The World," *NYT*, Feb. 19, 1956; "Statement on Shipping Tanks to Arabs," *NYT*, Feb. 19, 1956; "U.S. Does Not Bar Paris Plane Deal," *NYT*, Feb. 25, 1956.

33 William S. White, "Dulles Stresses Rise in Strength for Free World," *NYT*, Feb. 25, 1956.

34 "Excerpts from Dulles Testimony," *NYT*, Feb. 26, 1956.

35 Byroade to JFD, Feb. 23, 1956, *FRUS, 1955–57*, Vol. XV, no. 115, pp. 210–12 & footnote no. 5.

36 Ben-Gurion to DDE, Feb. 14, 1956, *FRUS, 1955–57*, Vol. XV, no. 103, pp. 185–87; DDE to Ben-Gurion & DDE to Nasser, Feb. 27, 1956, DDE Diary, B 13, Misc. (1), EL.

37 Meeting with Joint Chiefs, Feb. 10, 1956, WHOSS, Subject Series, Dept. of Defense Subseries, B 1, Dept. of Defense, Joint Chiefs of Staff (2), Jan.–Apr. 1956, EL.

38 Donald Neff, *Warriors at Suez* (New York: Linden Press/Simon & Schuster, 1981), p. 168.

39 NSC 277th Meeting, Feb. 27, 1956, B 7, EL.

40 W. H. Lawrence, "Eisenhower Word on Second Term Expected Today," *NYT*, Feb. 29, 1956.

41 Hoover summarized this phone call to JFD, March 1, 1956, *FRUS, 1955–57*, Vol. XV, no. 141, pp. 260–61.

42 The building had been constructed in the nineteenth century, the State Department's south wing completed in 1875. The Treaty Room had been the Navy's library and reception room. The original tenants gradually moved out, until the building was turned over to the White House and renamed the Executive Office Building in 1949 and renamed the Eisenhower Executive Office Building in 2002; see whitehouse.gov.

43 William S. White, "President Builds to Climax," *NYT*, March 1, 1956.

44 News Conference, Feb. 29, 1956, *PPP*, no. 47, pp. 263–73.

45 White, "President Builds to Climax," *NYT*, March 1, 1956.

46 ACW Diary Entry, Feb. 29, 1956, B 8, EL; Eisenhower, *Waging Peace*, pp. 3–4.

47 Radio and Television Address, Feb. 29, 1956, *PPP*, no. 48, pp. 273–79; James Reston, "Can Last 5 Years," *NYT*, March 1, 1956.

5. A TANGLE OF POLICY AND POLITICS

1 DDE to Hazlett, March 2, 1956, DDE Diary, B 14, Misc. (6) EL. In this letter, Eisenhower recalled that he had proposed to insert in his 1953 inaugural address that he intended to be a one-term president and had been talked out of it.

2 Conversation, March 2, 1956, DP, WH Memoranda Series, B 4, Meetings with Pres., (5), EL. For the president's schedule during period covered by this chapter, see Eisenhower, Appt. Schedules, Miller Ctr., UV, millercenter.org.

3 "U.S. Bars Tanks for Saudi Arabia," Feb. 17, *NYT*, Feb. 17, 1956; "The World," *NYT*, Feb. 19, 1956; "U.S. Does Not Bar Paris Plane Deal," *NYT*, Feb. 25, 1956.

4 "Egypt, Israel in Border Clash," *NYT*, Feb. 8, 1956; "Gaza Firing Reported," *NYT*, Feb. 13, 1956; Osgood Caruthers, "Pact for Red Arms to Syria Reported," *NYT*, Feb. 20, 1956; "Israel and Syria in a New Clash," *NYT*, Mar. 5, 1956; Steven Z. Freiberger, *Dawn over Suez: The Rise of American Power in the Middle East* (Chicago: Ivan R. Dee, 1992), pp. 122–23, 143–45; Peter L. Hahn, *Caught in*

the Middle East: U.S. Policy Toward the Arab-Israeli Conflict, 1945–1961 (Chapel Hill: University of North Carolina Press, 2004), pp. 186–87.

5   HH to JFD, Mar. 5, 1956, DP, WH Memos, B 4, Meetings with Pres. (4), EL; also in *FRUS, 1955–57*, Vol. XV, "Arab-Israeli Dispute," no. 161, pp. 292–94; "Syria's Border Guns Down Israeli Plane," *NYT*, March 6, 1956; Donald Neff, *Warriors at Suez* (New York: Linden Press/Simon & Schuster, 1981), p. 160.

6   Press Conference, March 7, 1956, *PPP*, no. 53, pp. 286–99.

7   NSC 279th Meeting, March 8, 1956, B 7, EL.

8   DDE Diary, March 8, 1956, B 9, Personal (1), EL; also in *DDEP*, no. 1773; JFD to HH, March 8, *FRUS, 1955–57*, Vol. XV, no. 176, pp. 325–26; Freiberger, *Dawn over Suez*, p. 236.

9   Eden to DDE, March 4, 1956, DDE Diary, B 14, Misc. (6), EL; DDE to Eden, Mar. 9, 1956, *DDEP*, no. 1774; also in *FRUS, 1955–57*, Vol. XV, no. 182, pp. 337–38.

10   DDE to JFD, March 10, 1956, DDE Diary, B 14, Misc. (4), EL.

11   Elie Abel, "Foreign Aid Plan Faces Stiff Test," *NYT*, March 11, 1956.

12   Conference, March 12, 1956, DDE Diary, B 13, Goodpaster, EL; HH to JFD, March 12, 1956, DP, WH Memos, B 4, Meetings with Pres. (4), EL.

13   DDE Diary, March 13, 1956, B 9, Personal (1), EL; also in *DDEP*, no. 1784, and *FRUS, 1955–57*, Vol. XV, no. 187, pp. 342–43.

14   Byroade to JFD, March 14, 1956, *FRUS, 1955–57*, Vol. XV, no. 191, pp. 348–51.

15   Memorandum, March 14, 1956, *FRUS, 1955–57*, Vol. XV, no. 192, pp. 352–55.

16   Special Message, March 19, 1956, *PPP*, no. 58, pp. 314–20; "The President's Message," *NYT*, March 20, 1956.

17   DDE Diary, March 19, 1956, *DDEP*, no. 1793; Eden to DDE, March 15, 1956, report dated March 12, 1956, *FRUS, 1955–57*, Vol. XV, no. 197, pp. 364–65.

18   Conversation, March 27, 1956, DP, WH Memos, B 4, Meetings with Pres. (4), EL; News Conference, March 21, 1956, *PPP*, no. 62, p. 335.

19   Ben-Gurion to DDE, March 16, 1956, *FRUS, 1955–57*, Vol. XV, no. 201, pp. 372–74; Conversation, March 26, 1956, DP, WH Memos, B 4, Meetings with Pres. (4), EL.

20   Conversation, March 28, 1956, *FRUS, 1955–57*, Vol. XV, no. 221, pp. 405–8.

21   Conference, March 28, 1956, DDE Diary, B 13, EL; also in *FRUS, 1955–57*, Vol. XV, no. 225, pp. 423–24.

22   JFD to DDE, March 28, 1956, DDE Diary, B 13, EL; also in DP, WH Memos, B 4, WH Corres.-Gen. (6), EL; also in *FRUS, 1955–57*, Vol. XV, Arab-Israeli Dispute, no. 223, pp. 419–21.

23   The Eisenhower administration flirted frequently with the idea of organizing a coup in Syria, not unlike what had transpired in Iran in 1953, but never carried it out; see Freiberger, *Dawn over Suez*, p. 179.

24   Conferences, March 28, 1956, *FRUS, 1955–57*, Vol. XV, nos. 224–25, pp. 421–24; DDE Diary, B 13, EL.

25   DDE Diary, March 28, 1956, B 9, Personal, (1), EL; also in *DDEP*, no. 1811.

26   Daun van Ee was an editor of *The Papers of Dwight David Eisenhower (DDEP)*, (Baltimore: Johns Hopkins University Press, 1970–2001).

27   DDE to Churchill, March 29, 1956, DDE Diary, B 14, Misc. (1), EL.

28   Churchill to DDE, April 16, 1956, DDE Diary, B 14, Misc. (3), EL.

29   Conversation, April 1, 1956, *FRUS, 1955–57*, Vol. XV, no. 232, pp. 435–39.

30   Osgood Caruthers, "Nasser Retaining Soviet Dam Offer Lest West Demur," *NYT*, April 2, 1956.

31 Dana Adams Schmidt, "Eisenhower Bans Arms," *NYT,* April 3, 1956, p. 1.

32 Thomas J. Hamilton, "U.N. Council Bids Hammarskjöld Survey Mideast," *NYT,* April 5, 1956; "Gaza Strip Fight Rages 10 Hours," *NYT,* April 6, 1956; "Israeli Towns Pounded, *NYT,* April 6, 1956; "Egypt Accuses Israel," *NYT,* April 7, 1956; "Zionists Assail Dulles," *NYT,* April 6, 1956.

33 Byroade to State Dept., April 8 & 9, 1956, *FRUS, 1955–57,* Vol. XV, no. 257, pp. 494–95; Byroade to JFD, April 9, 1956, *FRUS, 1955–57,* Vol. XV, no. 260, pp. 498–500.

34 "U.S. Promises to Oppose Middle East Aggression" & Dana Adams Schmidt, "Dulles to Brief Leaders," *NYT,* April 10, 1956.

35 DDE to JFD, April 10, 1956, DDE Diary, B 15, EL; also in ACW Diary, B 8 (2), EL; Dulles's side of the conversation is in DP, Tel. Conv., B 11, WH (4), EL.

36 Conversation, April 10, 1956, *FRUS, 1955–57,* Vol. XV, no. 265, pp. 504–11.

37 JFD to DDE, April 10, 1956, DP, Tel. Conv., WH, (4), EL.

38 JFD to DDE, April 11 & 12, 1956, DP, B 11, Tel. Conv., WH (4), EL.

39 Civil Defense Meeting, April 19, 1956, WHOSS, Subject Series, Alpha Subseries, B 23, President & Seaton Conference, EL.

40 For an account of the Eisenhower civil defense program, see Guy Oakes, *The Imaginary War: Civil Defense and American Cold War Culture* (New York: Oxford University Press, 1994), pp. 92–95.

41 "The Great Debate," Texts of Stevenson and Eisenhower Addresses at ASNE dinner, *NYT,* April 22, 1956; Eisenhower address also in *PPP,* no. 87, p. 411.

42 Neff, *Warriors at Suez,* p. 236.

43 DDE to Churchill, April 27, 1956, DDE Diary, B 14, Misc. (1), EL; also in *DDEP,* no. 1853.

44 William S. White, "2 Democrats Raise Obstacles to Plans for Wider U.S. Aid," *NYT,* April 28, 1956.

45 Dana Adams Schmidt, "Foreign Aid Drive Will Begin Today," *NYT,* April 30, 1956; "Text of Dulles Statement Urging Foreign Aid Program," *NYT,* May 1, 1956; Dana Adams Schmidt, "Eisenhower Joins Dulles in Pushing Foreign Aid Plan," *NYT,* May 1, 1956.

46 DDE to HH, May 2, 1956, *DDEP,* no. 1859.

47 HH to DDE, May 3, 1956, *FRUS, 1955–57,* Vol. XV, no. 323, p. 599.

48 Thomas J. Hamilton, "U.N. Chief Reports 'Positive Result' in Mideast Truce," *NYT,* May 4, 1956.

49 Conversation, May 7, 1956, DP, WH Memos, B 4, Meetings with Pres., (3), EL.

50 James Reston, "Bases of Dulles Policy," *NYT,* May 8, 1956; Elie Abel, "Dulles Sees Hope of Mideast Peace in Soviet Pledge," *NYT,* May 9, 1956.

51 Bricker Amendment, *Time,* March 19, 1956, www.time.com/time/magazine/article/0,9171,824007,00.html.

52 Conversation, May 7, 1956, DP, WH Memos, B 4, Meetings with Pres., (3), EL; Statement by President, May 8, 1956, DDE Diary, B 15, Misc. (4), EL.

53 Conversation, May 9, 1956, DP, WH Memos, B 4, Meetings with Pres., (3), EL.

54 NSC 284th Meeting, May 10, 1956, B 7, EL.

55 ACW Diary, May 11, 1956, B 8 (2), EL; Snyder Papers, Book Draft, B 11, EL; "President Accepts Bid," *NYT,* May 12, 1956.

56 Edwin L. Dale, Jr., "President Proves a Peripatetic Patient," *NYT,* May 12, 1956.

57 DDE's Ileitis Operation, June 1956, Snyder Papers, Book Draft, B 11, EL.

58 "Eisenhower Spends Quiet Day on Farm," *NYT,* May 14, 1956.

59 Allen Drury, "George Explains Decision to Quit," *NYT*, May 12, 1956; Edwin L. Dale, Jr., "George to Serve as Envoy to NATO," *NYT*, May 15, 1956.

60 Osgood Caruthers, "Egypt Assails West," *NYT*, May 15, 1956; "Egypt Gets Suez Airfields," *NYT*, May 17, 1956.

61 "Peiping Action Weighed," *NYT*, May 19, 1956; Osgood Caruthers, "Nasser Will Visit Communist China," *NYT*, May 25, 1956.

62 "House Unit Bars Eisenhower Plan on Long-Term Aid," *NYT*, May 18, 1956; William S. White, "Foreign Aid Bill Cut $1,109,000,000 by House Group," *NYT*, May 23, 1956.

63 "U.S. Order Halts 21 Army Vehicles Bound for Israel," *NYT*, May 19, 1956; "Israel Not to Act on Blocked Arms," *NYT*, May 20, 1956.

64 "Mideast Pressures," *NYT*, May 20, 1956.

65 JFD to DDE, May 22, 1956, DP, WH Memos, B 3, WH Corres.-Gen. (3), EL.

66 Elie Abel, "Dulles Reproves Nasser over Ties with Red Chinese," *NYT*, May 23, 1956.

67 Homer Bigart, "Ben-Gurion Bows," *NYT*, April 20, 1956; Editorial Note, *FRUS, 1955–57*, Vol. XV, no. 376, p. 691.

68 News Conference, June 6, 1956, *PPP*, no. 121, pp. 553–56; Dana Adams Schmidt, "Eisenhower Sees Merit in Attitude of Neutral Lands," *NYT*, June 7, 1956.

69 JFD to Hagerty, June 7, 1956, DP, B 11, Tel. Conv. WH (2), EL; a draft showing Eisenhower's edits of the June 7 statement is found in DP, Tel. Conv., B 11, WH, (2) EL; Edwin L. Dale, Jr., "Policy on Neutral Nations Clarified by White House," *NYT*, June 8, 1956.

70 An aphorism ascribed to journalist Michael Kinsley.

71 Neff, *Warriors at Suez*, p. 248; Snyder Papers, Book Draft, B 11, EL.

6. TROUBLE OVER ASWAN

1 Snyder Papers, Book Draft, B 11, EL. For the president's schedule during the period covered by this chapter, see Eisenhower, Appt. Schedules, Miller Ctr., UV, millercenter.org.

2 ACW Diary, June 8, 1956, B 8, EL; Hagerty to JFD, June 8 (mislabeled January), 1956, Dwight D. Eisenhower's Papers as President (Ann Whitman File), D-H, B 11, Tel. Conv., WH, (2), EL; Robert H. Ferrell, *Ill-Advised: Presidential Health and Public Trust* (Columbia: University of Missouri Press, 1992), p. 118; Robert E. Gilbert, *The Mortal Presidency: Illness and Anguish in the White House* (New York: Basic Books, 1992), pp. 99–101.

3 Snyder Papers, Book Draft, B 11, EL.

4 Goodpaster to JFD, June 8, 1956, D-H, B 11, Tel. Conv., WH (2), EL.

5 Snyder Papers, Book Draft, B 11, EL; ACW Diary, June 8, 1956, B 8, EL.

6 "Dulles Declares Neutrality Pose Is Obsolete Idea," & "Dulles Talk Aims to Assure Allies," *NYT*, June 10, 1956.

7 JFD to M. Snyder, June 8, 1956, D-H, B 11, Tel. Conv., WH (2), EL; Hagerty to JFD, June 8, 1956, D-H, B 11, Tel. Conv., WH (2), EL; JFD to Adams, June 8, 1956, D-H, B 11, Tel. Conv., WH (2), EL; JFD to DDE, June 8, D-H, B 7, (JFD June 1956), EL.

8 Snyder Papers, Book Draft, B 11, EL; Anthony Leviero, "President Undergoes Surgery," *NYT*, June 9, 1956.

9 Snyder Papers, Book Draft, B 11, EL; John S. D. Eisenhower, *Strictly Personal* (Garden City, NY: Doubleday, 1974), p. 186.

10 Snyder Papers, Book Draft, B 11, EL; ACW Diary, June 9–11, 1956, B 8, EL.

11 ACW Diary, June 8, 1956 B 8, EL.

12 Anthony Leviero, "President Undergoes Surgery," *NYT*, June 9, 1956; Edwin L. Dale, Jr., "Block 'Bypassed,' " *NYT*, June 10, 1956.

13 W. H. Lawrence, "Aides Close to Eisenhower Say Privately He Will Run," *NYT*, June 10, 1956; "Truman 'Very Happy' Operation Succeeded," *NYT*, June 10, 1956.

14 Goodpaster to White House Staff, DDE Diary, B 16, Misc. (3), EL.

15 JFD to Hagerty, June 12, 1956, Dulles Papers (DP), Tel. Conv., B 11, White House (WH) (2), EL; JFD to Adams, 2 calls on June 12, 1956, DP, B 11, Tel. Conv., WH (2), EL. Dulles's first full discussion with the president was held at Gettysburg on July 13, 1956, DP, WH, B 4, Meetings with Pres. (1), EL.

16 DDE to Paul Roy Helms, June 15, 1956, *DDEP*, no. 1894; Dwight D. Eisenhower, *The White House Years: Waging Peace, 1956–61* (Garden City, NY: Doubleday, 1965), p. 9.

17 Snyder Papers, Book Draft, B 11; EL; Richard M. Nixon, *Six Crises* (New York: Doubleday, 1962), p. 168; Gilbert, *The Mortal Presidency*, p. 102.

18 Adams to JFD, June 14, 1956, 3:11 PM, DP, B 11, Tel. Conv., WH (2), EL.

19 NSC 288th Meeting, June 15, 1956, B 7, EL; Molotov, a leftover from the Stalin era, was forced out of the foreign minister's position about June 1.

20 Sam Pope Brewer, "Russians Go All Out to Win Arab Friends, *NYT*, June 17, 1956; Osgood Caruthers, "Shepilov Renews Proposal for Helping Egypt on Dam," *NYT*, June 18, 1956.

21 Conversation, June 18, 1956, DP, WH, B 4, Meetings with Pres. (1), EL; Edwin L. Dale, Jr., "Eisenhower Sees Nixon and Dulles," *NYT*, June 19, 1956.

22 William S. White, "Dulles Stresses Peril in Aid Cut," *NYT*, June 20, 1956.

23 Adams to JFD, June 22, 1956, DP, B 11, Tel. Conv., WH (2), EL; ACW Diary, June 8 to July 16, B 8, EL.

24 Osgood Caruthers, "Nasser Asks U.S. Speed Aswan Bid," *NYT*, June 22, 1956.

25 Conversation, June 25, 1956, *FRUS, 1955–57*, "Arab-Israeli Conflict," Vol. XV, no. 410, pp. 748–49.

26 Eisenhower, *Waging Peace*, pp. 30–31; Telegram from State Department to American Embassy in Egypt, Dec. 16, 1955, *FRUS, 1955–57*, Vol. XIV, no. 461, pp. 868–70; "West Will Help Egypt Build Dam," *NYT*, Dec. 18, 1955.

27 Eugene Black Interview, May 13, 1975, OH-341, p. 10, EL.

28 Adams to JFD, June 20, 1956 and JFD to Adams, June 26, 1956, DP, B 11, Tel. Conv., WH (2), EL.

29 JFD to Allen and Hoover, June 27, 1956, DP, B 5, Tel. Conv. Gen. (1) EL.

30 NSC 289th Meeting, June 28, 1956, B 8, EL; Stassen had been appointed as a special presidential assistant in March 1955.

31 ACW Diary, June 8 to July 16, 1956, B 8, EL.

32 Secret Service Report on June 30, 1956, dated July 6, DDE Diary, B 16, July '56 Misc. (2), EL.

33 Memo for Record, DDE to JFD, July 5, 1956, WHOSS, Subject Series, Alphabetical Subseries, B 14, Intel Matters (2), EL; JFD to Adams, 2 Calls, June 12, 1956, DP, B 11, Tel. Conv., WH (2), EL; DDE to Robinson, July 9, 1956, DDE Diary, B 16, Misc. (3), EL.

34 Dana Adams Schmidt, "U.S. Re-Examines Ties with Egypt," *NYT*, July 9, 1956.

35 JFD to Embassy, July 9, 1956, *FRUS, 1955–57*, Vol. XV, no. 434, pp. 793–97.

36 DDE to Richardson, July, 10, 1956, DDE Diary, B 16, Misc. (3), EL.

37 Minutes of Legislative Meeting, July 10, 1956, ACW Diary, B 8, July '56, EL.

38 William S. White, "Conferees Accept 4 Billion Aid Bill," *NYT,* July 7, 1956.

39 William S. White, "President Pleads for Restoration of Aid Bill Funds," *NYT,* July 9, 1956.

40 "Why Shouldn't I?" *NYT,* July 15, 1956.

41 Byroade to State Department, July 10, 1956, *FRUS, 1955–57,* Vol. XV, no. 439, pp. 826–27; Freiberger, *Dawn over Suez,* p. 152.

42 Byroade to State Department, July 12, 1956, *FRUS, 1955–57,* Vol. XV, no. 449, pp. 823–24.

43 Byroade to State Department, July 13, 1956, *FRUS, 1955–57,* Vol. XV, no. 455, pp. 832–35.

44 Allen to State Department, July 13, 1956, *FRUS, 1955–57,* Vol. XV, no. 453, pp. 828–30.

45 Conversation, July 13, 1956, DP, WH, B 4, Meetings with Pres. (1), EL.

46 Conversation, July 13, 1956, *FRUS, 1955–57,* Vol. XV, no. 454, pp. 830–32.

47 Dana Adams Schmidt, "U.S. to Reshuffle Envoys," *NYT,* July 16, 1956; "Shake-Up Transfers U.S. Envoy to Egypt," *NYT,* July 25, 1956.

48 Knowland to JFD, July 13, 1956, DP, B 5, Tel. Conv. Gen. (6), EL; Dana Adams Schmidt, "Dulles Presents Last Plea for Aid," *NYT,* July 13, 1956; William S. White, "Senate Unit Adds 680 Million in Aid," *NYT,* July 14, 1956.

49 JFD to Chairman of Senate Appropriations Committee (Hayden), July 17, 1956, *FRUS, 1955–57,* Vol. XV, no. 466, pp. 848–49; William S. White, "Senate Committee Prohibits Aid Funds for Aswan Dam," *NYT,* July 17, 1956.

50 DDE to Woodruff, July 12, 1956, & DDE to David E., July 14, 1956, B 16, Misc. (3), EL; also *DDEP,* no. 1914.

51 ACW Diary, Summary July, 8–16, 1956, B 8, EL; DDE to Ellis D. Slater, July 16, 1956, DDE Diary, B 16, Misc. (2), EL.

52 JFD to Adams, July 17, 1956, DP, B 11, Tel. Conv., WH (1), EL; JFD to Hayden, July 17, 1956, *FRUS, 1955–57,* Vol. XV, no. 466, pp. 848–49.

53 Knowland to JFD, July 17, 1956, DP, B 5, Tel. Conv. Gen. (6), EL.

54 Allen to JFD, July 17, 1956, *FRUS, 1955–57,* Vol. XV, no. 467, pp. 849–53.

55 NSC 291st Meeting, July 19, 1956, B 8, EL.

56 Conversation, July 19, 1956, *FRUS, 1955–57,* Vol. XV, no. 473, pp. 861–62.

57 Conversation, July 19, 1956, *FRUS, 1955–57,* Vol. XV, no. 474, pp. 863–64.

58 Russell to JFD, July 19, 1956, *FRUS, 1955–57,* Vol. XV, no. 476, p. 865; JFD to AWD, July 19, 1956, *FRUS, 1955–57,* Vol. XV, no. 477, p. 866.

59 Conversation, July 19, 1956, *FRUS, 1955–57,* Vol. XV, no. 478, pp. 867–73.

60 Knowland to JFD, July 19, 1956, DP, B 5, Tel. Conv. Gen. (5), EL; JFD to AWD, July 19, 1956, DP, B 5, Tel. Conv. Gen. (5), EL.

61 Press Release, July 19, 1956, DP, Subject Series, B 6, Mid-East Inquiry; Dana Adams Schmidt, "U.S. Annuls Offer of Fund to Egypt to Build High Dam," *NYT,* July 20, 1956.

62 Interview, Eugene R. Black, May 13, 1975, OH-341, pp. 9, 15, EL.

63 Jackson Log, July 20, 1956, C. D. Jackson Papers, B 69 (3), EL.

64 Byroade to State Department, July 20, 1956, *FRUS, 1955–57,* Vol. XV, no. 484, p. 878; Andrew B. Foster to State Dept., July 20, 1956, *FRUS, 1955–57,* Vol. XV, no. 485, p. 879; Bohlen to State Dept., July 22, 1956, *FRUS, 1955–57,* Vol. XV, no. 486, pp. 879–80.

65 "U.S.-British Step a Shock to Cairo," *NYT,* July 21, 1956; Kennett Love, "Britain

Cancels Aswan Dam Offer in Line with U.S.," *NYT,* July 21, 1956; "U.S. Shift," *NYT,* July 22, 1956.
66 Brownell to JFD, June 28, 1956, DP, B 5, Tel. Conv. Gen. (1), EL; JFD to Adams, June 28, 1956, DP, B 11, Tel. Conv., WH (2), EL.
67 Hagerty to JFD, July 17, 1956, DP, B 11, Tel. Conv., WH (1), EL.
68 John Eisenhower, *Strictly Personal,* p. 187; Nixon, *Six Crises,* p. 169; Emmet John Hughes, *The Ordeal of Power: A Political Memoir of the Eisenhower Years* (New York: Atheneum, 1963), p. 176; Gilbert, *The Mortal Presidency,* pp. 102–3.
69 DDE to Mamie, approx. July, 22, 1956, DDE Diary, B 16, Misc. (1), EL.
70 JFD to HH, July 23, 1956, DP, B 5, Tel. Conv. Gen. (5), EL. The particular problem Hoover and Dulles were discussing is not specifically identified but it surely was their relief at the news of president's renewed vigor.
71 JFD to Nixon, July 30, 1956, PM, DP, B 5, Tel. Conv. Gen. (5), EL; Hughes, *Ordeal of Power,* p. 176; Gilbert, *The Mortal Presidency,* p. 102.
72 DDE Diary, July 25, 1956, B 16, EL.
73 "Shake-Up Transfers U.S. Envoy to Egypt," *NYT,* July 25, 1956; Byroade to State Department, July 24, 1956, *FRUS, 1955–57,* Vol. XV, no. 495, p. 890; Osgood Caruthers, "Nasser Says U.S. Lied in Explaining Bar to Aswan Aid," *NYT,* July 25, 1956.
74 Rountree to Hoover, July 25, 1956, *FRUS, 1955–57,* Vol. XV, no. 499, pp. 896–97; "Conferees Vote 3.7 Billion in Aid," *NYT,* July 26, 1956.
75 Cabinet Meeting, July 25, 1956, B 7, EL.
76 "Egypt Nationalizes Suez Canal; Will Use Revenues to Build Aswan Dam," *NYT,* July 27, 1956.

7. A GROWING RIFT
1 ACW Diary, July 27, 1956, B 8, EL; Conference, July 27, 1956, DDE Diary, B 16, July '56, Staff Memos, EL; also in *FRUS, 1955–57,* "Suez Crisis," Vol. XVI, no. 3, pp. 5–7; Foster to State Department, *FRUS, 1955–57,* Vol. XVI, no. 2, pp. 3–5; D-H, B 7, JFD, EL; Current Intelligence Bulletin, July 28, 1956, CREST, National Archives (NA), Archives II College Park Md. For the president's schedule during the period covered by this chapter, see Eisenhower, Appt. Schedules, Miller Ctr., UV, millercenter.org.
2 Donald Neff, *Warriors at Suez* (New York: Linden Press/Simon & Schuster, 1981), p. 281. For the Soviet response to the nationalization of the canal, see Aleksandr Fursenko and Timothy Naftali, *Khrushchev's Cold War: The Inside Story of an American Adversary* (New York: W. W. Norton, 2006), pp. 85–88.
3 Eden to DDE, July 27, 1956, *FRUS, 1955–57,* Vol. XVI, no. 5, pp. 9–11.
4 Dillon to State Department, July 27, 1956, D-H, B 7, JFD, EL; *FRUS, 1955–57,* Vol. XVI, no. 4, pp. 7–9; JFD to State Department, July 27, 1956, *FRUS, 1955–57,* Vol. XVI, no. 4, p. 9.
5 Cabinet Meeting, July 27, 1956, B 7, EL; DDE Diary, B 16, Misc. (1), EL.
6 State Dept. statement, July 27, 1956, *FRUS, 1955–57,* Vol. XVI, no. 3, p. 7.
7 Conference with President, July 27, 1956, DDE Diary, B 16, Staff Memos, EL; *FRUS, 1955–57,* Vol. XVI, no. 6, pp. 11–12.
8 Murphy was awarded the National Security Medal on Dec. 19, 1960, Dwight D. Eisenhower, the American Presidency Project, Citation Dec. 19, 1960, www.presidency.ucsb.edu/ws/index.php?pid=12034. See Dwight D. Eisenhower, *Cru-*

sade in Europe (Garden City, NY: Doubleday, 1949), pp. 85–86, for Murphy's role in the North Africa campaign in World War II.

9 DDE to Nixon, July 27, 1956, DDE Diary, B 16, Phone Calls, EL.

10 DDE to Eden, July 27, 1956, *DDEP*, no. 1932.

11 Calls, July 27, 1956, DDE Diary, B 16, Phone Calls, EL; HH to DDE, July 28, 1956, DDE Diary, B 16, Phone Calls, EL; Conversation, July 28, 1956, D-H, B 7, JFD, EL; there are two sets of Goodpaster notes on this conversation in DDE Diary, B 16, Staff Memos, EL.

12 ACW Diary, July 28, 1956, B 8, EL.

13 Dana Adams Schmidt, "Cairo Is Denounced by Dulles on Seizure," *NYT*, July 30, 1956; JFD to DDE, July 19, 1956, *FRUS, 1955–57*, Vol. XVI, no. 23, pp. 38–39.

14 Kennett Love, "Eden Firmly Bars Suez Canal Rule by Single Power," *NYT*, July 31, 1956.

15 Current Intelligence Bulletin, July 29, 1956, CREST, NA; Jack Raymond, "Khrushchev Appeals for Calm over Suez," *NYT*, Aug. 1, 1956.

16 ACW Diary, July 31, 1956, B 8, EL.

17 Murphy to JFD, HH, July 29, 1956, *FRUS, 1955–57*, Vol. XVI, no. 21, pp. 35–36.

18 Murphy to JFD, HH, July 29, 1956, 11 PM, *FRUS, 1955–57*, Vol. XVI, no. 24, pp. 30–41; D-H, B 7, JFD, EL.

19 Editorial note, *FRUS, 1955–57*, Vol. XVI, no. 26, pp. 45–46; DDE to JFD, July 30, 1956, *FRUS, 1955–57*, Vol. XVI, no. 27, pp. 46–47; JFD to Murphy, July 30, 1956, D-H, B 7, JFD, EL; JFD to Murphy, July 30, 1956, *FRUS, 1955–57*, Vol. XVI, no. 28, pp. 48–49; also D-H, B 7, JFD, EL.

20 Byroade to State Department, July 30, 1956, *FRUS, 1955–57*, Vol. XVI, no. 31, pp. 55–58.

21 Murphy to JFD, HH, July 31, 1956, *FRUS, 1955–57*, Vol. XVI, no. 33, pp. 60–62.

22 Conference, July 31, 1956, DDE Diary, B 16, Staff Memos, EL.

23 Dakar is the capital of Senegal, on the coast of West Africa.

24 Special National Intelligence Estimate, July 31, 1956, *FRUS, 1955–57*, Vol. XVI, no. 40, pp. 78–79; DDE to JFD, July 31, 1956, DDE Diary, B 16, July '56, Phone Calls, EL.

25 DDE to Eden, July 31, 1956, *DDEP*, no. 1935.

26 ACW Diary, July 31, 1956, B 8, EL.

27 Conversation, British Foreign Office, Aug. 1, 1956, *FRUS, 1955–57*, Vol. XVI, no. 41, pp. 94–97; Conversation, JFD & Eden, Aug. 1, 1956, *FRUS, 1955–57*, Vol. XVI, no. 42, pp. 98–100.

28 Footnote no. 3, *FRUS, 1955–57*, Vol. XVI, no. 41, p. 100.

29 News Conference, Aug. 1, 1956, *PPP*, no. 155, p. 635.

30 JFD to State Department, Aug. 2, 1956, *FRUS, 1955–57*, Vol. XVI, no. 44, pp. 102–5.

31 JFD to DDE, Aug. 2, 1956, D-H, B 7, JFD (2), EL; also *FRUS, 1955–57*, Vol. XVI, no. 48, pp. 110–11 (see footnote no. 2 for Eisenhower response).

32 Tripartite Statement, Aug. 2, 1956, *FRUS, 1955–57*, Vol. XVI, no. 53, pp. 126–27.

33 DDE to Hazlett, Aug. 3, 1956, DDE Diary, B 17, Misc. (4), EL; also *DDEP*, no. 1936.

34 Murray Snyder to JFD, Aug. 3, 1956, DP, B 11, Tel. Conv., WH, (1), EL; JFD to AWD, Aug. 3, 1956, DP, Tel. Conv. Gen. (4), EL; Editorial Note, *FRUS, 1955–57*, Vol. XVI, no. 57, pp. 131–32.

35 President's Remarks, Aug. 3, 1956, *PPP*, no. 164, pp. 647–48; "Eisenhower's Remarks and Dulles' Report on Suez," *NYT*, Aug. 4, 1956.

36 Byroade to State Department, Aug. 4, 1956, *FRUS, 1955–57*, Vol. XVI, no. 59, pp. 133–35.

37 Eden to DDE, Aug. 5, 1956, *FRUS, 1955–57*, Vol. XVI, no. 64, pp. 146–48.

38 ACW Diary, Aug. 6, 1956, B 8, EL; DDE to JFD, Aug. 6, 1956, DDE Diary, B 16, Aug. '56, Phone Calls, EL; Dulles notes of same conversation in DP, B 11, Tel. Conv., WH, (1), EL.

39 JFD to Bohlen, Aug. 6, 1956, *FRUS, 1955–57*, Vol. XVI, no. 66, pp. 149–50; also in DP, Chrono., B 14, JFD Chrono. (3), EL.

40 DDE to Bulganin, Aug. 6, 1956, DP, Chrono., B 14, JFD Chrono., Aug. '56 (3), EL; also in *DDEP*, no. 1938. Bohlen delivered Eisenhower's belated response to Nikolai Bulganin's June 6 letter on disarmament, rejecting the Soviet leader's proposal that, in response to Soviet troop reductions, the United States reduce NATO forces accordingly; DDE to Bulganin, Aug. 4, 1956, *DDEP*, no. 1937; JFD call to DDE, Aug. 6, 1956, DDE Diary, B 16, Phone Calls, EL.

41 Bohlen to State Department, Aug. 7, 1956, D-H, B 7, JFD (2), EL; also in *FRUS, 1955–57*, Vol. XVI, no. 69, pp. 156–60. For the Soviet view of the conference and participation, see Fursenko and Naftali, *Khrushchev's Cold War*, pp. 90–105.

42 Memo for Record, Monday, Aug. 6, 1956, DP, WH Memoranda Series, B 5, Meetings with Pres. (8), EL; WHO, OSANSA, Special Assistant Series, Chronological Subseries, B 9, State Dept., EL.

43 ACW Diary, Aug. 6, 1956, B 8, EL.

44 DDE Diary, Aug. 8, 1956, B 17, EL; also in *DDEP*, no. 1946.

45 Phone Calls, DDE & Dulles, DDE & Brownell, Aug. 8, 1956, DDE Diary, B 16, Phone Calls, EL; Press Conference Series, Draft statement dated Aug. 7, 1956, B 5, EL.

46 News Conference, Aug. 8, 1956, *PPP*, pp. 660–62.

47 Conversation, DDE and JFD, Aug. 8, 1956, *FRUS, 1955–57*, Vol. XVI, no. 71, pp. 163–64; Eden to DDE, n.d., cover note, Macomber to Phleger, Aug. 8, 1956, DP, Subject Series, B 7, Suez Problem (7), EL.

48 NSC 292nd Meeting, Aug. 9, 1956, B 8, EL.

49 Intelligence Report, Aug. 10, 1956, WHO, OSANSA, Special Assistant Series, Subject Subseries, B 9, Suez Canal (Aug. 1956), EL; Welles Hangen, "Soviet to Attend Suez Conference, but Challenges It," *NYT*, Aug. 10, 1956.

50 Conversation, Aug. 11, 1956, DP, WH Memos, B 5, Meetings with Pres. (8), EL.

51 Memo for record, Meeting with Pres., Aug. 12, 1956, DDE Diary, B 17, Staff Memoranda, EL.

52 Notes on Presidential-Bipartisan Congressional Leadership Meeting, Aug. 12, 1956, *FRUS, 1955–57*, Vol. XVI, no. 79, pp. 188–97.

53 White House Statement, Aug. 12, 1956, ACW Diary, B 8, (1), EL; also *PPP*, no. 184, pp. 687–89.

54 ACW Diary, Aug. 12, 1956, B 8, EL; Kennett Love, "Britain Airlifts Force to Mideast," *NYT*, Aug. 13, 1956; Kennett Love, *Suez: The Twice-Fought War* (New York: McGraw-Hill, 1969), p. 398.

55 Conversation, DDE & JFD, Aug. 14, 1956, *FRUS, 1955–57*, Vol. XVI, no. 81, pp. 198–99.

56 DDE to Larson, Aug. 15, 1956, DDE Diary, B 16, Phone Calls, EL.

57 JFD to DDE, Aug. 16, 1956, *FRUS, 1955–57*, Vol. XVI, no. 86, pp. 210–11.

58 DDE to Prescott Bush, Aug. 16, 1956, DDE Diary, B 16, Phone Calls. EL; DDE to Brownell, Aug. 19, 1956, ACW Diary, B 8, EL; "Text of the Republican Platform as Adopted by the Party's National Convention," *NYT*, Aug. 22, 1956.

59 JFD to DDE, Aug. 17, 1956, *FRUS, 1955–57,* Vol. XVI, no. 91, pp. 218–19; HH to JFD, Aug. 17, 1956, *FRUS, 1955–57,* Vol. XVI, no. 92, p. 220.

60 Robinson to DDE, Aug. 17, 1956, DDE Diary, B 16, Phone Calls, EL.

61 JFD to DDE, Aug. 18, 1956, *FRUS, 1955–57,* Vol. XVI, no. 94, p. 227; DDE to JFD, Aug. 18, 1956, *DDEP,* no. 1958.

62 JFD to DDE, Aug. 19, 1956, *FRUS, 1955–57,* Vol. XVI, no. 97, pp. 231–32; also D-H, B 7, JFD (2), EL; DDE to JFD, Aug. 19, 1956, *FRUS, 1955–57,* Vol. XVI, no. 98, pp. 232–33; also DDE Diary, B 17, Misc. (2), EL.

63 JFD to DDE, Aug. 20, 1956, *FRUS, 1955–57,* Vol. XVI, no. 100, pp. 236–37; DDE to JFD, Aug. 20, 1956, *DDEP,* no. 1962; Harold Callender, "Dulles Suez Plan Expected to Win Early Approval," *NYT,* Aug. 20, 1956.

64 JFD to DDE, Aug. 20, 1956, *FRUS, 1955–57,* Vol. XVI, no. 105, pp. 245–46; Conversation, JFD & Macmillan, Aug. 21, 1956, *FRUS, 1955–57,* Vol. XVI, no. 108, pp. 249–49; DDE to JFD, Aug. 20, 1956, *DDEP,* no. 1962.

65 JFD to DDE, Aug. 21, 1956, *FRUS, 1955–57,* Vol. XVI, no. 111, pp. 253–54; also in D-H, B 7, JFD (1), EL.

66 Russell Baker, "Convention Was 'Too Interesting' to Miss,' " *NYT,* Aug. 22, 1956.

67 HH to JFD, Aug. 22, 1956, *FRUS, 1955–57,* Vol. XVI, no. 114, pp. 257–58.

68 JFD to DDE, Aug. 22, 1956, *FRUS, 1955–57,* Vol. XVI, no. 117, pp. 261–62; also D-H, B 7, JFD (1), EL.

69 JFD to DDE, Aug. 23, 1956, D-H, JFD Aug. '56 (1); also in *FRUS, 1955–57,* Vol. XVI, no. 125, pp. 280–81, information on Menzies in footnote no. 3.

70 "G.O.P. Withholds Big Thrill to End," *NYT,* Aug. 24, 1956.

71 Acceptance Address, Aug. 23, 1956, *PPP,* no. 190, pp. 702–15.

72 Diary entry, Jan. 10, 1956, DDE Diary, B 9, Personal (2), EL; also in *DDEP,* no. 1681.

73 W. H. Lawrence, "Party of the Future," *NYT,* Aug. 24, 1956.

74 Editorial Note, *FRUS, 1955–57,* Vol. XVI, no. 128, pp. 284–85.

8. BETRAYAL OF TRUST

1 Harold Callender, "18 Nations Agree to Invite Egypt to Discuss Suez," *NYT,* Aug. 24, 1956. Henderson, known as an expert on the Soviet Union, had served as ambassador to Iraq and Iran and was involved with the 1953 coup that restored the Shah of Iran to power.

2 Lloyd and JFD Conversation, Aug. 23, 1956, *FRUS, 1955–57,* Vol. XVI, "The Suez Crisis," no. 126, p. 281; Eden and JFD conversation, Aug. 24, 1956, *FRUS, 1955–57,* Vol. XVI, no. 129, pp. 285–86.

3 Eden to DDE, Aug. 27, 1956, *FRUS, 1955–57,* Vol. XVI, no. 137, pp. 304–5; Henderson to State Dept., Aug. 28, 1956, *FRUS, 1955–57,* Vol. XVI, no. 142, pp. 312–13.

4 Conversation, JFD & DDE, Aug. 29, 1956, *FRUS, 1955–57,* Vol. XVI, no. 144, pp. 314–15; statement, Aug. 29, 1956, D-H, B 7; JFD (1), EL. For the president's schedule during the period covered by this chapter, see Eisenhower, Appt. Schedules, Miller Ctr., UV, millercenter.org.

5 ACW Diary, Aug. 30, 1956, B 8, EL; NSC 295th Meeting, Aug. 30, 1956, B 8, EL.

6 Statement, Aug. 29, 1956, D-H, B 7, JFD (1) EL; "Text of Nasser Statement," *NYT*, Aug. 31, 1956; JFD to DDE, Aug. 31, 1956, DDE Diary, B 16, Phone Calls, EL; also in *FRUS, 1955–57*, Vol. XVI, no. 155, pp. 340–41.

7 News Conference, Aug. 31, 1956, *PPP*, no. 193, pp. 717–18; John D. Morris, "President Clarifies His Suez Statement," *NYT*, Sept. 1, 1956.

8 Donald Neff, *Warriors at Suez* (New York: Linden Press/Simon & Schuster, 1981), p. 309; Kennett Love, *Suez: The Twice-Fought War* (New York: McGraw-Hill, 1969), p. 433.

9 DDE to Eden, Sept. 2, 1956, *DDEP*, no. 1972.

10 JFD to G. Humphrey, Sept. 13, 1956, DP, Tel. Conv., B 5, Tel. Conv. Gen. (2), EL.

11 Duck Island Memorandum, Sept. 2, 1956, *FRUS, 1955–57*, Vol. XVI, no. 161, pp. 351–52; Editorial Note, *FRUS, 1955–57*, Vol. XVI, no. 168, p. 365.

12 Summary of Suez Situation, Sept. 4, 1956, *FRUS, 1955–57*, Vol. XVI, no. 169, pp. 366–69; Summary no. 2, Suez Situation, Sept. 5, 1956, *FRUS, 1955–57*, Vol. XVI, no. 173, pp. 375–78.

13 Annex to Watch Committee Report No. 318, Sept. 5, 1956, *FRUS, 1955–57*, Vol. XVI, no. 174, pp. 378–81; Special National Intelligence Estimate, Sept. 5, 1956, *FRUS, 1955–57*, Vol. XVI, no. 175, pp. 382–91.

14 News Conference, Sept. 5, 1956, *PPP*, no. 198, p, 737.

15 These words are based on Henderson's cable 613, and provided in a summary report, Sept. 6, 1956, *FRUS, 1955–57*, Vol. XVI, no. 178, pp. 393–95; Conversation, Sept. 6, 1956, *FRUS, 1955–57*, Vol. XVI, no. 1779, pp. 392–93.

16 Henderson to State Dept., Sept. 6, 1956, *FRUS, 1955–57*, Vol. XVI, no. 180, pp. 398–400.

17 Eden to DDE, Sept. 6, 1956, *FRUS, 1955–57*, Vol. XVI, no. 181, pp. 400–3.

18 JFD to DDE, Sept. 7, 1956, DDE Diary, B 18, Phone Calls, EL; also in DP, Tel. Conv., B 11, Tel. Conv., White House (WH) (2), EL.

19 DDE to JFD, Sept. 7, 1956, DDE Diary, B 18, Phone Calls, EL; also in DP, B 11, Tel. Conv., WH (2), EL; also in *FRUS, 1955–57*, Vol. XVI, no. 183, p. 405; *FRUS, 1955–57*, Vol. XVI, no. 187, pp. 418–19.

20 JFD to DDE, Sept. 7, 1956, DP, B 11, Tel. Conv., WH (2), EL.

21 Conversations, DDE & JFD, Sept. 8, 1956, *FRUS, 1955–57*, Vol. XVI, nos. 191, 193, pp. 434–35, 438–51; Users Proposal, Sept. 9, 1956, *FRUS, 1955–57*, Vol. XVI, no. 198, p. 451–55.

22 DDE to Eden, Sept. 8, 1956, *DDEP*, no. 1982.

23 Henderson to JFD, Sept. 9, 1956, *FRUS, 1955–57*, Vol. XVI, no. 196, pp. 446–47; Editorial Note, *FRUS, 1955–57*, Vol. XVI, no. 194, pp. 441–43.

24 Selwyn Lloyd, *Suez 1956: A Personal Account* (New York: Mayflower, 1978), p. 170. JFD to DDE, Sept. 10, 1956, DDE Diary, B 18, Phone Calls, EL.

25 Pre–Press Conference Notes, Sept. 11, 1956, PC, B 5 EL. The original note said "key of dynamite," an obvious typographical error; see Conversation with President, Sept. 11, 1956, DDE Diary, B 17, Sept. '56 Daily Staff Memos, EL. Eisenhower received a report on tanker availability that addressed future plans for supertankers and new pipelines. Although the United States had substantial oil to meet its own needs, the future was not so secure. There had been a decline in American oil exploration, increased abandonment of wells in Texas, Oklahoma, and Kansas, and imports had been increasing. The report identified a "trend toward increasing dependency on foreign oil." Since the end of World War II, the

percentage of imported oil had moved from 5 to 20 percent. The following day, Eisenhower ordered Arthur Flemming, the director of the Office of Defense Mobilization, to convene an interdepartmental task force to study the long-term implications of oil supplies, given the Suez crisis, including development of supertankers and additional pipelines from the Middle East oilfields to the Mediterranean; Goodpaster to Flemming, Sept. 12, 1956, Dwight D. Eisenhower, Records as President, WH CF, Confidential File, Subject Series, Suez Canal Crisis (1), EL; Love, *Suez,* p. 433.

26 News Conference, Sept. 11, 1956, *PPP,* No. 205, pp. 756–57.

27 JFD to Makins, Sept. 11, 1956, DP, Tel. Conv., B 5, Tel. Conv. Gen. (2), EL; Summary No. 7, Sept. 12, 1956, *FRUS, 1955–57,* Vol. XVI, no. 211, pp. 484–85.

28 Editorial Note, *FRUS, 1955–57,* Vol. XVI, no. 212, pp. 486–87.

29 Annex to Watch Committee Report, No. 319, Sept. 12, 1956, *FRUS, 1955–57,* Vol. XVI, no. 214, pp. 488–89.

30 DDE to JFD, Sept. 13, 1956, DP, B 11, Tel. Conv., WH (2), EL.

31 Conversation, Sept. 13, 1956, *FRUS, 1955–57,* Vol. XVI, no. 216, pp. 491–92.

32 Press Conference, Sept. 13, 1956, D-H, B 7, JFD (2), EL.

33 Conversation, Sept. 13, 1956, *FRUS, 1955–57,* Vol. XVI, no. 217, pp. 492–94; JFD to DDE, Sept. 13, 1956, DP, B 11, Tel. Conv., WH (2), EL.

34 Dwight D. Eisenhower, *The White House Years: Waging Peace, 1956–61* (Garden City, NY: Doubleday, 1965), p. 33.

35 DDE to JFD, Sept. 6, 1956, letter Nils E. Lind to Charles Jones, Aug. 25, 1956, DP, WH Memoranda, B 3, WH Corres.-Gen. (2), EL. See also *DDEP,* No. 1976, footnote no. 1; Conversation, Sept. 17, 1956, *FRUS, 1955–57,* Vol. XVI, no. 224, pp. 505–6.

36 JFD to DDE, Sept. 15, 1956, delivered Sept. 17, D-H, B 7, JFD (2), EL; Eisenhower, *Mandate for Change,* p. 33.

37 NIE, Sept. 19, 1956, *FRUS, 1955–57,* Vol. XVI, no. 236, pp. 525–28.

38 Conversation, Sept. 20, 1956, *FRUS, 1955–57,* Vol. XVI, no. 245, pp. 545–46; JFD to DDE, Sept. 20, 1956, *FRUS, 1955–57,* Vol. XVI, no. 244, pp. 544–45; Steven Z. Freiberger, *Dawn over Suez: The Rise of American Power in the Middle East* (Chicago: Ivan R. Dee, 1992), p. 181.

39 Radio and Television Address, Sept. 19, 1956, *PPP,* No. 210, pp. 779–88.

40 NSC 297th Meeting, Sept. 20, 1956, B 8, EL.

41 Statement and Declaration, London, Sept. 21, 1956, *FRUS, 1955–57,* Vol. XVI, nos. 251–52, pp. 556–59.

42 Summary No. 7, Sept. 12, 1956, *FRUS, 1955–57,* Vol. XVI, no. 211, pp. 484–85; Summary No. 15, Sept. 24, 1956, *FRUS, 1955–57,* Vol. XVI, no. 260, pp. 569–70; JFD to Flemming, Sept. 25, 1956, DP, Tel. Conv., B 5, Memoranda of Tel. Conv. Gen. (1), EL.

43 JFD to DDE, Sept. 25, 1956, DDE Diary, B 18, Phone Calls, EL. Macmillan discusses this trip to the United States in detail in Harold Macmillan, *Riding the Storm, 1956–1959* (London: Macmillan, 1971), pp. 129–38. Neff, *Warriors at Suez,* pp. 321–23; Keith Kyle, *Suez: Britain's End of Empire in the Middle East* (London: I. B. Taurus, 1991, 2003), pp. 260, 266–68.

44 Eden to DDE, Oct. 1, 1956, *FRUS, 1955–57,* Vol. XVI, no. 287, pp. 618–19; Summary No. 21, Oct. 2, 1956, *FRUS, 1955–57,* Vol. XVI, no. 290, pp. 623–25.

45 Kyle, *Suez,* p. 263; Neff, *Warriors at Suez,* p. 313; Love, *Suez,* p. 387.

46 Conversation, Oct. 2, 1956, *FRUS, 1955–57,* Vol. XVI, no. 291, pp. 625–27.

47 Annex to Watch Committee Report, No. 322, Oct. 3, 1956, *FRUS, 1955–57,* Vol. XVI, no. 294, pp. 629–30.
48 NSC 299th Meeting, Oct. 4, 1956, B 8, EL.
49 Conversation, Oct. 5, 1956, *FRUS, 1955–57,* Vol. XVI, no. 300, pp. 639–45.
50 JFD to DDE, Oct. 5, 1956, *FRUS, 1955–57,* Vol. XVI, no. 302, pp. 648–50.
51 Jackson Log, Oct. 5, 1956, C. D. Jackson Papers, B 69, Log-1956 (4), EL.
52 Neff, *Warriors at Suez,* p. 335; Kyle, *Suez,* p. 277.
53 Editorial Note, *FRUS, 1955–57,* Vol. XVI, no. 299, pp. 638–39; HH to Rountree, Oct. 6, 1956, *FRUS, 1955–57,* Vol. XVI, no. 305, pp. 653–54; Conversation, Oct. 7, 1956, *FRUS, 1955–57,* Vol. XVI, no. 307, pp. 656–57.
54 James B. McCaffrey, "G.O.P. Is 'Scared,' Truman Asserts," *NYT,* Oct. 3, 1956; "Eisenhower Refrains from Comment on Suez," *NYT,* Oct. 6, 1956.
55 Hagerty to DDE, Oct. 8, 1956, D-H, B 7, JFD (2), EL; also in HP, B 8, Personal-Mr. Hagerty, EL.
56 DDE phone call to HH, Oct. 8, 1956, DDE Diary, B 18, Misc. (4), EL; also in *FRUS, 1955–57,* Vol. XVI, no. 310, pp. 661–62.
57 DDE letter to HH; Oct. 8, 1956, DDE Diary, B 18, Misc. (4); also in *FRUS, 1955–57,* Vol. XVI, no. 311, pp. 662–63, & *DDEP,* No. 2014.
58 HH to JFD, Oct. 9, 1956, DP, Tel. Conv., B 5, Tel. Conv. Gen. (4), EL; JFD to DDE, Oct. 10, 1956, *FRUS, 1955–57,* Vol. XVI, no. 323, p. 684.
59 DDE, JFD, HH conversation, Oct. 11, 1956, *FRUS, 1955–57,* Vol. XVI, no. 327, pp. 692–93.
60 News Conference, Oct. 11, 1956, *PPP,* No. 235, pp. 882–83.
61 Edwin L. Dale, Jr., "Eisenhower Says Policy on Suez Has Been Clear," *NYT,* Oct. 12, 1956.
62 JFD to McCardle, Oct. 11, 1956, DP, Tel. Conv., B 5, Tel. Conv. Gen. (4), EL; DDE to Eden, Oct. 11, 1956, *DDEP* No. 2024.
63 NSC 300th Meeting, Oct. 12, 1956, B 8, EL.
64 Editorial Note, *FRUS, 1955–57,* Vol. XVI, no. 337, pp. 712–13; JFD to DDE, Oct. 12, 1956, DP, B 11, Tel. Conv., WH (2), EL.
65 Television Broadcast, Oct. 12, 1956, *PPP,* no. 241, pp. 903, 910–11.
66 Editorial Notes, *FRUS, 1955–57,* Vol. XVI, nos. 341–42, pp. 718–20.
67 Dana Adams Schmidt, "Eisenhower, Dulles Optimistic on Suez," *NYT,* Oct. 15, 1956.
68 JFD to DDE, Oct. 14, 1956, DP, Chrono., B 14, JFD Chrono. (2), EL; also in *FRUS, 1955–57,* Vol. XVI, no. 343, p. 721; Freiberger, *Dawn over Suez,* p. 181; Love, *Suez,* pp. 450–52; Kyle, *Suez,* pp. 295–97.
69 Undated paper on "U.S. Opportunities in the Middle East," HH to DDE, Oct. 12, 1956, D-H, B 7, JFD (2) EL; also discussed in the NSC 300th meeting, Oct. 12, 1956, B 8, EL; Conversation, Oct. 15, 1956, DP, WH Memos, B 4, Meetings with Pres. (4), EL; Neff, *Warriors at Suez,* pp. 330–31.
70 Memo for Record, Oct. 15, 1956, DDE Diary, B 9, Personal (1), EL; also in ACW Diary, B 8, EL.
71 Lloyd to JFD, Oct. 15, 1956, *FRUS, 1955–57,* Vol. XVI, no. 348, pp. 738–40.
72 JFD to Lloyd, Oct. 15, 1956, DP, Chrono., B 14, JFD Chrono. (2), EL; also in *FRUS, 1955–57,* Vol. XVI, no. 347, pp. 734–37.
73 For Dulles's fearful instructions to the American ambassadors in London and Paris, see JFD to Aldrich and Dillon, Oct. 17, 1956, *FRUS, 1955–57,* Vol. XVI, no. 351, pp. 744–45.

74 Lloyd, *Suez 1956*, p. 173; Love, *Suez*, p. 453; Kyle, *Suez*, pp. 302–3; Freiberger, *Dawn over Suez*, pp. 181–82; Anthony Eden, *Full Circle: The Memoirs of Anthony Eden* (Cambridge: Riverside/Houghton Mifflin, 1960), pp. 569–74. On November 16, Christian Pineau, the French foreign minister, told Allen Dulles and Admiral Radford about these October 16 meetings; see *FRUS, 1955–57*, Vol. XVI, no. 379, pp. 1135–37, & WHOSS, Subseries Dept. of Defense, B 1, Dept. of Defense, Joint Chiefs (3), EL.

75 Minutes, Intelligence Advisory Committee, Oct. 16, 1956, CREST, NA.

76 DDE to Hazlett, March 2, 1956, DDE Diary, B 14, Misc. (6), EL.

77 DDE to JFD, Oct. 17, 1956, DP, B 11, Tel. Conv., WH (2), EL.

78 Lodge to JFD, Oct. 17, 1956, DP, Tel. Conv., B 5, Tel. Conv. Gen. (4), EL; JFD to DDE, Oct. 17, 1956, DP, B 11, Tel. Conv., WH (2), EL.

79 JFD to AWD, Oct. 18, DP, Tel. Conv., B 5, Tel. Conv. Gen. (4), EL; Joint Chiefs & State Dept. discussion, Oct. 19, 1956, *FRUS, 1955–57*, Vol. XVI, No. 355, pp. 749–51; Freiberger, *Dawn over Suez*, p. 182; Eden, *Full Circle*, p. 574; Kyle, *Suez*, p. 263.

80 Neff, *Warriors at Suez*, p. 341; Love, *Suez*, p. 455; William Taubman, *Khrushchev: The Man and His Era* (New York: W. W. Norton, 2003), pp. 293–94.

81 Aldrich to JFD, Oct. 19, 1956, *FRUS, 1955–57*, Vol. XVI, no. 356, pp. 751–53.

82 Dillon to JFD, Oct. 19, 1956, *FRUS, 1955–57*, Vol. XVI, no. 357, pp. 753–57.

83 JFD to Lloyd, Oct. 19, 1956, *FRUS, 1955–57*, Vol. XVI, no. 358, pp. 757–60; Aldrich to JFD, Oct. 19, 1956, *FRUS, 1955–57*, Vol. XVI, no. 356, pp. 751–53; Lodge to JFD, DP, Tel. Conv., B 5, Tel. Conv. Gen. (4), EL.

84 JFD to Adams, Oct. 19, 1956, DP, Tel. Conv., WH (2), EL; DDE to Bulganin, Oct. 21, 1956, no. 2041, footnote no. 1; "Bulganin Bids Eisenhower Study Ban on H-Bomb Test," *NYT*, Oct. 21, 1956; the Bulganin letter is in Dwight D. Eisenhower's Papers as President (Ann Whitman File), International Series, EL.

85 Calls on Oct. 21, 1956, DP, B 11, Tel. Conv., WH (2), EL; Harrison E. Salisbury, "Stevenson Asks for Suez 'Truth,'" *NYT*, Oct. 20, 1956.

86 Conversation with President, Oct. 21, 1956, DP, WH Memoranda, B 4, Meetings with Pres., (4), EL; DDE to Bulganin, Oct. 21, 1956, DDE Diary, B 18, Misc. (2), EL; also in *DDEP*, no. 2041.

87 Lodge to JFD, Oct. 22, 1956, Editorial Note, *FRUS, 1955–57*, Vol. XVI, no. 363, pp. 765–66; JFD to Dillon, Oct. 22, 1956, *FRUS, 1955–57*, Vol. XVI, no. 364, p. 766.

88 Lodge to JFD, Oct. 23, 1956, *FRUS, 1955–57*, Vol. XVI, no. 367, pp. 770–71.

89 "Nagy Is Renamed," *NYT*, Oct. 24, 1956; Love, *Suez*, p. 467; Neff, *Warriors at Suez*, pp. 341–42; Taubman, *Khrushchev*, p. 295; Aleksandr Fursenko and Timothy Naftali, *Khrushchev's Cold War: The Inside Story of an American Adversary* (New York: W. W. Norton, 2006), pp. 122–24.

90 Neff, *Warriors at Suez*, p. 342; Love, *Suez*, pp. 460–66; Lloyd, *Suez 1956*, p. 180.

91 Neff, *Warriors at Suez*, pp. 342–47; Lloyd, *Suez 1956*, pp. 180–87; Love, *Suez*, pp. 460–66; Kyle, *Suez*, pp. 314–31.

9. DOUBLE-CROSSING IKE

1 *FRUS, 1955–57*, Vol. XVI, "The Suez Crisis," no. 373, pp. 776–77; Keith Kyle, *Suez: Britain's End of Empire in the Middle East* (London: I. B. Taurus, 1991), p. 330; Kennett Love, *Suez: The Twice-Fought War* (New York: McGraw-Hill, 1969), p. 466; Donald Neff, *Warriors at Suez* (New York: Linden Press/

Simon & Schuster, 1981), p. 348. The details of the negotiations are found in Moshe Dayan, *Story of My Life* (New York: William Morrow, 1976), pp. 211–34.

2 *FRUS, 1955–57,* Vol. XVI, no. 372, pp. 775–76.

3 Dwight D. Eisenhower, *The White House Years: Waging Peace, 1956–61* (Garden City, N.Y.: Doubleday, 1965), p. 64; Elie Abel, "Deaths Put at 150," *NYT,* Oct. 25, 1956.

4 Chester L. Cooper, *The Lion's Last Roar: Suez 1956* (New York: Harper & Row, 1978), p. 158; Neff, *Warriors at Suez,* p. 348; Notes from Intelligence Advisory Committee meeting in Editorial Note, *FRUS, 1955–57,* Vol. XVI, no. 369, p. 773.

5 Conversation, Oct. 24, 1956, DP, WH Memoranda Series, B 4, Meetings with Pres. (4), EL; also in *FRUS, 1955–57,* Vol. XVI, no. 370, p. 774; Eisenhower, *Waging Peace,* pp. 64–65. For the president's schedule during the period covered by this chapter, see Eisenhower, Appt. Schedules, Miller Ctr., UV, millercenter.org.

6 Radio and Television Broadcast, Oct. 24, 1956, *PPP,* no. 268, pp. 1016–17.

7 Summary No. 37, Oct. 25, 1956, *FRUS, 1955–57,* Vol. XVI, no. 374, pp. 777–79; Hare to State Department, Oct. 25, 1956, *FRUS, 1955–57,* Vol. XVI, no. 377, pp. 782–83; the canal authority was the Egyptian administrative body running canal operations.

8 Aldrich to JFD, Oct. 25, 1956, RG 59, B 2697 (10-656), NA, Dillon to State Department, Oct. 25, 1956, *FRUS, 1955–57,* Vol. XVI, no. 375, pp. 779–81.

9 Robert E. Gilbert, *The Mortal Presidency: Illness and Anguish in the White House* (New York: Basic Books, 1992), pp. 104–5.

10 Eisenhower, *Waging Peace,* p. 65.

11 JFD to DDE, Oct. 25, 1956, DP, B 11, Tel. Conv., WH, (1), EL.

12 Address in Madison Square Garden, Oct. 25, 1956, *PPP,* no. 272, pp. 1020–27.

13 Eisenhower, *Waging Peace,* p. 66.

14 Editorial, *FRUS, 1955–57,* Vol. XVI, no. 382, p. 788; Lawson to State Department, Oct. 26, 1956, *FRUS, 1955–57,* Vol. XVI, no. 379, p. 785.

15 NSC 301st Meeting, Oct. 26, 1956, B 8, EL.

16 These comments come directly from the minutes of the NSC's Oct. 26 meeting; Eisenhower paraphrases them in *Waging Peace,* pp. 67–68.

17 Aldrich to JFD, Oct. 26, 1956, *FRUS, 1955–57,* Vol. XVI, no. 385, pp. 791–92.

18 JFD to Lodge, Oct. 26, 1956, *FRUS, 1955–57,* Vol. XVI, no. 383, pp. 789–90; JFD to Aldrich, Oct. 26, 1956, *FRUS, 1955–57,* Vol. XVI, no. 384, p. 790.

19 DDE & JFD, Oct. 26, 1956, DP, B 11, Tel. Conv., WH (1), EL; DDE Diary, Oct. 26, 1956, B 18, EL; also in *DDEP,* no. 2044.

20 Drew Pearson, "Ike's Check-Up Eyed as Political," *Washington Post & Times Herald,* Oct. 27, 1956; Hagerty comments, Oct. 26, 1956, B 18, EL; also in DDEP, no. 2044.

21 Snyder's Progress Reports, Oct. 16–18, 1956, Snyder Papers, B 3 (4), EL.

22 ACW Diary, Oct. 27, 1956, B 8, EL; Aldrich to JFD, Oct. 27, 1956, RG 59, B 2697 (10-656), NA; Lawson to JFD, Oct. 27, 1956, RG 59, B 2697 (10-656), NA; "A Look Back: U-2 Monitors Suez Crisis," News & Information, Featured Story Archives, cia.gov.

23 Conference, Oct. 27, 1956, DDE Diary, B 19, Staff Memos, EL.

24 DDE to Ben-Gurion, Oct. 27, 1956, *FRUS, 1955–57,* Vol. XVI, no. 388, p. 795.

25 JFD to embassies, Oct. 27, 1956, RG 59, B 2697, (10-656), NA; also in *FRUS, 1955–57,* Vol. XVI, no. 390, pp. 796–97.

26 Snyder Medical Diary, Oct. 27, 196, Snyder Papers, B 7, EL; Eisenhower, *Waging Peace*, p. 69.

27 Cooper, *The Lion's Last Roar,* pp. 159–61.

28 Dana Adams Schmidt, "Dulles Calls Charge of Soviet 'Tommyrot,' " *NYT,* Oct. 29, 1956; Eisenhower, *Waging Peace,* p. 70.

29 Snyder Papers, B 7 (1), EL; US Army to JFD, Oct. 28, 1956, RG 59, B 2697 (10-656), NA; Hitchcock to Intelligence Advisory Committee, Oct. 28, 1956, *FRUS, 1955–57,* Vol. XVI, no. 392, pp. 799–800; DDE to Ben-Gurion, Oct. 28, 1956, *DDEP,* no. 2048; also *FRUS, 1955–57,* Vol. XVI, no. 394, p. 801; Statement, Oct. 28, 1956, *PPP,* no. 276, pp. 1034–35; also HP, B 7 (Middle East, October 1956), EL.

30 Press Release, Oct. 28, 1956, HP, B 7, Medical-DDE, EL; also in Snyder Papers, B 1, Medical Reports on DDE 1956 (3), EL.

31 Entry, Oct. 28, 1956, ACW Diary, B 8, EL.

32 Emmet John Hughes, *The Ordeal of Power: A Political Memoir of the Eisenhower Years* (New York: Atheneum, 1963), pp. 212–13; Hughes Diary, Oct. 28, 1956, Emmet John Hughes Papers, Seely Mudd Library, Princeton University (S-M-P).

33 Conversation, Oct. 28, 1956, RG 59, B 2697 (10-656), NA; also in *FRUS, 1955–57,* Vol. XVI, no. 396, pp. 803–4.

34 Conversation, Oct. 28, 1956, RG 59, B 2697 (10-656), NA; also in *FRUS, 1955–57,* Vol. XVI, no. 397, pp. 805–6.

35 JFD to DDE, Oct. 28, 1956, DDE Diary, B 18, Phone Calls, EL.

36 DDE & JFD, Oct. 28, 1956, DP, Tel. Conv., B 11, Tel Conv., WH, EL.

37 Lodge to JFD & Lawson to JFD, Oct. 28, 1956, Dwight D. Eisenhower, Records as President, CF, Confidential File, Subject Series, B 82, Suez Canal Crisis (1) EL; also, RG 59, B 2697 (10-656), NA; Lawson to JFD, Oct. 28 & 29, 1956, RG 59, B 2697 (10-656), NA; Oct. 28 also in *FRUS, 1955–57,* Vol. XVI, no. 401 pp. 811–13.

38 ACW Diary, Oct. 29, 1956, B 8, EL; Dulles & DDE Phone Call, Oct. 29, 1956, DDE Diary, B 18, Phone Calls; also DP, Tel Conv., B 11, Tel. Conv., WH, EL.

39 JFD to Allen Dulles, Oct. 29, 1956, DP, Tel. Conv., B 5, Tel. Conv. Gen., EL.

40 Aldrich to State Dept., Oct. 29, 1956, *FRUS, 1955–57,* Vol. XVI, no. 405, pp. 817–20.

41 Dulles to Aldrich, Oct. 29, 1956, DP, Chrono., B 14, Oct. 1956 (1), EL; also RG 59, B 2697 (10-656), NA.

42 Eisenhower, *PPP,* 1956, no. 278, pp. 1038–45.

43 Address in Jacksonville, Oct. 29, 1956, *PPP,* no. 279, pp. 1045–54.

44 Suez Crisis, 1956, Center for Naval Analysis, Washington, D.C., Institute of Naval Studies, April 1974, p. 37; Interview with William M. Rountree, Foreign Affairs Oral History Collection of the Association for Diplomatic Studies and Training, Library of Congress, p. 2; Abba Solomon Eban, *Abba Eban: An Autobiography* (New York: Random House, 1977), p. 211.

45 Goodpaster to DDE, Oct. 29, 1956, HP, B 7 (Middle East, Oct. '56), EL; Eisenhower, *Waging Peace,* p. 71; "President to Continue to Seek World Peace," *NYT,* Oct. 30, 1956, p. 5.

46 Interview with Loy Henderson, OH 191, p. 47, EL.

47 JFD to Lodge, Oct. 29, 1956, DP, Tel. Conv., B 5, Tel. Conv. Gen., EL; Hare to State Dept., Oct. 29, 1956, *FRUS, 1955–57,* Vol. XVI, no. 408, pp. 827–28.

48 Conversation, Oct. 29, 1956, *FRUS, 1955–57*, Vol. XVI, no. 409, pp. 829–30.

49 Editorial, *FRUS, 1955–57*, Vol. XVI, no. 413, pp. 840–42; Lodge to JFD, Oct. 29, 1956, DP, Tel. Conv., B 5, Tel. Conv. Gen., EL.

50 Address at Byrd Field, Oct. 29, 1956, *PPP*, no. 280, pp. 1054–59; Hagerty to JFD, Oct. 29, 1956, DP, Tel. Conv., B 11, Tel. Conv., WH, EL.

51 Statement, Oct. 29, 1956, HP, B 7, Middle East, EL.

52 Knowland to JFD, Oct. 29, 1956, DP, Tel. Conv., B 5, Tel. Conv. Gen., EL.

53 Memorandum, Oct. 29, 1956, and Telegram, Joint Chiefs to Commanders, Oct. 29, 1956, *FRUS, 1955–57*, Vol. XVI, nos. 407, 415, pp. 826–27, 844–46.

54 Kennett Love, Interview with Eisenhower, Nov. 25, 1964, Dwight D. Eisenhower, Papers, Post-Presidential Papers, Signature File, B 4, PR-3, EL; also quoted in Love, *Suez*, p. 503; Neff, *Warriors at Suez*, p. 365; Conference with Pres., Oct. 29, 1956, DDE Diary, B 19, Staff Memos, EL; Eisenhower, *Waging Peace*, pp. 72–73.

55 Conferences with the President, 7:10 P.M. and 8:15 P.M., Oct. 29, 1956, DDE Diary, B 19, Staff Memos, EL; Eisenhower, *Waging Peace*, p. 73.

56 Press Release, Oct. 29, 1956, HP, B 7, Middle East, EL; Dana Adams Schmidt, "1950 Pledge Cited," *NYT*, Oct. 30, 1956.

57 Ben-Gurion to DDE, Oct. 30, 1956, RG 59, B 2697 (10-3056), NA; Eisenhower, *Waging Peace*, p. 74; Adams to JFD, two calls, Oct. 30, 1956, Dulles Tel. Conv., B 11, Tel. Conv., WH, EL; Press Release, Oct. 30, 1956, HP, B 7, Middle East, EL; Hughes, *The Ordeal of Power*, p. 215; Emmet John Hughes Diary, Oct. 30, 1956, Hughes Papers, B 5(5), S-M-P.

58 Conf. with Pres., Oct. 30, 1956, DDE Diary, B 19, Staff Memos; *FRUS, 1955–57*, Vol. XVI, no. 419, pp. 851–55.

59 DDE to Eden, Oct. 30, 1956, *FRUS, 1955–57*, Vol. XVI, no. 418, pp. 848–50.

60 Lodge to JFD, Oct. 30, 1956, DDE Diary, B 18, Phone Calls, EL.

61 Eden to DDE, Oct. 30, 1956, *FRUS, 1955–57*, Vol. XVI, no. 421, pp. 856–57.

62 Dulles to DDE, Oct. 30, 1956, DDE Diary, B 18, Phone calls, EL; DP, Tel. Conv., B 11, Tel. Conv., WH, EL.

63 DDE to Eden, Oct. 30, 1956, *FRUS, 1955–57*, Vol. XVI, no. 424, pp. 860–61.

64 "Eden's and Mollet's Talks on Suez Step," *NYT*, Oct. 31, 1956; Lodge to JFD, Oct. 30, 1956, RG 59, B 2697, 10-3056, NA; Egypt Letter to U.N. Security Council, Oct. 30, 1956, *United States Policy in the Middle East*, Sept. 1956–June 1957 (Washington, D.C.: Department of State), pp. 142–43; Editorial Note, *FRUS, 1955–57*, Vol. XVI, no. 420, pp. 855–56.

65 Dulles to DDE, Oct. 30, 1956, DDE Diary, B 18, Phone Calls, EL; DP Tel. Conv., B 11, Tel. Conv., WH, EL.

66 Dulles to DDE, 3:00 P.M. Oct. 30, 1956, DDE Diary, B 18, Phone Calls, EL; DP, Tel. Conv., B 11, Tel. Conv., WH, EL; DDE to Eden, Oct. 30, 1956, *FRUS, 1955–57*, Vol. XVI, no. 430, p. 866; James Reston "President in Plea," *NYT*, Oct. 31, 1956.

67 Eden to DDE, Oct. 30, 1956, *FRUS, 1955–57*, Vol. XVI, no. 434, pp. 871–73; DDE to Dulles, 3:40 P.M. (mislabeled 5:24 P.M.), Oct. 30, 1956, DDE Diary, B 18, Phone Calls, EL; DP, Tel. Conv., B 11, Tel. Conv., WH, EL; Dulles to DDE, Oct. 30, 1956, DDE Diary, B 18, Phone Calls, EL; Press Release, Oct. 30, 1956, HP, B 7, Middle East, EL.

68 Conference with the President, Oct. 30, 1956, DDE Diary, B 19, Staff Memos, EL; also in *FRUS, 1955–57*, Vol. XVI, no. 438, pp. 873–74.

69 DDE to JFD, DDE Diary, B 18, Phone Calls, EL; Hughes, *The Ordeal of Power*, p. 217; Hughes Diary, Oct. 30, 1956, Hughes Papers, B 5(5) S-M-P.

70 Three cables, Bohlen to JFD, Oct. 30, 1956, RG 59, B 2697, 10-3056, NA.

71 Adams to JFD, Oct. 30, 1956, DP, Tel. Conv., B 11, Tel. Conv., WH, EL.

72 Kathleen Teltsch, "Two Powers Bar U.S. Call for Israel to Leave Egypt," *NYT*, Oct. 31, 1956.

73 Drew Middleton, "Forces Take Off," *NYT*, Oct. 31, 1956.

74 *DDEP*, no. 2067, footnote no. 2; William J. Jorden, "Shift by Russia" & "Text of Soviet Statement," *NYT*, Oct. 31, 1956.

75 Eden to DDE, Oct. 30, 1956, *FRUS, 1955–57*, Vol. XVI, no. 440, pp. 882–83 & footnote no. 1.

76 DDE draft letter to Eden, DP, Tel. Conv., B 11, Tel. Conv., WH, EL; also in *FRUS, 1955–57*, Vol. XVI, no. 436, pp. 874–75.

77 James Reston, "President in Plea," *NYT*, Oct. 31, 1956.

78 Bohlen to JFD, Oct. 31, 1956, RG 59, B 2697, 10-3056, NA; Hare to JFD, Oct. 31, RG 59, B 2697, 10-3056, NA.

79 Nixon to JFD, Oct. 31, 1956, DP, Tel. Conv., B 5, Tel. Conv. Gen. (2), EL.

80 Hare Interview, Association for Diplomatic Studies Oral History, Library of Congress; Hare to JFD, Oct. 31, 1956, CF/Confidential File, Subject Series, B 82, Suez Canal Crisis (1), EL; also RG 59, B 2697, 10-3056, NA.

81 Knowland to JFD, Oct. 31, 1956, DP, Tel. Conv., B 11, Tel. Conv., WH, EL.

82 Knowland to DDE, Oct. 31, 1956, DDE Diary, B 18, Oct. '56, Phone Calls, EL.

83 Legation in Budapest to JFD, Oct. 31, D-H, B 7, JFD (1), EL; Eisenhower, *Waging Peace*, pp. 78–79.

84 Lodge to JFD, Oct. 31, 1956, DP, Tel. Conv., B 5, Tel. Conv. Gen. (2), EL; Lodge to DDE, Oct. 31, 1956, DDE Diary, B 18, Oct. '56, Phone Calls, EL.

85 Conversation, Oct. 31, 1956, *FRUS, 1955–57*, Vol. XVI, no. 445, pp. 888–90.

86 "Fighting in Egypt Disturbs Moscow," *NYT*, Oct. 31, 1956; William J. Jorden, "Moscow Assails 3 as Aggressors," *NYT*, Nov. 1, 1956.

87 Gregory W. Pedlow and Donald E. Welzenbach, *The CIA and the U-2 Program, 1954–1974* (Washington, D. C.: History Staff, Center for the Study of Intelligence, CIA, 1998), pp. 117–18; Eisenhower, *Waging Peace*, p. 80.

88 James Reston, "Washington Loses Grip," *NYT*, Oct. 31, 1956.

89 Dulles to Adams, Oct. 31, 1956, DP, Tel. Conv., B 11, Tel. Conv., WH, EL.

90 Eisenhower, *Waging Peace*, p. 80.

91 "Text of Stevenson Talk at Liberal Rally," *NYT*, Nov. 1, 1956.

92 Stevenson to DDE, Oct. 31, 1956, DP, Subject Series, B 7, Suez Problem (5), EL; Clayton Knowles, "Stevenson Warns of a Split in West," *NYT*, Nov. 1, 1956.

93 Hughes, *The Ordeal of Power*, pp. 219–21; Hughes Diary, Oct. 31, 1956, Hughes Papers, B 5(5), S-M-P.

94 Text of President's Report to the Nation, Oct. 31, 1956, HP, B 7, Middle East, EL; "Text of Eisenhower Broadcast on the Mideast Crisis," *NYT*, Nov. 1, 1956; Edwin L. Dale, Jr., "Speech to Nation," *NYT*, Nov. 1, 1956; Eisenhower, *PPP, 1956*, pp. 1060–66.

95 Clayton Knowles, "Stevenson Warns of a Split in West," *NYT*, Nov. 1, 1956.

96 Arthur Krock, "In the Nation," *NYT*, Nov. 1, 1956.

10. DAYS OF CRISIS

1 ACW Diary, Nov. 1, 1956, B 8, EL; Sherman Adams, *First-Hand Report: The Story of the Eisenhower Administration* (New York: Harper & Brothers, 1961), p. 205. For the president's schedule during the period covered by this chapter, see Eisenhower, Appt. Schedules, Miller Ctr., UV, millercenter.org.

2 Editorial Note, *FRUS, 1955–57*, Vol. XVI, "The Suez Crisis," no. 452, p. 900.

3 Joseph and Stewart Alsop, *New York Herald Tribune*, Nov. 2, 1956, Burke comments, cited in *Suez Crisis, 1956* (Center for Naval Analysis, Institute of Naval Studies, April 1974, Naval History and Heritage Command, Washington, D.C.), pp. 44, 48, 67.

4 Conversation, Oct. 31, 1956, *FRUS, 1955–57*, Vol. XVI, no. 447 pp. 891–93; Record of Decision, CF, Confidential File, Subject Series, B 82 Suez Canal Crisis (2), EL.

5 Dulles and DDE, DDE Diary, B 19, Phone Calls, EL; Dulles Papers, Tel. Conv., B 11, Tel. Conv., WH, EL; Dwight D. Eisenhower, *The White House Years: Waging Peace, 1956–61* (Garden City, NY: Doubleday, 1965), p. 83.

6 NSC 302nd Meeting, Nov. 1, 1956, B 8, EL; ACW Diary, B 8, EL; Harold Stassen had been appointed special assistant to the president in 1955, assigned to disarmament negotiations.

7 JFD to DDE, Nov. 1, 1956 DDE Diary, B 19, Nov. '56, Phone Calls, EL; DDE to JFD, Feb. 1, 1956, DDE Diary, B 12, Phone Calls, EL.

8 Dillon to State Department, Nov. 1, 1956, *FRUS, 1955–57*, Vol. XVI, no. 459, pp. 919–22.

9 Chester L. Cooper, *The Lion's Last Roar: Suez 1956* (New York: Harper & Row, 1978), p. 171; Harry Schwartz, "Soviet Faces Task of Deciding on Aid," *NYT,* Nov. 1, 1956.

10 Brownell to JFD, Nov. 1, 1956, DP, Tel. Conv., B 5, Tel. Conv. Gen. (2), EL.

11 JFD to AWD, Nov. 1, 1956, DP, Tel. Conv., B 5, Tel. Conv. Gen. (2), EL; JFD & Eban Conversation, Nov. 1, 1956, *FRUS, 1955–57*, Vol. XVI, no. 462, pp. 925–27.

12 DDE to Dulles, Nov. 1, 1956, not sent, DP, WH Memoranda Series, B 3, WH Corres.-Gen. (1), EL; also in *FRUS, 1955–57*, Vol. XVI, no. 461, pp. 924–25 & *DDEP,* no. 2057; see *FRUS* footnote no. 1, indicating no transcript had been found of the 12:50 P.M. meeting that led to Eisenhower recording his thoughts.

13 DDE to Eden, Nov. 1, 1956, *DDEP,* no. 2058; also *FRUS, 1955–57*, Vol. XVI, no. 460, pp. 922–24.

14 Leonard Ingalls, "Britons Condemn Attack on Egypt," *NYT,* Nov. 2, 1956; Keith Kyle, *Suez: Britain's End of Empire in the Middle East* (London: I. B. Taurus, 1991), pp. 404–7.

15 Aldrich to JFD, Nov. 1, 1956, CF, Confidential File, Subject Series, B 82, Suez Canal Crisis (1), EL.

16 "U.S. Holds Up Oil Plan to Aid Britain, France," *NYT,* Nov. 1, 1956, p. 22; Eisenhower had said this in a meeting with Arthur Flemming, Oct. 30, 1956, DDE Diary, B19, Oct. '56, Staff Memos, EL; also in *FRUS, 1955–57*, Vol. XVI, no. 438, pp. 873–74.

17 Bohlen to JFD, Nov. 1, 1956, Dept. of State, 684A.86/11-156, RG 59, B 2697, NA; Dillon to JFD, Nov. 1, 1956, CF, Confidential File, Subject Series, B 82, Suez Canal Crisis (1), EL; HH to JFD, Nov. 1, 1956, RG 59, B 2697, 11-156, NA.

18 Harry Schwartz, "Soviet Faces Task of Deciding on Aid," *NYT,* Nov. 1, 1956; Eisenhower, *Waging Peace,* p. 81.

19 Chairman's Staff Group to Radford, Nov. 1, 1956, RG 218, Records of U.S. Joint Chiefs of Staff, Chairman's File, Radford, B 38, File 381, Net Evaluation 1956, NA; WHOSS, Subject Series, Dept. of Defense Subseries, B 1, Dept. of Defense, Joint Chiefs of Staff, (2), Jan–Apr. 1956, EL.

20 ACW Diary, B 8, EL; Emmet John Hughes Diary, Nov. 1, 1956, Hughes Papers, B 5 (5), S-M-P.

21 Address in Convention Hall, Philadelphia, Nov. 1, 1956, *PPP,* no. 283, pp. 1066–74; Russell Baker, "President Calls Stevenson Plans Way to 'Disaster,' " *NYT,* Nov. 2, 1956.

22 Medical Diary, Nov. 1, 1956, Snyder Papers, B 7, EL.

23 Thomas J. Hamilton, "U.S. Move Backed," *NYT,* Nov. 2, 1956; Editorial Note, *FRUS, 1955–57,* Vol. XVI, no. 467, pp. 932–33.

24 Kyle, *Suez,* p. 404.

25 Eisenhower, *Waging Peace,* p. 84.

26 HH to DDE, DDE Diary, B 19, Phone Calls, EL.

27 Harrison E. Salisbury, "Stevenson Says U.S. Policy Fails," *NYT,* Nov. 2, 1956.

28 Hare to JFD, Nov. 2, 1956, RG 59, B 2697, 11-156, NA; Hare to JFD, Nov. 2, 1956, *FRUS, 1955–57,* Vol. XVI, no. 472, pp. 939–40.

29 DDE to HH, Nov. 2, 1956, DDE Diary, B 19, Phone Calls, EL; also DP, WH Memos, B 4, Meetings with Pres. (3), EL; also *FRUS, 1955–57,* Vol. XVI, no. 469, p. 935.

30 Conference with the President, Nov. 2, 1956 (notes dated Nov. 5), DDE Diary, B 19, Staff Memos, EL; also in *FRUS, 1955–57,* Vol. XVI, no. 470, pp. 936–37.

31 JFD to Rountree, DDE Diary, B 19, Phone Calls, EL.

32 JFD to Lodge, Nov. 2, 1956, *FRUS, 1955–57,* Vol. XVI, no. 471, p. 938.

33 Conversation, JFD & Heeney, Nov. 2, 1956, *FRUS, 1955–57,* Vol. XVI, no. 473, pp. 940–42.

34 AWD to JFD, two Calls, Nov. 2, 1956, DP, Tel. Conv., B 5, Tel. Conv. Gen. (2), EL.

35 John McCormack, "Nagy Quits Warsaw Pact," *NYT,* Nov. 2, 1956; Elie Abel, "Tanks Seal Border," *NYT,* Nov. 2, 1956.

36 Hare to JFD, Nov. 2, 1956, RG 59, B 2697, 11–256, NA.

37 Lodge to JFD, Nov. 2, 1956, D-H, B 8, JFD (2), EL.

38 Richard H. Immerman, *John Foster Dulles: Piety, Pragmatism and Power in U.S. Foreign Policy* (Wilmington: Scholarly Resources, 1999), p. 156.

39 Harrison E. Salisbury, "Stevenson Offers a Program to End Strife in Mideast," *NYT,* Nov. 3, 1956.

40 William M. Blair, "Nixon Hails Break with Allies' Policies," *NYT,* Nov. 3, 1956.

41 Eisenhower and Dulles had attempted to resolve that conflict with the Alpha plan in 1955, and had failed. DDE to Hazlett, Nov. 2, 1956, Name Series, Dwight D. Eisenhower's Papers as President (Ann Whitman File), B 18, EL; also *DDEP,* no. 2063.

42 DDE to Gruenther, Nov. 2, 1956, DDE Diary, B 20, Misc. (4), EL; also *DDEP,* no. 2064.

43 Sydney Gruson, "Troops Reported Crossing Poland," *NYT,* Nov. 3, 1956.

44 Eisenhower, *Waging Peace,* p. 86; U.S. Aim, to JFD, Nov. 3, 1956, RG 59, B 2697, 11-256, NA.

45 Cooper, *The Lion's Last Roar,* p. 182.

46 Immerman, *John Foster Dulles*, p. 156; ACW Diary, Nov. 3, 1956, B 8, EL; Cole C. Kingseed, *Eisenhower and the Suez Crisis of 1956* (Baton Rouge: Louisiana State University Press, 1995), pp. 114–15.

47 Cooper, *The Lion's Last Roar*, p. 182.

48 Conference, DDE Diary, B 19, Staff memos, EL; also *FRUS, 1955–57*, Vol. XVI, no. 477, pp. 947–49.

49 Statement by Eden, Nov. 3, 1956, *FRUS, 1955–57*, Vol. XVI, no. 476, p. 946.

50 Statement by Hagerty, Nov. 3, 1956, HP, B 7, Middle East, EL.

51 Conversation, Nov. 3, 1956, *FRUS, 1955–57*, Vol. XVI, no. 479, pp. 953–54.

52 Lodge to DDE, Nov. 3, 1956, *FRUS, 1955–57*, Vol. XVI, no. 481, pp. 956–57.

53 Editorial Note, *FRUS, 1955–57*, Vol. XVI, no. 485, pp. 960–64.

54 Report, Joint Middle East Planning Committee, Nov. 3, 1956, *FRUS, 1955–57*, Vol. XVI, no. 489, pp. 968–72.

55 DDE to Douglas, Nov. 3, 1956, DDE Diary, B 20, Misc. (4), EL.

56 "Mrs. Roosevelt Defends Israel," *NYT*, Nov. 4, 1956.

57 "6 Senators Score G.O.P. on Mideast," *NYT*, Nov. 3, 1956.

58 Harrison E. Salisbury, "Stevenson Holds President Lacks 'Energy' for Job," *NYT*, Nov. 4, 1956.

59 William J. Jorden, "Moscow Pledges Backing to Syria," *NYT*, Nov. 4, 1956.

11. A PERFECT STORM

1 For the president's schedule during the period covered by this chapter, see Eisenhower, Appt. Schedules, Miller Ctr., UV, millercenter.org.

2 AWD to JFD, two calls, Nov. 2, 1956, DP, Tel. Conv., B 5, Tel. Conv. Gen., Oct. 1, 1956 to Dec. 29, 1956 (2), EL; Legation in Budapest, message, Nov. 4, 1956, WHOSS, Subject Series, Dept. of State Subseries, B 1, EL; Dwight D. Eisenhower, *The White House Years: Waging Peace, 1956–61* (Garden City, NY: Doubleday, 1965), pp. 86–87; Cole C. Kingseed, *Eisenhower and the Suez Crisis of 1956* (Baton Rouge: Louisiana State University Press, 1995), p. 114; Aleksandr Fursenko and Timothy Naftali, *Khrushchev's Cold War: The Inside Story of an American Adversary* (New York: W. W. Norton, 2006), pp. 130–32.

3 HH to Embassy in Israel, Nov. 4, 1956, RG 59, B 2697, 11-256, NA; also *FRUS, 1955–57*, Vol. XVI, "The Suez Crisis," no. 490, p. 973; Eisenhower, *Waging Peace*, p. 87.

4 Conversation, Nov. 4, 1956, *FRUS, 1955–57*, Vol. XVI, no. 491, pp. 974–75. Eisenhower had made his wishes plain in a meeting with Flemming, Oct. 30, 1956, DDE Diary, B19, Staff Memos, EL; also in *FRUS, 1955–57*, Vol. XVI, no. 438, pp. 873–74.

5 Eisenhower, *Waging Peace*, pp. 88–89.

6 Conference, Nov. 4, 1956, DDE Diary, B 19, Staff Memos, EL; also *FRUS, 1955–57*, Vol. XVI, no. 493, pp. 976–77: Dana Adams Schmidt, "Eisenhower Sees His Top Advisers," *NYT*, Nov. 5, 1956.

7 Kathleen Teltsch, "Bid to UN Chief," *NYT*, Nov. 4, 1956. The minutes of the meeting indicate that Hoover said the vote was 55–0, and the subheading for the *Times* article said 59–0, but the vote was actually 57–0, as indicated in the text of Telsch's report.

8 DDE to Bulganin, Nov. 4, 1956, Hagerty Papers, B 7, Middle East, EL; also Eisenhower, *PPP, 1956*, no. 291, pp. 1080–81.

9 Statement, Eisenhower, *PPP, 1956*, no. 287, p. 1076.

10 Dana Adams Schmidt, "Eisenhower Sees His Top Advisers," *NYT*, Nov. 5, 1956.

11 Lodge to HH, Nov. 4, 1956, *FRUS, 1955–57*, Vol. XVI, no. 494, pp. 977–80; on November 3, Eden had stated his conditions for declaring a cease-fire: the Israeli and Egyptian governments had to agree to accept a United Nations force and accept Anglo-French troops stationed between them until that force was constituted—a de facto occupation of the Canal Zone; statement by Eden, Nov. 3, 1956, *FRUS, 1955–57*, Vol. XVI, no. 476, p. 946.

12 Hare to State Department, Nov. 4, 1956, *FRUS, 1955–57*, Vol. XVI, no. 492, p. 975.

13 Lodge to State Dept., Nov. 4, 1956, *FRUS, 1955–57*, Vol. XVI, no. 494, pp. 977–80.

14 Eisenhower, *Waging Peace*, p. 89.

15 Eden to DDE, Nov. 5, 1956, Dwight D. Eisenhower's Papers as President (Ann Whitman File), International Series, B. 21, EL; Eisenhower, *Waging Peace*, p. 88.

16 Conference, Nov. 5, 1956, DDE Diary, B 19, Staff Memos, EL.

17 Draft letter DDE to Eden, Nov. 5, 1956, *FRUS, 1955–57*, Vol. XVI, no. 502, pp. 989–90. See footnote no. 1 for reason the letter was not sent; also in *DDEP*, no. 2068.

18 Cuomo to the Secretary of State, Nov. 7, 1956 (report on Nov. 5 situation), RG 59, B 2698, 11-656, NA; Eisenhower, *Waging Peace*, p. 89.

19 Remarks, Nov. 5, 1956, *PPP*, no. 290, pp. 1079–80.

20 Text of Message, Bulganin to Eden, Nov. 5, 1956, CF, Confidential File, B 82, Suez Canal Crisis (2), EL; Kingseed, *Eisenhower and the Suez Crisis of 1956*, pp. 118–19; William J. Jorden, "Moscow Aroused," *NYT*, Nov. 6, 1956; Eisenhower, *Waging Peace*, p. 89; Fursenko and Naftali, *Khrushchev's Cold War*, pp. 133–34.

21 Editorial Note, *FRUS, 1955–57*, Vol. XVI, no. 504, p. 992.

22 Bulganin to DDE, Nov. 5, 1956, International Series, B 50, Bulganin, EL; *FRUS, 1955–57*, Vol. XVI, no. 505, pp. 993–94; Eisenhower, *Waging Peace*, p. 89.

23 Bohlen to State Dept., Nov. 5, 1956, *FRUS, 1955–57*, Vol. XVI, no. 506, pp. 995–96.

24 Conference, Nov. 5, 1956, DDE Diary, B 19, Staff Memos, EL; Eisenhower, *Waging Peace*, pp. 89–90.

25 Emmet John Hughes, *The Ordeal of Power: A Political Memoir of the Eisenhower Years* (New York: Atheneum, 1963), p. 224; Hughes Diary, Nov. 5, 1956, Hughes Papers, B5[5], S-M-P.

26 White House Statement, Nov. 5, 1956, HP, B 7, Middle East, EL. This statement is not provided in *PPP* but is mentioned in a footnote in the Nov. 5, 1956 (no. 291, p. 1081), message to Bulganin urging the withdrawal of Soviet forces from Hungary.

27 Dana Adams Schmidt, "Washington Firm," *NYT*, Nov. 5, 1956.

28 Memorandum, Secretary of Joint Chiefs to Chairman, Nov. 5, 1956, RG 218, Records of Joint Chiefs, Chairman's File, Radford, B 14, File 091 Palestine, NA; *FRUS, 1955–57*, Vol. XVI, no. 510, p. 1002; Kingseed, *Eisenhower and the Suez Crisis of 1956*, pp. 119–20. Jeffrey Barlow, at the Naval History and Heritage Command in Washington, D.C., confirms that the president ordered American forces in the Mediterranean and later the Eastern Atlantic placed on alert. The order applied especially to the Sixth Fleet, whose forward-deployed attack car-

riers were equipped with fully operational nuclear weapons. Even after the crisis faded, the Sixth Fleet did not go off its twenty-four-hour alert until mid-December 1956. Barlow's conclusion is confirmed in a declassified study, *Suez Crisis, 1956* (Center for Naval Analysis, Institute of Naval Studies, April 1974, Washington, D.C.).

29 Editorial Note, *FRUS, 1955–57*, Vol. XVI, no. 514, pp. 1010–11.
30 Snyder, Medical Diary (often labeled "Progress Reports" during this period), Nov. 5, 1956, Snyder Papers, B 7, EL.
31 Closed-Circuit TV Remarks, Nov. 5, 1956, *PPP*, no. 292, pp. 1082–85.
32 Harrison E. Salisbury, "Democrat Ends Campaign," *NYT,* Nov. 6, 1956; Robert E. Gilbert, *The Mortal Presidency: Illness and Anguish in the White House* (New York: Basic Books, 1992), p. 105.
33 Radio and Television Remarks, Nov. 5, 1956, *PPP,* no. 293, p. 1088: Russell Baker, "President Visits Aides," *NYT,* Nov. 6, 1956.
34 Snyder, Medical Diary, Nov. 5, 1956, Snyder Papers, B 7, EL.
35 Snyder, Medical Diary, Nov. 6, 1956, B 7, EL.
36 Conference, Nov. 6, 1956, DDE Diary, B 19, Staff Memos, EL; Eisenhower, *Waging Peace,* p. 90.
37 Special National Intelligence Estimate, "Sino-Soviet Intentions in the Suez Crisis," Nov. 6, 1956, *FRUS, 1955–57*, Vol. XVI, nos. 521–22, pp. 1018–21.
38 Dillon to State Dept., Nov. 6, 1956, *FRUS, 1955–57*, Vol. XVI, no. 515, p. 1012.
39 Conversation, Nov. 6, 1956, D-H, B 8, JFD, Nov. '56, EL; also in *FRUS, 1955–57,* Vol. XVI, no. 524, pp. 1023–25.
40 *Suez Crisis, 1956,* Center for Naval Analysis, Institute of Naval Studies, April 1974, p. 71.
41 Editorial Note, *FRUS, 1955–57*, Vol. XVI, no. 516, pp. 1012–13; also see Harold Macmillan, *Riding the Storm, 1956–1959* (London: Macmillan, 1971), pp. 163–64. According to *FRUS*, the documents reflecting this denial of the return of IMF funds were not found in State Department records.
42 Lloyd, *Suez 1956,* p. 211; Diane B. Kunz, *The Economic Diplomacy of the Suez Crisis* (Chapel Hill: University of North Carolina Press, 1991), pp. 131–33; James A. Boughton, "Was Suez in 1956 the First Financial Crisis of the Twenty-first Century?," *Finance and Development,* September 2001, Vol. 38, no. 3.
43 ACW Diary, Nov. 6, 1956, B 8, Nov. '56 (2), EL; *Suez Crisis, 1956,* Center for Naval Analysis, Institute of Naval Studies, April 1974, pp. 52, 81; Kingseed, *Eisenhower and the Suez Crisis of 1956,* p. 121.
44 Bohlen to Secretary of State, Nov. 6, 1956, CF, Confidential File, Subject Series, B 82, Suez Canal Crisis (1), EL.
45 ACW Diary, Nov. 6, 1956, B 8, EL.
46 Memorandum for Radford, Nov. 6, 1956, RG 218, B 14, Records of Joint Chiefs of Staff, Chairman's File, Radford, File 091 Palestine, NA.
47 ACW Diary, Nov. 6, 1956, B 8, EL; Eisenhower, *Waging Peace,* p. 91; Gregory W. Pedlow and Donald E. Welzenbach, *The CIA and the U-2 Program, 1954–1974* (Washington, D.C.: History Staff, Center for the Study of Intelligence, CIA, 1998), p. 120.
48 Aldrich reported that Eden had told him he was planning to communicate to the Secretary-General that if the Egyptian and Israeli governments agreed and a competent international force could secure the situation, the British government would consider ceasing military operations, "unless they are attacked." Eden told Aldrich

that British troops were in control of the situation but he was concerned about the possibility of Russians moving into Syria; see Aldrich to Secretary of State, Nov. 6, 1956, CF/Confidential File, Subject Series, B 82, Suez Canal Crisis (1), EL.

49 The account of the meeting in the Cabinet Room is in a memorandum for the record by Goodpaster, Nov. 6, 1956, DDE Diary, B 19, Staff Memos, EL; the transcript of this meeting, missing for many years, was only recently located and declassified by the staff at the Eisenhower Library. Until then, the only account of the meeting was in Eisenhower, *Waging Peace*, p. 91.

50 Robert Murphy, *A Diplomat Among Warriors: The Unique World of a Foreign Service Expert* (Garden City, NY: Doubleday, 1964), pp. 390–91.

51 DDE to Eden, Nov. 6, 1956, DDE Diary, B 19, Phone Calls, EL; also ACW Diary, B 8, EL. Transatlantic cable telephone service had been inaugurated just a month and a half earlier, on September 25.

52 DDE to Eden, Nov. 6, 1956, *DDEP*, no. 2071; Eden to DDE, Nov. 7, 1956, *FRUS, 1955–57*, Vol. XVI, no. 535, p. 1039.

53 DDE to Mollet, Nov. 6, 1956, *DDEP*, no. 2073.

54 Bohlen to Secretary of State, Nov. 6, 1956, CF, Confidential File, Subject Series, B 82, Suez Canal Crisis (1), EL; also RG 59, B 2698, 11-656, NA.

55 Aldrich to Secretary of State two messages, Nov. 6, 1957, RG 59, B 2697 & 2698, 11-656, NA.

56 Meeting, Nov. 6, 1956, *FRUS, 1955–57*, Vol. XVI, no. 529, pp. 1030–32; Hoover to Hare, Nov. 6, 1956, *FRUS, 1955–57*, Vol. XVI, no. 530, pp. 1032–33.

57 Dillon to Secretary of State, Nov. 6, 1956, RG 59, B 2698, 11-656, NA; also *FRUS, 1955–57*, Vol. XVI, no. 531, pp. 1033–34.

58 Joint Chiefs to Certain Commanders, Nov. 6, 1956, *FRUS, 1955–57*, Vol. XVI, no. 533, pp. 1035–36.

59 Remarks Following Election Victory, Nov. 7, 1956, Eisenhower, *PPP*, pp. 1089–91; Russell Baker, "Eisenhower Vows to Toil for Peace, *NYT*, Nov. 7, 1956.

12. A RELUCTANT WITHDRAWAL

1 "Eisenhower by a Landslide," *NYT*, Nov. 7, 1956; ACW Diary, B 8, EL. For the president's schedule during the period covered by this chapter, see Eisenhower, Appt. Schedules, Miller Ctr., UV, millercenter.org.

2 Eden to DDE, Nov. 7, 1956, ACW Diary, B 8, EL.

3 Memorandum for Record, Nov. 7, 1956, DDE Diary Series, B 19, Staff Memos, EL; DP, WH Memoranda, Meetings with the President, EL; ACW Diary, Nov. 7, 1956, B 8, EL.

4 DDE to Eden, Nov. 7, 1956, ACW Diary, B 8, EL; *FRUS, 1955–57*, Vol. XVI, "Suez Crisis," no. 540, pp. 1045–46.

5 Conversation, Secretary Dulles's Room, Walter Reed Hospital, Nov. 7, 1956, *FRUS, 1955–57*, Vol. XVI, no. 542, pp. 1049–53; DDE to Eden, Nov. 7, 1956, *DDEP*, no. 2076; *FRUS, 1955–57*, Vol. XVI, no. 545, p. 1056.

6 Editorial Note, *FRUS, 1955–57*, Vol. XVI, no. 534, p. 1038.

7 Hoover to DDE, Nov. 7, 1956, *FRUS, 1955–57*, Vol. XVI, no. 549, pp. 1062–63; Notes, CF, Confidential File, B 82, Sub-Series Suez Canal Crisis (1), EL; an expanded set of minutes, including Shiloah's responses, is found in *FRUS, 1955–57*, Vol. XVI, no. 551, pp. 1065–67.

8 DDE to Ben-Gurion, Nov. 7, 1956, HP, B 7, Middle East, EL; *DDEP*, no. 2077; *PPP*, no. 295, pp. 295–96; *FRUS, 1955–57*, Vol. XVI, no. 550, pp. 1063–64;

Ben-Gurion to DDE, Nov. 8, 1956, HP, B 7, Middle East, EL; *FRUS, 1955–57,* Vol. XVI, no. 560, pp. 1095–96; DDE to Ben-Gurion, footnote no. 4.

9 Hare to State Department, Nov. 8, 1956, *FRUS, 1955–57,* Vol. XVI, no. 561, pp. 1096–97.

10 *Suez Crisis, 1956,* Center for Naval Analysis, Washington, D.C., Institute of Naval Studies, April 1974, p. 54.

11 NSC 303rd Meeting, Nov. 8, 1956, B 8, EL.

12 Record of NSC Actions, Nov. 8, 1956, WHOSS, Sub-Series Alpha, B 19, NSC, Vol. 2 (6), EL.

13 DDE to Douglas, Nov. 30, 1956, DDE Diary Series, B 20, Misc. (1), EL; *DDEP,* no. 2124A.

14 Anthony Nutting, *No End of a Lesson: The Story of Suez* (London: Constable, 1967), p. 144.

15 Christian Pineau, Video interview, *The Eisenhower Legacy: Dwight D. Eisenhower's Military and Political Crusades,* Part 4: "Commander in Chief, 1953–1961," Starbright Media Corp, eisenhowerlegacy.com.

16 Memorandum, Nov. 8, 1956, DDE Diary Series, B 19, EL; *DDEP,* no. 2076.

17 DDE to Humphrey, Nov. 8, 1956, *FRUS, 1955–57,* Vol. XVI, no. 558, p. 1092.

18 Bipartisan Legislative Meeting, Nov. 9, 1956, DDE Diary Series, B 20, Misc. (3), EL; AWD to Higgs, Nov. 13, 1956, Status Report on the Near East, presented to bipartisan congressional leadership, Nov. 9, 1956, CREST CIA Files, NA.

19 James Reston, "President May Bid Congress Endorse Force in Mideast," & "U.S. Drafts Mideast Plan to Check Soviet with Aid and if Needed, with Force," *NYT,* Dec. 28 & 30, 1956.

20 HH to DDE, JFD to DDE, Nov. 9, 1956, DDE Diary, B 19, Phone Calls, EL; DDE to Edgar E., Nov. 12, 1956, DDE Diary Series, B 20, Misc. (3), EL.

21 DDE to Bulganin, Nov. 11, 1956, *DDEP,* no. 2084.

22 *Suez Crisis, 1956,* Center for Naval Analysis, p. 55; AWD to HH, *FRUS, 1955–57,* Vol. XVI, no. 564, pp. 1101–2.

23 Ike could not understand why else the British had so bungled the military planning for the invasion of Egypt when, in his experience, they had always been "meticulous military planners"; conversation, DDE & JFD, Nov. 12, 1956, *FRUS, 1955–57,* Vol. XVI, no. 570, pp. 1112–14.

24 HH to DDE, Nov. 13, 1956, DDE Diary Series, B 19, Phone Calls, EL. This directive from Eisenhower resulted in State Department officials, over the coming six weeks, preparing a series of papers on the American position in the Middle East, moving toward preparation of the Eisenhower Doctrine.

25 News Conference, Nov. 14, 1956, *PPP,* no. 298, pp. 1095–1108. At his pre–press conference briefing that morning, the group anticipated that reporters might ask the president if Secretary Dulles's August 26, 1955, statement on a peace settlement in the Middle East (the Alpha plan) was still valid. Ike took time in the meeting to read Dulles's long statement and then quipped, "If I go over there with all these papers, I will need a brief case and then I will look like a State Department guy." Pre–Press Conference Briefing, Nov. 14, 1956, Press Conference series, B 5, EL.

26 ACW Diary, B 8, EL: "Shepilov Charges New Attack Plot," *NYT,* Nov. 29, 1956.

27 Conversation, Nov. 17, 1956, DP, WH Memos, B 4, Meetings with Pres. (3), EL.

28 Aldrich to HH, Nov. 19, 1956, *FRUS, 1955–57,* Vol. XVI, no. 588, pp. 1150–52.

29 Aldrich to DDE, Nov. 19, 1956, DDE Diary Series, B 19, Phone Calls, EL.

30 HH to DDE, Nov. 19, 1956, DDE Diary Series, B 19, Phone Calls, EL. Ike called Treasury Secretary Humphrey, saying he wanted to remind him of "a remote possibility," apparently referring to Eden's impending fall from grace. Humphrey said he hated to see Eden "stick in there, & go to a vote of confidence & get licked." Referring to the possibility of dealing with a government run by the Labour Party, Humphrey worried that "if they throw him out, then we have these Socialists to lick." DDE to Humphrey, Nov. 19, 1956, 3:45 P.M., DDE Diary Series, B 19, Phone Calls, EL.

31 Aldrich to Hoover, Nov. 19, 10:00 p.m., *FRUS, 1955–57*, Vol. XVI, no. 593, p. 1163.

32 Conference, Nov. 20, 1956, DP, WH Memos, Meetings with Pres., B 4, EL; *FRUS, 1955–57*, Vol. XVI, no. 596, pp. 1166–69.

33 Aldrich to HH, Nov. 21, 1956, *FRUS, 1955–57*, Vol. XVI, no. 598, pp. 1172–72; DDE to Humphrey, Nov. 21, 1956, *FRUS, 1955–57*, Vol. XVI, no. 599, pp. 1172–73.

34 Conference, Nov. 21, 1956, DDE Diary Series, B 19, Staff Memos, EL.

35 HH to DDE, Nov. 21, 1956, "An Outline of Short-Term and Long-Term United States Plans in the Middle East," D-H, B 8, Dulles, Foster (1), EL.

36 For a detailed examination of the Al Buraimi dispute, see Daniel C. Williamson, *Separate Agendas: Churchill, Eisenhower, and Anglo-American Relations, 1953–55* (London: Lexington, 2006), pp. 75–105.

37 Conference, Nov. 23, 1956, noon, *FRUS, 1955–57*, Vol. XVI, no. 604, pp. 1178–80.

38 Conference, Nov. 25, 1956, *FRUS, 1955–57*, Vol. XVI, no. 612, pp. 1194–95.

39 DDE to JFD, Nov. 27, 1956, *FRUS, 1955–57*, Vol. XVI, no. 618, pp. 1202–3; Humphrey to DDE, Nov. 26, 1956, DDE Diary Series, B 19, Phone Calls, EL.

40 Churchill to DDE, Nov. 23, 1956, International Series, B 20, EL; *DDEP* footnote no. 2, no. 2118.

41 DDE to Churchill, Nov. 27, 1956, *DDEP*, no. 2118.

42 Aldrich to Sec. of State, Nov. 29, 1956, CF, Confidential File, Subseries Suez Canal Crisis, B 82 (3), EL.

43 Circular Telegram, Department of State, Nov. 29, 1956, *FRUS, 1955–57*, Vol. XVI, no. 624, pp. 1214–15; Harold Callendar, "Washington Wins Support in Paris," *NYT*, Dec. 1, 1956; Edwin L. Dale, Jr., "Shipments Rising," *NYT*, Dec. 1, 1956; "Statement by Hagerty," *NYT*, Dec. 1, 1956. A glitch in these announcements infuriated Eisenhower. His plan had been for the Augusta White House to issue a statement, followed by the Office of Defense Mobilization statement elaborating on the president's announcement. On Saturday morning, December 1, Ike called Flemming from Augusta to ask how in the world the ODM office had managed to issue the oil statement first, thereby making the White House's statement appear "ridiculous." Ike said he wanted Flemming "to call in whoever was responsible and give him unshirted hell." DDE to Flemming, Dec. 1, 1956, DDE Diary Series, B 20, Phone Calls, EL.

44 "White House Statement, Dec. 1, 1956, *NYT*, Dec. 2, 1956.

45 W. H. Lawrence, "President, Dulles Express Optimism on Mideast Peace," *NYT*, Dec. 3, 1956.

46 Aldrich to HH, Dec. 3, 1956, *FRUS, 1955–57*, Vol. XVI, no. 633, pp. 1238–39; "Text of Statement by Lloyd," *NYT*, Dec. 4, 1956.

47 DDE to JFD, Dec. 3, 1956, *FRUS, 1955–57*, Vol. XVI, no. 634, p. 1240.

48 Russell Baker, "U.S. Seeks Speed in Clearing Suez," *NYT*, Dec. 4, 1956.

49 Kyle, *Suez*, pp. 514–15; Freiberger, *Dawn over Suez*, p. 203; Drew Middleton, "Eden, Home, Urges Speed in Suez Job," *NYT*, Dec. 15, 1956; Neff, *Warriors at Suez*, p. 435.

50 Homer Bigart, "British, French Are out of Suez," *NYT*, Dec. 23, 1956; "Statue of de Lesseps Dynamited," *NYT*, Dec. 25, 1956; Love, *Suez*, pp. 656–57; Kyle, *Suez*, p. 522.

51 DDE Diary, Dec. 6, 1956, B 20, Misc., EL.

CONCLUSION: WAGING PEACE IN THE MIDDLE EAST

1 Quoted in Patrick Anderson, *The Presidents' Men: White House Assistants of Franklin D. Roosevelt, Harry S. Truman, Dwight D. Eisenhower, John F. Kennedy, and Lyndon B. Johnson* (Garden City, NY: Doubleday, 1968), p. 179; Eisenhower apparently meant that no soldier died in traditional combat (see endnote no. 13). He makes a similar, more complex statement in his memoir, *The White House Years: Waging Peace, 1956–1961* (Garden City, NY: Doubleday, 1965), p. 624: "The United States lost no foot of the Free World to Communist aggression, made certain that Soviets and China understood the adequacy of our military power, and dealt with them firmly but not arrogantly. We regarded our friends as respected partners and valued partners and tried always to create mutual confidence and trust, well knowing that without these ingredients alliances would be of little enduring value."

2 Memorandum, Nov. 8, 1956, DDE Diary Series, Dwight D. Eisenhower's Papers as President (Ann Whitman File), B 19, EL; *DDEP*, no. 2076.

3 Notes on Bipartisan Congressional Leadership Meeting, Jan. 1, 1957, Legislative Meetings Series, B 2 (1), EL; Special Message to Congress, Jan. 5, 1957, *PPP*, no. 6, pp. 6–16; State of the Union Address, Jan. 10, 1957, *PPP*, no. 8, p. 28; Middle East Resolution, Jan. 5, 1957, DP, Subject Series, B 6, EL; Eisenhower, *Waging Peace*, pp. 178–81. For perspectives of diplomatic historians on the Eisenhower Doctrine, see Salim Yaqub, *Containing Arab Nationalism: The Eisenhower Doctrine and the Middle East* (Chapel Hill: University of North Carolina Press, 2004); Peter L. Hahn, *Caught in the Middle East: U.S. Policy Toward the Arab-Israeli Conflict, 1945–1961* (Chapel Hill: University of North Carolina Press, 2004), pp. 223–47; and Douglas Little, *American Orientalism: The United States and the Middle East Since 1945* (Chapel Hill: University of North Carolina Press, 2002), pp. 132–37, 181–83.

4 William S. White, "Rayburn Backing Plan on Mideast," *NYT*, Jan. 17, 1957; King Saud's comment is noted in Hahn, *Caught in the Middle East*, p. 272; Eisenhower's detailed notes on his talks with Saud are in DDE Diary, B 21, EL; also *DDEP*, 1957, no. 13; Eisenhower, *Waging Peace*, p. 182.

5 William S. White, "Johnson Warns President Against 'Coercing' Israel,' " *NYT*, Feb. 19, 1957; Bipartisan Congressional Meeting, Feb. 20, 1957, DDE Diary, B 21, Misc. (2), EL; Eisenhower, *Waging Peace*, pp. 184–91; Address to Nation, Feb. 20, 1957, *PPP*, no. 35, pp. 147–55; W. H. Lawrence, "President Says U.N. Has No Choice," *NYT*, Feb. 21, 1957.

6 John D. Morris, "President Signs Mideast Doctrine," *NYT*, March 10, 1957.

7 Eisenhower's notes on Bermuda conference, March 21, 1957, DDE Diary, B 22, Misc. (2), EL; also in *DDEP*, no. 78.

8 Eisenhower, *Waging Peace*, pp. 191–93.

9 The situation with Syria is discussed in some detail in Eisenhower, *Waging Peace*, pp. 196–204.

10 Eisenhower devotes an entire chapter to the Lebanon landing in *Waging Peace*, pp. 262–91.

11 John Lewis Gaddis, *The Cold War: A New History* (New York: Penguin, 2005), pp. 62–64; Eisenhower commented extensively in his diary regarding a report on projected nuclear casualties, received on Jan. 23, 1956; DDE Diary, B 9, Personal (2), EL; also *DDEP*, no. 1708.

12 Eisenhower used the "keg of dynamite" phrase in his pre–press conference briefing, Sept. 11, 1956, Press Conference Series, B 5, EL.

13 One soldier was killed by a sniper in Lebanon in 1958; see endnote no. 1; Lieutenant Colonel Gary H. Wade, Research Survey No. 3, Rapid Deployment Logistics: Lebanon, 1958, United States Army Command and General Staff College (Combat Studies Institute, October 1984).

14 Gaddis, *The Cold War*, p. 64.

15 DDE to Douglas, Nov. 30, 1956, DDE Diary Series, B 20, Misc. (1), EL: also *DDEP*, no. 2124A.

16 Conference with President, Sept. 11, 1956, DDE Diary, B 17, Staff Memoranda, EL; Goodpaster to Flemming, Sept. 12, 1956, Dwight D. Eisenhower, Records as President, White House CF, Confidential File, Subject Series, Suez Canal Crisis (1), EL; DDE Diary Entry, Jan. 11, 1956, *DDEP*, No. 1684; DDE to Hazlett, Aug. 3, 1956, DDE Diary, B 17, Misc. (4), EL; also *DDEP*, no. 1936.

17 Bipartisan Congressional Leadership Meeting, Jan. 1, 1957, Legislative Meetings Series, B 2 (1), EL; Diary entry, July 15, 1958, DDE Diary, B 34, EL.

18 Eisenhower, *Waging Peace*, pp. 288–91.

19 Conversation, Sept. 26, 1960, *FRUS, 1958–60*, Vol. XIII, "Arab-Israeli Dispute," no. 264, pp. 600–607; Eisenhower, *Waging Peace*, p. 584; Yaqub, *Containing Arab Nationalism*, pp. 265–67.

20 White House Statement, Nov. 5, 1956, Hagerty Papers, B 7, Middle East, EL; Address to Nation, Feb. 20, 1957, *PPP*, no. 35, pp. 147–55.

21 Conversation, Oct. 3, 1955, *FRUS, 1955–57*, Vol. XIV, no. 323, pp. 543–49.

22 JFD to DDE, March 28, 1956, DDE Diary, B 13, EL; also in *FRUS, 1955–57*, Vol. XV, Arab-Israeli Dispute, no. 223, pp. 419–21.

23 JFD conversation with DDE, July 19, 1956, *FRUS, 1955–57*, Vol. XV, no. 473, pp. 861–62; JFD with Egyptian ambassador, July 19, 1956, *FRUS, 1955–57*, Vol. XV, no. 478, pp. 867–73.

24 JFD and congressional leaders, April 10, 1956, *FRUS, 1955–57*, Vol. XV, no. 265, pp. 504–11; Eugene Black Interview, May 13, 1975, OH-341, p. 10, EL.

25 Minutes, Intelligence Advisory Committee, Oct. 16, 1956, CREST, NA.

26 Eisenhower, *Waging Peace*, p. 58; Eisenhower often made this point about planning, particularly in a civil defense meeting on April 19, 1956, WHOSS, Subject Series, Alpha Subseries, B 23, President & Seaton Conference, EL.

27 JFD to DDE, Oct. 30, 1956, DDE Diary, B 18, Phone Calls, EL; DP, Tel. Conv., B 11, Tel. Conv., WH, EL., Richard Nixon is on record on several occasions that he believed that Eisenhower, in the years after his presidency, believed that his failure to support the British and French was a mistake. However, there is little evidence for this conclusion, including in Eisenhower's memoirs; for one example, see Julian Amery, "The Suez Group: A Retrospective on Suez," in S. I. Troen

and M. Shemesh, eds., *The Suez-Sinai Crisis 1956: Retrospective and Reappraisal* (New York: Columbia University Press, 1990), p. 125.

28 Conference with the President, Oct. 30, 1956, DDE Diary, Staff Memos, EL; also in *FRUS, 1955–57,* Vol. XVI, no. 438, pp. 873–74.

29 Ike made the "ashes" remark in his diary after reviewing a report on projected casualties resulting from a nuclear exchange, Jan. 23, 1956, DDE Diary, B 9, Personal (2), EL; also *DDEP*, no. 1708; campaign address in Philadelphia, Nov. 1, 1956, Eisenhower, *PPP*, no. 283, pp. 1066–74.

30 Eisenhower's January 17, 1961, farewell address to the nation is famed for its warning about the dangers of "the military-industrial complex." That theme was not new with him. Throughout his presidency Ike had worried that the demands of prosecuting the Cold War might turn the United States into "a garrison state"; see the Joint Chiefs Conference with the President, March 13, 1956, DDE Diary Series, Box 13, March '56 Goodpaster, EL.

PHOTO CREDITS

★ ★ ★ ★ ★ ★

INDEX

★ ★ ★ ★ ★ ★

ABOUT THE AUTHOR

★ ★ ★ ★ ★ ★

DAVID A. NICHOLS, a leading expert on the Eisenhower presidency, is the author of *A Matter of Justice: Eisenhower and the Beginning of the Civil Rights Revolution* and *Lincoln and the Indians.* He is a veteran of thirty-five years in higher education as a professor and administrator, including eleven years as an academic dean at Southwestern College in Kansas. Nichols lives in Winfield, Kansas.